WHAT'S WRONG WITH LEADERSHIP?

Leadership practitioners and those who seek to develop leadership are concerned with whether they are using evidence-based best practices to develop leadership capacity in themselves and others. Are we indeed using best practices in the study, practice, and development of leadership? This book seeks to draw attention to the limitations of extant work on leadership and to provide suggestions for a way forward. Presenting chapters on topics ranging from research methodology, gender, and cross-cultural issues in leadership studies, and the role of the humanities in our understanding of leadership, the book represents a rigorous multidisciplinary collaboration.

This is a must-read for graduate students studying leadership, leadership consultants and trainers, leadership scholars, and anyone who practices, teaches, or seeks to develop leadership. It will help to expand the horizons of how we think about and practice leadership.

Ronald E. Riggio is Henry R. Kravis Professor of Leadership and Organizational Psychology at the Kravis Leadership Institute, Claremont McKenna College. Dr. Riggio is a leadership scholar, author or editor of more than a dozen books, as well as more than 150 articles and book chapters. His research interests are leadership, organizational communication, and social competence. He is part of the Fullerton Longitudinal Study, examining leadership development across the lifespan (from first birthday through to middle adulthood). Besides research on leadership development, he has been actively involved in training young (and not-so-young) leaders.

Leadership: Research and Practice Series
A James MacGregor Burns Academy of Leadership Collaboration

Series Editors

Georgia Sorenson, Ph.D, Møller Leadership Scholar and Møller By-Fellow, Churchill College, University of Cambridge, Founder of the James MacGregor Academy of Leadership at the University of Maryland, and co-founder of the International Leadership Association.

Ronald E. Riggio, Ph.D, Henry R. Kravis Professor of Leadership and Organizational Psychology and former Director of the Kravis Leadership Institute at Claremont McKenna College.

The Global Hillary
Women's Political Leadership in Cultural Contexts
Edited by Dinesh Sharma

Teaching Leadership
An Integrative Approach
Barbara C. Crosby

College Student Leadership Development
Valerie I. Sessa

Exploring Distance in Leader-Follower Relationships
When Near is Far and Far is Near
Edited by Michelle C. Bligh and Ronald E. Riggio

Women's Leadership Journeys
Stories, Research, and Novel Perspectives
Edited by Sherylle J. Tan and Lisa DeFrank-Cole

Snapshots of Great Leadership
Second Edition
Jon P. Howell and Isaac Wanasika

What's Wrong with Leadership? (And How to Fix It)
Edited by Ronald E. Riggio

For more information about this series, please visit: https://www.routledge.com/psychology/series/LEADERSHIP

WHAT'S WRONG WITH LEADERSHIP?

Improving Leadership Research and Practice

Edited by Ronald E. Riggio

Routledge
Taylor & Francis Group
NEW YORK AND LONDON

First published 2019
by Routledge
711 Third Avenue, New York, NY 10017

and by Routledge
2 Park Square, Milton Park, Abingdon, Oxon, OX14 4RN

Routledge is an imprint of the Taylor & Francis Group, an informa business

© 2019 Taylor & Francis

The right of Ronald E. Riggio to be identified as the author of the editorial material, and of the authors for their individual chapters, has been asserted in accordance with sections 77 and 78 of the Copyright, Designs and Patents Act 1988.

All rights reserved. No part of this book may be reprinted or reproduced or utilised in any form or by any electronic, mechanical, or other means, now known or hereafter invented, including photocopying and recording, or in any information storage or retrieval system, without permission in writing from the publishers.

Trademark notice: Product or corporate names may be trademarks or registered trademarks, and are used only for identification and explanation without intent to infringe.

Library of Congress Cataloging-in-Publication Data
Names: Riggio, Ronald E., editor.
Title: What's wrong with leadership? : improving leadership research and practice / edited by Ronald E. Riggio.
Description: 1 Edition. | New York, NY : Routledge, 2019. | Series: Leadership: research and practice series | Includes bibliographical references and index.
Identifiers: LCCN 2018022141 | ISBN 9781138059399 (hb : alk. paper) | ISBN 9781138059405 (pb : alk. paper) | ISBN 9781315163604 (eb)
Subjects: LCSH: Leadership. | Leadership—Research.
Classification: LCC HD57.7 .W45598 2019 | DDC 658.4/092—dc23
LC record available at https://lccn.loc.gov/2018022141

ISBN: 978-1-138-05939-9 (hbk)
ISBN: 978-1-138-05940-5 (pbk)
ISBN: 978-1-315-16360-4 (ebk)

Typeset in Bembo
by Swales & Willis Ltd, Exeter, Devon, UK

CONTENTS

About the Contributors   *viii*
Acknowledgements   *xv*
Foreword   *xvi*

Introduction: What's Wrong with Leadership?
Improving Leadership Theory, Research, and Practice   1
Ronald E. Riggio

PART I
Improving Leadership Methodology, Assessment, and Selection   7

1 Leadership Research Methods: Progressing back to Process   9
Maureen E. McCusker, Roseanne J. Foti, and Elsheba K. Abraham

2 Leadership and Levels of Analysis: Clarifications and Fixes for What's Wrong   41
Francis J. Yammarino and Shelley D. Dionne

3 Leadership Assessment Can Be Better: Directions for Selection and Performance Management   58
Manuel London

4 Self-selection Bias in Leadership: Understanding
    Reluctant Leaders   89
    Olga Epitropaki

PART II
Increasing the Scope of Leadership Research   **105**

 5 Leadership and Ethics: You Can Run, but You
    Cannot Hide from the Humanities   107
    Joanne B. Ciulla

 6 Leadership Is Male-centric: Gender Issues in the
    Study of Leadership   121
    Stefanie K. Johnson and Christina N. Lacerenza

 7 Are Leadership Theories Western-centric? Transcending
    Cognitive Differences between the East and the West   138
    Kenta Hino

 8 Leadership and the Medium of Time   150
    Robert G. Lord

 9 Leaders Are Complex: Expanding Our Understanding
    of Leader Identity   173
    Stefanie P. Shaughnessy and Meredith R. Coats

10 Turning a Blind Eye to Destructive Leadership:
    The Forgotten Destructive Leaders   189
    Birgit Schyns, Pedro Neves, Barbara Wisse, and Michael Knoll

PART III
**Improving Leadership Practice and Expanding
Our Thinking about Leadership**   **207**

11 Leadership Development Starts Earlier Than We Think:
    Capturing the Capacity of New Leaders to Address
    the Leader Talent Shortage   209
    Susan E. Murphy

12 What Is Wrong with Leadership Development and
    What Might Be Done about It?   226
    David V. Day and Zhengguang Liu

13 Solving the Problem with Leadership Training: Aligning
    Contemporary Behavior-based Training with Mindset
    Conditioning   241
    Alex Leung and Thomas Sy

14 Critical Leadership Studies: Exploring the Dialectics of
    Leadership   260
    David L. Collinson

15 Leadership for What?   279
    Eric Guthey, Steve Kempster, and Robyn Remke

Index   *299*

ABOUT THE CONTRIBUTORS

Elsheba K. Abraham is a doctoral candidate in industrial-organizational psychology at Virginia Polytechnic Institute and State University (known as Virginia Tech). Her Masters' thesis focused on the self-regulation of emotions and subsequent expressions of racial bigotry. Additional research interests include emotion regulation in leadership settings, the influence of behavioral interactions on the leadership process, and understanding new methods for measuring leadership and diversity-related attitudes. Born and raised in Malaysia, Elsheba is enjoying her time in Virginia, and when she is not conducting research or writing, she is looking for opportunities to travel and discover new cities.

Joanne B. Ciulla is a professor of leadership ethics and academic director of the Institute for Ethical Leadership at Rutgers University Business School. Prior to joining Rutgers, she was part of the founding faculty at the Jepson School of Leadership Studies, University of Richmond. Ciulla has written extensively on leadership ethics and business ethics. Holding B.A., M.A., and Ph.D. degrees in philosophy, she best known for her work in developing the field of leadership ethics. Ciulla has served as president of both the International Society for Business, Economics, and Ethics (ISBEE), and The Society for Business Ethics (SBE). She sits on the editorial boards of *The Leadership Quarterly*, *Leadership*, *Leadership and the Humanities*, and *Business Ethics Quarterly*, and she edits the New Horizons in Leadership Studies series for Edward Elgar.

Meredith R. Coats is a doctoral fellow working with the U.S. Army Research Institute through the Consortium Research Fellows Program. She is currently a doctoral candidate at The George Washington University, where she earned an M.Phil. in industrial-organizational psychology. Ms. Coats specializes in leadership and longitudinal analyses. Her research interests include leader developmental experiences, high potentials in the workplace, and incorporating time into research.

David L. Collinson is a distinguished professor of leadership and organization at Lancaster University Management School, UK. He is the founding co-editor (with Keith Grint) of SAGE journal *Leadership* and founding co-organizer of The International Studying Leadership Conference. Previously holding positions at the universities of Manchester, Warwick, St Andrews, and South Florida, David has published extensively on critical approaches to leadership and management, power and identity, and gender and masculinity.

David V. Day is a professor of psychology and academic director of the Kravis Leadership Institute at Claremont McKenna College, where he also holds the titles Steven L. Eggert "82 P"15 Professor of Leadership and George R. Roberts Fellow. He is a Fellow of the American Psychological Association (APA), American Psychological Society (APS), International Association of Applied Psychology (IAAP), and the Society for Industrial and Organizational Psychology (SIOP). Day was awarded the 2010 Walter F. Ulmer Research Award by the Center for Creative Leadership for outstanding career-long contributions to applied leadership research.

Shelley D. Dionne is a professor of Leadership and Organizational Behavior in the School of Management at Binghamton University, and Associate Director of the Center for Leadership Studies. She has received multiple grants from the National Science Foundation and Army Research Institute to study leadership, multidisciplinary team building and collective decision making. She is a former Associate Editor for the *Leadership Quarterly*. She received her Ph.D. and MBA from Binghamton University's School of Management and her research interests include leadership, team development, collective dynamics and levels of analysis issues, and her publications include articles in the *Journal of Applied Psychology, Organizational Research Methods, Leadership Quarterly* and *Complexity*.

Olga Epitropaki is a professor of management at Durham University Business School. She has research interests in the areas of implicit leadership theories, leader–member exchange (LMX), creative leadership, and identity, as well as whether psychological contracts wane employability. Her research has been published in top refereed journals. She is senior associate editor of *The Leadership Quarterly* and associate editor of the *British Journal of Management*. She is also the founder and organizer of the annual Interdisciplinary Perspectives on Leadership Symposium (www.leadership-symposium.com).

Roseanne J. Foti is a professor of psychology at Virginia Tech. Her research interests focus on social cognition, memory processes, and dyadic/group processes related to leadership. She is also interested in person-oriented theory and methodologies as they apply to the study of leadership. Her research has been published in top refereed journals, including the *Journal of Applied Psychology*, *The Leadership Quarterly*, and *Organizational Behavior and Human Decision Processes*, among others. Her research has received financial support from various funding agencies, including the National Science Foundation (NSF), the U.S. Army Research Institute, the Leverhulme Trust, and the Agency for Healthcare Research and Quality (AHRQ). Roseanne is a fellow of SIOP.

Eric Guthey is an associate professor at Copenhagen Business School in Denmark. His research and teaching leverage his years of experience at business schools in the United States, Europe, and the Pacific Rim, as well as his background in the humanities and cultural history, to develop interdisciplinary perspectives on leadership, management, and cultural dynamics in a variety of organizational and social contexts. Eric's current research focuses on the competitive and cultural dynamics of the leadership industries, and on the connections between these commercial/industrial/professional dynamics and prevailing conceptions of leadership itself.

Kenta Hino is a professor of organization studies within the Department of Business Administration, Komazawa University, in Tokyo. He was educated and has worked throughout his life in Japan, other than one year during which he visited Durham Business School. Studying organization theory, organizational behavior, and business management, he received a Ph.D. in commerce from Waseda University in 2009. His research interests are in leadership theories (especially implicit leadership theories and social identity perspective on leadership), organizational behavior, and organization theory. His recent works include *Leadership and Follower Approach* (in Japanese), a co-translation of Mary Jo Hatch's *Organization Theory* (3rd ed., Routledge), and articles published in the *Leadership and Organization Development Journal* and in Japanese journals.

Stefanie K. Johnson is an associate professor of management at Leeds School of Business, University of Colorado, Boulder. Dr. Johnson studies the intersection of leadership and diversity, focusing on (a) how unconscious bias affects the evaluation of leaders and (b) the strategies that leaders can use to mitigate bias. Stefanie has published some 40 journal articles and book chapters in outlets such as *Harvard Business Review*, the *Journal of Applied Psychology*, and the *Academy of Management Journal*.

Steve Kempster is a professor of leadership learning and development at Lancaster University Management School, UK. He has authored the books *LEADing*

Small Business (Edward Elgar) and *How Managers Have Learnt to Lead* (Palgrave Macmillan), and has co-edited (with Brigid Carrol) *Responsible Leadership: Realism and Romanticism* (Routledge), and he has published widely in *The Leadership Quarterly, Management Learning, Leadership*, and other top-ranking journals. Steve's first career was as a chartered surveyor, during which time he ran his own practice. In his second career, his research and engagement interests span leadership learning, responsible leadership, the relevance gap in leadership research, and how to bridge that gap by asking "Leadership for what?"

Michael Knoll is a researcher and lecturer at Chemnitz University of Technology. Before joining Chemnitz University, he held positions at Universität Leipzig, Martin Luther Universität Halle-Wittenberg, and Durham University Business School. His main research interests include employee silence and voice, authenticity, leadership, and the role of culture in organizations.

Christina N. Lacerenza is an assistant professor of organizational leadership and information analytics at Leeds School of Business, University of Colorado, Boulder. Her work focuses on teamwork and leadership, with an emphasis on emergent and shared leadership, leadership development, and diversity. Her work appears in outlets such as the *Journal of Applied Psychology* and *Organizational Behavior and Human Decision Processes*, and has been presented at various professional meetings, including a National Academy of Sciences (NAS) workshop. She earned her Ph.D. from Rice University, with a dissertation focused on deep- and surface-level leader traits within self-managed teams.

Alex Leung is a doctoral candidate in the psychology department at the University of California, Riverside. His research focuses on understanding how conceptions of leaders and followers may trigger expectancy effects, such as self-fulfilling prophecies, that shape employee performance outcomes. His research is published in a variety of scientific outlets. Alex also has experience collaborating with a variety of organizations, such as Zappos and the U.S. Army. Alex aims to apply findings from his research to inform leadership training and development, including programs for diversity and inclusion.

Zhengguang Liu, is a visiting scholar in the Kravis Leadership Institute (KLI) at Claremont McKenna College. Marko is currently a full-time researcher at KLI, and his research interests include leader emergence, leadership effectiveness, leadership assessment, and life-span leadership development. He is also a fourth-year Ph.D. candidate in developmental psychology at Beijing Normal University, China. Funded by a Chinese government scholarship, he is studying in the United States for 20 months. Prior to his doctoral study, Marko had five years' working experience in human resource management in business, focusing on organizational development and talent management.

Manuel London is the dean of the College of Business and a Distinguished Professor of Management at the State University of New York at Stony Brook. He received his A.B. from Case Western Reserve University, and his M.A. and Ph.D. in industrial and organizational psychology from Ohio State University. He taught at the University of Illinois in Champaign-Urbana before joining AT&T, where he conducted research and designed programs for management assessment, performance evaluation, and leadership development. London has been on the Stony Brook faculty since 1989, during which time he has served as deputy to the president, associate provost for enrollment & retention management, director of the Undergraduate College of Leadership & Service, associate dean of the College of Business, and, for the last eight years, dean. He is the author of 18 books and the editor of 10, and the author of more than 130 articles in the areas of performance evaluation, job feedback, career motivation, leadership development, and group learning. His books and articles have won awards from the Association for Human Resource Development (AHRD) and the Society for Human Resource Management (SHRM).

Robert G. Lord obtained his Ph.D. in social-organizational psychology from Carnegie-Mellon University in 1975. His undergraduate degree in economics was obtained from the University of Michigan. He joined the Psychology Department at the University of Akron in 1974 and worked there for 38 years, leaving in 2013 to assume a post with Durham University Business School in the UK. His research uses cognitive science to understand leadership processes, self-regulation, emotions, and identity as they affect applied work and social processes. He is the recipient of the International Leadership Association Lifetime Achievement Award (2017), the Distinguished Scientific Contribution Award from SIOP (2012), and *The Leadership Quarterly* Distinguished Scholar Award for Career Contribution to the Study of Leadership (2009).

Maureen E. McCusker is a Post-doctoral Research Fellow with CRFP at the Army Research Institute. Her research interests lie broadly in the relational processes of leadership, and in team and dyadic composition. Maureen uses a variety of non-traditional research methods (for example, unobtrusive measurement, text and communication analysis, sequential and event-based techniques, and social network analysis) to better understand how and why leadership and group perceptions emerge and become effective. She earned her Ph.D. in psychology from Virginia Tech.

Susan E. Murphy is chair in leadership development and head of the Organisation Studies Group at University of Edinburgh Business School. She was formerly the director of the School of Strategic Leadership Studies at James Madison

University and a professor of leadership studies. She has published numerous articles and book chapters on leadership, leadership development, and mentoring. Her most recent co-edited volume (with Rebecca Reichard) is *Early Development and Leadership: Building the Next Generation of Leaders* (Routledge), and she has co-authored (with Ellen Ensher) *Power Mentoring: How Successful Mentors and Protégés Make the Most of Their Relationships* (Jossey-Bass). She also serves on the editorial board of *The Leadership Quarterly*.

Pedro Neves is an associate professor at Nova School of Business and Economics, and is currently the director of the Ph.D. program in management. He has published in journals such as the *Journal of Applied Psychology*, the *Journal of Occupational and Organizational Psychology*, and *The Leadership Quarterly*. His research interests focus on interpersonal relationships in the workplace, change management, toxic workplaces, leadership, and entrepreneurship.

Robyn Remke is a lecturer in leadership and organizational communication at Lancaster University Management School, UK. Her research combines interdisciplinary interests in communication, gender, and organizational studies to examine the role of, and potential for, leadership in specific organizational contexts. Robyn's current research projects focus on diversity and inclusion practices in the public sector, women in enterprise in West Africa, and gender inclusivity and women's leadership in European business schools. Robyn has taught and conducted research in the United States, Europe, Africa, and Asia, and she is a past president of the Organization for the Study of Communication, Language, and Gender (OSCLG).

Birgit Schyns is a professor in organizational behavior at Neoma Business School. Her research focus is on leadership – particularly the follower side of leadership, as well as the dark side of leadership. Birgit has edited several special issues of journals and four books. She was associate editor for the *European Journal of Work and Organizational Psychology* (until 2011) and the *British Journal of Management* (until 2013), and she is currently associate editor for *Applied Psychology: An International Review*. Birgit serves on several editorial boards.

Stefanie P. Shaughnessy is a research psychologist at the U.S. Army Research Institute for the Behavioral and Social Sciences. She received her M.Sc. and Ph.D. in industrial-organizational psychology from Purdue University. Dr. Shaughnessy is a member of the Basic Research Team within the Foundational Science Research Unit, where she works at the intersection of the academic and applied worlds, focusing on the long-term research needs of the U.S. Army. She is responsible for conducting her own innovative research in the area of leader development, as well as supporting research efforts in academic settings through the Institute's "Leader Development" portfolio.

Thomas Sy is an award-winning scholar, teacher and consultant. He teaches and conducts research on leadership, teams, mindsets, and diversity at the Psychology Department, University of California (Riverside). His research is published in a variety of top scientific and popular media outlets. He has advised diverse organizations, including Google, Zappos, General Electric, Ford, IBM, U.S. Marine Corp Special Operations Command, and among others. Dr. Sy completed his PhD in Organizational Psychology at the University of Michigan. He was an advisor with a top-tier global management consultancy. Dr. Sy has also served in the U.S. Army Special Forces (Green Beret).

Barbara Wisse is a professor of organizational psychology at the University of Groningen and a chaired professor of management at Durham University, UK. Her work focuses explicitly on power and leadership processes, and often revolves around topics such as ethics and morality, emotions, "dark triad" personality traits, and the psychological effects of change.

Francis J. Yammarino is SUNY Distinguished Professor of Management and Director, Center for Leadership Studies, at Binghamton University, State University of New York. He was senior editor of The Leadership Quarterly and co-editor of Research in Multi-Level Issues, has served on nine scholarly journal editorial review boards, and is a Fellow of the Society for Industrial and Organizational Psychology, American Psychological Association, Association for Psychological Sciences, and Society for Organizational Behavior. His research focuses on leadership and levels of analysis issues and has been funded by the Army Research Institute, Office of Naval Research, National Science Foundation, and National Aeronautics and Space Administration, among others. In 2010, Dr. Yammarino received the Eminent (Distinguished) Leadership Scholar Award from The Leadership Quarterly and Academy of Management Network of Leadership Scholars for outstanding career contributions to the study of leadership.

ACKNOWLEDGEMENTS

Robert Lord would like to thank Rosalie J. Hall, Ronald Riggio, Xiaotong Zheng, and Yanjun Guan for helpful comments on an earlier version of his chapter.

Stefanie P. Shaughnessy and Meredith R. Coats would like to acknowledge that their research was sponsored in part by U.S. Army Research Institute Cooperative Agreement #W911NF-16-2-0092. The views, opinions, and/or findings contained in their chapter are those of the authors and should not be construed as an official U.S. Department of the Army position, policy, or decision.

FOREWORD

This new book is well positioned to provide a formative evaluation of the field of leadership studies, and it offers corrective direction in both theory and practice. That is to say: It's a must-read for anyone interested in the field of leadership.

The authors – established scholars brought together by senior scholar Robert Lord – examine the omissions in theoretical development (the humanities, gender, a focus on leaders rather than leadership, nonwestern views, introverts and non-charismatics, etc.) and the dearth of agreed-upon best practices (or the overlooking of such), as well as the limitations of leadership evaluation research.

In short, this summation (necessitated by the editor's extensive overview and rationale in the Introduction) is a ruthlessly honest view, meant not to discredit the work done to date, of which many of us are architects, but to shore it up. Good gardeners pull up the plant by the roots in spring, simply to see how things are going down there. This book offers a perfectly timed deracination, and it accomplishes the true spirit of editor Ronald Riggio's intention: "Taking a look at what's *wrong* with leadership will help students to better understand what's *right* with leadership."

Professor Georgia Sorenson, Ph.D.
Churchill College, University of Cambridge

INTRODUCTION

What's Wrong with Leadership? Improving Leadership Theory, Research, and Practice

Ronald E. Riggio

The study of leadership is both immensely fascinating and enormously complex. A major concern that troubles all leadership scholars is whether the scope of our theories and the methods that we use to study leadership are broad enough to capture its complexity and precise enough to actually understand the phenomenon. Leadership practitioners, and those who seek to develop leadership, are concerned with whether they are using evidence-based best practices to develop leadership capacity in themselves and others. Are we indeed using best practices in the study, practice, and development of leadership? This book seeks to draw attention to the limitations of this work and to attempt to provide suggestions for a way forward.

The impetus for this book came from conversations among a group of international leadership scholars who were drawn together, under the direction of renowned scholar Robert Lord, to collaborate on advancing theorizing and research on implicit leadership theories. This work was supported first by the Leverhulme Foundation and later by the U.S. Army Research Institute. As we proceeded in our discussions about leadership research, the limitations of some of the methods and approaches to studying leadership became clear. In addition to the members of the scholar group, other noted leadership researchers were recruited to author chapters focusing on their areas of specialization. The result is this collection.

What's Wrong with Leadership?

Criticisms of how we conceptualize and study leadership stretch back to the very beginning of its scientific study. Stogdill (1948) criticized the prevailing emphasis on studying leader traits, which altered the future course of research.

Meindl, Ehrlich, and Dukerich (1985) argued that leadership is socially constructed, which led to new ways of thinking about leadership (and followership). More recently, there have been criticisms of the current state of leadership research (for example, Avolio, Walumbwa, & Weber, 2009; Collinson, 2014) and practice (for example, Kellerman, 2012), with suggestions about the way forward.

Looking even further back, there is imbalance in the study of leadership. Research on leadership has been dominated in the past several decades by the social sciences – particularly psychology, management, and political science, with contributions from sociology, education, public administration, and other disciplines. Yet the humanities – particularly philosophy – have focused on leadership since ancient times. Classic literature, from the Bible to Shakespeare, and modern literature as well feature leadership as a common theme (Cronin & Genovese, 2012), and leadership is depicted and studied in the arts and in film (Warner, 2014; Warner & Riggio, 2012). So it is clear that one important theme in moving leadership forward is the need for multidisciplinary and interdisciplinary collaboration. For today's scholars, it is important to use a broad lens to study and understand leadership. Focusing too narrowly is limiting. Leadership scholars need to be broadly educated and aware of research across a range of academic disciplines.

The first part of this book focuses on issues related to leadership research methodology and what research tells us about best practices in assessing and choosing leaders. Chapter 1, by Maureen McCusker, Roseanne Foti, and Elsheba Abraham, takes a broad-brush approach to the limitations of how social scientists have studied leadership in the past half-century. A primary theme is the need to shift from a study of leaders (and the impact their behavior has on followers) to a study of the process of leadership – incorporating the followers and the context into the equation. Leadership is dynamic, not static, and our research methods should reflect that. The chapter also foreshadows some of the methodological limitations that will be dealt with in-depth in forthcoming chapters, such as the need to consider time and levels of analysis, and to view leadership as a relationship (as well as to learn from other disciplines that study interpersonal relationships). The authors also argue for more qualitative research, case studies, and ethnographic and historiometric methods. We are also given a glimpse into the future, with discussion of the use of computational modeling to try to capture the complex, dynamic process of leadership.

In Chapter 2, Francis Yammarino and Shelley Dionne urge scholars to recognize that leadership is a multilevel phenomenon and to incorporate that into conceptualizing studies and data analyses. They offer guidelines both for improving leadership research and for the way in which we think about and practice leadership.

When it comes to the application of state-of-the-art methods for assessing leadership, Manuel London's chapter (Chapter 3) discusses the ways in which we currently measure leadership potential and performance, and it suggests that there are best practices that are not used often enough. In particular, the use of assessment centers for leader selection are advocated. In addition, the melding of 360-degree performance feedback with ongoing leader development processes (for example coaching) is emphasized as having the potential to create an integrated system for evaluating and improving leadership across the organization.

In Chapter 4, Olga Epitropaki focuses on self-selection bias, which influences both the leaders who are studied and those who are tagged and selected for leadership positions in organizations. She argues that most of our attention is directed toward those who are more "visible" (such as extraverts, charismatics) or those who seek to claim leadership positions (such as narcissists). As a result, many individuals with substantial leadership potential are overlooked. This leads to bias, in terms of both those who attain leadership positions and those who are targeted for leader development (that is, "high potentials"). Suggestions for encouraging reluctant leaders to step forward are provided.

The second part of this book deals with the limitations of leadership research. These range from perspectives on leadership research that are too narrow, through systematic biases in how we conceptualize leadership, to limitations in the measured variables that are typically investigated. The section begins with an important contribution by Joanne Ciulla (Chapter 5), who emphasizes the social sciences bias in the majority of studies of leadership and notes that, even when investigating topics such as leadership ethics, the contributions of philosophy specifically, and the humanities in general, are typically ignored. She urges us to take a more multidisciplinary and interdisciplinary approach to leadership research.

In the same vein, Stefanie Johnson and Christina Lacerenza (Chapter 6) note the perennial male-centric bias in the investigation of leadership (as well as its prevalence in leadership positions worldwide). The authors argue for a more gender-neutral approach to the study and practice of leadership. Their conclusion is that removing the male-centric bias from leadership will lead to greater leadership resources and will "level the playing field" for women leaders.

Kenta Hino (Chapter 7) takes an interesting perspective on the predominance of Western (particularly U.S.) views of leadership and the limitations that are caused by this cultural bias. Kenta focuses on the cognitive differences, contrasting Western perspectives with those of East Asians. One important point made in this chapter is that eastern perspectives on leadership are more inclusive of followers and context than are Western approaches. This is consistent with the trend in leadership research that is widening the lens to incorporate the situation and followers into the leadership equation.

Expanding the scope of research on leadership, Robert Lord emphasizes in Chapter 8 that scholars have not adequately considered the construct of time when studying leadership. Whether in terms of the speed at which leaders make decisions, the length of a leader's developmental trajectory, or how leaders (and followers) envision and prepare for future events, time is an important variable. Although much of this chapter focuses on research, Lord also suggests that practicing leaders carefully consider time as a key factor, and he concludes the chapter with a number of questions that every leader should consider.

Continuing to expand our thinking about leadership, Stefanie Shaughnessy and Meredith Coats (Chapter 9) explore the complexities of leader identities. Moreover, these authors suggest that identities are quite flexible, and that they change and develop over time. Much research on leader identity views it as static, so looking at trajectories of leader identity development and change across the lifespan will increase the depth of our understanding of the images that leaders have of themselves. This has important implications for both research and practice.

In Chapter 10, Birgit Schyns, Pedro Neves, Barbara Wisse, and Michael Knoll focus on negative, destructive leaders. They caution us to not fall prey to the bias in leadership research, theory, and practice that focuses – almost exclusively – on exemplary leaders and leadership. Schyns and colleagues emphasize that destructive leadership is complex, and that we need to expand our thinking and our research perspectives to better understand the depth and scope of destructive leadership.

The third part of the book looks at ways of both improving the practice of leadership and more broadly expanding our thinking about leadership. Although several other chapters draw attention to the fact that leadership is a developmental process, Susan Murphy focuses, in Chapter 11, on the earliest developmental roots of leadership. For the most part, research on leadership has dealt almost exclusively with adult leaders. Murphy reminds us that if we want to fully understand leader development, we need to look early in life at the influence of parents, peers, educational systems, and the structured opportunities and activities offered to youth. She suggests that incorporating early-life leadership experiences into our leadership development of the next generation of workers will help us to fill the impending shortage of leaders with high potential.

In Chapter 12, David Day and Zhengguang Liu discuss what's wrong with our approach to leadership development, and they offer solutions. In Chapter 13, Alex Leung and Tom Sy complement Day and Liu's work by focusing on the specific methods used to train leadership. Drawing on research – particularly work on leader mindsets – Leung and Sy suggest that there is a strong connection between how we think about leadership and leadership behavior. In addition, they provide guidelines for leadership training in organizations.

David Collinson (Chapter 14) discusses the discipline of critical leadership studies, which has called into question the prevailing theories and methodologies in the bulk of leadership research. Critical leadership studies broadens our understanding of the complexities of leadership and of the intricate power dynamics between leaders and followers. The result is a critical re-evaluation of past leadership research and a more complex, nuanced understanding of leadership that will impact on research and practice.

The book closes with a chapter that asks the important question: "Leadership for what?" In other words, it asks: Why study leadership at all if the end game is simply to better understand the phenomenon and to predict leadership effectiveness? In Chapter 15, Eric Guthey, Steve Kempster, and Robyn Remke note that all of the research, as well as the time and money spent developing leadership – what Kellerman (2012) calls "the leadership industry" – is for naught if leadership does not have a positive impact on people and society. This chapter provides a framework for collaboration, marshaling the expertise of leadership scholars and practitioners to collaboratively solve major social problems.

Who Is This Book for?

There are three important audiences for this book. The first is leadership scholars. There are many lessons here for academics who study leadership, regardless of discipline or methodology. A major theme in the first part of the book is best research practices, but throughout the book there is an emphasis on widening the lens through which to study leadership, to open up a broad perspective on leadership processes and to foster interdisciplinarity.

A second audience is students of leadership – particularly (but not only) graduate students. Again, regardless of discipline, there are important lessons to be learned about the broad field of leadership. All too often, leadership is presented in an "ideal" way – what exemplary leadership looks like, what are the best practices, etc. Taking a look at what's *wrong* with leadership will help students to better understand what's *right* with leadership.

Finally, this book should appeal to leadership practitioners of all types. The conclusions and recommendations for practice are solidly grounded in the latest research and are authored by renowned experts in the field. A leader who wants to be fully informed about the state of leadership research and practice will find no better source. Hopefully, together, we can all advance our understanding of leadership and make it better.

References

Avolio, B.J., Walumbwa, F.O., & Weber, T.J. (2009). Leadership: Current theories, research, and future directions. *Annual Review of Psychology, 60*, 421–469.

Collinson, D. (2014). Dichotomies, dialectics and dilemmas: New directions for critical leadership studies? *Leadership, 10*(1), 36–55.

Cronin, T.E., & Genovese, M.A. (2012). *Leadership matters: Unleashing the power of paradox*. Boulder, CO: Paradigm.

Kellerman, B. (2012). *The end of leadership*. New York: HarperCollins.

Meindl, J.R., Ehrlich, S.B., & Dukerich, J.M. (1985). The romance of leadership. *Administrative Science Quarterly, 30*, 78–102.

Stogdill, R.M. (1948). Personal factors associated with leadership: A survey of the literature. *Journal of Psychology, 25*, 35–71.

Warner, N.O. (2014). Picturing power: The depiction of leadership in art. *Leadership and the Humanities, 2*, 4–26.

Warner, N.O., & Riggio, R.E. (2012). Italian-American leadership in Hollywood films: Images and realities. *Leadership, 8*(3), 211–227.

PART I
Improving Leadership Methodology, Assessment, and Selection

1

LEADERSHIP RESEARCH METHODS

Progressing back to Process

Maureen E. McCusker, Roseanne J. Foti, and Elsheba K. Abraham

The term *leadership* is much used, but poorly understood. In 1974, Ralph Stogdill stated that there are almost as many different definitions of leadership as there are persons who have defined it. More than 100 years of leadership research has led to many paradigm shifts (Antonakis & Day, 2018), as well as calls for more integrative strategies (Hernandez, Eberly, Avolio, & Johnson, 2011). Today, there exists an interactive development of leadership theories and methodologies (Lord, Day, Zaccaro, Avolio, & Eagly, 2017); thus, to discuss leadership research methods, we first have to define what we mean by *leadership*. Given its many definitions, we selected three quotes with which to begin our chapter and to illustrate our own definition.

Leadership places its emphasis:

> . . . not on a set of personal characteristics or on particular kinds of leadership behavior, but upon the circumstances under which groups of people integrate and organize their activities toward objectives, and upon the way in which that integration and organization is achieved. Thus, the leadership function is analyzed and understood in terms of a dynamic relationship.
>
> *(Knickerbocker, 1948, p. 26)*

> An early element of confusion in the study of leadership was the failure to distinguish it as a process from the leader as a person who occupies a central role in that process. Leadership constitutes an influence relationship between two, or usually more, persons who depend upon one another for the attainment of certain mutual goals within a group situation.
>
> *(Hollander & Julian, 1969, p. 388)*

> Leadership is no longer simply described as an individual characteristic or difference, but rather is depicted in various models as dyadic, shared, relational, strategic, global, and a complex social dynamic.
> *(Avolio, Walumbwa, & Weber, 2009, p. 423)*

All of these definitions share a common theme: moving beyond characteristics of a single individual towards a dynamic influence process. The first quote is from Knickerbocker (1948); the second, from Hollander and Julian (1969), was published 21 years later; the third quote, from Avolio and colleagues (2009), some 40 years later. Thus the distinction between leaders and leadership, as well as a focus on dynamic processes, spans more than 60 years. As these quotes illustrate, leadership is not simply a person, a behavior, or an outcome, but a socio-perceptual and relational process.

Now let us turn from the conceptualization of the leadership process to the methods used to study it. The "typical" leadership research study, as described by Hunter, Bedell-Avers, and Mumford (2007), generally begins with the distribution of a self-report questionnaire. The typical questionnaire is a pre-developed, behaviorally-based leadership assessment. These questionnaires are completed by individuals reporting on their immediate supervisor's behavior. Generally, the results of these questionnaires are then correlated with outcomes such as job satisfaction and perceived effectiveness. This "typical" leadership study is in sharp contrast to early leadership research, such as Bales' (1953) inter-action process analysis and Browne's (1949, 1950, 1951) series of studies of the relational and communication patterns of executive leadership.

Consistent with the typical leadership study, when Lowe and Gardner (2000) summarized the research methods used in empirical articles published in the first ten years of *The Leadership Quarterly*, they found that 64 percent of them used a questionnaire-based approach. An analysis of the second ten years of publications in the journal revealed that the most prevalent research strategy for empirical articles was still the sample survey (Gardner, Lowe, Moss, Mahoney, & Cogliser, 2010). This state of affairs led Kaiser, Hogan, and Craig (2008) to conclude that most leadership research concerns how individual leaders are regarded and provides little information about the process of leadership.

Thus the conceptualization of leadership as a process has remained mostly unchanged, while the typical leadership study has largely ignored process variables and methods. By not aligning our research methods with our conceptualization, we are drifting further away from a better understanding of the process of leadership and how and why it happens, leaving us with only a narrow and incomplete understanding of leadership. Furthermore, when studying leadership, researchers typically study the outcome of the process, not the process itself. In the case of leadership emergence, this involves studying who emerged as a leader in a group by, for example, measuring perceptions of who emerged as a leader using questionnaire-based measures of the outcome of the leadership process (Acton, Foti, Lord, & Gladfelter, 2019). In the case of leadership effectiveness, ratings of the effectiveness of leaders or the job satisfaction of subordinates are used as measures of the outcome of leadership. To study the process itself means to focus on the mediating mechanism that explains the causal relationship between inputs (for example, leader behaviors) and outputs (for example, effective performance), following an input–process–output logic (Fischer, Dietz, & Antonakis, 2017).

The main purpose of this chapter is to help research to get back on the path to understanding the dynamic process of leadership – that is, the *how* and the *why* of leadership. Thus our chapter is both retrospective and prospective. We first discuss what it means to study leadership as a process, noting the key elements that are critical when conducting process-oriented leadership research. We then provide recommendations and examples of process-oriented research methodology that addresses each of the key elements.

Key Elements of the Leadership Process

The process orientation of leadership research methods certainly lags behind that of leadership conceptualization. However, as academics, we are not incapable of conducting leadership research using process-oriented methods. History is replete with examples of early research involving much more process-oriented methods than today's "typical leadership study" (Hunter et al., 2007). Additionally, technological advancements have equipped us with the tools to design, collect, and analyze process-oriented data more feasibly than ever before (Tan, Shiyko, Li, Li, & Dierker, 2012). But if leadership is generally understood to be a socio-perceptual and relational process, and we have the ability to research process dynamics, then why are we rarely employing process-oriented methods? One reason may be that the core concepts underlying the study of leadership as a process are underdeveloped or lacking in terms of current leadership theory and measurement (Kozlowski, Mak, & Chao, 2016). This suspected lack of clarity of the critical components, or elements, of the leadership process in turn hinder the effective implementation of process-oriented methods. In what follows, we aim to begin to unpack what a leadership process *actually means* by identifying some of the critical elements involved.

Rather than developing yet another definition of leadership as a process, we use existing definitions of leadership to uncover the critical elements. We conducted a review of leadership literature conceptualizing leadership as a process, extracted definitions of leadership, and identified commonalities among the critical elements involved in the process of leadership. Our results are laid out in Table 1.1. Our review yielded four critical elements of the leadership process: interpersonal interactions, time, levels, and context. While we recognize that these are not the only elements involved in leadership processes, these four were the most critical and the most common elements represented in our analysis. Next, we discuss each of these elements in more detail.

TABLE 1.1 Examples of process-oriented definitions of leadership, published between 2010 and 2017

Author (Year)	Journal/Book chapter	Definition	Relational interactions	Time	Levels	Context
Avolio et al. (2009)	Annual Review of Psychology	A dyadic, shared, relational, strategic, global, and complex social dynamic	x	x	x	
Day (2012)	Chapter	Requires a social interaction between people, traditionally labeled as leaders and followers, within a situational context	x			x
DeRue & Ashford (2010)	Academy of Management Review	Multiple individuals engaged in a process of interpersonal and mutual influence that is ultimately embedded within some collective	x		x	
Dinh et al. (2014)	The Leadership Quarterly	A complex phenomenon that operates across multiple levels of analysis (Cho & Dansereau, 2010; Wang & Howell, 2010), involves multiple mediating and moderating factors (e.g. DeRue, Nahrgang, Wellman, & Humphrey, 2011), and takes place over substantial periods of time (Day & Sin, 2011; Lord & Brown, 2004)		x	x	x
Fischer et al. (2017)	Journal of Management	A social and goal-oriented influence process, unfolding in a temporal and spatial milieu	x	x		x
Gardner et al. (2010)	The Leadership Quarterly	A complex, multilevel and socially constructed process	x		x	
Gooty et al. (2012)	The Leadership Quarterly	Inherently a multilevel phenomenon involving a leader and a follower, or a group of followers, organized via groups or departments, acting in a coordinated and interconnected manner	x		x	

Hazy & Uhl-Bien (2015)	Leadership	The recognizable pattern of organizing activity among autonomous individuals as they form a system of action	×		×	
Hosking (1988)	Journal of Management Studies	The structuring of interactions and relationships, activities and sentiments; processes in which definitions of social order are negotiated, found acceptable, implemented, and renegotiated; a certain kind of organizing activity	×			
Uhl-Bien & Ospina (2012)	Chapter	Co-created in relational interactions between people, and that . . . is dynamic, developing, and changing over time	×	×		
Yammarino (2013)	Journal of Leadership & Organizational Studies	A multilevel (person, dyad, group, collective) leader–follower interaction process that occurs in a particular situation (context) in which a leader (e.g. a supervisor) and followers (e.g. subordinates, direct reports) share a purpose (vision, mission) and jointly accomplish things (i.e. goals, objectives, tasks) willingly (i.e. without coercion)	×	×	×	×
Yukl (2012)	Academy of Management Perspectives	Influencing and facilitating individual and collective efforts to accomplish shared objectives		×		×

Interpersonal Interactions

Leadership, especially in the informal sense, is an emergent phenomenon. The concept of *emergence* is rooted in multilevel theory (Kozlowski & Klein, 2000) and is defined as a process by which higher-level, collective phenomena arise from the dynamic interactions of lower-level elements over time (Cronin, Weingart, & Todorova, 2011; Kozlowski & Klein, 2000). Thus leadership, the *emergent product*, comes into existence as a result of a series of simultaneous emergent processes occurring within and across multiple levels. For example, the constructions of cognitive self-structures of leadership occur within individuals (Lord & Chui, 2018), interpersonal interactions unfold among dyads (DeRue & Ashford, 2010), and dynamic group-level processes and states frame and constrain these lower-level processes (Day & Antonakis, 2012). While leadership researchers most commonly study the outcome of what has emerged (van Knippenberg & Sitkin, 2013), studying leadership as a process means studying how all of these congruent micro-dynamic processes within and between actors produce the emergent product (Rost, 1995).

Researchers have long argued that interpersonal interactions are the crux of any social process, including leadership. For instance, in one of the earliest interaction studies, Stogdill and Shartle (1948) used direct observation among other methods to categorize leadership behaviors into "planning" and "coordination." This created a framework for systematically assessing effective behavioral interactions, which could be carried out by any member of the group, not only those assigned to formal leadership roles. What followed from Stogdill and Shartle's research, and similar research by contemporaries, was a recognition that interactions among all group members were a defining characteristic of the process producing leadership relationships. As stated by Peter Blau (1964), social structures (that is, leadership) emerge(s) through interpersonal exchanges, and understanding how those structures emerge cannot be reduced to studying only individual characteristics, attributes, or behaviors.

Individual interactions and their complexities progress over time. Early work by Robert Bales (1950), Hollander and Willis (1967), and Karl Weick (for example, 1978, 1979) established the importance of sequences, or patterns, of behavioral interactions (that is, acts, interacts, and double interacts) as the organizing processes in social groups. Since this time, a group of leadership and communication researchers have focused on behavioral interactions among group members as the means of unpacking the process through which leadership is enacted (Lehmann-Willenbrock & Allen, 2018). For example, Fairhurst's work on discursive leadership focuses on assessing and understanding the patterns of speech that underlie and characterize leader–follower relationships (Fairhurst, 2007; Fairhurst & Uhl-Bien, 2012). DeRue and Ashford's (2010) leadership identity construction theory claims that dyadic leadership relationships emerge from a series of reciprocal and iterative, mutual-influence behaviors consisting of "claims" and "grants" of leadership. Individuals within a social context grow to recognize these patterns of behavior and co-construct identities as leaders, which result in the formation of dyadic leader–follower perceptions. These perceptions, cognitions, and identities influence, and are influenced by, the behavioral interactions, producing the complex, reciprocal process of leadership (DeRue, 2011).

The key to studying leadership processes as interactions is a focus on the interactional behaviors of pairs or groups of individuals (DeRue, 2011). While there is an extensive literature on leadership behavior (for example, Bass, 1985; Morgeson, DeRue, & Karam, 2010), the unit of analysis is most commonly the individual, with frequencies or types of behavior aggregated within an individual, often over time. While this technique is useful for understanding and defining leadership behaviors in general, it provides little insight into the *process* of how particular behaviors influence leader–follower relationships (Weingart, 1997). Alternatively, by measuring sequences or patterns of interpersonal behavior (Fairhurst & Uhl-Bien, 2012; Lehmann-Willenbrock & Allen, 2018; Marchiondo, Myers, & Kopelman, 2015; Leenders, DeChurch, & Contractor, 2015) over time, we can more precisely identify and understand the dynamic, active interactions between people impacting on leadership relationships (Shamir, 2011). We discuss specific research methods for doing so later in the chapter.

Time

The following phrases are included in Merriam-Webster's (2018) definitions of *process*: "phenomenon marked by gradual changes," "a continuous operation or treatment," "a continuing natural or biological activity," and "a series of actions or operations." All of these definitions invoke a sense of temporality, suggesting that all processes are inherently tied to time. The leadership process is no different, as noted in the process-orientated definitions we compiled at the outset of this chapter. The enactment of behavioral interactions, the development of leader or follower identities, the formation of relational perceptions, and the impact of leadership inputs on outcomes all take time to unfold (Shamir, 2011). While leadership is defined as a process necessitating time, leadership theories are largely atemporal (Kozlowski, Watola, Nowakowski, Kim, & Botero, 2008), as are the vast majority of research methods used to test the theories (Bluedorn & Jaussi, 2008). This represents misalignment between the conceptualization of the construct and its measurement (Dinh et al., 2014; Kozlowski & Klein, 2000; Ployhart, Holtz, & Bliese, 2002) and inhibits the ability to make causal inferences about leadership relationships (Day, 2014).

To study leadership as a process, we must incorporate time into our research methods. According to Castillo and Trinh (2018, p. 169), the predominant research methods of cross-sectional surveys "have blurred the effects of time" for three reasons: Their retrospective nature introduces major individual biases; the time frame of the construct being measured is rarely specified; and the leadership constructs being assessed (for example, behaviors) are treated as wholes, assuming that they are stable and global (Grand, Braun, Kuljanin, Kozlowski, & Chao, 2016), rather than dynamic. In particular, cross-sectional research contributes very little toward an understanding of how long it takes for leadership to emerge, stabilize, become effective, or develop successfully (Shamir, 2011). Addressing these issues requires employing longitudinal methods targeting the pace, duration, nonlinearity, and change triggers of leadership (Alipour, Mohammed, & Martinez, 2017; Castillo & Trinh, 2018). Additionally, it requires attention to be paid to how best to design temporal leadership studies to capture such change and development – that is, the ideal length of a leadership study, the number of data collection points, and the duration between data collection points (Day, 2014).

It is possible to build temporality into leadership and methods, but we must be more deliberate and strategic. In Chapter 8 of this volume, Lord highlights five thought-provoking aspects or dimensions of time for which we need to account. His chapter urges researchers to consider various mediums of temporality, and then to evaluate and embed them in theories of leadership. Accordingly, we urge researchers in turn to deliberately align leadership research methods with those temporal considerations. One way in which we might do so is this: Instead of setting time points based on convenience, researchers should be more purposeful about when to collect leadership data. For example, we might implement intensive longitudinal designs (Tan et al., 2012) by collecting many (at least ten) time points over the course of a study, or we might take a "shortitudinal" approach, in which multiple time points are taken in short periods of time (Dormann & Griffin, 2015), or we even may choose to set fewer, more dispersed time points (Miscenko, Guenter, & Day, 2017) – or we might combine any of the three approaches. This would allow us to better understand time lags, pace, and the nonlinearity of time. One historical example of this method is an early process-oriented research design by Bass (1949), in which group interactions were observed and tracked for 20-minute sessions over the course of six weeks. Findings produced insight on when leaders emerged in leaderless groups over time. Another option to consider the role of time in process-oriented research methods is to examine phases of the leadership processes, which is common in teams research (Gersick, 1988; Hollander, 1992; Marks, Mathieu, & Zaccaro, 2001). Early behavioral observation research work by Fisher (1970) showed the group decision-making process to be composed of multiple different phases, each characterized by different types of behavioral interaction among group members. More recently, Bergman, Small, Bergman, and Bowling (2014) found differential relationships between individual behavior and leadership emergence over the course of different team phases.

Levels

The predominant approach to leadership has been leader-centric, treating the source of leadership at an individual level – typically, that of the leader. This is not to say that leadership researchers have ignored the others involved in the leadership process. In particular, the influence of the social psychologists in the mid-twentieth century drew attention to the social context in which leadership occurs (Day & Zaccaro, 2007). Many studies were conducted in groups, highlighting the important influence of all group members on leadership processes (for example, Bass, 1949; Sample & Wilson, 1965). Both Murphy (1941) and Browne (1951) used sociometric methods, which inherently involve multiple levels, to derive a group structure of dyadic leadership perceptions and communication involving all group members.

While levels have not been historically absent from leadership research, the last several decades have driven a growing recognition that leadership can manifest at multiple different levels beyond the individual (Wang, Zhou, & Liu, 2014), such as at the dyad level as a relationship (Carter, DeChurch, Braun, & Contractor, 2015), at the group level as a structure (Mehra, Smith, Dixon, & Robertson, 2006), or at the within-individual level (Hoffman & Lord, 2013).

Conceptualizing leadership as a socio-perceptual process, we conceive leadership as:

1. an inherently dyadic perception (Foti & Hauenstein, 2007); and
2. socially constructed by means of the social relations among those in a social context (Uhl-Bien, 2006).

Accordingly, the leadership process involves at least two levels – the individual and the dyad (Uhl-Bien, 2006) – and is nested within a larger system – the collective (Yammarino, 2013). So the leadership process involves factors originating within and crossing multiple levels (Dinh et al., 2014): the leader; the follower (for example, Felfe & Schyns, 2009); the dyad (for example, Uhl-Bien, 2006); the team (Kozlowski et al., 2016); and the context – both social (for example, Bono & Anderson, 2005) and environmental (for example, Oc, 2018).

More than 20 years ago, Rousseau (1985) called for a deeper recognition of multiple levels in organizational research, calling organizational research on levels "messy" and "underdeveloped." Since Rousseau's critique, leadership research as a field has made great strides in the developing of multilevel theory both generally (Kozlowski & Klein, 2000) and within leadership (Dionne et al., 2014). But, in the leadership domain, multilevel theory is ahead of the data (Yammarino, Dionne, Chun, & Dansereau, 2005), and it is ahead of leadership research methods more generally. As Yammarino and Dionne explicate in Chapter 2 of this volume, leadership research must consider levels throughout the entirety of the research process, from theory development, through methodology, to implementation and practice. As they show, the vast majority of leadership research methods are conducted at the individual level, and those that do involve multilevel methods are improperly conducted.

Adding complexity to multilevel leadership research methods, Fischer and colleagues (2017) emphasize the importance of considering multiple simultaneous processes within the global leadership process. In other words, they recognize that leadership necessarily involves numerous processes occurring across levels at the same time. They argue that, to study the leadership process, we must construct multi-process and multilevel models of leadership. Thus the consideration of levels and the combination of levels (see Yammarino & Dionne, Chapter 2 of this volume) is critical for understanding the leadership process, as well as the multiple simultaneous sub-processes involved.

Context

The context of leadership has historically been considered to be a concern that is secondary to the study of leaders and leadership (Jepson, 2009; Porter & McLaughlin, 2006). Treated mainly as exogenous of the leader, context was considered to be an interactional variable (Fiedler, 1966; House, 1971) and treated seemingly as an afterthought, poorly defined in terms of levels, types, and complexity (Eberly, Johnson, Hernandez, & Avolio, 2013). In reality, context is an incredibly broad and complex phenomenon from which leadership cannot be divorced (Oc, 2018). Context can take a variety of forms and mediums, including person, place, culture, history, situational environments, and so on. It can exist at all levels of analysis (Hernandez et al., 2011), and it can involve interactive effects across all levels (Jepson, 2009). Context can be both distal and proximal to leadership (Avolio, 2007), and it can be treated as an antecedent, mediator, moderator, or outcome of leadership (Mowday & Sutton, 1993; Oc, 2018).

Regardless of how *context* is defined, conceptualized, or modeled, it is clear that it is inexorably intertwined with the process of leadership. Process-oriented approaches to leadership view context as comprising forces that not only constrain and facilitate the leadership processes, but also guide the meaning, relevance, and interpretation of the behavioral interactions that in turn define and produce leadership (Eberly et al., 2013; Uhl-Bien, 2006; Uhl-Bien, Marion, & McKelvey, 2007); hence studying the leadership process necessarily means studying context *in conjunction* with leadership (Carter et al., 2015). While recent researchers have made calls for more completely incorporating the social, cultural, and environmental context into leadership research (Antonakis et al., 2004; Yammarino, 2013), we strongly believe that the process of leadership cannot be understood without simultaneously understanding the complexity of the context in which it is embedded.

Recommendations for Process-oriented Methods

Taking into consideration the critical components we have reviewed so far, we next need to ask: How do we advance leadership research methods? Opportunities present themselves both within our own field's history and within other fields or disciplines (Mathieu & Chen, 2011). To answer the question, we examined previous leadership process-oriented studies in an effort to resurrect some of the methods, as well as analytical techniques, used. We also turned to other related fields studying similarly complex processes. What we found there mapped well onto the key elements of relational processes of leadership; thus we discuss them in that order.

Observational Methods

Behavioral approaches to leadership and followership have traditionally focused on what leaders and followers do, or how they behave. However, unpacking the leadership process may best be achieved by focusing attention on the micro-enactments of parties' interactions with each other. Observational research methods that focus on capturing verbal interaction behavior are one option (Fairhurst & Uhl-Bien, 2012). We discuss one example, which aims to capture how control is exchanged among dyads (for example, relational control). To use this type of research method, first, the verbal behaviors of group members can be coded (Hazy & Silberstang, 2009) to assess the frequency, pattern, and types of behavior and interaction. Many schemes exist for coding verbal behavior, dating back to Bales (1950). More recently, Silberstang and Hazy (2008) described how micro-enactments, which consist of the individual behaviors of group members as they interact with one another, create organized programs of action that are subject to evolving group dynamics and show how this process can be described as self-organizing. Seven micro-enactments are described, along with a framework for examining how they assemble, intersect, and influence one another to enable organized learning, action, innovation, and change, at both the group and the organizational levels.

In the team context, Lehmann-Willenbrock, Meinecke, Rowold, and Kauffeld (2015) developed a coding scheme to examine leader–follower communication dynamics during team interactions. Their goal was to investigate the relationship of transformational leader behaviors to functional and dysfunctional team processes. In a related context, Kolbe, Burtscher, and Manser (2013) developed a coding scheme for capturing task-relevant verbal *and* nonverbal behavioral interactions in healthcare action teams. Similarly to Lehmann-Willenbrock and colleagues (2015), Kolbe's team's (2013) scheme allows for assessment of the occurrence and timing of coordination behavior, thus providing the basis on which to study the dynamics of the coordination process, revealing insights into the immediate functions of specific behaviors for ongoing team interaction.

The popularity of verbal discourse analysis has grown over the years and has recently been applied to the study of leadership (see Fairhurst & Uhl-Bien, 2012, for an overview of these approaches). For our second example, we highlight one particular technique: relational control (Rogers & Escudero, 2004; Rogers & Farace, 1975). This system codes each conversation in turn for whether it asserts control (designated as a single upward arrow), acquiesces or requests control (designated as a single downward arrow), or neutralizes the control move of the previous utterance (designated as a single transverse arrow). In this scheme, the form of the utterance is important, not the content. As noted by Wiley (1988), to understand social structure, however, knowing what people do individually is not sufficient; rather, we must understand what group members do in conjunction with other members in an interaction – that is, "we need to know the answers to questions, whether proposals were accepted, rejected, or modified, and the like" (Courtright, Fairhurst, & Rogers, 1989, p. 777).

With interaction data, relational control focuses on sequenced behavior, similar to the way in which Weick (1979) described the "act," "interact," and "double interact." In this familiar scheme, an "act" is the behavior of one person, an "interact" is the response of another to that behavior, and a "double interact" is the response to the response. Relational control analyses also have the capacity to examine more extended interactional sequences through Markov chain or lag sequential analyses. So-called first-order transitions or interacts occur when one relational control code directly follows the previous one (lag1). In other words, transition probabilities indicate the likelihood that B's response is triggered by A within the interaction process.

In relational control, constructs such as emergent leadership evolve from interaction patterns that leadership research typically assumes are measured through self-report. Thus, similar to Hirsh, Mar, and Peterson (2012), the emergence of a collective structure reflects a reduction over time of entropy in terms of the probability of who will exert the next leadership behavior (that is, a better prediction of who will perform the next leadership act). Consequently, we recommend the use of both organizational discourse and relational control analysis to capture the process of leadership emergence, because these methods can capture the micro-level interactions that underlie leadership emergence.

Person-oriented Methods

Osborn, Hunt, and Jauch (2002, p. 797) argued that current leadership research is not invalid, but is incomplete, advocating that "leadership and its effectiveness, in large part, is dependent upon the context." Since then, the vast majority of research has focused on the influence of context on leadership, or on relationships between leadership and both individual and organizational outcomes. For example, contingency theories portray leaders as most effective when they adapt to their environment (for example, Fiedler, 1966; House & Mitchell, 1974).

Common across these contingency theories is an assumption that the context supplies the variation to which leaders must adapt and that this "variation is exogenous to the leadership process" (DeRue, 2011, p. 130). There are two main issues with this perspective: First, the leadership process may influence the contextual conditions that enable or constrain group effectiveness; and second, this perspective views the relationship between leadership and context from a variable-oriented perspective (Block, 1971). Specifically, research in leadership has focused on understanding relationships between separate dimensions of people (for example, values, traits, beliefs, perceptions, behaviors) and separate dimensions of context (for example, disruptive events, follower ability, task structure) and work-related outcomes. Moreover, when *context* is included in leadership studies, it is mostly modeled using a *person × context* interaction term, ignoring the idea that individuals' structure and dynamics are in part defined by their context (Bergman & Magnusson, 1997). If leadership is socially constructed *in* a context, then patterns (over time) must be considered; hence this presents a great opportunity for person-oriented research.

Person-oriented research treats the individual as an organized system of dynamically interacting variables, which form a pattern within a person over time (Magnusson, 1995). The person-oriented approach is concerned with individuals and how individuals operate in, or are influenced by, the context in which they exist (Magnusson, 1988). In other words, the person in the environment is just as important as the person × environment interaction and the environment itself. A hallmark characteristic of the person-oriented approach is that variables have limited meaning in and of themselves (Bergman & Magnusson, 1997); rather, it is the configuration of these variables as part of an indivisible pattern that allows them to take on meaning and begin to describe individuals. Finally, each variable takes its meaning from the other variables in the pattern to form the coherent whole. Thus, when we assume that the relationships among variables are not uniform across all of the values that a variable might take, we can develop profiles, patterns, or configurations that describe individuals, not scores on the variables (Bogat, 2009). Instead of addressing questions about the individual components of people *or* contexts, the person-oriented approach seeks to address questions related to a whole person, as a coherent, organized totality (Bergman & Magnusson, 1997). Thus a prototypic person-oriented approach has three characteristics: configuration focus, a focus on the individual, and a process focus.

This way of thinking is more closely aligned with the conceptualizations and research questions of processes and individuals as holistic systems. It captures the reciprocal nature of interactions between individuals and their environments, such that the concept under study becomes a "person–environment system" (Magnusson & Stattin, 2006, p. 425). In addition, the variables forming the patterns within the system do not have to be at the same level of analysis. A final advantage is that examining many different components of the process in combination can result in a more complete understanding of leadership processes, as well as the potential for greater predictive accuracy (MacDougall, Bauer, Novicevic, & Buckley, 2014).

A classic example of the person-oriented approach is Gustafson and Magnusson's (1991) study of female life careers. This study demonstrated that patterns of variables reflecting the girls' intelligence, achievement, and self-perceived academic competence, as well as traditional measures of socio-economic conditions (primarily their parents' income and education) and family climate (relationships, norms, joint activities), jointly produced psychologically meaningful descriptions of the girls' abilities and school adaptation during adolescence. Interpreting individual variables in these *patterns* at two different ages revealed information and suggested differential developmental processes that might have been "masked by more traditional, linear-model-based methodology" (Gustafson & Magnusson, 1991, p. 37). By analyzing the girls' *patterns* across certain variables, instead of "assessing girls' relative standing on a series of group variables and then relating their rank on one variable to their ranks on others," Gustafson and Magnusson (1991, p. 4) had defined the "individual-in-the environment" as the analytic unit.

Another avenue for the advancement of leadership process research is therefore a better integration of context, and the person-oriented approach provides a methodology with which to do so. Context, in leadership research, can refer to the environment, the situation, the task, other individuals, or other dyads in a system. Recently, Oc (2018) proposed a framework to provide a broad, but systematic, understanding of how contextual factors that shape human behavior can be categorized and how the effect of such factors can be studied in organizational research. Oc (2018) elaborated on John's (2006) two-level framework: the omnibus context and the discrete context. The omnibus level involves when, where, and who is being led; the discrete level involves the task, social, physical, and temporal variables that influence attitudes, behaviors, and cognitions. In addition, Oc's (2018) review discussed how context impacts leadership, finding that most research regards context as modifiers of, not partners in, the leadership process. Since context is regarded as part of a holistic unit using the pattern-oriented approach, there is no need to specify context as a modifier, as in variable-oriented research. Furthermore, even when context is identified, it is unlikely that it is soundly measured and properly defined (Bogat, 2009). Here, Oc's (2018) categorization of context and identification of how context is typically studied within leadership can help to guide future research. Moreover, as noted by Wang and colleagues (2014), inconsistencies in research findings may be reconciled by considering the potential heterogeneity in the population studied. Taking a person-oriented perspective may help us to achieve this aim.

Finally, the importance of both time and context can be highlighted with the notion of trajectories of profiles over time. Recent analytical advances in longitudinal extensions of latent class and latent profile analyses – for example, repeated measures latent class analysis (Collins & Lanza, 2010), latent class/profile growth analysis (Vandenberg & Stanley, 2009), or growth mixture modeling (Muthén, 2004) – offer immense opportunity for understanding patterns in how leadership changes over time and situations (Foti & McCusker, 2017).

Dyadic Methods

To reflect the multilevel nature of leadership processes, multiple levels of analysis must be examined simultaneously (Batistič, Černe, & Vogel, 2017; Contractor, Wasserman, & Faust, 2006). This means accounting for and explaining leadership phenomena occurring at the micro, meso, and macro levels of analysis (Kozlowski & Klein, 2000). Of all of the levels involved in leadership, that arguably is most in need of methodological advancement is the meso level, or the dyad, which, according to Yammarino and Gooty (2017, p. 229), is "the most neglected and poorly understood level of analysis in leadership research." Because leadership originates as a dyadic perception, there should be a plethora of research conducted at the dyadic level – and yet dyadic-level research is the least prevalent (Krasikova & LeBreton, 2012) and most frequently misaligned in the theory, measurement, and analysis of leadership (Gooty, Serban, Thomas, Gavin, & Yammarino, 2012). In what follows, we describe methods for advancing process-oriented leadership methods at the dyadic level.

A handful of organizational scholars have consistently advocated for more dyadic leadership research to further the multilevel agenda of leadership processes (for example, Dansereau, 1995; Gooty & Yammarino, 2011; Krasikova & LeBreton, 2012; Tse & Ashkanasy, 2015; Uhl-Bien, 2006) and have discussed different methods of conducting it as such. The first is by collecting data at the individual level, but using dyadic data analysis techniques, such as the actor–partner interdependence model (APIM), the social relations model (SRM) (Kenny, 1994), one-with-many (OWM) designs (Kenny, Kashy, & Cook, 2006), within and between analyses (WABA) (Dansereau, Alutto, & Yammarino, 1984), and advanced random coefficient modeling, such as hybrid and cross-classification models (Luo & Kwok, 2009). For this method to be considered dyadic, perceptions and behaviors must be collected reciprocally, as opposed to unilaterally (Duncan, Kanki, Mokros, & Fiske, 1984) – that is, instead of asking only one dyad member about perceptions of leadership, as is most common, data must be collected from *both dyad members* (Krasikova & LeBreton, 2012).

Unilaterally collecting and analyzing dyadic data is problematic because its theoretical misalignment is a mis-specified model (that is, leadership is inherently dyadic, but is measured by one individual), resulting in biased standard errors (Kline, 2005). If data is collected from both dyad members, but analyzed without any of the dyadic data analysis techniques listed above, the assumption of independence of the dyad members is violated. Similarly, if dyads are nested in larger groups and the analysis strategy does not account for higher-order dependencies in the dyad (for example, if dyads share members), the assumption of independence of the dyads is violated. Both cases produce inaccurate standard errors, error rates, and false conclusions (Bliese & Hanges, 2004).

While each of the aforementioned techniques is best suited for different types of leadership data (for when to use which technique, see Gooty & Yammarino, 2011; Krasikova & LeBreton, 2012; Tse & Ashkanasy, 2015), all advance leadership research methods by incorporating an emphasis on the dyad (and sometimes the group) in the analysis of leadership data. Furthermore, by accounting for nesting, dependencies, and interactions within and between dyads, these methods more closely align with the multilevel nature of leadership processes.

Some leadership scholars argue that if leadership research is to be fully dyadic, the *unit of measurement* ought to be dyadic – that is, the unit of measurement ought to be the relationship itself (Fairhurst & Antonakis, 2012). Instead of estimating "relationship effects," or the effects and variances unaccounted for by dyad members and error, relational measurement directly captures that which is exchanged, shared, or connected between the two individuals. Historically, one of the most common ways of capturing dyadic relational data was behavioral observation. As discussed earlier in the chapter, behavioral observation is effective in capturing the verbal exchange and discourse among dyads, where the unit of analysis is a dyadic "interact," but behavioral observation is not limited to verbal relational data collection. Nonverbal interactions can also be coded to elicit the dyadic measurements involved in leadership processes, such as friendship, relationship quality/strength, closeness, emotional relations, and relational identities.

Looking outside of the leadership realm generates ample unconventional (and often less obtrusive) ways of measuring and collecting relational data among dyads. For example, in political science research, a relatively common method is coding textual negotiations and diplomatic exchanges between entities (for example, Bonham, 1993). From the applied field and sociological/socio-psychological domain, there comes a growth in scraping and coding dyadic data through social media, community forums, and other forms of online trace data (Avolio, Sosik, Kahai, & Baker, 2014). Finally, in the teams literature, there is a heavy focus on understanding group processes and states using unobtrusive measures (Hill, White, & Wallace, 2014). One tool useful for capturing dyadic leadership processes is sociometric badges (Olguín et al., 2009; Paradiso et al., 2010) and other mobile devices, which, in addition to a host of other capabilities, measure the frequency, duration, and expression of individuals in dyads and groups.

These dyadic data collection methods produce units of analysis at the relationship or relational event levels, which open doors towards more process-oriented, multilevel analysis methods. For example, in social network analysis (SNA), a dyadic relationship, or "tie," is the unit of analysis. A tie can represent a variety of inherently relational constructs (for example, perceptions, interactions, or relationships), and since each dyadic tie is analyzed in conjunction with all other ties in the group, this technique can account for the social embeddedness of each tie. With advanced predictive and longitudinal extensions of SNA – for example, the temporal exponential random graph model (TERGM) or simulation investigation for empirical network analysis (SIENA) – we can now model more of dyadic complexities, such as how relationships change, evolve, and emerge. Additionally, sequential synchronization analysis (Murase, Poole, Asencio, & McDonald, 2017) and relational event modeling (Pilny, Schecter, Poole, & Contractor, 2016), among others, have the capacity to capture the *pattern* of the unfolding dyadic relational processes of leadership emergence, effectiveness, and development. Together with dyadic analysis of individual data, these methods reflect a step in the right direction toward growing a much-needed body of research of leadership at the dyadic and, ultimately, multiple levels of analysis.

Within-person Methods

Short-longitudinal, or "shortitudinal," studies can be used to explicitly acknowledge the role of time when studying the leadership process (Acton, McCusker, Foti, & Braun, 2017). Characterized by a study design with multiple waves of measurements at short time intervals, shortitudinal studies can be a viable alternative to longitudinal studies for examining causal effects (Dormann & Griffin, 2015). To better understand the dynamics of leadership processes, shortitudinal designs can model an event-level approach, in which the variability within an individual across time or events is measured (Hoffman & Lord, 2013). This shifts the temporal focus from traditional units, such as days and weeks, to a more micro perspective. Events are understood as units of activity rooted in a particular time and place, with distinct beginnings and ends (Zacks, Tversky, & Iyer, 2001). Hoffman and Lord (2013) provide a more in-depth review of event-level approaches, along with a taxonomy for the seven identified event dimensions involved in studying various constructs.

One method for studying within-person constructs is experience sampling measurement (ESM). Refocusing attention back on examination of daily experiences, Csikszentmihalyi, Larson, and Prescott (1977) identified their efforts to study daily adolescent activity through use of electronic pagers as ESM. This method involves intensive, repeated assessments taken by means of handheld devices or surveys, at brief intervals between measurements, for a study duration that could span as short a time as several hours or as long as a couple of weeks (Beal, 2015). The measurement time intervals in ESM can vary. Depending on the construct and research question, assessments can be done daily, multiple times in a day, or even with continuous ratings within one event. (For an in-depth review of different temporal levels in ESM, see Beal & Gabriel, 2018.) With ESM, a researcher avoids the assumption that a construct is stable; instead, the researcher obtains deeper insight into how a construct fluctuates over time and into the factors potentially contributing to these changes. As such, ESM is a valuable tool for understanding the leadership process. It is also a method of studying leadership in context. Respondents answer questions guided by their fresh work experiences, and it records episodic-based memories that capture truer assessments of actual leadership behaviors. Additionally, ESM provides a more representative sampling of a construct, which offers insight into the within-person process and how immediate events impact it (Beal, 2015).

While ESM is often employed for measuring attitudinal constructs, there is a growing recognition of the unique advantages that ESM has for leadership research – particularly in understanding the context-specific and dynamic processes. For example, Foti, Hansbrough, Epitropaki, and Coyle (2017) highlight the specific need for such methods in understanding implicit leadership theories (ILT) and implicit followership theories (IFT). They propose that ESM can help in determining in which circumstances individuals rely on implicit perceptions rather than processing leader behaviors as they occur, as well as in tracking how changes in perceptions of leaders or followers occur. Additionally, using ESM to measure current opinions about leaders based on immediate past experiences can help to distinguish between real perceptions of leader effectiveness and the actual performance of leader behaviors (Hoffman & Lord, 2013).

In leadership research, ESM has been used only occasionally – mainly in the area of transformational leadership research. Because transformational leadership theorizes unique leader interactions with each follower, measuring it daily captures its dynamic nature more accurately. Tepper and colleagues (2018) carried out daily ESM by administering online surveys at the end of each workday over a period of three weeks to assess the person–supervisor fit between transformational leadership required by the subordinate and what was received from the supervisor. For more frequent measurements, researchers might use the episodic approach and signal respondents periodically during the workday to complete assessments. For example, Nielsen and Cleal (2011), and Bono, Foldes, Vinson, & Muros (2007), assessed the antecedents and moderating effects of transformational leadership, respectively. This allowed respondents to assess the immediate cognitive, emotional, and situational factors that influenced their perceptions regarding transformational leadership. If the research focus is on understanding the variability of a construct within an event, researchers can employ the continuous rating assessment (CRA) approach. In a notable example from outside of the transformational leadership literature, Naidoo and Lord (2008) had participants continuously rate their current perceptions of a leader's charisma as they listened to an audio speech recording.

Leadership research can benefit greatly from the use of ESM, especially for understanding the leadership process within an individual – that is, how events have an immediate impact on subsequent perceptions and behaviors. However, when choosing between the different ESM methods, with their respective time intervals, it is important to align method with theory and research question (George & Jones, 2000; Ployhart & Vandenberg, 2010). This allows a true assessment of the function of time within a leadership construct. Furthermore, implementing an events-level approach by means of ESM can provide a within-person perspective on traditionally person-level constructs. Measuring perceptions of a construct as an event that is rooted in context over different time points provides a more organic understanding of the leadership process as it develops, instead of supplying only an aggregation of those perceptions, which may be biased (Hoffman & Lord, 2013).

Moving beyond Quantitative Approaches to Leadership Research Methods

Axelrod (1997) claimed there are three ways of practicing science: quantitative, qualitative, and computational simulation. In the study of organizational leadership, quantitative analysis is undoubtedly the dominant strategy, but we believe that qualitative research methods and computational simulations cannot be neglected. We believe that both have a particularly important place in improving process-oriented leadership methods, because they can advance knowledge in all of the key areas discussed in this chapter. Accordingly, we devote the last section to illustrating their importance.

Qualitative Methods

Although some researchers have long highlighted the strengths of qualitative methods for leadership research (Conger, 1998; Bryman, 2004), qualitative research only makes up 24 percent of leadership research designs (Gardner et al., 2010). Because of its inductive nature, qualitative research promotes understanding of the interactional, dynamic, multilevel, and contextual elements of the leadership process and their associated complexities (Conger, 1998). If used correctly, qualitative methods afford researchers various strengths over and above traditional quantitative research. First, because most qualitative research is conducted *in situ*, it allows various factors to be uncovered that influence leadership within its natural context and over time. Second, it has the flexibility of capturing leadership constructs even if they are unexpected, because the data informs findings. Finally, qualitative research requires a researcher to immerse themselves in the study setting, providing an in-depth exploration of leadership longitudinally (Bryman, 1995) and contextually, allowing for deeper insight into the symbolic and social implications of leadership constructs (Parry, Mumford, Bower, & Watts, 2014). With this holistic understanding of leadership-related events, qualitative approaches better position the researcher to understand the hypothetical "black box" of leadership process (Parry et al., 2014).

Qualitative research can be categorized in a variety of ways – for example, by research paradigm, such as positivism (see Klenke, 2016), or by type of analysis, such as qualitative analysis on quantitative data (see Parry et al., 2014). However, we limit our discussion to five of the most commonly used qualitative methods in leadership research. First, *content analysis* is a popular technique, in which the content of text or interview data is analyzed for themes that provide insight into the research question of interest. For example, Aas, Ellingsen, Lindøe, and Möller (2008) content-analyzed transcripts of interviews with both subordinates and supervisors to identify specific leadership behaviors that encouraged smooth transitions back to work for those returning from long-term leave. By first identifying specific leadership characteristics and then organizing them into broad thematic categories, the researchers contributed to an understanding of effective leadership in such contexts.

Second, in *grounded theory*, the aim is to develop a theory from data that is systematically collected. This form is highly inductive, because the researcher begins analysis without any prior assumptions; instead, understanding of a construct is derived from the ongoing observation and interpretation of the data. Hunt and Ropo (1995) used this method to understand the challenges in leadership experienced in a multilevel organization. They studied a case narrative of Roger Smith's tenure as chief executive officer (CEO) of General Motors as he interacted with individuals from various levels. Based on this narrative, they developed propositions using additional existing literature and applying a levels-of-analysis framework for further analysis.

Next, another strategy is to conduct a *case analysis*. Case study methodology is most often employed for exploratory purposes: It enables better understanding of new issues on which theory is underdeveloped, of complex phenomena, or of events that are influenced by a variety of contextual factors (Parry et al., 2014). Galli and Müller-Stewens (2012) carried out a case analysis to unpack the process through which leadership development practices contributed to an organization's social capital. They first analyzed collected observational data and interview transcripts with employees; they then developed propositions to answer the research question, while keeping in mind the contextual factors that influenced their findings.

Fourth, *ethnographical research* is less often used in our field, but it is a powerful tool whereby researchers completely immerse themselves in the contexts of the social systems they are studying to better understand how they operate. It is especially useful in examining interactions between individuals in a natural setting, allowing more accurate interpretations of behaviors and language, with the cultural and organizational factors in mind. For example, Smit (2014) conducted an ethnographical study in a South African school to understand relational leadership from the perspective of its female school principal. From interview transcripts and observational notes, Smit was able to capture leadership qualities that were embodied by that principal, in addition to explicating the interactions the leader had with the school and community at large.

Finally, *historiometric studies* are gaining popularity as a qualitative research method of choice in leadership (for example, DeChurch et al., 2010; O'Connor, Mumford, Clifton, Gessner, & Connelly, 1995). By interpreting historical texts and the biographies of past leaders, historiometric approaches aim to use history to predict future expected attributes of interest (see Ciulla, Chapter 5 in this volume).

Thus qualitative research can be applied to a variety of research questions and capture different dimensions of the leadership process. It is essential to understand the nature of the research question and data before deciding which qualitative method to use. Klenke (2016), Parry and colleagues (2014), Bryman (2004), and Conger (1998) are all excellent resources for more information about the strengths and challenges of qualitative research, and for general guidance. Qualitative research can be tedious and time-consuming, but if carried out correctly, it holds much potential for furthering the field of leadership research – especially when it comes to understanding the leadership process.

Computational Modeling

Computational models are an additional means of studying organizational phenomena, and its prevalence is growing in the organizational sciences (Weinhardt & Vancouver, 2012). Computational models are mathematical representations of complex, dynamic processes, which specify "what, how, and when events or actions happen" (Grand et al., 2016, p. 8). Using computer software, complex social systems can be modeled and simulated to allow a researcher to understand the underlying processes of emergence. While there exist multiple different types of computational models (Vancouver & Weinhardt, 2012), of particular utility for studying leadership as a process is agent-based modeling (Dionne, Sayama, Hao, & Bush, 2010; Hazy & Uhl-Bien, 2014). In agent-based modeling, "agents" – that is, entities often representing individuals or organizations in a social system – are assigned certain characteristics or properties and interact based on a set of preassigned rules that govern their interactional behavior. From the agents' interactions, collective-level properties and states emerge, and researchers are able to manipulate the various input parameters and rules to better understand how lower-level mechanisms interact in context to produce system-level outcomes.

Agent-based modeling is particularly well suited to studying leadership as a process, in part because it addresses all four of the key components of the leadership process mentioned earlier in the chapter. Agent-based modeling aims to explain how agents at one level interact over time in a particular environment or situation to produce phenomena at a higher level (Vancouver & Weinhardt, 2012); hence this method simultaneously incorporates the study of interpersonal, or "interagent," interaction, as it develops over time, across multiple levels, and as a factor of context. For example, in an agent-based study by Dionne and

Dionne (2008) examining the impact of leadership on *group* decision-making, results showed that groups' decision quality, as well as the *time* it took for groups to reach decisions, varied based on the number of *interactions* among group *members* and the *context* of leadership style – that is, participative, individualized, leader–member exchange (LMX), and ideal. Another example is a study by Black, Oliver, Howell, and King (2006), which used agent-based modeling to examine the emergence process of a group's context for learning (CFL) based on characteristics of the leader, follower, and group. Researchers first specified the agents (leaders, followers, and group), the agents' characteristics, and the agents' learning behavior, then examined the developmental trajectories toward reaching a CFL. Results showed that groups followed different developmental paths towards CFL depending on the leader–follower combinations specified.

While agent-based modeling specifically, and computer simulation in general, are not perfect replications of reality (Axelrod, 1997), their controlled manipulation of multilevel mechanisms and rules allows for an understanding of how dynamic, nonlinear, and temporal components of leadership of the leadership process unfold (Castillo & Trinh, 2018).

Conclusion

After reviewing leadership trends over the past 100 years, Lord and colleagues (2017) identified several directions for leadership research in the future. They predicted that leadership will be more multidisciplinary, will emphasize the coproduction of leadership by multiple individuals, and will have an emergent and shared nature. Thus the process of leadership – specifically, multilevel dynamic frameworks – will be particularly important to the future of leadership.

There have been several recent reviews of leadership research that have been critical of both theory and methodology (Fischer et al., 2017; Lord, 2017). A focus on process can help us to address many of these criticisms. First, a process focus may be one promising approach to finding commonalities across various leadership theories. For example, Meuser and colleagues (2016) integrated 49 focal leadership constructs into six theoretical perspectives. They concluded that the integration of leadership theories is still in its infancy and suggested that integration could be accomplished "with approaches in which the fabric of each theory is interwoven" (Meuser et al., 2016, p. 1395). We believe process to be that fabric.

Second, a focus on process can move us beyond the "typical" leadership study with its questionnaire measures that can distort inferences about time, interactions, and levels.

Third, a focus on process can help us to move past the notion that leadership is localized in leaders, rather than a result of social and relational systems. It can encourage us to see the nexus of leadership in processes that link entities.

Finally, a focus on process can aid us in linking theory, methodology, measurement, and analysis.

References

Aas, R.W., Ellingsen, K.L., Lindøe, P., & Möller, A. (2008). Leadership qualities in the return to work process: A content analysis. *Journal of Occupational Rehabilitation*, *18*(4), 335–346.

Acton, B.P., Foti, R.J., Lord, R.G., & Gladfelter, J. G. (2019). Putting emergence back in leadership emergence: Integrating leadership emergence research into a multilevel, process-oriented framework. *The Leadership Quarterly* (in review).

Acton, B., McCusker, M.E., Foti, R.J., & Braun, M.T. (2017, April). *Behind the times: Examining the development of shared leadership emergence.* Poster presented at the 32nd Annual Conference of the Society for Industrial and Organizational Psychology, Orlando, FL.

Alipour, K.K., Mohammed, S., & Martinez, P.N. (2017). Incorporating temporality into implicit leadership and followership theories: Exploring inconsistencies between time-based expectations and actual behaviors. *The Leadership Quarterly*, *28*(2), 300–316.

Antonakis, J., & Day, D.V. (Eds.). (2018). *The nature of leadership.* Thousand Oaks, CA: Sage.

Antonakis, J., Schriesheim, C.A., Donovan, J.A., Gopalakrishna-Pillai, K., Pellegrini, E.K., & Rossomme, J.L. (2004). Methods for studying leadership. In J. Antonakis, A.R. Cianciolo, & R.J. Sternberg (Eds.), *The nature of leadership* (pp. 48–70). Thousand Oaks, CA: Sage.

Avolio, B.J. (2007). Promoting more integrative strategies for leadership theory-building. *American Psychologist*, *62*(1), 25–33.

Avolio, B.J., Sosik, J.J., Kahai, S.S., & Baker, B. (2014). E-leadership: Re-examining transformations in leadership source and transmission. *The Leadership Quarterly*, *25*(1), 105–131.

Avolio, B.J., Walumbwa, F.O., & Weber, T.J. (2009). Leadership: Current theories, research, and future directions. *Annual Review of Psychology*, *60*, 421–449.

Axelrod, R. (1997). Advancing the art of simulation in the social sciences. In R. Conte, R. Hegselmann, & P. Terna (Eds.), *Simulating social phenomena* (pp. 21–40). Berlin: Springer-Verlag.

Bales, R.F. (1950). *Interaction process analysis: A method for the study of small groups.* Cambridge, MA: Addison Wesley Press.

Bales, R.F. (1953). A theoretical framework for interaction process analysis. In D. Cartwright and A. Zander, (Eds.), *Group dynamics: Research and theory* (pp. 29–38). Evanston, IL: Row Peterson.

Bass, B.M. (1949). An analysis of the leaderless group discussion. *Journal of Applied Psychology*, *33*(6), 527–533.

Bass, B.M. (1985). *Leadership and performance beyond expectations.* New York: Free Press.

Batistič,, S., Černe, M., & Vogel, B. (2017). Just how multi-level is leadership research? A document co-citation analysis 1980–2013 on leadership constructs and outcomes. *The Leadership Quarterly*, *28*(1), 86–103.

Beal, D.J. (2015). ESM 2.0: State of the art and future potential of experience sampling methods in organizational research. *Annual Review of Organizational Psychology and Organizational Behavior*, *2*, 383–407.

Beal, D.J., & Gabriel, A.S. (2018). Looking within: An examination, combination, and extension of within-person methods across multiple levels of analysis. In S.E. Humphrey & J.M. LeBreton (Eds.), *The handbook for multilevel theory, measurement, and analysis* (in press). Washington, D.C.: American Psychological Association.

Bergman, L.R., & Magnusson, D. (1997). A person-oriented approach in research on developmental psychopathology. *Development and Psychopathology, 9*(2), 291–319.

Bergman, S.M., Small, E.E., Bergman, J.Z., & Bowling, J.J. (2014). Leadership emergence and group development: A longitudinal examination of project teams. *Journal of Organizational Psychology, 14*(1) 111–126.

Black, J.A., Oliver, R.L., Howell, J.P., & King, J.P. (2006). A dynamic system simulation of leader and group effects on context for learning. *The Leadership Quarterly, 17*(1), 39–56.

Blau, P.M. (1964). *Exchange and power in social life*. New York: John Wiley.

Bliese, P.D., & Hanges, P.J. 2004. Being both too liberal and too conservative: The perils of treating grouped data as though they were independent. *Organizational Research Methods, 7*(4), 400–417.

Block, J. (1971). *Lives through time*. Berkeley, CA: Bancroft Books.

Bluedorn, A.C., & Jaussi, K.S. (2008). Leaders, followers, and time. *The Leadership Quarterly, 19*(6), 654–668.

Bogat, G.A. (2009). Is it necessary to discuss person-oriented research in community psychology? *American Journal of Community Psychology, 43*(1–2), 22–34.

Bonham, G.M. (1993). Cognitive mapping as a technique for supporting international negotiation. *Theory and Decision, 34*(3), 255–273.

Bono, J.E., & Anderson, M.H. (2005). The advice and influence networks of transformational leaders. *Journal of Applied Psychology, 90*(6), 1306–1314.

Bono, J.E., Foldes, H.J., Vinson, G., & Muros, J.P. (2007). Workplace emotions: The role of supervision and leadership. *Journal of Applied Psychology, 92*(5), 1357–1367.

Browne, C.G. (1949). Study of executive leadership in business, I: The R, A, and D scales. *Journal of Applied Psychology, 33*(6), 521–526.

Browne, C.G. (1950). Study of executive leadership in business, III: Goal and achievement index. *Journal of Applied Psychology, 34*(2), 82–87.

Browne, C.G. (1951). Study of executive leadership in business, IV: Sociometric pattern. *Journal of Applied Psychology, 35*(1), 34–37.

Bryman, A. (1995). Qualitative methods in leadership research: Introduction. *The Leadership Quarterly, 6*(4), 491–493.

Bryman, A. (2004). Qualitative research on leadership: A critical but appreciative review. *The Leadership Quarterly, 15*(6), 729–769.

Carter, D.R., DeChurch, L.A., Braun, M.T., & Contractor, N. (2015). Social network approaches to leadership: An integrative conceptual review. *Journal of Applied Psychology, 100*(3), 597–622.

Castillo, E.A., & Trinh, M.P. (2018). In search of missing time: A review of the study of time in leadership research. *The Leadership Quarterly, 29*(1), 165–178.

Cho, J., & Dansereau, F. (2010). Are transformational leaders fair? A multi-level study of transformational leadership, justice perceptions, and organizational citizenship behaviors. *The Leadership Quarterly, 21*(3), 409–421.

Collins, L.M., & Lanza, S.T. (2010). *Latent class and latent transition analysis: With applications in the social, behavioral, and health sciences*. New York: John Wiley & Sons.

Conger, J.A. (1998). Qualitative research as the cornerstone methodology for understanding leadership. *The Leadership Quarterly, 9*(1), 107–122.

Contractor, N.S., Wasserman, S., & Faust, K. (2006). Testing multitheoretical, multi-level hypotheses about organizational networks: An analytic framework and empirical example. *Academy of Management Review, 31*(3), 681–703.

Courtright, J.A., Fairhurst, G.T., & Rogers, L.E. (1989). Interaction patterns in organic and mechanistic system. *Academy of Management Journal, 32*(4), 773–802.

Cronin, M.A., Weingart, L.R., & Todorova, G. (2011). Dynamics in groups: Are we there yet? *Academy of Management Annals, 5*(1), 571–612.

Csikszentmihalyi, M., Larson, R., & Prescott, S. (1977). The ecology of adolescent activity and experience. *Journal of Youth and Adolescence, 6*(3), 281–294.

Dansereau, F. (1995). A dyadic approach to leadership: Creating and nurturing this approach under fire. *The Leadership Quarterly, 6*(4), 479–490.

Dansereau, F., Alutto, J.A., & Yammarino, F.J. (1984). *Theory testing in organizational behavior: The varient approach*. Englewood Cliffs, NJ: Prentice Hall.

Day, D.V. (2012). Leadership. In S.J. Kozlowski (Ed.), *The Oxford handbook of organizational psychology* (pp. 696–733). New York: Oxford University Press.

Day, D.V. (2014). Time and leadership. In A.J. Shipp & Y. Fried (Eds.), *Time and work: How time impacts groups, organizations, and methodological choices* (pp. 30–52). New York: Psychology Press.

Day, D.V., & Antonakis, J. (2012). Leadership: Past, present, and future. In D.V. Day & J. Antonakis (Eds.), *The nature of leadership* (2nd ed.) (pp. 3–25). Thousand Oaks, CA: Sage.

Day, D.V., & Sin, H.P. (2011). Longitudinal tests of an integrative model of leader development: Charting and understanding developmental trajectories. *The Leadership Quarterly, 22*(3), 545–560.

Day, D.V., & Zaccaro, S.J. (2007). Leadership: A critical historical analysis of the influence of leader traits. In L.L. Koppes (Ed.), *Historical perspectives in industrial and organizational psychology* (pp. 383–405). Mahwah, NJ: Lawrence Erlbaum.

DeChurch, L.A., Burke, C.S., Shuffler, M.L., Lyons, R., Doty, D., & Salas, E. (2011). A historiometric analysis of leadership in mission critical multiteam environments. *The Leadership Quarterly, 22*(1), 152–169.

DeRue, D.S. (2011). Adaptive leadership theory: Leading and following as a complex adaptive process. *Research in Organizational Behavior, 31*, 125–150.

DeRue, D.S., & Ashford, S.J. (2010). Who will lead and who will follow? A social process of leadership identity construction in organizations. *Academy of Management Review, 35*(4), 627–647.

DeRue, D.S., Nahrgang, J.D., Wellman, N., & Humphrey, S.E. (2011). Trait and behavioral theories of leadership: An integration and meta-analytic test of their relative validity. *Personnel Psychology, 64*(1), 7–52.

Dinh, J.E., Lord, R.G., Gardner, W.L., Meuser, J.D., Liden, R.C., & Hu, J. (2014). Leadership theory and research in the new millennium: Current theoretical trends and changing perspectives. *The Leadership Quarterly, 25*(1), 36–62.

Dionne, S.D., & Dionne, P.J. (2008). Levels-based leadership and hierarchical group decision optimization: A Monte Carlo simulation. *The Leadership Quarterly, 19*(2), 212–234.

Dionne, S.D., Gupta, A., Sotak, K.L., Shirreffs, K.A., Serban, A., Hao, C., . . . Yammarino, F.J. (2014). A 25-year perspective on levels of analysis in leadership research. *The Leadership Quarterly, 25*(1), 6–35.

Dionne, S.D., Sayama, H., Hao, C., & Bush, B.J. (2010). The role of leadership in shared mental model convergence and team performance improvement: An agent-based computational model. *The Leadership Quarterly, 21*(6), 1035–1049.

Dormann, C., & Griffin, M.A. (2015). Optimal time lags in panel studies. *Psychological Methods, 20*(4), 489–505.

Duncan, S., Kanki, B.G., Mokros, H., & Fiske, D.W. (1984). Pseudounilaterality: Simple rate variables and other ills to which interaction research is heir. *Journal of Personality and Social Psychology*, 46(6), 1335–1348.

Eberly, M.B., Johnson, M., Hernandez, M., & Avolio, B.J. (2013). An integrative process model of leadership: Examining loci, mechanisms, and event cycles. *American Psychologist*, 68(6), 427–443.

Fairhurst, G.T. (2007). *Discursive leadership: In conversation with leadership psychology*. Thousand Oaks, CA: Sage.

Fairhurst, G.T., & Antonakis, J. (2012). Dialogue: A research agenda for relational leadership. In M. Uhl-Bien & S. Ospina (Eds.), *Advancing relational leadership research: A dialogue among perspectives* (pp. 433–459). Charlotte, NC: Information Age.

Fairhurst, G.T., & Uhl-Bien, M. (2012). Organizational discourse analysis (ODA): Examining leadership as a relational process. *The Leadership Quarterly*, 23(6), 1043–1062.

Felfe, J., & Schyns, B. (2009). Followers' personality and the perception of transformational leadership: Further evidence for the similarity hypothesis. *British Journal of Management*, 21(2), 393–410.

Fiedler, F.E. (1966). The effect of leadership and cultural heterogeneity on group performance: A test of the contingency model. *Journal of Experimental Social Psychology*, 2(3), 237–264.

Fischer, T., Dietz, J., & Antonakis, J. (2017). Leadership process models: A review and synthesis. *Journal of Management*, 43(6), 1726–1753.

Fisher, B.A. (1970). Decision emergence: Phases in group decision-making. *Communications Monographs*, 37(1), 53–66.

Foti, R.J., & Hauenstein, N.M.A. (2007). Pattern and variable approaches in leadership emergence and effectiveness. *Journal of Applied Psychology*, 92(2), 347–355.

Foti, R.J., & McCusker, M.E. (2017). Person-oriented approaches to leadership: A roadmap forward. In B. Schyns, R.J. Hall, & P. Neves (Eds.), *Handbook of methods in leadership research* (pp. 195–228). Cheltenham: Edward Elgar.

Foti, R.J., Hansbrough, T.K., Epitropaki, O., & Coyle, P.T. (2017). Dynamic viewpoints on implicit leadership and followership theories: Approaches, findings, and future directions. *The Leadership Quarterly*, 28(2), 261–267.

Galli, E.B., & Müller-Stewens, G. (2012). How to build social capital with leadership development: Lessons from an explorative case study of a multibusiness firm. *The Leadership Quarterly*, 23(1), 176–201.

Gardner, W.L., Lowe, K.B., Moss, T.W., Mahoney, K.T., & Cogliser, C.C. (2010). Scholarly leadership of the study of leadership: A review of *The Leadership Quarterly*'s second decade, 2000–2009. *The Leadership Quarterly*, 21(6), 922–958.

George, J.M., & Jones, G.R. (2000). The role of time in theory and theory building. *Journal of Management*, 26(4), 657–684.

Gersick, C.J.G. (1988). Time and transition in work teams: Toward a new model of group development. *Academy of Management Journal*, 31(1), 9–41.

Gooty, J., & Yammarino, F.J. (2011). Dyads in organizational research: Conceptual issues and multi-level analyses. *Organizational Research Methods*, 14(3), 456–483.

Gooty, J., Serban, A., Thomas, J.S., Gavin, M.B., & Yammarino, F.J. (2012). Use and misuse of levels of analysis in leadership research: An illustrative review of leader–member exchange. *The Leadership Quarterly*, 23(6), 1080–1103.

Grand, J.A., Braun, M.T., Kuljanin, G., Kozlowski, S.W., & Chao, G.T. (2016). The dynamics of team cognition: A process-oriented theory of knowledge emergence in teams. *Journal of Applied Psychology*, *101*(10), 1353–1385.

Gustafson, S.B., & Magnusson, D. (1991). *Female life careers: A pattern approach*. Mahwah, NJ: Lawrence Erlbaum.

Hazy, J.K., & Silberstang, J. (2009). Leadership within emergent events in complex systems: Micro-enactments and the mechanisms of organizational learning and change. *International Journal of Learning and Change*, *3*(3), 230–247.

Hazy, J.K., & Uhl-Bien, M. (2014). Changing the rules: The implications of complexity science for leadership research and practice. In D.V. Day (Ed.), *Oxford handbook of leadership and organizations* (pp. 709–732). Oxford: Oxford University Press.

Hazy, J.K., & Uhl-Bien, M. (2015). Towards operationalizing complexity leadership: How generative, administrative and community-building leadership practices enact organizational outcomes. *Leadership*, *11*(1), 79–104.

Hernandez, M., Eberly, M.B., Avolio, B.J., & Johnson, M.D. (2011). The loci and mechanisms of leadership: Exploring a more comprehensive view of leadership theory. *The Leadership Quarterly*, *22*(6), 1165–1185.

Hill, A.D., White, M.A., & Wallace, J.C. 2014. Unobtrusive measurement of psychological constructs in organizational research. *Organizational Psychology Review*, *4*, 147–173.

Hirsh, J.B., Mar, R.A., & Peterson, J.B. (2012). Psychological entropy: A framework for understanding uncertainty-related anxiety. *Psychological Review*, *119*(2), 304–320.

Hoffman, E.L., & Lord, R.G. (2013). A taxonomy of event-level dimensions: Implications for understanding leadership processes, behavior, and performance. *The Leadership Quarterly*, *24*(4), 558–571.

Hollander, E.P. (1992). Leadership, followership, self, and others. *The Leadership Quarterly*, *3*(1), 43–54.

Hollander, E.P., & Julian, J.W. (1969). Contemporary trends in the analysis of leadership processes. *Psychological Bulletin*, *71*(5), 387–397.

Hollander, E.P., & Willis, R.H. (1967). Some current issues in psychology of conformity and nonconformity. *Psychological Bulletin*, *68*(1), 62–76.

Hosking, D.M. (1988). Organizing, leadership and skilful process, 1. *Journal of Management Studies*, *25*(2), 147–166.

House, R.J. (1971). A path–goal theory of leadership effectiveness. *Administrative Science Quarterly*, *16*(3), 321–328.

House, R.J., & Mitchell, T. (1974). Path–goal theory of leadership. *Journal of Contemporary Business*, *3*(4), 81–98.

Hunt, J.G.J., & Ropo, A. (1995). Multi-level leadership: Grounded theory and mainstream theory applied to the case of General Motors. *The Leadership Quarterly*, *6*(3), 379–412.

Hunter, S.T., Bedell-Avers, K.E., & Mumford, M.D. (2007). The typical leadership study: Assumptions, implications, and potential remedies. *The Leadership Quarterly*, *18*(5), 435–446.

Jepson, D. (2009). Studying leadership at cross-country level: A critical analysis. *Leadership*, *5*(1), 61–80.

Johns, G. (2006). The essential impact of context on organizational behavior. *Academy of Management Review*, *31*(2), 386–408.

Kaiser, R.B., Hogan, R., & Craig, S.B. (2008). Leadership and the fate of organizations. *American Psychologist*, *63*(2), 96–110.

Kenny, D.A. (1994). *Interpersonal perception: A social relations analysis.* New York: Guilford Press.

Kenny, D.A., Kashy, D.A., & Cook, W.L. (2006). *Dyadic data analysis.* New York: Guilford Press.

Klenke, K. (2016). *Qualitative research in the study of leadership.* Bingley: Emerald Group.

Kline, R.B. (2005). *Principles and practice of structural equation modeling* (2nd ed.). New York: Guilford.

Knickerbocker, I. (1948). Leadership: A conception and some implications. *Journal of Social Issues*, *4*, 23–40.

Kolbe, M., Burtscher, M.J., & Manser, T. (2013). Co-ACT: A framework for observing coordination behavior in acute care teams. *BMJ Quality and Safety*, *22*(7), 596–605.

Kozlowski, S.W.J., & Klein, K.J. (2000). A multilevel approach to theory and research in organizations: Contextual, temporal, and emergent processes. In K.J. Klein & S.W.J. Kozlowski (Eds.), *Multilevel theory, research, and methods in organizations: Foundations, extensions, and new directions* (pp. 3–90). San Francisco, CA: Jossey-Bass.

Kozlowski, S.W.J., Mak, S., & Chao, G.T. (2016). Team-centric leadership: An integrative review. *Annual Review of Organizational Psychology and Organizational Behavior*, *3*, 21–54.

Kozlowski, S.W.J., Watola, D., Nowakowski, J.M., Kim, B., & Botero, I. (2008). Developing adaptive teams: A theory of dynamic team leadership. In E. Salas, G.F. Goodwin, & C.S. Burke (Eds.), *Team effectiveness in complex organizations: Cross-disciplinary perspectives and approaches* (pp. 113–155). Mahwah, NJ: Lawrence Erlbaum.

Krasikova, D., & LeBreton, J.M. (2012). Just the two of us: Misalignment of theory and methods in examining dyadic phenomena. *Journal of Applied Psychology*, *97*(4), 739–757.

Leenders, R., DeChurch, L.A., & Contractor, N. (2016). Once upon a time: Understanding team dynamics as relational event networks. *Organizational Psychology Review*, *6*(1), 92–115.

Lehmann-Willenbrock, N., & Allen, J.A. (2018). Modeling temporal interaction dynamics in organizational settings. *Journal of Business and Psychology*, *33*(3), 325–344.

Lehmann-Willenbrock, N., Meinecke, A.L., Rowold, J., & Kauffeld, S. (2015). How transformational leadership works during team interactions: A behavioral process analysis. *The Leadership Quarterly*, *26*(6), 1017–1033.

Lord, R.G. (2017). Leadership in the future and the future of leadership. In B. Schyns, R.J. Hall, & P. Neves (Eds.), *Handbook of methods in leadership research* (pp. 403–429). Cheltenham: Edward Elgar.

Lord, R.G., & Brown, D.J. (2004). *Leadership processes and follower self-identity.* Mahwah, NJ: Lawrence Erlbaum.

Lord, R.G., & Chui, S.L. (2018). Dual process models of self-schemas and identity: Implications for leadership and followership processes. In D.L. Ferris, R.E. Johnson, & C. Sedikides (Eds.), *The self at work* (pp. 341–362). New York: Routledge.

Lord, R.G., Day, D.V., Zaccaro, S.J., Avolio, B.J., & Eagly, A.H. (2017). Leadership in applied psychology: Three waves of theory and research. *Journal of Applied Psychology*, *102*(3), 434–451.

Lowe, K.B., & Gardner, W.L. (2000). Ten years of *The Leadership Quarterly*: Contributions and challenges for the future. *The Leadership Quarterly*, *11*(4), 459–514.

Luo, W., & Kwok, O.M. (2009). The impacts of ignoring a crossed factor in analyzing cross-classified data. *Multivariate Behavioral Research, 44*(2), 182–212.

MacDougall, A.E., Bauer, J.E., Novicevic, M.M., & Buckley, M.R. (2014). Toward the pattern-oriented approach to research in human resources management: A review of configurational and category theorizing, methods and applications. *Research in Personnel and Human Resources Management, 32*, 177–240.

Magnusson, D. (1988). *Individual development from an interactional perspective: A longitudinal study*. Mahwah, NJ: Lawrence Erlbaum.

Magnusson, D. (1995). Individual development: An integrated model. In P. Moen, G.H. Elder Jr., & Luscher (Eds.), *Examining lives in context: Perspectives on the ecology of human development* (pp. 19–60). Washington, D.C.: American Psychological Association.

Magnusson, D., & Stattin, H. (2006). The person in context: A holistic-interactionistic approach. In R.M. Lerner & W. Damon (Eds.), *Handbook of child psychology, vol. 1: Theoretical models of human development* (6th ed.) (pp. 404–464). Hoboken, NJ: Wiley.

Marchiondo, L.A., Myers, C.G., & Kopelman, S. (2015). The relational nature of leadership identity construction: How and when it influences perceived leadership and decision-making. *The Leadership Quarterly, 26*(5), 892–908.

Marks, M.A., Mathieu, J.E., & Zaccaro, S.J. (2001). A temporally based framework and taxonomy of team processes. *Academy of Management Review, 26*(3), 356–376.

Mathieu, J., & Chen, G. (2011). The etiology of the multilevel paradigm in management research. *Journal of Management, 37*(2), 395–403.

Mehra, A., Smith, B.R., Dixon, A.L., & Robertson, B. (2006). Distributed leadership in teams: The network of leadership perceptions and team performance. *The Leadership Quarterly, 17*(3), 232–245.

Merriam-Webster. (2018, June 17). Process. Retrieved from www.merriam-webster.com/dictionary/process

Meuser, J.D., Garnder, W.L., Dinh, J.E., Hu, J., Liden, R.C., & Lord, R.G. (2016). A network analysis of leadership theory: The infancy of integration. *Journal of Management, 42*(5), 1374–1403.

Miscenko, D., Guenter, H., & Day, D.V. (2017). Am I a leader? Examining leader identity development over time. *The Leadership Quarterly, 28*(5), 605–620.

Morgeson, F.P., DeRue, S.D., & Karam, E.P. (2010). Leadership in teams: A functional approach to understanding leadership structures and processes. *Journal of Management, 36*(1), 5–39.

Mowday, R.T., & Sutton, R.I. (1993). Organizational behavior: Linking individuals and groups to organizational contexts. *Annual Review of Psychology, 44*, 195–229.

Murase, T., Poole, M.S., Asencio, R., & McDonald, J. (2017). Sequential synchronization analysis. In A. Pilny & M.S. Poole (Eds.), *Group processes* (pp. 119–144). New York: Springer.

Murphy, A.J. (1941). A study of the leadership process. *American Sociological Review, 6*(5), 674–687.

Muthén, B. (2004). Latent variable analysis: Growth mixture modeling and related techniques for longitudinal data. In D. Kaplan (Ed.), *Handbook of quantitative methodology for the social sciences* (pp. 345–368). Thousand Oaks, CA: Sage.

Naidoo, L.J., & Lord, R.G. (2008). Speech imagery and perceptions of charisma: The mediating role of positive affect. *The Leadership Quarterly, 19*(3), 283–296.

Nielsen, K., & Cleal, B. (2011). Under which conditions do middle managers exhibit transformational leadership behaviors? An experience sampling method study on the predictors of transformational leadership behaviors. *The Leadership Quarterly*, 22(2), 344–352.

O'Connor, J., Mumford, M.D., Clifton, T.C., Gessner, T.L., & Connelly, M.S. (1995). Charismatic leaders and destructiveness: An historiometric study. *The Leadership Quarterly*, 6(4), 529–555.

Oc, B. (2018). Contextual leadership: A systematic review of how contextual factors shape leadership and its outcomes. *The Leadership Quarterly*, 29(1), 218–235.

Olguín, D.O., Waber, B.N., Kim, T., Mohan, A., Ara, K., & Pentland, A. (2009). Sensible organizations: Technology and methodology for automatically measuring organizational behavior. *IEEE Transactions on Systems, Man, and Cybernetics, Part B*, 39(1), 43–55.

Osborn, R.N., Hunt, J.G., & Jauch, L.R. (2002). Toward a contextual theory of leadership. *The Leadership Quarterly*, 13(6), 797–837.

Paradiso, J.A., Gips, J., Laibowitz, M., Sadi, S., Merrill, D., Aylward, R., . . . & Pentland, A. (2010). Identifying and facilitating social interaction with a wearable wireless sensor network. *Personal and Ubiquitous Computing*, 14(2), 137–152.

Parry, K., Mumford, M.D., Bower, I., & Watts, L.L. (2014). Qualitative and historiometric methods in leadership research: A review of the first 25 years of *The Leadership Quarterly*. *The Leadership Quarterly*, 25(1), 132–151.

Pilny, A., Schecter, A., Poole, M.S., & Contractor, N. (2016). An illustration of the relational event model to analyze group interaction processes. *Group Dynamics: Theory, Research, and Practice*, 20(3), 181–195.

Ployhart, R.E., & Vandenberg, R.J. (2010). Longitudinal research: The theory, design, and analysis of change. *Journal of Management*, 36(1), 94–120.

Ployhart, R.E., Holtz, B.C., & Bliese, P.D. (2002). Longitudinal data analysis: Applications of random coefficient modeling to leadership research. *The Leadership Quarterly*, 13(4), 455–486.

Porter, L.W., & McLaughlin, G.B. (2006). Leadership and the organizational context: Like the weather? *The Leadership Quarterly*, 17(6), 559–576.

Rogers, L.E., & Escudero, V. (2004). *Relational communication: An interactional perspective to the study of process and form*. Mahwah, NJ: Lawrence Erlbaum.

Rogers, L.E., & Farace, R.V. (1975). Relational communication analysis: New measurement procedures. *Human Communication Research*, 1(3), 222–239.

Rost, J.C. (1995). Leadership: A discussion about ethics. *Business Ethics Quarterly*, 5(1), 129–142.

Rousseau, D. (1985). Issues of level in organizational research: Multilevel and cross-level perspectives. *Research in Organizational Behavior*, 7, 1–37.

Sample, J.A., & Wilson, T.R. (1965). Leader behavior, group productivity, and rating of least preferred co-worker. *Journal of Personality and Social Psychology*, 1(3), 266–270.

Shamir, B. (2011). Leadership takes time: Some implications of (not) taking time seriously in leadership research. *The Leadership Quarterly*, 22(2), 307–315.

Silberstang, J., & Hazy, J.K. (2008). Toward a micro-enactment theory of leadership and the emergence of innovation. *The Innovation Journal: The Public Sector Innovation Journal*, 13(3), art. 5.

Smit, B. (2014). An ethnographic narrative of relational leadership. *Journal of Sociology and Social Anthropology*, 5(2), 117–123.

Stogdill, R.M. (1974). *Handbook of leadership: A survey of theory and research*. New York: Free Press.

Stogdill, R.M., & Shartle, C.L. (1948). Methods for determining patterns of leadership behavior in relation to organization structure and objectives. *Journal of Applied Psychology, 32*(3), 286–291.

Tan, X., Shiyko, M., Li, R., Li, Y., & Dierker, L. (2012). A time-varying effect model for intensive longitudinal data. *Psychological Methods, 17*(1), 61–77.

Tepper, B., Dimotakis, N., Lambert, L., Koopman, J., Matta, F.K., Park, H., & Goo, W. (in press). Examining follower responses to transformational leadership from a dynamic, person-environment fit perspective. *Academy of Management Journal*.

Tse, H.H., & Ashkanasy, N.M. (2015). The dyadic level of conceptualization and analysis: A missing link in multilevel OB research? *Journal of Organizational Behavior, 36*(8), 1176–1180.

Uhl-Bien, M. (2006). Relational leadership theory: Exploring the social processes of leadership and organizing. *The Leadership Quarterly, 17*(6), 654–676.

Uhl-Bien, M., & Ospina, S. (2012). Paradigm interplay in relational leadership: A way forward. In M. Uhl-Bien & S. Ospina (Eds.), *Advancing relational leadership research: A dialogue among perspectives* (pp. 537–580). Charlotte, NC: Information Age.

Uhl-Bien, M., Marion, R., & McKelvey, B. (2007). Complexity leadership theory: Shifting leadership from the industrial age to the knowledge era. *The Leadership Quarterly, 18*(4), 298–318.

van Knippenberg, D., & Sitkin, S.B. (2013). A critical assessment of charismatic–transformational leadership research: Back to the drawing board? *Academy of Management Annals, 7*(1), 1–60.

Vancouver, J.B., & Weinhardt, J.M. (2012). Modeling the mind and the milieu: Computational modeling for micro-level organizational researchers. *Organizational Research Methods, 15*(4), 602–623.

Vandenberg, R.J., & Stanley, L.J. (2009). Statistical and methodological challenges for commitment researchers: Issues of invariance, change across time, and profile differences. In H.J. Klein, T.E. Becker, & J.P. Meyer (Eds.), *Commitment in organizations: Accumulated wisdom and new directions* (pp. 383–416). Florence, KY: Routledge.

Wang, M., Zhou, L., & Liu, S. (2014). Multilevel issues in leadership research. In D.V. Day (Ed.), *The Oxford handbook of leadership and organizations* (pp. 146–166). New York: Oxford University Press.

Wang, X.H., & Howell, J.M. (2010). Exploring the dual-level effects of transformational leadership on followers. *Journal of Applied Psychology, 95*(6), 1134–1144.

Weick, K.E. (1978). The spines of leaders. In M. McCall and M. Lombardo (Eds.), *Leadership: Where else can we go?* (pp. 37–61). Durham, NC: Duke University Press.

Weick, K.E. (1979). *The social psychology of organizing*. Reading, MA: Addison-Wesley.

Weingart, L. (1997). How did they do that? The ways and means of studying group process. *Research in Organizational Behavior, 19*, 189–239.

Weinhardt, J.M., & Vancouver, J.B. (2012). Computational modeling and organizational psychology: Opportunities abound. *Organizational Psychology Review, 2*(4), 267–292.

Wiley, N. (1988). The micro–macro problem in social theory. *Sociological Theory, 6*(2), 254–261.

Yammarino, F.J. (2013). Leadership past, present, and future. *Journal of Leadership & Organizational Studies, 20*(2), 149–155.

Yammarino, F.J., & Gooty, J. (2017). Multi-level issues and dyads in leadership research. In B. Schyns, R.J. Hall, & P. Neves (Eds.), *Handbook of methods in leadership research* (pp. 229–255). Cheltenham: Edward Elgar.

Yammarino, F.J., Dionne, S.D., Uk Chun, J., & Dansereau, F. (2005). Leadership and levels of analysis: A state-of-the-science review. *The Leadership Quarterly, 16*(6), 879–919.

Yukl, G. (2012). Effective leadership behavior: What we know and what questions need more attention. *Academy of Management Perspectives, 26*(4), 66–85.

Zacks, J.M., Tversky, B., & Iyer, G. (2001). Perceiving, remembering, and communicating structure in events. *Journal of Experimental Psychology: General, 130*(1), 29–58.

2

LEADERSHIP AND LEVELS OF ANALYSIS

Clarifications and Fixes for What's Wrong

Francis J. Yammarino and Shelley D. Dionne

While there are no doubt many things that are *right* about leadership, there are nevertheless many things that are *wrong*. Key among these is that leadership research and practice often ignores, misunderstands, and misrepresents levels of analysis. Simply, leadership theory without levels of analysis is *incomplete*, leadership data without levels of analysis is *incomprehensible*, and leadership practice without levels of analysis is *ineffective*. The *fixes* are to explicitly specify and address levels of analysis in all phases of research (that is, in theory/conceptualization, sampling/measurement, data analyses, and inference drawing) and in professional practice (that is, in application and implementation). As such, our purpose here is to highlight these fixes by introducing and explaining some basic levels of analysis issues, noting how to explicitly include levels in leadership work, and offering some guidelines for leadership researchers and professionals.

What's Wrong?

The State of the Field

Beginning in the 1980s and through the early 2000s, numerous publications attempted to explain levels of analysis and their importance theoretically and empirically to organizational science scholars in general, and to leadership researchers in particular (for example, Dansereau & Yammarino, 1998a, 1998b, 2000; Dansereau, Alutto, & Yammarino, 1984; Dansereau, Yammarino, & Kohles, 1999; Dansereau, Yammarino, & Markham, 1995; Klein & Kozlowski, 2000; Klein, Dansereau, & Hall, 1994; Rousseau, 1985; Schriesheim, 1995; Schriesheim, Castro, Zhou, & Yammarino, 2001; Yammarino, 1998). After some two decades of effort on educating the field about levels-of-analysis issues, in a state-of-the-science review of leadership and levels of analysis examining about 350 articles across 17 areas of leadership research, Yammarino, Dionne, Chun, and Dansereau (2005) reached a stunning conclusion: Few studies, in any of the areas of leadership research reviewed, addressed levels-of-analysis issues appropriately in theory, measurement, data analysis, and inference drawing. In particular, they found that:

- less than 30 percent of the publications displayed an explicit or appropriate inclusion of levels of analysis in theoretical development and conceptualization;
- some 50 percent reflected levels-of-analysis issues appropriately in measurement – that is, specified concepts and measures at the same level of analysis or aggregated correctly specified measures at one level to the level of the concept;
- only 15 percent appropriately reflected levels-of-analysis issues in data analysis – that is, used some multilevel data analytic technique at the correct level(s) of analysis;
- some 40 percent reflected an appropriate alignment of theory and data in terms of levels of analysis – that is, theory and data aligned at the correct level(s) of analysis; and
- only 9 percent of all publications addressed levels-of-analysis issues appropriately in all four areas of theory and hypothesis formulation, measurement, data analysis, and inference drawing.

Given this relatively weak state of affairs, additional publications tried to extend our knowledge and to explain the importance of levels in leadership and related work (for example, Dansereau & Yammarino, 2006; Dansereau, Cho, & Yammarino, 2006; Dionne & Dionne, 2008; Dionne et al., 2012; Gooty & Yammarino, 2011; Gooty, Serban, Thomas, Gavin, & Yammarino, 2012; Yammarino & Dansereau, 2008, 2009, 2010, 2011). After another decade, in a 25-year retrospective on leadership and levels of analysis involving examination of 790 articles across 29 areas of leadership research, Dionne and colleagues (2014) reached a very similar conclusion: Relatively few studies, in any of the areas of leadership research reviewed, addressed levels-of-analysis issues appropriately in theory, measurement, data analysis, and inference drawing. In particular, for conceptual leadership articles, they found that less than 40 percent explicitly stated the level of analysis in theory development. For empirical leadership articles, they found that:

- only 30 percent explicitly stated the level of analysis in theory and hypothesis development;
- some 80 percent appropriately incorporated levels into measurement – an improvement over the prior review, although most work was solely at the individual level;

- less than 20 percent used multilevel techniques appropriately, realizing that the majority of leadership research has been at the individual level of analysis; and
- some 80 percent had an appropriate alignment between theory and data – also an improvement over the previous review, but again primarily involving only the individual level.

Thus, while there was some overall improvement over time in the incorporation of levels for some aspects of research, again only a small percentage of all publications addressed levels-of-analysis issues appropriately in all four areas of theory and hypothesis formulation, measurement, data analysis, and inference drawing, and most of these were solely at the individual level. Dionne and colleagues (2014) noted that any celebration, despite some positive trends, was premature, and there was still room for great improvement in the understanding and incorporating of levels-of-analysis and multilevel issues in leadership work.

The Problem

Why does this poor (but slightly improving) state of affairs still exist? Perhaps it is because levels of analysis and multilevel issues are difficult to understand and implement. The complexity of the key issues involved, as well as some technical and analytical fixes, have been outlined by Gooty and Yammarino (2011) and Yammarino and Gooty (2017, 2018), among others. Without getting technical, however, it is still possible to clarify and simplify levels-of-analysis issues so that additional fixes can start to be applied to the leadership field.

What Are Levels of Analysis and Why Are Multilevel Issues Important for Leadership?

Simply, leadership is inherently multilevel and levels-related: You can't be a leader without at least one follower; and, to be a leader, the leader (individual level) has to link with others either on a one-to-one basis (dyad level) or on a one-to-many basis (group/team and collective/organization levels) and within a context (multiple levels). As such, leadership is a multilevel phenomenon involving not only variables and processes, but also individuals, dyads, groups/teams, collectives/organizations, and multiple levels simultaneously.

Levels of analysis or entities, inherent in theoretical formulations in leadership, can be implicit or assumed, or explicitly incorporated, and can be used to specify boundary conditions on theories. If we understand how and when levels are specified, then an examination of the potential or degree of prevalence of theoretical mis-specification can be explored. Also, identification of relevant levels-of-analysis issues can help to account for inconsistent and contradictory findings in prior leadership research. With explicit incorporation of levels-of-analysis issues, complete conceptual understanding of a construct or phenomena is plausible, which can then lead to sound measures, appropriate data analytic techniques, valid inference drawing and conclusions, and, ultimately, effective professional practice. As such, *leadership theory without levels of analysis is incomplete, leadership data without levels of analysis is incomprehensible, and leadership practice without levels of analysis is ineffective.*

Clarifications and Understandings

Definitions and Basics

More specifically, *leadership* is a multilevel (person, dyad group, collective) leader–follower interaction process that occurs in a particular situation (context) in which a leader (for example, superior, supervisor) and followers (for example, subordinates, direct reports) share a purpose (vision, mission) and jointly accomplish things (for example, goals, objectives, tasks) willingly (for example, without coercion). And *levels of analysis* are the entities, units, or objects of study (for example, person, dyad, group/team, and collective/organization) that must be incorporated in theory and conceptualization (including definitions and specification of relationships among constructs and variables), research design, operationalization (including measurement), sampling and data analysis, inference drawing, and professional practice. Levels are typically hierarchically ordered, with lower-level entities, such as persons, nested or embedded in higher-level entities, such as dyads or groups.

In leadership work, there are four critical levels of analysis or perspectives on the human beings who comprise organizations. First, independent *individuals* or *persons* (for example, leaders or followers) allow for the exploration of individual differences. In this case, focus can be on a leader or a follower/subordinate, or on how leaders or followers differ from one another. Some relevant leadership elements for this levels perspective are the knowledge, skills, abilities, and affective and cognitive processes of leaders and followers, as well as various leader behaviors and styles.

Second, *dyads*, a special case of groups, are a two-person group with interpersonal relationships (for example, leader–follower roles) that involve one-to-one interdependence between individuals (that is, dyadic partners). In this case, focus can be on superior–subordinate dyads, leader–follower dyads, or other interpersonal relationships (for example, peer–peer dyads), independent of the formal work group. Some relevant leadership elements for this levels perspective are interpersonal exchange or attraction processes, empowerment, and providing support for and developing others.

Third, *groups*, including workgroups and teams, are a collection of individuals who are interdependent and interact on a face-to-face, or "virtual" (non-co-located), basis with one another. While there are some potential differences between groups and teams, they are viewed similarly here. Formal work groups or teams generally consist of a leader and their immediate direct reports. Some relevant leadership elements for this levels perspective are: group climate, norms, and cohesiveness; shared team mental models and team building; and consideration, participation, delegation, and structural elements applied to the group/team.

Fourth, *collectives* are clusterings of individuals that are larger than groups and whose members are interdependent based on a hierarchical structuring, or a set of common or shared expectations. Collectives can include groups of groups, departments, functional areas, strategic business units, organizations, firms, and industries. Collectives do not necessarily involve direct interaction among people (as in groups and teams), but are held together by echelons or hierarchies, or even networks. Some relevant leadership elements for this levels perspective are: organizational factors, such as the form, tasks, and communication system; organizational culture and values; and strategic leadership.

These four levels of analysis constitute different "lenses" for the examination, both conceptually and empirically, of people in organizations. Because of the hierarchical and nested structure of levels, viewing people from increasingly higher levels of analysis necessarily means that the number of entities decreases (for example, there are fewer groups than persons in an organization) and the size of the entity increases (for example, there are a larger number of people in collectives than in groups). So, as the perspectives change, so do the number of entities involved.

In this way, levels of analysis are *not* levels of management; rather, levels are the multiple lenses on the organization chart, which is the management structure. An illustration of levels of analysis can be made in terms of nodes, representing individuals, and the connections among them, represented by line segments. As shown in Figure 2.1, for the four levels of management in the upper portion, these nodes and line segments in the lower portion can then be viewed through different lenses, or as different levels, representing 15 persons, 14 dyads (one-to-one connections or relationships), 7 groups or teams (of 3 individuals each in this case), 2 collectives (for example, departments of 7 individuals each in this case, with the center individual/node connecting them), and a single organization (comprising 15 individuals).

Dyads, Collectives, and Networks

While individuals, groups, and teams are relatively well understood, given a long and rich history of research about them, dyads, collectives (unless perhaps when viewed as "organizations"), and the connection of levels of analysis to networks are less well known. Some elaboration for each of these may be helpful.

Dyads may be the most neglected level, often confused with the individuals who comprise them or the groups/teams into which they can emerge, and

Levels of management: Organizational chart (4 levels)

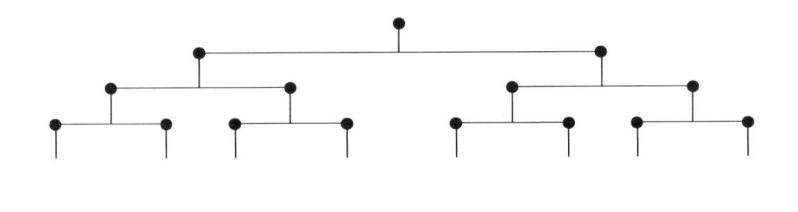

Levels of analysis: 15 persons, 14 dyads, 7 groups, 2 collectives, 1 organization

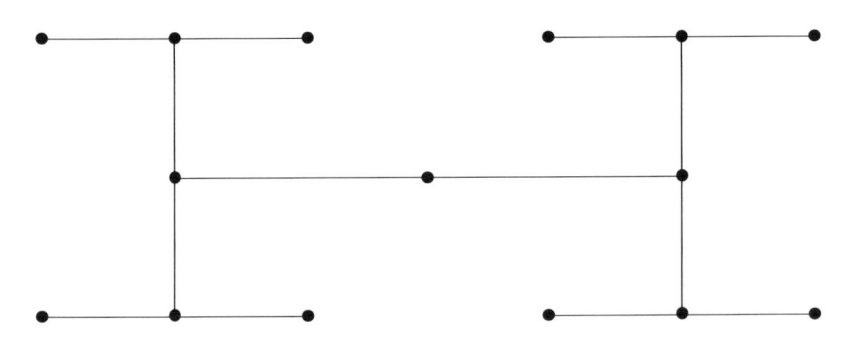

FIGURE 2.1 Levels of management and levels of analysis.

because they are typically the hardest to conceptualize clearly, operationalize precisely, and test accurately. However, there have been some recent attempts to address this level of analysis fully (for example, Gooty & Yammarino, 2011; Yammarino & Dansereau, 2009; Yammarino & Gooty, 2017). A key notion here is the one-to-one interdependence between dyadic partners (for example, leader and follower) and the aspects or interpersonal dimensions of that interdependence, which creates a unique relationship, specific to a particular dyad, that is independent or removed from any group or team to which the partners may also belong. This uniqueness, coupled with the notion that dyads in organizations are also embedded with various groups/teams, however, requires conceptual (for example, is there one dyadic member – a leader, for instance – who may be a member of more than one dyad within a group/team?), measurement (for example, are operationalizations/measurements obtained on all constructs from both dyadic members or not?), and analytic (for example, are appropriate/advanced dyadic data analytic tools used or not?) enhancements to better understand dyads, and these improvements have begun to take hold in the leadership field.

Collectives may be the most misunderstood level, often because so many different types of unit can viewed as collectives and because collectives can comprise so many different types of unit (as noted above). But, again, there has been some recent work conceptually clarifying and empirically testing collectives and the notions linked to collectives, especially when they are not organizations per se (for example, McHugh et al., 2016; Yammarino & Dansereau, 2009, 2010). A key notion here is that, while often confused with groups and teams, collectives are different from these other entities in four main ways: size (more members), expertise (more of it and more diverse), level of interaction (typically less direct and less intensive), and number of one-to-one connections (many more). The latter two differences define the nature of interdependence in a collective, which is characterized by the relationships among members being weaker and members acting more independently than in a group or team. Again, this uniqueness requires conceptual (for example, what specifically are the units involved, and how are they defined, in the collectives of interest?), measurement (for example, have all or only some collective members provided data, and how are the operationalizations accomplished?), and analytic (for example, are advanced multilevel or simulation/modeling tools used?) enhancements to better understand collectives, and these improvements have begun to take hold in the leadership field.

Networks are also relevant to leadership and levels of analysis in general, and to collectives in particular. We define networks in line with discrete mathematics, a key historical root within network science, as consisting of a set of actors/nodes and a set of ties/edges that connect actors/nodes (Sayama, 2015). While "network level of analysis" has been used in prior research (cf. Provan, Fish, & Sydow, 2007; Rothaermel & Hess, 2007), it is not clear that a network represents its own unique entity or level of analysis; rather, networks may be an advanced and expanded means of examining entities, particularly collectives, because collectives may be comprised of other units/entities (for example, individuals, dyads, groups/teams).

With regard to entities such as dyads, groups, and collectives, connections among components – or, more specifically, the heterogeneity or homogeneity among the connected components – is a key defining feature. Where networks serve to advance and extend our understanding of entities is their ability to focus on both connectedness and interactions among the components – that is, on the entity (entities) and its (their) dynamical properties. A network perspective can evaluate nonhomogeneous connectivity, where some components are connected and others are not, as well as allow for the number of components in the network to dynamically increase or decrease over time. As such, networks are relevant for examining not only dynamic group-level issues, but also dynamic collective-level issues. Thus a focus on connectedness and interactions (that is, networks) may not be a level in and of itself, but rather an enhanced view of existing levels of analysis.

Consider the traditional view of entities – collective entities, in particular – prior to the infusion of network science into organizational science. This traditional view of collectives allowed for the notion that different units exist within a collective level of analysis. However, traditional views did not necessarily account for scale and time issues within the collective. Thus networks provide entities with a means to model dynamism across typical and atypical structures. For example, typical dyads that comprise the network are two individuals as connected nodes. Atypical dyads have individual–group/team, group/team–group/team, agent–agent, or entity–entity as connected nodes. Typical and atypical structures are not inconsistent with the notion of interdependence within a collective level of analysis. However, a network perspective of the collective level allows for a more complicated and complete view of interdependence – that is, the study of nontrivial relationships between the system's properties at different scales (that is, emergence) (Bar-Yam, 1997), as well as time, in the sense of accounting for dynamic processes as time progresses (Sayama, 2015).

The strength of a network perspective is its ability to flexibly capture dynamism and/or connections within levels of analysis. Evaluating a network within a collective as a static snapshot in time does not represent a new and different level of analysis, but rather the structure underlying the collective. Conversely, examining the dynamic connectedness and interactions within a collective does not produce a new entity, but rather a more coherent and realistic view of interdependence within the collective. Both the static and dynamic views of networks have greatly enhanced organizational science and leadership, but we assert, in the interest of scientific parsimony, that there remain four key entities of interest (that is, individual, dyad, group, and collective), with networks providing a powerful means for examining interdependence and dynamism within the traditional entities.

Multiple Levels in Combination

In leadership work, effects can be masked or falsely indicated when we assume or choose only one level of analysis without consideration of other levels (for example, Dansereau et al., 1984; Dionne et al., 2014; Yammarino & Dansereau, 2009, 2011; Yammarino et al., 2005). Levels – especially in organizational settings – are typically nested or somehow linked, and these linkages necessitate that multiple levels and their effects be considered simultaneously.

Micro versus macro leadership theories, processes, and concepts, depending on various levels formulations, can be viewed as analogous or in contrast to one another, because adjacent levels can align, misalign, or oppose one another via complicated processes. To understand this linking of multiple levels, level-specific, emergent, and cross-level formulations and effects are important for leadership work.

First, relationships among constructs may hold at a lower level (for example, person), but not at a higher level (for example, group). This is a discontinuity thesis, a *level-specific* formulation, or, empirically, a disaggregated, individual, or level-specific effect. As such, the higher level of analysis is not relevant for understanding the leadership phenomena. For example, at the individual level, aspects of an individual's personality may be associated with their leadership style; at the group level, a team's cohesiveness can be related to that team's performance.

Second, relationships among constructs may not hold at a lower level, but manifest at a higher level of analysis. This is also a type of discontinuity thesis, an *emergent* formulation that holds at a higher level (for example, group), but is not found to hold at a lower level (for example, person), or, empirically, a higher-level effect that does not disaggregate or which is an emergent effect. The lower level of analysis is not relevant for understanding the leadership phenomena. For example, the notions of group cohesion, shared mental models, and shared and team leadership, as well as their potential associations, make sense only at the team (and not individual) level.

Third, relationships among constructs also may hold at both higher (for example, collective) and lower (for example, group) levels of analysis. This is a homology thesis, or, empirically, an aggregated or ecological effect, and a traditional *cross-level* explanation. (Note that the use here of "cross-level" is different from how the term is used in much contemporary work. For a historical explanation and technical details, see Yammarino & Gooty, 2018.) For example, work effort exerted by an employee can be positively related to that employee's performance at the individual level. This association is also plausible at multiple higher levels, including the dyad (for example, both a follower and leader exert higher effort leading to better dyadic performance), group (for example, team effort is associated with team performance), and organization (for example, organizational productivity/effort is associated with organizational performance) levels. In the physical sciences, an example is Einstein's $E = mc^2$, which holds from very micro to very macro levels. These cross-level notions specify patterns of relationships replicated across levels of analysis, and they are uniquely powerful and parsimonious because the same (leadership) phenomenon occurs at more than one level of analysis.

Dynamics and Analytics

Furthermore, levels, like leadership variables and processes, can shift, change, or remain stable over time. We should view leadership from a dynamic perspective if we are to fully understand relevant phenomena that develop over time. Relatively little has been written, however, about changing levels of analysis over time (for exceptions, see Dansereau et al., 1984, 1999; Yammarino & Dansereau, 2009, 2011). For example, for various levels of analysis, Dansereau and colleagues (1999) define and illustrate four types of stable condition, three types of change that move from a lower to a higher level, and three types of change that move from a higher to a lower level, as well as three types of change that indicate the beginning of a level (that is, "emergents") and three that indicate the end of a level (that is, "ends").

Given these dynamics and various levels issues for leadership research, a variety of multilevel methods and data analytic tools are available for measuring and testing these notions. Although beyond the scope of this chapter, a key issue is the potential dependency among observations that may not be independent as a result of nesting, embeddedness, and cross-classification of entities at multiple levels of analysis (see Dansereau et al., 1984; Gooty & Yammarino, 2011). For analyzing levels-related notions in leadership work, tools that are appropriate include various measurement approaches to aggregation, agreement, and consensus assessment – for example, various intraclass correlation (ICC) and r_{wg} notions – as well as approaches for testing substantive associations with random coefficient models (RCM) via hierarchical linear modeling (HLM) and hierarchical cross-classified models (HCM), multilevel routines in Mplus and Stata, multilevel structural equation models (MLSEM), within and between analysis (WABA), and multilevel routines in the R software package. (For details and leadership examples, see Dansereau & Yammarino, 2000, 2006; Dansereau et al., 1984, 2006; Gooty & Yammarino, 2011, 2016; Klein & Kozlowski, 2000; Yammarino, 1998; Yammarino & Markham, 1992.) Within these various measurement and analytic approaches (for example, RCM, WABA, MLSEM), there are also procedures for testing multilevel mediation and moderation (with mediators and moderators at the same level as, or higher levels than, the independent and dependent variables), and longitudinal leadership notions (with changing variables and changing levels of analysis over time), while accounting for the dependencies in the data (for example, resulting from the nesting or embeddedness of entities).

Another appropriate analytic tool for levels-related leadership work is dynamic computational modeling (see Sayama, 2015), including agent-based modeling and simulation (for example, Dionne & Dionne, 2008; Dionne, Sayama, Hao, & Bush, 2010; McHugh et al., 2016). For example, Dionne and Dionne (2008) generated a computational model for a dynamic group decision-making optimization scenario using a levels-based comparison of four types of leadership at the individual, dyad, and group levels. Computational modeling (via agent-based modeling and simulation, for example) of complex, nonlinear, dynamic relations among various leadership behaviors, properties, processes, and environmental characteristics is a growing area of leadership work. The real advantage of these approaches is their ability to account for potential dependencies among entities as a result of multiple embedded or interrelated levels of analysis. In particular, for various leadership aspects of interest, these computational approaches can model the dynamic and changing nature of entities (for example, individuals, dyads, teams) and networks over time, building in all of the potential connections and influences among various entities, individual members, or agents within networks, and even entities within networks when the entities are not simply individuals (see Sayama, 2015). For example, Dionne and colleagues (2010) illustrated how the complexity of mental model development and team performance could be examined within the context of individual development, leader–follower exchanges, and follower–follower exchanges embedded within social networks. Computational models allowed multiple interrelated levels of analysis to be examined across a dynamic mental model development process.

Fixes and Guidelines

As an initial step, the clarifications and understandings presented thus far provide some key fixes for addressing what's wrong with leadership and levels of analysis. Beyond these, however, additional fixes and some guidelines for leadership research and professional practice can be developed to further address the problems associated with leadership and levels of analysis.

For Leadership Research

To begin to better link leadership notions to levels of analysis, Yammarino and Dansereau (2009) provided a general and parsimonious conceptualization of numerous complex leadership ideas, based on multiple levels of analysis. Starting with the scientific premise that "simple is beautiful," they offer four general theoretical formulations, as summarized in Table 2.1, each based simply on two constructs and their association about a level of analysis. They then extend and develop these general constructs and levels to more specific theoretical formulations to account for numerous additional models, constructs, variables, and associations for understanding leadership via levels of analysis.

Briefly, the first notion is about leadership in terms of individual behavior and decision making – that is, option cutting and commitment are positively associated, based on differences between persons (inter-individual differences): a level-specific formulation at the individual level of analysis. In other words,

TABLE 2.1 Leadership and levels of analysis

Form of leadership	Levels of analysis	Key constructs
Individual behavior & decision making	Individuals & level-specific	Option cutting + Commitment
Interpersonal relations	Dyads & emergent	Investments + Returns
Group dynamics/team processes & norms	Groups/teams & emergent	Interdependence + Cohesion
Collectivized processes & roles	Collectives/organizations & cross-level	Titles + Expectations

when leaders or followers are faced with a decision to make, they examine choices and options, cut off those options that are not feasible for a variety of reasons (for example, time, resources, pragmatism), and thus become committed to a particular (remaining) option, resulting in the actual decision or choice they make. This could yield commitment to a course of action, a particular managerial philosophy, the job, a leader, a co-worker, the organization, etc.

The second notion is about leadership in terms of interpersonal relationships – that is, investments and returns are positively associated, based on differences between dyads: a level-specific formulation that emerges at the dyad level of analysis. In this case, independently of the group/team of which they are members, within each leader–follower or supervisor–subordinate pairing, a leader makes investments in (for example, support, resources) and receive returns from (for example, performance) a follower; likewise, a follower makes investment in (for example, performance) and receives returns from (for example, support, resources) a leader; and these investment–return cycles help to build and develop the dyadic relationship over time.

The third notion is about leadership in terms of group dynamics and team processes and norms – that is, interdependence and cohesion are positively associated, based on differences between groups: a level-specific formulation that emerges at the group level of analysis. In other words, within a group or team, task-based interdependence from inputs and process, and outcome interdependence from goals and rewards, can enhance group/team potency, efficacy, and effort, and are the basis for shared mental models, understandings, beliefs, and emotional tone (affect) that solidifies the group/team.

Finally, the fourth notion is about leadership in terms of collectivized processes and roles – that is, titles and expectations are positively associated, based on differences between collectives: a cross-level formulation (in the traditional sense noted above) from individual to dyad to group to collective levels of analysis. In this case, because all collectives can be named or titled (for example, "ABC Company," "Production Department," "XYZ Professional Association"), this naming creates a set of shared expectations or commonalities for the members with which they identify. This connection allows collective members to function in their prescribed roles and responsibilities by providing information and norms for role completion.

These four theoretical notions and their more detailed specifics (see Yammarino & Dansereau, 2009) clearly are not the only plausible notions about leadership – but they are leadership notions that integrate large amounts of the leadership literature by specifically linking different constructs to different levels of analysis. As such, these connections between leadership constructs and various levels of analysis could be the basis for future refined theorizing and testing in leadership research.

In addition, and more generally, to further address the problem of leadership research ignoring or misunderstanding levels of analysis, the following guidelines for conducting future levels-of-analysis research in the realm of leadership are offered (see also Dionne et al., 2014; Yammarino & Dansereau, 2010; Yammarino & Gooty, 2017, 2018; Yammarino et al., 2005).

For *leadership theory building* (that is, theory, conceptualization, model specification, propositions, hypotheses), first define the relevant levels of analysis for the associated concepts, constructs, variables, and relationships, and then provide a theoretical justification for these decisions. Also, specify the boundary conditions, including and based on levels of analysis, for these theoretical elements as well. For example, if a researcher is interested in some type of dyadic leadership approach, then the constructs involved need to be conceptualized and defined at the dyad (and not solely individual) level of analysis, and the associations involved need to be conceptualized and justified at the dyad (and not solely individual) level of analysis. In terms of the boundary conditions on this dyadic approach, elements at the group/team or organizational levels that may alter or constrain the dyadic leadership notions also need to be considered. Following a dyadic leadership approach, this means that theory should not reflect only a follower's characteristic and/or perspective, or only a leader's characteristics and/or perspective; rather, dyadic leadership theory building is about developing theory related to the unique association between a leader and a follower.

For *leadership theory testing* (that is, sampling, design, measurement, data cleaning, and data analyses), employ observations, assessments, and manipulations, and construct measures, at the same level of analysis depicted in the theory, models, and hypotheses. If this is not feasible, employ appropriate aggregation, agreement, and consensus techniques, and justify the use of these techniques. Then, permit the conceptualization and design to determine the appropriate multilevel method and analytic technique(s) to be used for testing the entities of interest. For example, a researcher interested in some type of dyadic leadership approach should sample dyads (not individuals), manipulate dyads (not individuals) if an experiment is being conducted, measure variables at the dyad level (for example, gathering data from both dyadic partners on all variables) and/or justify aggregation to the dyad level (via ICCs, r_{wg}s, or WABA), and then conduct analyses at the dyad level using an appropriate dyadic analysis tool (see Gooty & Yammarino, 2011). Again, dyadic leadership theory cannot be sufficiently tested relying only on follower respondents or using only leader assessments; rather, each leader and follower is assessed jointly regarding the phenomena of interest.

For *leadership inference drawing* (that is, linking theory building to theory testing), remember that it is not simply about constructs/variables and relationships for theory–data alignment. Constructs/variables and relationships, in terms of both theory and testing, must include levels of analysis – that is, inference drawing is a levels-based research process. For our researcher interested in some type of dyadic leadership approach, this should be straightforward if the leadership theory building and leadership theory testing recommendations noted above have been implemented, because variables, relationships, and levels of analysis (entities) are all accounted for and included.

For Leadership Practice

The alignment of theory building and theory testing involving levels of analysis, after extensive validation of a particular leadership approach, then permits the consideration of levels of analysis in managerial and professional practice regarding leadership. Policies, procedures, practices, changes, innovations, training and development, education programs, etc. must be designed, implemented, monitored, and managed at the level(s) at which they are determined to operate (based on research, of course). What does this mean, or "look like," at various levels of analysis for the professional practice of leadership?

For leadership and individuals: "*There are only two options regarding commitment. You're either IN or you're OUT. There is no such thing as life in-between.*" (Pat Riley, head coach, LA Lakers)

Leaders must help followers to become committed to the job, organization, even the leader themselves, via option-cutting – that is, helping followers to identify and evaluate options, so that they can make good choices and decisions. Leaders must also inspire followers, treat followers as individuals, spark followers intellectually, and pick a "good #2" to develop to replace them and thus, over time, eliminate their own job, allowing the #2 to take over, freeing the leader to do things that others cannot do.

For leadership and dyads: "*Some players you pat their butts, some players you kick their butts, some players you leave alone.*" (Pete Rose, manager, Cincinnati Reds)

Leaders must focus on their own and their followers' investments and returns to develop others, realizing that followers develop in their own way, at their own pace, and by valuing different things. Leaders can help to develop the self-worth of followers by supporting them, and by providing them with attention, time, resources, and challenging work. By doing these things, high performance – perhaps even outstanding performance – will follow.

For leadership and groups/teams: "*Teamwork is really a form of trust. It's what happens when you surrender the mistaken idea that you can go it alone and realize that you won't achieve your individual goals without the support of your colleagues.*" (Pat Summitt, women's basketball head coach, Tennessee Volunteers)

Leaders must build group/team cohesion via interdependence – whether task-, relationship-, and/or outcome-based interdependence – among all team members. One way of accomplishing this is by group/team members sharing leadership responsibilities, authority, and tasks. Leaders must also foster a welcoming, positive climate in which cooperation is the key to group/team success.

For leadership and collectives/organizations: "*A great football coach has to have the vision to see, the faith to believe, the courage to do . . . and 25 great players.*" (Marv Levy, head coach, Buffalo Bills)

Because leadership titles create and set expectations for others, as a leader, you must meet these expectations, as well as share and endorse them widely within the collective. Leaders "at the top" (not restricted only to the top of the organization) must provide a vision and direction for their unit, and must set the mission, goals, and objectives. Moreover, they must be the moral and ethical compass – a model of integrity – for the collective involved. And leaders need not only to focus on the short-run bottom line, but also to think about the long-term financial and nonfinancial implications facing their collectives.

Conclusion

So, what's wrong with leadership? Leadership research and professional practice often ignore, misunderstand, and misrepresent levels of analysis. It's clear, however, that without levels of analysis, leadership theory, data, and practice are incomplete, incomprehensible, and ineffective, respectively.

So, how do we fix it? The ideas, fixes, and guidelines developed in this chapter are intended to promote a fuller understanding, as well as an explicit specification, to address levels of analysis in all phases of leadership research and leadership professional practice. We hope that our work gets the leadership field closer to that end.

References

Bar-Yam, Y. (1997). *Dynamics of complex systems*. Boston, MA: Addison-Wesley.

Dansereau, F., & Yammarino, F.J. (Eds.) (1998a). *Leadership: The multiple-level approaches, Part A – Classical and new wave*. Stamford, CT: JAI Press.

Dansereau, F., & Yammarino, F.J. (Eds.) (1998b). *Leadership: The multiple-level approaches, Part B – Contemporary and alternative*. Stamford, CT: JAI Press.

Dansereau, F., & Yammarino, F.J. (2000). Within and between analysis: The varient paradigm as an underlying approach to theory building and testing. In K.J. Klein & S.W.J. Kozlowski (Eds.), *Multilevel theory, research, and methods in organizations: Foundations, extensions, and new directions* (pp. 425–466). San Francisco, CA: Jossey Bass.

Dansereau, F., & Yammarino, F.J. (2006). Is more discussion about levels of analysis really necessary? When is such discussion sufficient? *The Leadership Quarterly, 17*, 537–552.

Dansereau, F., Alutto, J.A., & Yammarino, F.J. (1984). *Theory testing in organizational behavior: The varient approach*. Englewood Cliffs, NJ: Prentice Hall.

Dansereau, F., Cho, J., & Yammarino, F.J. (2006). Avoiding the "fallacy of the wrong level": A within and between analysis (WABA) approach. *Group and Organization Management, 31*(5), 536–577.

Dansereau, F., Yammarino, F.J., & Kohles, J. (1999). Multiple levels of analysis from a longitudinal perspective: Some implications for theory building. *Academy of Management Review, 24*(2), 346–357.

Dansereau, F., Yammarino, F.J., & Markham, S.E. (1995). Leadership: The multiple-level approaches. *The Leadership Quarterly, 6*(2), 97–109.

Dionne, S.D., & Dionne, P.J. (2008). Levels-based leadership and hierarchical group decision optimization: A Monte Carlo simulation. *The Leadership Quarterly*, *19*(2), 212–234.

Dionne, S.D., Chun, J.U., Hao, C., Serban, A., Yammarino, F.J., & Spangler, W.D. (2012). Levels of analysis incorporation and publication quality: An illustration with transformational/charismatic leadership. *The Leadership Quarterly*, *23*(6), 1012–1042.

Dionne, S.D., Gupta, A., Sotak, K.L., Shirreffs, K., Serban, A., Hao, C., . . . & Yammarino, F.J. (2014). A 25-year perspective on levels of analysis in leadership research. *The Leadership Quarterly*, *25*(1), 6–35.

Dionne, S.D., Sayama, H., Hao, C., & Bush, B.J. (2010). The role of leadership in shared mental model convergence and team performance improvement: An agent-based computational model. *The Leadership Quarterly*, *21*(6), 1035–1049.

Gooty, J., & Yammarino, F.J. (2011). Dyads in organizational research: Conceptual issues and multi-level analyses. *Organizational Research Methods*, *14*(3), 456–483.

Gooty, J., & Yammarino, F.J. (2016). The leader–member exchange relationship: A multi-source, cross-level investigation. *Journal of Management*, *42*, 915–945.

Gooty, J., Serban, A., Thomas, J.S., Gavin, M.B., & Yammarino, F.J. (2012). Use and misuse of levels of analysis in leadership research: An illustrative review of leader–member exchange. *The Leadership Quarterly*, *23*(6), 1080–1103.

Klein, K.J., & Kozlowski, S.W.J. (2000). *Multilevel theory, research, and methods in organizations: Foundations, extensions, and new directions* (SIOP Frontiers Series). San Francisco, CA: Jossey-Bass.

Klein, K.J., Dansereau, F., & Hall, R.J. (1994). Levels issues in theory development, data collection, and analysis. *Academy of Management Review*, *19*(2), 195–229.

McHugh, K.A., Yammarino, F.J., Dionne, S.D., Serban, A., Sayama, H., & Chatterjee, S. (2016). Collective decision making, leadership, and collective intelligence: Tests with agent-based simulations and a field study. *The Leadership Quarterly*, *27*(2), 218–241.

Provan, K.G., Fish, A., & Sydow, J. (2007). Interorganizational networks at the network level: A review of the empirical literature on whole networks. *Journal of Management*, *33*(3), 479–516.

Rothaermel, F.T. & Hess, A.M. (2007). Building dynamic capabilities: Innovation driven by individual-, firm-, and network-level effects. *Organization Science*, *18*(6), 896–921.

Rousseau, D.M. (1985). Issues of level in organizational research: Multilevel and cross-level perspectives. *Research in Organizational Behavior*, *7*, 1–37.

Sayama, H. (2015). *Introduction to the modeling and analysis of complex systems*. New York: Open SUNY Textbooks.

Schriesheim, C.A. (1995). Multivariate and moderated within- and between-entity analysis (WABA) using hierarchical multiple linear regression. *The Leadership Quarterly*, *6*(1), 1–18.

Schriesheim, C.A., Castro, S.L., Zhou, X.T., & Yammarino, F.J. (2001). The folly of theorizing "A" but testing "B": A selective level-of-analysis review of the field and a detailed leader-member exchange illustration. *The Leadership Quarterly*, *12*(4), 515–551.

Yammarino, F.J. (1998). Multivariate aspects of the varient/WABA approach: A discussion and leadership illustration. *The Leadership Quarterly*, *9*(2), 203–227.

Yammarino, F.J., & Dansereau, F. (2008). Multi-level nature of and multi-level approaches to leadership. *The Leadership Quarterly*, *19*(2), 135–141.

Yammarino, F.J., & Dansereau, F. (2009). A new kind of OB (organizational behavior). *Research in Multi-level Issues*, *8*(2), 13–60.

Yammarino, F.J., & Dansereau, F. (2010). Multi-level issues in organizational culture and climate research. In N.M. Ashkanasy, C.P.M. Wilderom, & M.F. Peterson (Eds.), *Handbook of organizational culture and climate* (2nd ed.) (pp. 50–76). Thousand Oaks, CA: Sage.

Yammarino, F.J., & Dansereau, F. (2011). Multi-level issues in evolutionary theory, organization science, and leadership. *The Leadership Quarterly, 22*(6), 1042–1057.

Yammarino, F.J., & Gooty, J. (2017). Multi-level issues and dyads in leadership research. In B. Schyns, R. Hall, & P. Neves (Eds.), *Handbook of methods in leadership research* (pp. 229–255). Cheltenham: Edward Elgar.

Yammarino, F.J., & Gooty, J. (2018). Cross-level models. In S.E. Humphrey & J.M. LeBreton (Eds.), *Handbook for multilevel theory, measurement, and analysis* (in press). Washington, D.C.: American Psychological Association.

Yammarino, F.J., & Markham, S.E. (1992). On the application of within and between analysis: Are absence and affect really group-based phenomena? *Journal of Applied Psychology, 77*(2), 168–176 (correction, 77(4), 426).

Yammarino, F.J., Dionne, S.D., Chun, J.U., & Dansereau, F. (2005). Leadership and levels of analysis: A state-of-the-science review. *The Leadership Quarterly, 16*(6), 879–919.

3

LEADERSHIP ASSESSMENT CAN BE BETTER

Directions for Selection and Performance Management

Manuel London

Leadership assessment is a central process in organizations. It is the heart of executive selection and performance evaluation for decision making (compensation, promotion, assignment, and outplacement), as well as for identifying managers with leadership potential for career development. However, methods and processes for leadership assessment have been criticized (cf. Adler et al., 2016; Pulakos, Hanson, Arad, & Moye, 2015; Reynolds, McCauley, & Tsacoumis, 2018). In particular, consider the following key problems.

- The formality and structure of formal performance appraisals do not take into account the dynamic nature of leadership.
- Relying on multiple sources of input for measurement introduces potential biases and inaccuracies.
- Limiting assessment to annual or semi-annual rituals linked to "hot" outcomes, such as compensation and promotion, introduces political and interpersonal dynamics that limit their value.
- Ratings, as data points, have little meaning in and of themselves.

This chapter considers ways in which organizations have been changing leader assessment methods to be more flexible, to focus on behaviors and performance outcomes, and to take into account changing demands in line with organizational needs and goals for leadership development. The chapter offers directions for a happy medium that delivers reliable and valid input for decision making and feedback for development, while taking into account the complex and continuously changing conditions and demands of leadership.

What to Assess

Examining best practices for leadership assessment, London, Smither, and Diamante (2006) recommended taking a multilevel perspective measuring individual, team, and organizational level behaviors and outcomes. The individual level includes abilities, skills, knowledge, motivation, and values. The team level includes interpersonal relationships, group performance, and cross-team partnerships. The organizational level includes aspects of organizational dynamics and outcomes, such as business unit profitability. London and colleagues (2006) emphasized measuring both performance *processes* (how executives do their jobs) and *outcomes* (the results they achieve).

DeNisi and Smith (2014) pointed out the value of performance measurements that are tied to strategic organizational and team goals to transform generic knowledge, skills, and abilities (KSAs) into specific individual level KSAs that improve firm performance. Silzer and Church (2009) suggested a hierarchical "blueprint" of characteristics for assessment, covering *foundational* dimensions (personality and cognitive abilities), *growth* dimensions (learning, including openness and adaptability, and motivation, including energy and drive), and *career* dimensions (leaders competencies, such as inspiring others, developing teams, and having an international mindset, as well as technical/functional competencies of business). Thornton, Johnson, and Church (2017), building on Kirpatrick and Locke (1991), suggested assessment of a comprehensive set of leadership capabilities that indicate high potential and executive success, and which can be assessed in relation to specific conditions in an organization. Traits that distinguish successful leaders include drive (characteristics such as achievement motivation, ambition, energy, tenacity, and initiative), leadership motivation (the desire to lead), honesty and integrity, self-confidence, and business knowledge. These are characteristics that prompt leaders to be continuous learners, to formulate and communicate a clear and compelling vision, and to implement plans to make their vision a reality. The range of characteristics points to the value of using a multi-trait, multi-method approach to assessment (Church & Rotolo, 2013, cited in Thornton et al., 2017).

Leadership Traits in Context

Leadership is a dynamic process, changing over time, and differing between organizations and situations within an organization. Rapid shifts in business environments require "catalyst leaders," who "ignite a flame in others, gain their commitment, and drive productivity" (Byham & Wellins, 2016, p. 22). These competencies include fostering innovation, building trust, collaborating, developing others, aligning action with strategy, energizing, mobilizing, empowering, asking, listening, and providing balanced feedback. Leaders need to understand how value is created in their organization through innovation, and they should be able to use real-time predictive analytics to identify trends. They also need to become more agile in the face of the rapid pace of change (Frigo & Snellgrove, 2016)

Zaccaro and Klimoski (2001) argued for a leader assessment model that links leader characteristics to performance requirements. In other words, leadership occurs within a context of performance demands based on the nature of the industry, organization, and environment. The context determines:

> ... ways that leaders acquire information in their roles and go on to make sense of this information. It changes if and when (and then how and what) leaders plan appropriate collective responses. It changes the nature and role of key processes such as how leaders influence and manage their followers.
> *(Zaccaro & Klimoski, 2001, p. 13)*

Performance requirements include cognitive, social, political, personal, financial, technological, and staffing dynamics of the talent, structure, and culture of the organization and the economy in which it operates.

This context needs to be considered in identifying relevant assessment measures. This is not simply a matter of identifying current situational conditions and finding leaders who have the personal characteristics to match, or who have the ability to diagnose the situation and adapt their leadership style to meet current needs. Recognizing performance requirements is especially important at top executive levels, where the situation is dynamic, often changing rapidly. Performance demands are likely to be more idiosyncratic at the level of the C-suite. At the lowest level of management, performance requirements are likely to be more structured and stable. At middle levels of the organization, managers translate strategic goals and initiatives from the top, implementing them at lower levels. Each level of the organization, then, is likely to have different performance requirements (Katz & Kahn, 1978).

Zaccaro (2007, pp. 7–8) argued for consideration of traits as important sources of variance in leader effectiveness: "Leader traits can be defined as relatively coherent and integrated patterns of personal characteristics, reflecting a range of individual differences, that foster consistent leadership effectiveness across a variety of group and organizational situations." Cognitive abilities, personality, motives, and values are distal antecedents of leader performance. They influence antecedents that are more proximal to leader performance, such as problem-solving abilities, social appraisal skills, expertise, and tacit knowledge, which, in turn, affect leader emergence, effectiveness, and potential to advance (Zaccaro, Kemp, & Bader, 2004, cited in Zaccaro, 2007). The attributes that have the strongest relationships with leader performance are those that reflect an individual's stable tendency to lead in different ways across different organizational situations (Zaccaro, 2007).

Global Leadership

Characteristics for leadership success and assessment increasingly include global dimensions. International executives learn to be "global" as they prepare for, and perform in, jobs abroad. Critical dimensions for global leadership include continuous learning and the role of mentors to help to overcome culture shock (McCall & Hollenbeck, 2002). Cultural assimilation training involves exposing executives to cultural explanations for different reactions of people from different cultures in a range of scenarios (Bhagat, Triandis, & McDivitt, 2012; Bhawuk, Podsiadlowski, Graf, & Triandis, 2002). Trainers provide feedback to participants about their opinions, explaining cultural factors that underlie the ways in which people behave and how theories about culture explain norms, such as differences in leading teams in collectivistic cultures compared to those in individualistic cultures. Assessments for leaders' readiness to work in another culture or across cultures can include awareness of cultural differences, experiences in different cultures, and accuracy in interpreting behaviors and recognizing what to expect in different cultures. Assessment results can be used for selection and training, and can be validated against behaviors and performance once the executives have worked in international assignments (Adsit, London, Crom, & Jones, 1997).

Competency Models

The dynamic context in which leadership occurs poses a challenge to establishing the leadership characteristics that an organization wants to promulgate and reward. Competency modeling is a method that organizations have adopted to communicate characteristics that the organization expects of its leaders. An organization's competency model defines characteristics that are important to leadership in the organization. Although an organization's leader competency model may include generic characteristics of leadership, the model needs to be specific to the culture and demands of the organization. Competency models drive all elements of a performance/talent management system. Graber (2016) outlined the value of competency models, as follows.

- They cover management in all parts of the organization with a common core of competencies.
- They recognize differences between business units and the possibility of changes in job requirements.
- They include both easily identifiable or visible skills and subtle differences that may be critical competencies.
- They include components that are appropriate for different jobs and roles in managerial and technical career paths.
- They distinguish between core competencies, leadership competencies for top managers and executives, technical competencies for each function, and job-specific competencies.

- They provide a basis for managers to encourage their employees to focus on their strengths – applying them and developing those skills – and they recognize new skills needed as job demands and career opportunities change (and if organization goals change, the common core of competencies can be revised).

Although competency models give organizations a common language of leadership performance dimensions that are tied to organizational goals and strategies, how they are implemented, or what can be viewed as the antecedents of competencies, are likely to lie in the leader's personality.

Identifying and Assessing Personality Antecedents of Leadership Style

Consider how dimensions of leader behavior are driven by personality characteristics. Transformational and transactional leadership dimensions is a principal way of delineating leadership styles (Bass, 1985). Transformational leadership has four dimensions, including being a charismatic role model (idealized influence), articulating a clear and inspiring vision (inspirational motivation), questioning assumptions to stimulate subordinates' creativity (intellectual stimulation), and recognizing and supporting subordinates' needs (individual consideration). These can be assessed through leadership behavior questionnaires (Bass, 1995, 1999). There is also evidence that transformational leadership is related to personality, suggesting that personality measures may predict ability to be or to become a transformational leader. For instance, in a sample of leaders in a wide range of organizations, extraversion and agreeableness positively predicted transformational leadership (Judge & Bono, 2000), however these relationships were moderate (for example, $r = .40$) (Judge & Bono, 2000; Judge, Bono, Ilies, & Gerhardt, 2002), perhaps because personality does not directly reflect (is distal or distant from) leader behavior.

Maner and Mead (2010) distinguished between "dominant" leaders and "prestige" leaders (see also Korkki, 2016). *Dominant leaders* are brash, speak more often and more loudly than others, can bully subordinates and others, hoard information, micro-manage, and keep employees socially isolated, preventing them from forming social bonds with colleagues (for instance, assigning the same project to several individuals or teams and insisting that they not communicate). Steve Jobs was thought to exemplify a dominant leadership style. A dominant style works well if the leader's goal is to move the organization quickly in one direction to accomplish a singular vision: that of the leader. In contrast, *prestige leaders* listen to and empower others. They are less forceful. A prestige style works well if expertise and brainstorming new ideas are important in the organization, for innovation. The prestige leader does not have a singular vision of any strength, but needs employees to generate innovative and creative goals and strategies. The prestige leader facilitates the team's vision. A leader who shows humility seeks feedback for a true understanding of themselves, and also seeks to understand others' strengths and ability to learn (Owens, Johnson, & Mitchell, 2013). A disadvantage of prestige leadership, however, is that the leader may pay more attention to building relationships and may make popular decisions rather than giving people negative feedback when they need it (Case & Maner, 2014).

In summary, assessing leaders and establishing desired leadership characteristics across an organization require a differentiated view of leader characteristics. Competency models can be useful for articulating sets of leader characteristics that apply across an organization. Personality characteristics are likely to underlie leadership styles, and suggest the value of a "deep dive" to understand leaders' competences and to predict their likely behavior and performance under different situations. Next, we turn to ways of measuring leader characteristics for prediction, evaluation, and career development.

Assessment Methods

All too often, organizations create leader assessments and leave them in place for years, without determining whether they are producing anything of value. For instance, with regard to formal annual performance appraisals, the organization may assume that managers and executives are following standard policies and procedures by evaluating their subordinates' performance (for example, rating them on several performance dimensions), documenting performance (for example, supplementing ratings with written comments) for purposes of administrative decisions (rewards, advancement, dismissal, etc.), and holding meaningful feedback discussions with their subordinates (London, 1996). The value of leader assessments in an organization needs to be examined continuously (London et al., 2006). This includes determining whether standards were followed in the development of the assessment methods (for example, APA, 2002; AERA, APA, & NCME, 2014; International Task Force on Assessment Center Guidelines, 2015), whether the measures have construct validity, and the economic value of the assessment to the organization and as feedback to the individual(s) who were assessed. Assessment methods differ in terms of data collected, the degree of quantitative and qualitative results, reliability, validity (face and predictive), and usefulness for selection, evaluation, and development (London & McFarland, 2017). Common methods are summarized in Table 3.1.

The field of leadership assessment has well-validated technology, which may not be used enough. As Table 3.1 points out, there are strengths and weaknesses of each method, and situations for which the methods are most appropriate. The next sections include a critical analysis of assessment centers, 360-degree feedback surveys, and leader development programs as structured methods for comprehensive leader assessment.

TABLE 3.1 Assessment methods, and their strengths and weaknesses

Assessment method	Strengths	Weaknesses
Interviews	Situational judgments; can standardize interview	Difficult to quantify
Cognitive and personality tests	Produce objective result with percentiles, and with norms within the company and with national samples	Validity requires large samples in similar situations
Integrity tests	Ethical leadership is important in all organizations, especially when leaders are responsible for financial assets	Apply in limited situations (e.g. where assets, such as money or goods, are at risk, as in banks or retail establishments); may require justification to candidates in selection situations
Test batteries	Can produce comprehensive picture of candidates, and can be a basis for coaching and development; can be administered and scored electronically	Results can be complex, and certainly require professional input to administer and interpret
Biodata	Valuable to assess experience and to guide candidates for better preparation for future opportunities	Difficult to know what background information is predictive; need to focus on behaviors that are likely to be repeated
Assessment centers	Good basis for in-depth, integrative view of candidates' strengths and weaknesses for selection and development; multiple methods can be delivered and integrated through online technology, retaining qualitative depth and saving costs	Produce complex results; expensive

Multisource (360-degree) feedback surveys collecting performance ratings from subordinates, supervisors, peers, and/or customers, as well as self-ratings	Reflect performance expectation and value of performance management in the organization, and build culture of performance management and improvement	Need to be integrated into organization's performance management system and culture; results vary depending on role of the rater; acceptance and use by the recipient depend on support for development
Supervisor nominations and performance appraisals	Supervisors understand performance expectations and are accountable for results of their judgments	Potentially biased by rater errors and limited exposure to candidates, even subordinates; may be viewed by candidates as unfair, and may lead to politicking and impression management
Performance in a leadership development program	Program is a basis for assessment, similar to an assessment center	Evaluations are not systematic, as they are in an assessment center; observations are subject to rater biases similar to performance appraisals; simulations and exercises may be viewed as artificial, not reflective of actual job conditions and demands

Source: Adapted from London and colleagues (2006)

Assessment Centers

Assessment centers have a long history of use in leadership assessment. They are expensive to develop and administer. However, they have substantial validity, and new technology makes them more cost-effective. Assessment centers are used to identify managers who have the potential to become leaders (Bray, 1982; Bray & Grant, 1966; Byham & Thornton, 1986; Howard & Bray, 1988) and for assessing managers' career motivation (London & Bray, 1984). Assessment centers are used to screen external candidates for selection and internal candidates for promotion (Thornton & Gibbons, 2009). Personality and motivational measures from assessment centers have been shown to be strongly related to key managerial abilities, demonstrating the validity of the managerial assessment center (Klimoski & Brickner, 1987).

In assessment centers, multiple trained assessors observe assessees as they participate in complex organizational simulations. The assessors rate the candidates' performance on dimensions that have been found, in job analyses, to be important for entry and higher-level positions and/or competency models. The dimensions are defined in terms of observable behaviors, which are incorporated into the assessment center simulations. The assessors may be managers from the company, human resource managers, psychologists, and/or external consultants. Methods for integrating the results include assessors reviewing and discussing their ratings and agreeing on a common set of ratings, or they may be mechanically combined from ratings made by the assessors after the different exercises. The exercises can be viewed as work samples, and assessors can assign overall performance scores for each exercise, rather than rate distinct dimensions within each exercise, which tends to result in strong exercise effects rather than dimension effects across exercises (Thornton & Gibbons, 2009). Online technology now provides a cost-effective means of evaluating candidates, with candidates participating in assessment exercises on the Web (Collins & Hartog, 2011; Rupp, 2014). These can include the asynchronous administration of exercises, as well as synchronous administration, with candidates participating in team exercises and interacting with assessors as interviewers or in role-playing exercises.

Executive Assessment

The problem with executive assessment is that executive functions are complex, diverse, and situation-specific in continuously changing, global, and highly competitive environments (Jeaneret & Silzer, 1998; McPhail & Jeanneret, 2012; Thornton et al., 2017). As such, there is no one set of behavioral competencies that applies to all positions at the highest echelons of an organization: the vice presidential, "C-suite" level, comprising chief operating officer (COO), chief executive officer (CEO), and chair of the board. Hollenbeck (2009) recognized this, arguing that executive selection should be viewed as a judgment and decision-making problem. Executive selection methods assess a candidate's character, which includes a combination of moral, intellectual, and emotional qualities, such as honesty, integrity, and values, as well as a moral compass for doing the "right thing" and putting "the greater good" first (Klann, 2007; Tichy & Bennis, 2007). Selection methods also assess a candidate's competence – that is, what they can do. A candidate's fit with the organization's culture becomes especially important. The complexity of executive positions in global organizations is quite different than the job structures at lower levels of the organizational hierarchy. At the top of the organization, there is a loose relationship between behavior and results, and between results and organizational performance. There is no "right way" of doing the position. Assessment therefore tries to predict behaviors only after character and competences are assessed first.

The "character first" model begins with the decision maker's viewpoint. Decision makers who are selecting an executive start by asking what they need to know about the position, the organization, and the external environment. They then ask what they need to know about the candidates, how to find this out, and how to integrate this information to make a decision.

Methods for Assessing Executives

Individual assessments may be commissioned by the board of an organization searching for a CEO or other top executives. Fortunately, reliable and valid assessment methods are available to examine personality, leadership, and the ability to develop interpersonal relationships (emotional intelligence) in a variety of contexts, including the global arena. Darker characteristics that may be "derailers" can also be assessed, such as paranoia, passive-aggressiveness, narcissism, arrogance, dominance, poor team playing or collaborating, inflexibility, an inability to get along with co-workers, a lack of self-awareness, difficulty functioning during periods of stress and change, and a lack of clear vision or strategy (cf. Dalal & Nolan, 2009; Hogan & Hogan, 2001; Hogan, Hogan, & Kaiser, 2011; Johnson, 2016).

The interview can be a source of information on character and competence by asking candidates to describe themselves and their experiences, and to provide evidence of the judgments they have made and how they made them (Hollenbeck, 2009). Interviews get at critical experiences, learning, and outcomes that were developmental (McCall, Lombardo, & Morrison, 1988). Other methods for assessing character and competence include personality and cognitive tests, assessment centers, and 360-degree feedback surveys (giving feedback, and observing reactions to feedback and coaching). Assessment and development programs combine these methods during a week-long experience. An example is the Center for Creative Leadership's "Leadership at the Peak" program (Center for Creative Leadership, 2018).

Online assessments provide new avenues for emersion assessments of character and competence. Fenestra is an example (Collins & Hartog, 2011; Rupp, 2014). Developed by consulting psychologist Sandra Hartog and associates, companies can contract to have candidates assessed for leadership positions. Instead of the expense of bringing candidates and assessors together for a day or more, candidates use their computers to access tests and simulations. Online business simulations incorporate different media (video and text) and electronic communication, with actors playing roles and assessors conducting interviews, communicating electronically in real time. Another assessment process simply involves executives discussing and comparing leaders – activities that General Electric called "Session Cs" (Freedman, 2004) – incorporating different viewpoints and recognizing different contexts.

Giving Candidates Assessment Feedback

All too often, candidates do not receive assessment feedback. Data that are collected mainly for administrative decisions have value for the individual's self-evaluation and their own use for learning and professional growth. Candidates may not seek the feedback, especially when they are uncertain about the situation and the implications of the feedback results (Anseel, Beatty, Shen, Lievens, & Sackett, 2015) and when they are not open to learning about themselves (Diamante & London, 2002; Dweck, 2006). Whatever assessment measures are adopted to make decisions about individuals, participants should receive feedback on the results and guidance for applying the results to their career development.

London and McFarland (2017) described the value of providing – indeed, the obligation to provide – feedback of assessment results to candidates for leadership positions. This may not be the prime purpose of the assessment, but there are a number of reasons why candidates should receive feedback about their performance, as follows.

- Feedback informs candidates about the process – that is, that it is fair, that it is a chance to demonstrate their strengths, that it focuses on job-relevant characteristics, and that the organization has standards of excellence.
- Feedback protects a candidate's self-image (for example, reminding them about the tough competition, and that the goal is the best fit for the candidate and the organization).
- Feedback gives candidates a positive impression of the organization because of the care, accuracy, and fairness of the process.
- Feedback helps candidates to make career decisions (for example, whether to accept a job offer or search for other types of position that make better use of their skills).
- Feedback maintains the focus on job-relevant abilities.

- Feedback helps the organization to guard against discrimination based on characteristics that are not related to the position, and maintains the reliability and validity of the assessment methods.
- Feedback increases the value of the assessment, given the cost to the organization and the candidate's time and energy.

Of course, feedback cannot be done in a way that compromises the security of the assessment process. Alternative forms of selection can be valuable in this regard. However, knowing the methods in advance does not necessarily compromise the validity of the assessment, since leadership assessment is usually highly behavioral, measuring characteristics of the candidates in a range of situations and on a variety of personality, cognitive, and attitudinal traits that do not have right or wrong answers. A question arises as to whether the organization is obligated to give feedback to candidates and also to help them to use the feedback for their development. This is especially the case for internal candidates, for whom the assessment results are for both selection and career development.

Tests and assessment centers are methods for specific purposes — whether leader selection at executive or managerial levels, administrative decisions internal to an organization (promotion or job placement), and/or career development. Supervisor and co-worker ratings are another type of assessment method that can be used for evaluation and development. Next, we consider the pros and cons of 360-degree feedback, then we turn to programs for learning and performance appraisal, which often incorporate 360-degree feedback.

360-degree Feedback

Multisource, or 360-degree, feedback surveys have become a ubiquitous method of leader assessment in organizations without sufficient determination of whether they actually improve a leader's performance. Ostensibly, they are used to given managers formative feedback about strengths and weaknesses, as well as directions for learning, to make decisions about them, or — aggregated across units or the organization as a whole — to assess the leadership capabilities resident in the organization and the need for team or organizational-level development.

> 360° Feedback is a process for collecting, quantifying, and reporting coworker observations about an individual (that is, a ratee) that facilitates/enables three specific data-driven/based outcomes: (a) the collection of rater perceptions of the degree to which specific behaviors are exhibited; (b) the analysis of meaningful comparisons of rater perceptions across multiple ratees, between specific groups of raters for an individual ratee, and for ratee changes over time; and (c) the creation of sustainable individual, group, and/or organizational changes in behaviors valued by the organization.
>
> *(Bracken, Rose, & Church, 2015, p. 764)*

One goal of a 360-degree survey feedback process is to create sustainable change at the individual, team, and organization levels (Bracken, Timmreck, Fleenor, & Summers, 2001). Measures reflect and communicate the dimensions of performance that are valued by the organization. As such, the process influences goals for development, and it focuses raters' and ratees' attention of aspects of performance. Also, multisource surveys aggregated within units allow the comparison of units, as well has offer information about overall levels of performance and areas for development.

360-degree survey results should be accompanied by guidance on interpretation of the results, development planning, resources for development, and tracking mechanisms (for example, other performance measures and later feedback surveys). Sharing the results is a way of enhancing accountability, so that leaders use the results and commit to improvements (London, Smither, & Adsit, 1997). Indeed, lack of follow-up coaching to help ratees to use the results for behavior change can produce negative outcomes, such as the ratees ignoring valuable ideas, not achieving their potential for advancement, and even engaging in dysfunctional behaviors (Goldsmith & Morgan, 2004).

In addition to using them for career development, companies use multisource feedback surveys to make decisions about employees, such as to identify young managers who have the potential for leadership advancement and to evaluate senior executives for succession planning, in particular pinpointing those who are (or are not) aligned with the organization's strategies and culture (Adsit et al., 1997; Church & Rotolo, 2013; Church, Rotolo, Ginther, & Levine, 2015; Rose, 2011; Silzer & Church, 2010). When 360-degree feedback is incorporated into an organization's performance management program, the processes of rating, feedback, sharing results, using results for decisions and development, and continued follow-up all contribute to successful performance management (Bracken, Rose, & Church, 2015).

The Pros and Cons of 360-degree Surveys

The upside of 360-degree feedback is that it provides managers with a better understanding of their performance than they could get from their supervisor alone (Atwater, Brett, & Charles, 2007; Smither, London, & Reilly, 2005). 360-degree feedback helps team members to work together more effectively because team members become more accountable to each other. Serving as a giver, as well as recipient, of 360-degree feedback is a way in which managers can recognize how their individual career development relates to the organization's performance goals, and it provides input for managers to take responsibility for their own career development rather than relying on a supervisor or the company to manage their careers (Heathfield, 2016). Managers receiving 360-degree feedback see the assessment as more accurate and reflective of their performance than feedback from their supervisor alone. Also, because feedback comes from a number of different sources, there is less risk of bias or rating errors from one source (for example, supervisors basing their evaluations on the most recent event, which ignores performance throughout the year). Feedback directly from customers, whether internal or external, provides information for improving service. When averaged across people, 360-degree feedback gives the organization information about training needs.

TABLE 3.2 Limitations and advice for implementing 360-degree feedback surveys

Suggested by Heathfield (2016):
- 360-degree feedback surveys alone should not be viewed as a final annual evaluation;
- the managers who will use a 360-degree system should be involved in its development, because imposing the system (survey items, delivery of feedback) without input may meet resistance;
- the items rated and use of the results should be related to the strategic goals of the organization, i.e. ratings of competencies that matter to the organization and for which there are developmental opportunities;
- 360-degree feedback should be accompanied by support (e.g. one-on-one coaching, training of supervisors to help subordinates to understand the developmental value of the results), rather than a desk drop of a report (Smither, London, Flautt, Vargas, & Kucine, 2003, 2004);
- feedback recipients may be inclined to focus on negative results and dwell on their weaknesses, rather than recognize the positive results and implications for developing strengths;
- raters may not receive sufficient training to make ratings, deliver results, and receive results – one main reason why organizations are moving away from formal evaluation processes to more in-the-moment feedback; and
- 360-degree ratings can be complex, with multiple raters and different items to rate for raters in different roles (supervisors, subordinates, co-workers, customers), although technology helps – and even mobile applications are available.

Suggested by Jackson (2012):
- supervisors who were not involved in the process of developing the 360-degree feedback process may discourage subordinates from taking the results seriously;
- the survey questions may seem too generic to be useful;
- written responses may be too personal and not focused on behaviors that the ratee can change;
- the ratee may not use the results to formulate a development plan and put the plan in place;
- the 360-degree ratings are a one-time measure and not followed up with regular feedback over time;
- raters may worry that their ratings will not be confidential despite assurances to the contrary; and
- self-ratings are often collected as part of the 360-degree process, but these are likely to be inflated and, like other ratings, are subject to biases such as the halo effect.

Several authors have described the limitations of 360-degree feedback and ways of guarding against its downsides. These are summarized in Table 3.2. Despite these limitations, organizations find that 360-degree feedback surveys are valuable as a stimulus for leader development and performance management. In isolation, they are limited, as noted; their value emerges when they are incorporated into coaching programs and used over time to inculcate a feedback-oriented performance management culture in which areas for performance improvement are a regular topic of conversation (London & Smither, 2002; Smither et al., 2005). Employees are likely to take feedback to heart and to form a more objective view of themselves when they work with leaders to discuss the results and use the results to establish plans for their career development (London, 2015; London, Mone, & Scott, 2004; Wohlers, Hall, & London, 1993). The next two sections consider assessment for leader development and performance management.

Assessment and Leader Development

Leadership development is too often based on executives' judgments about what leaders need, or on leadership concepts that become popular, but have no sound basis in research showing their relationship to leadership success. Assessments can show gaps in leadership competence and provide directions for leadership development (Elmholdt, Elmholdt, Tanggaard, & Mersh, 2016). The leadership dimensions that are evaluated, how they are evaluated (ratings, narrative exemplars of rating scale points called behavioral anchors, averages across items, open-ended qualitative descriptions from evaluators), and how they are presented to the managers who are evaluated all influence how leadership is defined in an organization. Assessments convey those aspects of performance and behaviors that are valued by the organization. Assessment tools can be integral to the way in which leadership is defined and developed in the organization, or they can be superfluous. If these tools are abstract in method and content, and if they have little to do with actual day-to-day challenges, demands, and routines, or with the realities of career management and advancement, they are not likely to be valued by the raters or the ratees. Leaders will not see the measures and the ratings as informative of their learning about leadership or their actual leadership. They may see the dimensions measured as an aspirational ideal espoused by the organization, but not reflective of reality (Wenger, 1998, cited in Elmholdt et al., 2016). The goal may be to have leaders conform to an ideal expressed by the assessment tool leaving little opportunity for individual reflection or consideration of particular situations in which leaders find themselves. The assessment becomes the record of learning and performance, with no alignment with how they practice leadership, which may include balancing subject-matter expertise with day-to-day problem solving, as well as the design and implementation of long-term strategies in alignment with organizational goals. Leaders then have little connection with the assessment.

Role transition from subject-matter expert to leader is likely to require relinquishing one's identity as subject-matter expert, co-worker, and friend (Maurer & London, 2015). Organizations can facilitate or hinder this transition process (wittingly or unwittingly). Rewards and job demands may push individuals into leadership positions. However, practices that reward individual or team innovation, rather than leadership of teams, can discourage leaders from concentrating on the leader role. Assessments that evaluate leadership, but reward individual contribution as a subject-matter expert, devalue the assessment process; alternatively, the outcome would say little about the value of leadership success nor would it facilitate using the results to guide learning and development.

Another potential disconnect is the link (or lack thereof) between behavioral dimensions that are measured, day-to-day practice, and the content of leadership development programs. A training program will be of little value if it is not tied to the stresses and demands of leadership (for example, deadlines, strained resources, inadequate talent, sudden shifts in organizational goals and strategies for accomplishing them). Assessments of leadership learning will be of limited value if they measure abstract concepts that either are not covered in the leadership program or represent an unrealistic ideal. If assessment tools represent an aspirational ideal, individuals engaged in leadership development will compare themselves to that ideal as conditions change, and as they evolve and grow as leaders. The assessment tool may not capture the different ways in which people engage with the leadership role.

There are different degrees of "undoing" as an individual moves into the role of leader (Nicholson & Carroll, 2013). Promotion into a leadership role may be a frame-breaking adjustment that shakes up the leader's self-image and behavior. Leaders may concentrate on enacting core leadership competencies while they continue to flourish in their comfortable expert roles – or they may flounder. The assessment process needs to recognize different degrees of change and adjustment during the leader development phase for a new leader, and the continued role churn of an experienced leader, for that matter.

Leader development and being a leader is analogous to an acculturation process. Acculturating to a new role is like moving into a new cultural environment. The effect of such a dislocation and adjustment is not a single, uniform process, but depends on a number of factors such as condition (reason for the change, place, status, demands, competition), individual differences (gender, personality, cognitive ability, adaptability), time (age, prior experiences), process (socialization, learning, opportunities, coaching), and life domain (for example, work–family balance), as well as the interaction among these (cf. Bornstein, 2017).

Leader development takes place within the context of the organization's performance management culture. Assessment is an ongoing performance management process that is both *summative* (that is, for use in making decisions about leaders) and *formative* (as input for development). In the final section, we consider how leadership assessment is an integral component of performance management.

Assessment in Managing Leader's Performance

Performance management systems are criticized for their structure, formality, and lack of attention to what is actually happening that affects a leader's day-to-day performance. Performance management refers to the organizational policies, programs, and practices for recruiting, developing, evaluating, and compensating employees. Although performance management applies to employees at all levels, we will consider issues in managing a leader's performance. Performance evaluation refers to different types of appraisal – especially the annual performance appraisal and feedback review. For managers and executive leaders, the appraisal is generally a form, comprising ratings on key leadership dimensions of performance and narrative about performance, areas for improvement, and development plans completed by the target individual's immediate supervisor, and then used by the supervisor and other executives to make compensation and promotion decisions (or other decisions, such as reassignment or termination). Additional forms may collect ratings from other sources, including peers, subordinates, and other supervisors (that is, 360-degree, multisource ratings). Other surveys may measure employee engagement and satisfaction, as well as team and organization unit climate and culture, which, when the results are aggregated across employees within units, speaks to the performance of the unit's leader. Of course, objective data may be available, such as sales, costs, and indicators of financial accomplishments, such as return on investment or assets. Executives and supervisors may meet to discuss the performance of the leaders/managers in their units, defend their ratings, and rank order the leaders/managers. Other information may be available, such as performance in a leadership development program.

Say Adler and colleagues (2016, p. 215): "Performance feedback represents the ultimate lose-lose scenario. It is extremely difficult to do well, and if it was done well, the recipients would be likely to dismiss their feedback as inaccurate and unfair." Typically, performance management in many organizations consists of an annual review cycle, which starts with goal setting and concludes with a performance appraisal, feedback discussion, and some outcomes, such as a salary increase or bonus commensurate with the performance evaluation (Pulakos et al., 2015). The discussion will include areas for development – that is, learning or improving skills to increase performance and/or opportunities for advancement, as well as a review of career opportunities for the individual inside, or possibly outside, the organization. Feedback throughout the year is infrequent, and even the formal appraisal feedback discussion itself is completed quickly, going through the motions to affirm that it was done in compliance with organizational policies.

The rating process is time-consuming and replete with chances for error, or for cursory and incomplete information. Concerns about traditional performance management processes, including 360-degree feedback and annual performance appraisals, have become among the "top 10" concerns of organizational psychologists (SIOP Administrative Office, 2016). Following the lead of corporations, psychologists are examining alternative means of leader assessment as a basis for making decisions about them and as input for leaders' career development.

Organizations' complaints about the formal annual appraisal center on several characteristics of performance management systems. Common frustrations are as follows.

- The assessments may direct leaders' attention to a limited set of behaviors, paying less attention to other decisions and behaviors. They may focus on easily visible skills, ignoring others that are subtler, yet more important for individual projects or jobs (Graber, 2016).
- Ratings are given once a year on a limited series of performance dimensions that do not capture the full range of the individual's performance. Key events are forgotten. Recent events are weighted more heavily. Detailed information is lost. Irrelevant information may affect evaluations. Dimensions are meant to summarize an amalgam of information.
- Ratings are not behaviors nor are they objective indicators of actual performance.
- Different sources of information have different perspectives and make different errors. Raters may be influenced by a number of factors (rater characteristics, such as leniency or central tendency) and biases (for example, favoritism, recent performance affecting overall ratings, or discrimination based on nonjob-related characteristics of the individual evaluated, such as gender, race, and age).
- Feedback discussions are not done, or are not done well, and are confounded by discussions of compensation – although keeping discussions about pay separate from discussions about development may help (DiDonato, 2014; Meyer, 1975).
- Too much time is spent on the annual appraisal, boiling the evaluation down to a limited set of numbers that have little meaning in and of themselves.
- People work in different teams and make different contributions to those team projects. Overall, the performance appraisal process does not capture day-to-day performance or performance on a set of projects.
- Forced rankings may demoralize or stigmatize employees who are ranked low and do not allow for the possibility that all or most employees might be high performers.
- There is a difference between ratings for evaluating past performance versus ratings for performance improvement and career development. Ratings are backward-looking, not focused on improving performance or identifying

employees who are not making it and should leave the organization. Ratings do not have the desired effect of improving performance, goal setting, and career development at the individual or organizational levels.
- Supervisors can use ratings to justify decisions already made about subordinates.

Aligning Goals and Assessment: The Balanced Scorecard

The balanced scorecard is a method that evolved in the 1990s to cascade goals from executives through the managerial ranks of an organization and to provide a basis for comprehensive performance assessment that takes context into account (Kaplan & Norton, 1992, 2004; Lawrie & Cobbold, 2004). The method was intended to go beyond financial indicators of success to add goals and measures related to customers and other external stakeholders, internal business processes, and learning and growth. The process calls for establishing objectives, measures, targets, and initiatives for each element. Examples of measures of finance include cash flow, sales growth, operating income, and return on equity relative to stockholder expectations. Examples of measures of customer focus include percentage of sales from new products and on-time delivery. Examples of measures of operational processes include time for new product introduction and unit cost. Examples of measures of learning and growth include learning new skills and knowledge at the individual level, the introduction of needed new talent at the team level, and engagement and culture at the organizational level. The objectives are derived from departmental objectives and strategies, which in turn are derived from business unit or organizational objectives, thereby cascading goals and measures down to the team and individual levels. A leader's scorecard can be examined periodically for progress, updated as the situation changes, and used for annual assessment of accomplishments.

The benefits of the balanced scorecard are that the method focuses managers on organizational strategy, structure, and vision. It encompasses nonfinancial goals and metrics for a holistic and aligned approach to factors that contribute to organizational success. Also, it provides a basis for managers to monitor individual and team contributions to business unit and organizational success (Madsen & Stenheim, 2014).

However, a number of limitations have been cited in relation to the balanced scorecard, as summarized by Awadallah and Allam (2015), citing criticisms raised by several commentators (for example, Antonsen, 2010; Hoque, 2014; Madsen & Stenheim, 2014; Voelpel, Leibold, Eckhoff, & Davenport, 2006; Molleman, 2007). These include:

- difficulty in coordination and communication;
- rigidity, limiting performance measures to specific categories and measures that become the focus of managers' attention to the exclusion of others

that may emerge as more important, as well as failing to take into account cross-perspectives, such as customers and competition affecting the drive for innovation;
- insufficient flexibility in organizations that are in highly dynamic environments;
- merely listing metrics that make implementation difficult;
- not recognizing that innovation stems from advancements in technology, competition, partnerships, collaborators, and other external linkages; and
- creating work overload simply to set and keep track of performance measures, frustrating employees.

Other problems include that the scorecard process is viewed as a "quick fix," without proper guidance for implementation over time (BPM Institute, n.d.). As a result, metrics are poorly defined, there is a lack of efficient data collection and reporting, there is no formal review structure to integrate scorecards across leaders and units, there is no process improvement methods in relation to the goals articulated in a scorecard, and there is too much internal focus. These limitations may be resolved over time, with sufficient resources and patience, proper attention to the process, ongoing communication and coordination within and between teams and units, and flexibility in recognition of uncertain and/or changing internal and external conditions.

Arguments for Eliminating Annual Performance Appraisals

A solution to the limitations of the annual performance appraisal is to eliminate annual appraisals altogether. Adler and colleagues (2016) offered the reasons why this might be a good idea, as well as reasons for retaining the annual performance appraisal and improving the process (summarized in Table 3.3). Redesigned performance management systems rely less on annual performance appraisals and more on frequent feedback and coaching to improve performance (SIOP Administrative Office, 2016). Performance management becomes an ongoing process that focuses more on feedback in the moment – that is, daily, in the form of discussions of events; weekly, in the form of progress reports; and when major project deadlines are reached and accomplishments achieved (or not). This depends on leaders acquiring the skills to be effective sources of feedback and coaching, and on the organization inculcating feedback and development into its culture – as simply the way it does business. Assessing and developing subordinates in leadership roles become a key, if not a vital, role of leaders throughout the organization. Documentation to justify decisions and demonstrate fairness in compliance with organizational policies is still needed. This can be met by maintaining annual evaluations and documenting reviews, feedback, and coaching throughout the year.

TABLE 3.3 Summary of Adler and colleagues' (2016) analysis of performance management

Reasons for Eliminating Annual Performance Appraisal Ratings

- Disappointing interventions
- Multiple raters may disagree when evaluating the same individual.
- The ratings may not be comparable with other performance criteria.
- The use(s) of the ratings may conflict (e.g. for compensation, for development).
- Ratings may fail to reflect practice, i.e. how people are treated for promotion.
- Raters usually have no formal training to sift, sort, analyze, weigh, and aggregate the performance information that occurred throughout a year to make an overall judgment of a person's performance, which opens opportunities for bias – or at least inaccuracies (e.g. ignoring some important information or giving less important information more weight than it deserves).
- Raters may vary the goals they have in mind when rating – e.g. to improve task performance, to improve interpersonal relations among subordinates, to increase the ratee's standing in the organization – as well as have different beliefs about how ratings should be made (e.g. a desire to be seen as a tough rater).
- Assessments that emphasize differences between people are different than assessments emphasizing differences in strengths and weaknesses within individuals.
- Feedback from ratings may not necessarily be heard and/or acted upon, since people often have inflated views of themselves, i.e. leaders' personal characteristics (e.g. their autocratic, egotistical tendencies compared to their participative, humble tendencies) may affect the extent to which they seek, listen to, and accept feedback.
- Raters may have their own goals that wittingly or unwittingly influence ratings, whether as a result of factors such as favoritism, political gains, or impression management (i.e. aiming to impress senior managers with low ratings that reflect the rater's own high performance standards).
- Ratings may have different purposes – for development, compensation decisions, evidence of readiness for promotion – which may influence a rater's judgment on different dimensions of performance, succession planning, legal compliance, etc. as a basis for decisions, and their ability to demonstrate fairness and nondiscrimination
- Rating guidelines are confusing, i.e. training in frame of reference, behavioral examples, and rating errors has not improved their use in practice.
- Rating forms may be overengineered to achieve too much and, in the process, achieve less than they should.
- Ratings for development require comparisons within individuals, i.e. of strengths and weaknesses, and changes over time, rather than comparisons between individuals.

Arguments for Retaining Ratings

- Eliminating ratings is not likely to affect other aspects of performance management.
- Performance is evaluated in one way or another in any case.
- Developing a system that results in useful ratings is admittedly difficult, but this is no reason to eliminate them.
- Ratings from different perspectives may be valuable, since there are different dimensions of job performance that vary in their applicability from different vantage points. For example, subordinates may have different views of a manager's performance than that manager's peers, and different subordinates

may have different needs, e.g. subordinates who are new to the group or who are on resource-intensive projects with tight schedules may need more oversight than experienced subordinates or those in positions or on projects that are less demanding.
- The changing nature of work and the frequent movement of employees from one assignment or job to another makes performance documentation important.
- Not having ratings may be worse than having them.

Ideas for Improved Performance Management

- Hold calibration meetings among raters to arrive at common understandings of the meanings of different dimensions of performance and standards.
- Form performance review panels to discuss each individual rated from different perspectives and at which the principal rater (the immediate supervisor, usually) can defend the ratings.
- Develop competency models that describe the key behavioral dimensions of performance, expectations, and clear meanings for each rating level.
- Use 360-degree ratings as input for performance management. They can be particularly valuable when considerable work is done in teams with matrix reporting relationships or remotely, where the immediate supervisor has less opportunity to evaluate each subordinate's performance than peers or other co-workers and customers. The feedback results can help managers to achieve a more systems-level orientation to their performance, i.e. how their behaviors and decisions affect key stakeholders, providing a wider range of input (sources) and performance dimensions (individual behavior, teamwork, corporate citizenship behaviors) (Campion, Campion, & Campion, 2015).
- Measure team-level performance and provide feedback to the team (London & Sessa, 2006), and follow up with team discussions about the ways in which different team members influence the team's performance, how different members can be leaders for activities at which they are most expert, and the interdependent nature of the roles of team members in influencing overall team results.
- Simplify forms, reducing dimensions and ratings categories.
- Recognize that performance management is a continuous process that includes formal appraisal and feedback processes (the annual or semi-annual performance review and discussion), as well as informal dynamics (daily interactions, weekly check-ins on performance, gathering reactions from others, as well as the employee, and having "in the moment" discussions about events).
- Evaluate and reward leaders, in formal and informal ways, for their role as managers and developers of the people who report to them.
- Remove barriers to success, i.e. provide support, guidance, and advice for improving performance as an individual, couching the advice in terms of achieving better results for the department, highlighting for the employee the importance of behaviors and activities to the department's or organization's goals and discussing ways of improving the organization's results.
- Regardless of the methods for leadership assessment and review, recognize that what is important is the use of the ratings, the performance discussions that ensue from feedback, and that changes in behavior and performance that result.

Some Examples

Several companies have replaced annual performance reviews with continued oversight and feedback, driving continuous improvement. Consider some examples.

Lear – a global company in the automotive seating and electrical distribution systems business, with more than 110,000 employees in more than 200 manufacturing facilities – replaced annual performance reviews with quarterly sessions in which supervisors speak with subordinates about their past and future work, with a focus on learning new skills and limiting the effects of weaknesses. No mention is made of pay (DiDonato, 2014). The company believes that this avoids creating a blame-oriented culture that works against cooperative problem solving and collegiality.

Kimberly-Clark's performance management program pushes employees to constantly improve, tracking progress and addressing laggards (Weber, 2016). The company has created a sharper focus on high-performing employees and a routine "culture of accountability," training leaders to give and receive tough feedback. Leaders reinforce positive behavior, praising coworkers who exert effort and achieve, and welcoming and showing appreciation for feedback.

Coca-Cola encourages leaders to conduct a monthly "reflection" for every immediate subordinate. Supervisors answer several question, such as "Given [their] performance, would you assign this associate to increased scale, scope, and responsibilities?" and "Is this associate at risk for low performance?" (Weber, 2016).

Adobe Systems also scrapped the backward-looking annual appraisal in favor of encouraging leaders to engage in real-time, ongoing, and attentive discussions about performance (Armitage & Parray, 2013).

Accounting firm Deloitte adopted three interlocking "rituals" to recognize, see, and fuel performance: weekly check-ins; the quarterly, or per-project, performance snapshot; and the annual compensation decision (Buckingham & Goodall, 2015). This shifts performance evaluation from a batched focus on the past to a continual focus on the future, with regular evaluations and frequent check-ins. Executives check in with team leaders and members at the week's end, when projects near completion, and when projects are complete. They review priorities and expectations for each team member – what great work is and how each person contributed to the team. As at Lear, compensation decisions are separated from day-to-day performance management.

A risk of the current trend in performance management relying on leaders for informal evaluations and feedback rather than following a formal, structured process is that leaders have an implicit belief that they can evaluate and predict human behavior because of their experience. This results in an overreliance on intuition and a reluctance to question their own judgments or to rely on analytical approaches (Highhouse, 2008).

Gender Bias in Leadership Assessment

Assessment and feedback may be tied to gender and power differences, and this may explain a gender gap in leadership (Bear, Cushenbery, London, & Sherman, 2017; Heilman, 2001). Evaluating others and giving them feedback inherently imposes a power dynamic between the giver and receiver of feedback. The evaluator and source of feedback may be inclined, knowingly or otherwise, to use the situation to retain or advance a higher power status over the individual evaluated. This may be stronger when the leader doing the evaluation is male and the subordinate leader being evaluated is female. In that case, cultural norms and stereotypes favor men as leaders. Also, men are likely to have stronger social networks within the organization than women. The result can be women facing higher performance standards than men, receiving patronizing feedback, and/or being penalized for counter-normative behavior (for example, criticized for being aggressive when the same behavior would be lauded in men). Also, as recipients of feedback, women may be more likely than men to internalize negative feedback, to interpret ambiguous feedback as negative, and to give more weight to interpersonal aspects of the job than do men (Bear et al., 2017). The result is that women may be more likely than men to opt out of opportunities for leadership development and advancement, and will be less likely to be identified as high-potential managers ready for, or on a path toward, increased leadership responsibilities.

Directions for Improved Performance Management

Instead of doing away with performance assessments, the goal should be improving the process for performance evaluation, decision making, and development and developing initiatives to the benefit of all of the elements of the performance management process, including informal evaluations and feedback (Adler et al., 2016). The main problem with ratings, according to Pulakos and O'Leary (2011), is that the processes of rating, documenting, and goal setting are inconsistent with ongoing performance management – that is, providing frequent, credible, and useful performance feedback. Companies have been strengthening their performance management systems to provide real-time feedback, performance review discussions with the recipients of the feedback, and team collaboration for goal setting. Examples are goal-setting and performance check-ins as projects evolve and move to completion – that is, the process implemented by Deloitte. Although a focus on improving the rating process should be part of the overall improvements, organizations should give more attention to what drives leader effectiveness. Organizations need a common language, common perceptions of what is important, and a common process for development discussions.

Conclusion

Leadership assessment tries to capture the complex and often changing nature of leadership positions at multiple organizational levels and situations. To be useful, assessments need to examine the skills, knowledge, cognitive abilities, and personality characteristics that are important to the position. Competency models identify the abilities that are needed and valued across an organization. Assessment centers and individual assessment for executive positions often combine methods for a comprehensive view of the leader. Individual assessments are tailored to measure the leadership potential of prospective executives. Candidates for positions can learn about themselves and their fit for opportunities by providing them with feedback on assessment results. Multisource, 360-degree feedback surveys are a commonly used method to evaluate the performance of leaders from multiple perspectives and to give them feedback for development, although results are often used for decision-making purposes. The dimensions of performance that are rated in a 360-degree survey communicate the behaviors that the organization values. Leadership development programs may begin with a 360-degree survey as input for development. Participation in development exercises, with feedback and coaching, can support an individual's transition process from subject-matter expert to leader. Leader assessment is at the heart of managerial and executive performance management. The structured processes for appraisal, however, has led to resistance in many corporations that are instituting more flexible, in-the-moment feedback and coaching. Formal appraisal processes can be combined with informal and frequent leader assessments. This builds a culture of assessment, feedback, and coaching, and it highlights the roles of manager and executive as leadership coach and developer. Structured methods of appraisal and rater training can avoid biases, and can ensure fair and consistent assessments.

The future of leadership assessment for performance management can be practical and valuable for leaders and managers at all levels of an organization (Pulakos et al., 2015). In such an environment, discussions about goals and performance are frequent, recognizing that goals need to be adjusted or changed completely as organizational objectives and strategies shift. Leaders and their subordinates can discuss development frequently – even daily or several times a day – focusing on what they learn from experiences. Feedback is in real time, and ideas for improvement are just in time for impending tasks and projects. Leaders attend training programs to learn and practice elements of performance management, and performance ratings and feedback discussions focus on behaviors and outcomes that are clearly aligned with organizational goals.

References

Adler, S., Campion, M., Grubb, A., Murphy, K., Ollander-Krane, R., & Pulakos, E.D. (2016). Getting rid of performance ratings: Genius or folly? A debate. *Industrial and Organizational Psychology: Perspectives on Science and Practice, 9*(2), 219–252.

Adsit, D.J., London, M. Crom, S., & Jones, D. (1997). Cross-cultural differences in upward ratings in a multinational company. *International Journal of Human Resource Management*, 8(4), 385–401.

American Educational Research Association (AERA), American Psychological Association (APA), & National Council on Measurement in Education (NCME). (2014). *Standards for educational and psychological testing*. Washington, D.C.: AERA/APA/NCME.

American Psychological Association (APA). (2002). *Ethical principles of psychologists and code of conduct*. Washington, D.C.: APA.

Anseel, F., Beatty, A.S., Shen, W., Lievens, F., & Sackett, P.R. (2015). How are we doing after 30 years? A meta-analytic review of the antecedents and outcomes of feedback-seeking behavior. *Journal of Management*, 41(1), 318–348.

Antonsen, Y. (2010). The downside of the balanced scorecard: A case study from Norway. *The Scandinavian Journal of Management*, 30(1), 40–50.

Armitage, A., & Parray, D. (2013). Reinventing performance management: Creating purpose-driven practices. *People & Strategy*, 36(2), 26–33.

Atwater, L.E., Brett, J.F., & Charles, A.C. (2007). Multisource feedback: Lessons learned and implications for practice. *Human Resource Management*, 46(2), 285–307.

Awadallah, E.A., & Allam, A. (2015). A critique of the balanced scorecard as a performance measurement tool. *International Journal of Business and Social Science*, 6(7), 91–99.

Bass, B.M. (1985). *Leadership and performance beyond expectations*. New York: Free Press.

Bass, B.M. (1995). Theory of transformational leadership redux. *The Leadership Quarterly*, 6(4), 463–478.

Bass, B.M. (1999). Two decades of research and development in transformational leadership. *European Journal of Work and Organizational Psychology*, 8(1), 9–32.

Bear, J.B., Cushenbery, L., London, M., & Sherman, G.D. (2017). Performance feedback, power retention, and the gender gap in leadership. *The Leadership Quarterly*, 28(6), 721–740.

Bhagat, R.S., Triandis, H.C., & McDivitt, A.S. (2012). *Managing global organizations: A cultural perspective*. Northampton, MA: Edward Elgar.

Bhawuk, D.P.S., Podsiadlowski, A., Graf, J., & Triandis, H.C. (2002). Corporate strategies for managing diversity in the global workplace. In G.R. Ferris, M.R. Buckley, & D.B. Fedor (Eds.), *Human resource management: Perspectives, context, functions, and outcomes* (pp. 112–145). Englewood Cliffs, NJ: Prentice-Hall.

Bornstein, M.H. (2017). The specificity principle in acculturation science. *Perspectives on Psychological Science*, 12(1), 3–45.

Bracken, D.W., Rose, D.S., & Church, A.H. (2015). The evolution and devolution of 360° feedback. *Industrial and Organizational Psychology*, 9(4), 761–794.

Bracken, D.W., Timmreck, C.W., Fleenor, J.W., & Summers, L. (2001). 360° feedback from another angle. *Human Resource Management Journal*, 40(1), 3–20.

Bray, D.W. (1982). The assessment center and the study of lives. *American Psychologist*, 37(2), 180–189.

Bray, D.W., & Grant, D.L. (1966). The assessment center in the measurement of potential for business management. *Psychological Monographs: General and Applied*, 80(17), 1–27.

Buckingham, M., & Goodall, A. (2015). Reinventing performance management. *Harvard Business Review*, 93(4), 40–50.

Business Process Management Institute (BPM Institute). (n.d.). Problems implementing a balanced scorecard. (n.d.). Retrieved from www.bpminstitute.org/resources/articles/problems-implementing-balanced-scorecard

Byham, T.M., & Wellins, R.S. (2016). Sink or swim: Setting first-time leaders up for success. *Chief Learning Officer, 15*(9), 21–22.

Byham, W.C., & Thornton III, G.C. (1986). Assessment centers. In R.A. Berk (Ed.), *Performance assessment: Methods and applications* (pp. 143–166). Baltimore, MD: Johns Hopkins University Press.

Campion, M.C., Campion, E.D., & Campion, M.A. (2015). Improvements in performance management through the use of 360° feedback. *Industrial and Organizational Psychology: Perspectives on Science and Practice, 8*(1), 85–93.

Case, C.R., & Maner, J.K. (2014). Divide and conquer: When and why leaders undermine the cohesive fabric of their group. *Journal of Personality and Social Psychology, 107*(6), 1033–1050.

Center for Creative Leadership. (2018). Leadership at the peak. Retrieved from https://solutions.ccl.org/Leadership_at_the_Peak

Church, A.H., & Rotolo, C.T. (2013). How are top companies assessing their high-potential and senior executives? A talent management benchmark study. *Consulting Psychology Journal: Practice and Research, 65*(3), 199–223.

Church, A.H., Rotolo, C.T., Ginther, N.M., & Levine, R. (2015). How are top companies designing and managing their high-potential programs? A follow-up talent management benchmark study. *Consulting Psychology Journal: Practice and Research, 67*(1), 17–47.

Collins, L., & Hartog, S. (2011). Assessment centers: A blended adult development strategy. In M. London (Ed.), *The Oxford handbook of lifelong learning* (pp. 231–250). Oxford: Oxford University Press.

Dalal, D.K., & Nolan, K.P. (2009). Using dark side personality traits to identify potential failure. *Industrial and Organizational Psychology: Perspectives on Science and Practice, 2*(4), 434–436.

DeNisi, A., & Smith. C.E. (2014). Performance appraisal, performance management, and firm-level performance: A review, a proposed model, and new directions for future research. *Academy of Management Annals, 8*(1), 127–179.

Diamante, T., & London, M. (2002). Expansive leadership in the age of digital technology. *Journal of Management Development, 21*(6), 404–416.

DiDonato, T. (2014, July 10). Stop basing pay on performance reviews. *Harvard Business Review*. Retrieved from https://hbr.org/2014/01/stop-basing-pay-on-performance-reviews

Dweck, C. (2006). *Mindset: The new psychology of success*. New York: Random House.

Elmholdt, K., Elmholdt, C., Tanggaard, L., & Mersh, L.H. (2016). Learning and good leadership: A matter of assessment? *Human Resource Development International, 19*(5), 406–428.

Freedman, A. (2004, October 16). The Session C strategy. *Human Resource Online*. Retrieved from www.hreonline.com/HRE/view/story.jhtml?id=5359233

Frigo, M.L., & Snellgrove, D. (2016, October 1). Why innovation should be every CFO's top priority. *Strategic Finance*. Retrieved from http://sfmagazine.com/post-entry/october-2016-why-innovation-should-be-every-cfos-top-priority/

Goldsmith, M., & Morgan, H. (2004). Leadership is a contact sport: The "follow-up" factors in management development. *Strategy + Business, 36*, 71–79.

Graber, J. (2016). Creating layers of competency. *Chief Learning Officer, 15*(1), 40–41, 43.

Heathfield, S. (2016, January 4). *360 degree feedback: See the good, the bad and the ugly*. Retrieved from www.thebalance.com/360-degree-feedback-information-1917537

Heilman, M.E. (2001). Description or description: How gender stereotypes prevent women's ascent up the organizational ladder. *Journal of Social Issues, 57*(4), 657–674.

Highhouse, S. (2008). Stubborn reliance on intuition and subjectivity in employee selection. *Industrial and Organizational Psychology: Perspectives on Science and Practice, 1*(3), 333–342.

Hogan, J., Hogan, R., & Kaiser, R.B. (2011). Management derailment. In S. Zedeck (Ed.), *APA handbook of industrial and organizational psychology, Vol. 3: Maintaining, expanding, and contracting the organization* (pp. 555–575). Washington, D.C.: American Psychological Association.

Hogan, R., & Hogan, J. (2001). Assessing leadership: A view from the dark side. *International Journal of Selection and Assessment, 9*(1–2), 40–51.

Hollenbeck, G.P. (2009). Executive selection: What's right . . . and what's wrong. *Industrial and Organizational Psychology: Perspectives on Science and Practice, 2*(2), 266–267.

Hoque, Z. (2014). 20 years of studies on the balanced scorecard: Trends, accomplishments, gaps and opportunities for future research. *The British Accounting Review, 46*(1), 33–59.

Howard, A., & Bray, D.W. (1988). *Managerial lives in transition: Advancing age and changing times.* New York: Guilford Press.

International Task Force on Assessment Center Guidelines. (2015). Guidelines for ethical considerations for assessment center operations. *Journal of Management, 41*(4), 1244–1273.

Jackson, E. (2012, August 17). The 7 reasons why 360 degree feedback programs fail. *Fortune.* Retrieved from www.forbes.com/sites/ericjackson/2012/08/17/the-7-reasons-why-360-degree-feedback-programs-fail/#18cc28344b98

Jeanneret, R., & Silzer, R. (1998). An overview of individual psychological assessment. In R. Jeanneret & R. Silzer (Eds.), *Individual psychological assessment: Predicting behavior in organizational setting* (pp. 3–26). San Francisco, CA: Jossey-Bass.

Johnson, R. (2016, March 1). *The top 10 leadership derailers and how to best mitigate those risks* [Blog post]. Retrieved from http://info.growingyourleaders.com/blog/the-top-10-leadership-derailers-and-ho-best-to-mitigate-those-risks

Judge, T.A., & Bono, J.E. (2000). Five-factor model of personality and transformational leadership. *Journal of Applied Psychology, 85*(5), 751–765.

Judge, T.A., Bono, J.E., Ilies, R., & Gerhardt, M.W. (2002). Personality and leadership: A qualitative and quantitative review. *Journal of Applied Psychology, 87*(4), 765–780.

Kaplan, R.S., & Norton, D.P. (1992). The balanced scorecard: Measures that drive performance. *Harvard Business Review, 70*(1), 71–79.

Kaplan, R.S., & Norton, D.P. (2004). *Strategy maps: Converting intangible assets into tangible outcomes.* Boston, MA: Harvard Business School Press.

Katz, D., & Kahn, R.L. (1978). *The social psychology of organizations* (2nd ed.). New York: John Wiley & Sons.

Kirpatrick, S.A., & Locke, E.A. (1991). Leadership: Do traits matter? *Academy of Management Executive, 5*(2), 48–60.

Klann, G. (2007). *Building character.* San Francisco, CA: Jossey-Bass.

Klimoski, R., & Brickner, M. (1987). Why do assessment centers work? The puzzle of assessment center validity. *Personnel Psychology, 40*(2), 243–260.

Korkki, P. (2016, October 30). Bossy vs buddy: Each has its place a work. *New York Times*, p. BU6.

Lawrie, G.J.G, & Cobbold, I. (2004). 3rd generation balanced scorecard: Evolution of an effective strategic control tool. *International Journal of Productivity and Performance Management, 53*(7), 611–623.

London, M. (1996). Redeployment and continuous learning in the twenty-first century: Hard lessons and positive examples from the downsizing era. *Academy of Management Executive, 10*(4), 67–79.

London, M. (2015). *The power of feedback: Giving, seeking, and using feedback for performance improvement.* New York: Routledge.

London, M., & Bray, D.W. (1984). Measuring and developing young managers' career motivation. *Journal of Management Development, 3*(3), 3–25.

London, M., & McFarland, L.A. (2017). Assessment feedback. In J.L. Farr & N.T. Tippins (Eds.), *Handbook of employee selection* (2nd ed.) (pp. 406–426). New York: Routledge.

London, M., & Sessa, V.I. (2006). Group feedback for continuous learning. *Human Resource Development Review, 5*(3), 303–329.

London, M., & Smither, J.W. (2002). Feedback orientation, feedback culture, and the longitudinal performance management process. *Human Resource Management Review, 12*(1), 81–100.

London, M., Mone, E.M., & Scott, J.C. (2004). Performance management and assessment: Methods for improved rater accuracy and employee goal setting. *Human Resource Management, 43*(4), 319–336.

London, M., Smither, J.W., & Adsit, D.J. (1997). Accountability: The Achilles' heel of multisource feedback. *Group and Organization Management, 22*(2), 162–184.

London, M., Smither, J.W., & Diamante, T. (2006). Best practices in leadership assessment. In J.A. Conger & R.E. Riggio (Eds.), *The practice of leadership: Developing the next generation of leaders* (pp. 41–63). San Francisco, CA: Jossey-Bass.

Madsen, D.O., & Stenheim, T. (2014). Perceived benefits of balanced scorecard implementation: Some preliminary evidence. *Problems and Perspectives in Management, 12*(3), 81–90.

Maner, J.K., & Mead, N.L. (2010). The essential tension between leadership and power: When leaders sacrifice group goals for the sake of self-interest. *Journal of Personality and Social Psychology, 99*(3), 482–497.

Maurer, T.J., & London, M. (2015). From individual contributor to leader: A role identity shift framework for leader development within innovative organizations. *Journal of Management, 44*(4), 1426–1452.

McCall, M.W., Jr., & Hollenbeck, G.P. (2002). *Developing global executives.* Boston, MA: Harvard Business School Press.

McCall, M.W., Lombardo, M.M., & Morrison, A.M. (1988). *The lessons of experience: How successful executives develop on the job.* New York: Free Press.

McPhail, S.M., & Jeanneret, P.R. (2012). Individual psychological assessment. In N. Schmitt (ed.), *Oxford handbook of personnel, assessment, and selection* (pp. 411–442). New York: Oxford University Press.

Meyer, H.H. (1975). The pay for performance dilemma. *Organizational Dynamics, 3*(3), 39–50.

Molleman, B. (2007, February 2). *The challenge of implementing the balanced scorecard.* Paper presented at the 6th TwenteStudent Conference on IT, Enschede. Retrieved from http://referaat.cs.utwente.nl/conference/6/paper/6800/the-challenge-of-implementing-the-balanced-scorecard.pdf

Nicholson, H., & Carroll, B. (2013). Identity undoing and power relations in leadership development. *Human Relations, 66*(9), 1225–1248.

Owens, B.P., Johnson, M., & Mitchell, T. (2013). Expressed humility in organizations: Implications for performance, teams, and leadership. *Organization Science*, *24*(5), 1517–1538.

Pulakos, E.D., & O'Leary, R.S. (2011). Why is performance management so broken? *Industrial and Organizational Psychology: Perspectives on Science and Practice*, *4*(2), 146–164.

Pulakos, E.D., Hanson, R.M., Arad, S., & Moye, N. (2015). Performance management can be fixed: An on-the-job experiential learning approach for complex behavioral change. *Industrial and Organizational Psychology: Perspectives on Science and Practice*, *8*(1), 51–76.

Reynolds, D.H., McCauley, C.D., & Tsacoumis, S. (2018). A critical evaluation of the state of assessment and development for senior leaders. *Industrial and Organizational Psychology: Perspectives on Science and Practice*, *11*(4) (in press).

Rose, D.S. (2011, April 14–16). Using strategically aligned 360-degree feedback content to drive organizational change. Paper presented at the 26th Annual Conference of the Society for Industrial Organizational Psychology, Chicago, IL.

Rupp, D. (2014, October 24). *The evolving role of technology in assessment*. Paper presented at the 38th International Congress on Assessment Center Methods, Alexandria, VA. Retrieved from www.assessmentcenters.org/Assessmentcenters/media/2014/2014-Final-Presentations/The-Evolving-Role_of-Technology-in-Assessment_Panel.pdf

Silzer, R., & Church, A.H. (2009). The pearls and perils of identifying potential. *Industrial and Organizational Psychology: Perspectives on Science and Practice*, *2*(4), 130–143.

Silzer, R., & Church, A.H. (2010). Identifying and assessing high potential talent: Current organizational practices. In R. Silzer & B.E. Dowell (Eds.), *Strategy-driven talent management: A leadership imperative* (pp. 213–279). San Francisco, CA: Jossey-Bass.

Smither, J.W., London, M., & Reilly, R.R. (2005). Does performance improve following multisource feedback? A theoretical model, meta-analysis, and review of empirical findings. *Personnel Psychology*, *58*(1), 33–66.

Smither, J.W., London, M., Flautt, R., Vargas, Y., & Kucine, I. (2003). Can executive coaches enhance the impact of multisource feedback on behavior change? A quasi-experimental field study. *Personnel Psychology*, *56*(1), 23–44.

Smither, J.W., London, M., Flautt, R., Vargas, Y., & Kucine, I. (2004). Does discussing multisource feedback with raters enhance performance improvement? *Journal of Management Development*, *23*(5), 456–468.

Society for Industrial and Organizational Psychology (SIOP) Administrative Office. (2016, 20 December). *SIOP announces top 10 workplace trends for* 2017. Retrieved from www.siop.org/article_view.aspx?article=1610

Thornton, G.C., & Gibbons, A.M. (2009). Validity of assessment centers for personal selection. *Human Resource Management Review*, *19*(3), 169–187.

Thornton, G.C., III, Johnson, S.K., & Church, A.H. (2017). Selecting leaders: Executives and high-potentials. In J.L. Farr & N.T. Tippins (Eds.), *Handbook of employee selection* (2nd ed.) (pp. 833–852). New York: Routledge.

Tichy, N.M., & Bennis, W.G. (2007). *Judgment: How winning leaders make great calls*. New York: Penguin.

Voelpel, S.C., Leibold, M., Eckhoff, R.A., and Davenport, T.H. (2006). The tyranny of the balanced scorecard in the innovation economy. *Journal of Intellectual Capital*, *7*(1), 43–60.

Weber, L. (2016, August 21). At Kimberly-Clark, "dead wood" workers have nowhere to hide. *Wall Street Journal*. Retrieved from www.wsj.com/articles/focus-on-performance-shakes-up-stolid-kimberly-clark-1471798944

Wenger, E. (1998). *Communities of practice: Learning, meaning, and identity.* New York: Cambridge University Press.

Wohlers, A.J., Hall, M J., & London, M. (1993). Subordinates rating managers: Organizational and demographic correlates of self/subordinate agreement. *Journal of Occupational and Organizational Psychology, 66*(3), 263–275.

Zaccaro, S.J. (2007). Trait-based perspectives of leadership. *The American Psychologist, 62*(1), 6–16.

Zaccaro, S.J., & Klimoski, R.J. (2001). The nature of organizational leadership. In S.J. Zaccaro & R.J. Klimoski (Eds.), *The nature of organizational leadership: Understanding the performance imperatives confronting today's leaders* (pp. 3–41). San Francisco, CA: Jossey-Bass.

Zaccaro, S.J., Kemp. C., & Bader, P. (2004). Leader traits and attributes. In J. Antonakis, A.T. Cianciolo, & R.J. Sternberg (Eds.), *The nature of leadership* (pp. 101–124). Thousand Oaks, CA: Sage.

4
SELF-SELECTION BIAS IN LEADERSHIP

Understanding Reluctant Leaders

Olga Epitropaki

Despite the popular notion that leadership is a desired role that individuals aspire to and would be happy to embrace, the literature on talent management and leadership development (for example, Bhanugopan, Wang, Lockhart, & Farrell, 2017; DeRue & Ashford, 2010; Gentry, Logan, & Tonidandel, 2014) indicates that this may not be the case. Organizations suffer from a leadership shortage, and several reports (for example, Deloitte, 2017; Schwartz, Bohdal-Spiegelhoff, Gretczko, & Sloan, 2016) indicate that leadership pools are insufficient. Talented employees – who are, by all accounts, successful individual contributors – are not willing to step up into managerial positions and claim leadership. Even royals express reluctance. In a recent *Newsweek* interview (Levin, 2017), Prince Harry commented: "Is there any one of the royal family who *wants* to be king or queen? I don't think so, but we will carry out our duties at the right time."

The question of who chooses – or chooses not – to step up into leadership positions is of paramount importance because it defines the pool from which future organizational leaders are drawn, with important implications for organizational decisions and future outcomes (for example, Barling & Weatherhead, 2016). Those who are willing to step up do not always do it for the right reasons, and others hide away from leadership for the wrong reasons. There are also bias concerns for leadership research samples because we may over-rely on those who have chosen leadership as their path. This chapter will attempt to cast light on the individual factors that influence "stepping up to leadership" – hinting at a possible "self-selection bias" in leadership positions and further identify the main sources of leadership reluctance.

Claiming Leadership

Leadership emergence literature (for example, Ensari, Riggio, Christian, & Carslaw, 2011; Foti & Hauenstein, 2007) can help us to understand the key factors underlying stepping up to leadership versus leadership reluctance – although the question of "who claims leadership" is not exactly the same as "'who emerges as a leader." Leadership emergence addresses both the claiming of leadership and the granting of leadership by others. The vast majority of past leadership emergence research examined *others' perceptions* of a person as an emergent leader in group settings (for example, Côté, Lopes, Salovey, & Miners, 2010; Lemoine, Aggarwal, & Steed, 2016; Riggio, Riggio, Salinas, & Cole, 2003), and thus it helps to explain when and why group members *grant leadership* to someone. Relatively fewer leadership emergence studies address the question of *claiming leadership* and cast light on the factors that predispose certain individuals to seek leadership positions (for example, Barling & Weatherhead, 2016; Ensari et al., 2011; Li, Arvey, & Song, 2011; Strang & Kuhnert, 2009). These factors include individual differences such as personality traits (especially narcissism), gender, and socio-economic status, as well as biological factors. The following section briefly reviews each of these factors, which may introduce a *self-selection bias* into leadership positions.

Claiming Leadership and Individual Differences: Narcissism

Past research has consistently shown that intelligence, dominance, masculinity–femininity, and self-monitoring are strong predictors of leadership (for example, Foti & Hauenstein, 2007; Rueb, Erskine, & Foti, 2008). Several other studies and meta-analyses have shown the "Big Five" dimensions to influence leadership emergence. For example, Taggar, Hackett, and Saha (1999) found that conscientiousness, extraversion, and emotional stability were related to emergent leadership. Judge, Bono, Ilies, and Gerhardt (2002) showed that neuroticism, extraversion, openness to experience, and conscientiousness predicted leadership emergence, with extraversion being the strongest predictor. Ensari and colleagues (2011) further focused on leaderless group discussions (LGD), and found individual differences such as extraversion and authoritarian personality to predict leader emergence in such settings.

More recent studies have focused on the role of narcissism. The assumption that narcissism enhances the chances that an individual will emerge as a leader has been supported by several studies (for example, Grijalva, Harms, Newman, Gaddis, & Fraley, 2015; Harms, Spain, & Hannah, 2011; Judge, LePine, & Rich, 2006). Narcissism has generally been associated with social skills and charisma under conditions of brief acquaintance (for example, Nevicka, De Hoogh, Van

Vianen, Beersma, & McIlwain, 2011; Paulhus & Williams, 2002), and narcissists are more likely to be singled out as having leadership potential (for example, Brunell et al., 2008). There is also evidence that narcissists desire leadership roles, for reasons ranging from fantasies of power and status (Raskin & Novacek, 2006) and self-reported dominance (for example, Raskin, Novacek, & Hogan, 1991), to viewing themselves as leaders in organizations (Judge et al., 2006). Narcissists also appear prevalent in "C-suite" leadership roles, including as chief executive officers (CEOs) and presidents (for example, Deluga, 1997). Brunell and colleagues (2008) further found that the *power* factor of narcissism (and not exhibitionism) was a reliable and relatively unique predictor of emergent leadership. They concluded that "narcissism predicts seeking leadership positions, which are able to confer social status and dominance to the narcissist" (Brunell et al., 2008, p. 1674).

There is, however, an interesting oxymoron in the relationship between narcissism and leadership: Although narcissists desire and claim leadership, and are likely to be quickly granted leadership by others in leaderless groups, they are not necessarily effective as leaders. Studies often fail to find support for a positive relationship between narcissism and leadership effectiveness (for example, Brunell et al., 2008; Grijalva et al., 2015). Grijalva and colleagues' (2015) meta-analysis specifically found an inverted U-shaped relationship between narcissism and leadership effectiveness. Leaders were more effective when they had moderate levels of narcissism (rather than very high or very low levels).

Claiming Leadership and Gender

Research has consistently identified the role of gender in leadership emergence. Males are more likely to emerge as leaders than females (for example, Eagly & Karau, 1991) – a tendency that increases over time (Daly, Delaney, Egan, & Baumeister, 2015) and with the level of organizational hierarchy (for example, Barling & Weatherhead, 2016; Fitzsimmons, Callan, & Paulsen, 2014). Prior research has consistently documented the prejudice that women experience when they claim leadership as a result of the lack of fit of gender and leader construals, in accordance with *role congruity theory* (Eagly & Karau, 2002; Rosette & Tost, 2010) and the lack-of-fit model (Heilman, 2001). Observers' perceptions and stereotypes can act as barriers to women's advancement (for example, Ayman & Korabik, 2010; Schein, 1973), but there is also evidence for a *stereotype threat* (for example, Davies, Spencer, & Steele, 2005) that limits women's self-views as leaders and undermines their own leadership aspirations (for example, Elprana, Felfe, Stiehl, & Gatzka, 2015). Research also points to the importance of gender-role orientation and social pressure toward gender-role conformity (for example, male-agentic versus female-communal behaviors) in leadership positions (Barling, 2014).

Claiming Leadership and Socio-economic Status

Socio-economic status (SES) is another factor that may influence an individual's decision to step up in leadership. It has generally been defined by material wealth, occupation, and participation in educational and social institutions (for example, Kraus, Piff, & Keltner, 2009). Three main indicators of SES have been utilized in past studies examining early influences of SES on leadership emergence: family income, parental education, and parental occupation (Barling & Weatherhead, 2016). Evidence suggests that those coming from low-SES backgrounds are more likely to drop out of school early (for example, van Ewijk & Sleegers, 2010), to have difficulty finding employment, and to be more likely to be in low-paid jobs (Rumberger & Lamb, 2003). Polidano, Hanel, and Buddelmeyer (2013) further contended that family-born aspirations may result in intergenerational effects – that is, that the parents' low or high aspirations transfer to the children. Early exposure to poverty and financial hardship limits access to institutional and environmental resources (for example, Bradley & Corwyn, 2002). The quality of schools that low-SES students attend also plays an important role because they most often offer few opportunities (for example, fewer advanced placement classes or extracurricular school activities). Using the National Longitudinal Study of Youth and multiwave/multisource data for a sample of 4,536 (1,533 leaders; 3,003 nonleaders), Barling and Weatherhead (2016) found that persistent exposure to poverty during childhood limited later leadership role occupancy through the indirect effects of quality of schooling and personal mastery. They further noted that children in poverty may experience SES-based stereotype threat, which may undermine their motivation to seek leadership positions. Conversely, children of high-SES backgrounds have higher access to resources and schools of higher quality, are more likely to participate in extracurricular activities that require leadership skills (for example, sports teams, school clubs and societies), and are more likely to be exposed to positive leadership models in their immediate environment that may shape their leadership aspirations and leadership efficacy.

Biological Factors and Claiming Leadership

There are also a series of biological factors that may positively predispose individuals toward leadership. Results from twin studies have shown that 20–30 percent of the variance in leadership emergence is genetic (for example, Arvey, Rotundo, Johnson, Zhang, & McGue, 2006). De Neve, Mikhaylov, Dawes, Christakis, and Fowler (2013) also employed a twin design and estimated the heritability of leadership role occupancy at 24 percent. They even identified a specific gene (rs4950) that increased the likelihood that people will occupy a leadership position by 50 percent! Li and colleagues (2015) also showed that a dopamine transmitter (DAT1) indirectly influenced leader-role occupancy.

Such biological factors would surely offer certain people a leadership advantage over others who do not possess such genetic makeup.

In sum, all four factors reviewed in the previous sections – that is, narcissism, gender, SES, and biology – are more or less stable and hard to change, and they inevitably introduce a self-selection bias into leadership positions. A possible answer to the question of "who claims leadership?" posed earlier in this chapter could be that individuals with certain characteristics (for example, higher levels of narcissism, male, from a privileged SES background, and of a specific genetic makeup) will more readily claim and step up to leadership positions, and thus will self-select as leaders. However, their eagerness does not necessarily guarantee their leadership success (for example, Grijalva et al., 2015). It is also possible that organizations do not search further than these self-selected individuals and miss out on an untapped pool of reluctant leaders – that is, individuals less eager (for various reasons) to step up, but who are potentially effective in leadership roles when they are offered the chance to lead.

The following section explores some of the main reasons for leadership reluctance and discusses practical implications for leadership selection and development.

Understanding Reluctant Leaders: Refusing Leadership

The previous section discussed some of the underlying factors that explain why some individuals may be more attracted to leadership positions than others. In this section, we will try to understand what drives people away from leadership positions and to cast light on key sources of reluctance. We will specifically argue that reluctance relates to four interconnected constructs: (a) leader identity uncertainty and self-discrepancy, (b) motivation to lead, (c) developmental readiness and leader efficacy, and (d) leadership skills. In contrast to the constructs reviewed in the previous section, which were mainly dispositional, biological, or socio-economic, and thus less malleable, all of those presented in this section are open to change and can respond to systematic development efforts.

Leader Identity as a Source of Leadership Reluctance

One key explanation for an individual's reluctance to step up into leadership positions relates to leader identity salience. Individuals may refuse leadership because they simply do not see themselves as leaders. A leader identity arises when people internalize the meanings associated with a leadership role and personalize them, imbuing them with unique meaning (Ramarajan, 2014). In their review of the leader identity literature, Epitropaki, Kark, Mainemelis, and Lord (2017, p. 107) defined leader identity as "a sub-component of one's working self-concept that includes leadership schemas, leadership experiences and future representations of oneself as a leader." Day and Lance (2004) stressed the importance of integrating the leader identity into one's global self-schema for leadership development. Individuals develop as leaders when their leader sub-identity becomes differentiated, more complex, and integrated within a global identity. Transitions in a new (or even the same) organizational context may trigger a dynamic interplay among leader identities, follower identities, and social-structural contextual characteristics, and individuals may experience uncertainty regarding their leadership ability (for example, Lord, Brown, Harvey, & Hall, 2001). Epitropaki and colleagues (2017) argued that successful leadership development will involve active identity uncertainty reduction, as well as effective management of the identity tensions and successful integration of both leader and follower identities into one's self-concept. Prospective leaders need to increase the salience of their leader identity, if they are to be willing to claim leadership, and to actively seek out experiences to enact and develop that aspect of the self. Individuals with the characteristics reviewed in the previous section (for example, narcissism) have a higher leader identity salience at baseline and thus are more willing to seek leadership. Reluctant leaders experience high levels of self-uncertainty when facing an opportunity for a managerial transition.

According to identity uncertainty theory (Hogg, 2000), people find feelings of uncertainty – particularly about themselves and things that reflect or relate to their identity and self-concept – aversive and thus are motivated to reduce or fend of self-uncertainty. The easy way of reducing uncertainty is to distance oneself from the situation that triggers self-uncertainty – in this case, the potential leadership position. Not claiming leadership is a way of reducing uncertainty. It is a form of self-enhancement (for example, Leary, 2007) via which the individual maintains the previous positive self-concept as an individual contributor and follower. Other motivational drivers, such as self-expansion (Aron & Aron, 1996), can help to overcome leadership reluctance and increase leader identity salience. Reluctant leaders may expand themselves in various ways: They may actively seek opportunities for leadership development (for example, executive coaching and training programs) or incorporate a "significant other" (for example, a leader role model) in their self-concept. Self-enhancement will require active leader identity work (for example, Ashforth & Schinoff, 2016). It will also require reluctant leaders to resolve possible self-discrepancies between their "actual self" and "ideal self" (Higgins, 1987), and to further tackle relevant emotions. A reluctant leader may believe that their actual attributes do not match the ideal state they hope to attain (that is, a leadership position) and may thus experience an "actual/own versus ideal/own" discrepancy. According to Higgins (1987), in this case the person will be vulnerable to dejection-related emotions such as disappointment and dissatisfaction. It is also possible for a reluctant leader to believe that their actual attributes do not match the ideal state that they believe a significant other (for example, the manager who has recommended the reluctant leader for a promotion) wishes they could attain. In this case, the person will experience an "actual/own versus ideal/other" discrepancy and will be vulnerable to dejection-related emotions such as shame and embarrassment. Reluctant leaders need to tackle such self-discrepancies both cognitively and emotionally to increase their leader identity salience and leader efficacy. Systematic coaching could be a possible mechanism through which this might happen (for example, Ely et al., 2010; Wasylyshyn, 2005; Boyatzis, Smith, & Blaize, 2006).

Ely, Ibarra, and Kolb (2011) emphasized women's identity work as a way of overcoming leadership reluctance. They highlighted the challenges that women face in internalizing a leader identity and urged organizations to offer "identity spaces" for women to engage in identity work. Finally, Hammond, Clapp-Smith, and Palanski (2017) proposed a theory of leader identity development through cross-domain experiences. Such experiences can potentially help individuals to overcome leadership reluctance. They portrayed the development of leader identity as a sense-making process that entails four stages: *noticing* (experiencing a triggering event), *interpreting* (cognitive processing of connections and disconnections across domains), *authoring* (modifying identities and personal narratives), and *enacting* (the newly modified identities in leadership situations).

Motivation to Lead and Leadership Reluctance

Closely related to leader identity salience is a reluctant leader's motivation to lead (MTL). Motivation to lead is an individual difference construct that influences the intensity of effort at leading (Chan & Drasgow, 2001; Felfe & Schyns, 2014). Chan and Drasgow (2001) proposed that MTL consisted of three dimensions. The *affective component* is characterized by an individual's desire to take charge and to enjoy leading. Affective MTL is likely to be a product of a strong personal belief in ones' own leadership qualities. *Social normative* motivation to lead can be understood as a sense of responsibility or duty requiring them to take on leadership. Third, the *non-calculative* aspect emphasizes overlooking the personal risk of engaging in leadership. Popper and Mayseless (2007) proposed that MTL has its roots in the conditions of growth during childhood, and it is shaped via a process of internalizing expectations from influential others (such as parents and teachers), socialization, and learning experiences with leaders. High motivation to lead has been found to predict future career ambitions, leadership emergence, and possibly performance (Felfe & Shyns, 2014; Lent & Brown, 2006).

Leadership reluctance may stem from low levels of motivation to lead – but what predicts MTL? Chan and Drasgow (2001) proposed various variables as possible antecedents of MTL, including personality, general cognitive ability, and socio-cultural values, as well as leadership experience and leadership self-efficacy. Kark and Van Dijk (2007) suggested another possible antecedent: self-regulatory focus. Promotion-focused individuals are motivated mainly by internal motives such as growth and self-actualization, whereas prevention-focused individuals are motivated by external motives such as social pressures and obligations. Individuals with a prevention focus will be more likely to express reluctance to lead in the absence of a strong external motive. They will lead if they have to, out of necessity or duty, but are unlikely to seek leadership of their own accord.

Implicit leadership theories (ILTs) – that is, cognitive structures specifying traits and attributes that characterize leaders (for example, Epitropaki, Sy, Martin, Tram-Quon, & Topakas, 2013; Lord & Maher, 1991; Shondrick & Lord, 2010) – can also be another relevant antecedent of motivation to lead. For example, Guillén, Mayo, and Korotov (2015) examined individuals' comparisons of themselves to their own standards of leadership and their impact on leadership motivation. Their results showed that both self-comparisons with concrete, influential leaders of the past or present (self-to-exemplar comparisons), as well as comparisons with more general representations of leadership (self-to-prototype comparisons), related to motivation to lead. When people viewed high discrepancy between their leadership prototypes and their own characteristics, their motivation to lead decreased. Thus reluctant leaders may view themselves as falling short of their own leadership standards and thus view themselves as inadequate for leadership positions.

Affective motivation to lead may also decrease when individuals perceive high interpersonal risk associated with leadership. In a qualitative study, Unsworth, Miscenko, and Johnston-Billings (2016) found that new leaders experienced psychological conflict between their leader and friend identities that resulted in them feeling vulnerable to exploitation or fear of using their power. Individuals may be reluctant to step up to leadership positions because they will jeopardize their friendship relationships with members of their work group. The more calculative a person is about the costs of leading versus the benefits, the more reluctant they will be in claiming leadership.

Developmental Readiness, Leader Efficacy, and Leadership Reluctance

Reluctance to lead may also stem from lack of developmental readiness of a potential leader – that is, the ability to benefit from experiences that can help them to develop as a leader. Hannah and Avolio (2010, p. 1182) defined it as "the ability and motivation to attend to, make meaning of, and appropriate new leader KSAAs (knowledge, skills, abilities, and attributes) into knowledge structures along with concomitant changes in identity to employ those KSAAs." The role of developmental readiness in accelerating leadership development and strengthening leadership efficacy beliefs has been highlighted (Avolio & Hannah, 2008). An individual with low levels of developmental readiness will be less likely to frame many of the challenging developmental experiences they tackle as leadership development experiences; instead, they will merely view them as job-related. Thus the successful handling of such challenges will not increase leader efficacy beliefs.

Leadership self-efficacy (LSE) refers to an individual's perceptions regarding their own ability to lead (Murphy, 1992) and is of critical importance when we try to understand leadership reluctance. According to Hannah, Avolio, Luthans, and Harms (2008), it is a specific form of efficacy associated with the level of confidence in the knowledge, skills, and abilities associated with leading others. High LSE has been reported to result in more positive leadership ratings by instructors, peers, and observers, and more attempts by the individual to lead, as well as positive effects on group performance. With relation to gender, Hoyt (2005) reported that women with a high LSE demonstrated a heightened association with the leadership domain and increased ability to handle stressful situations.

Organizations can increase reluctant leaders' efficacy via various methods, such as long-term feedback and executive training. During a series of five-week interventions, Hannah (2006) raised levels of generalized leader efficacy through mastery experiences, social persuasion, and guided reflection; leader efficacy then predicted MTL, transformational leadership, and performance over a 34-week span. Hannah and colleagues (2008) further suggested that LSE (being state-like) can be developed through role modeling, vicarious learning, persuasion, arousal, raising the perceived utility and salience of leadership means, and focused mastery training interventions.

Leader Skills and Leadership Reluctance

Leader skills are closely related to the constructs of leader identity, MTL, developmental readiness, and efficacy previously reviewed, and they can further help us to understand reluctance. Individuals may express reluctance to lead when they believe that their leadership skills are underdeveloped. Mumford, Todd, Higgs, and McIntosh (2017) identified nine key leadership skills necessary to address leadership problems: problem definition, cause/goal analysis, constraint analysis, planning, forecasting, creative thinking, idea evaluation, wisdom, and sense-making/visioning. They further stressed that effective execution of these cognitive skills is strongly related to measures of both leader problem solving and overall leader performance (with correlation coefficients of between .40 and .50). Mastering these leadership skills can increase a person's leadership efficacy and further strengthen the salience of a leader identity. Lord and Hall (2005) stressed the connection between skill and identity and conceptualized leadership skill in terms of how leaders access and use information, as well as the knowledge content of the tasks and social issues related to leadership. They argued that the development of leadership skills occurs over an extended period of time, with multiple loosely connected skills effortfully attempted at first, in the case of novice leaders. These skills become increasingly proceduralized and contextualized, and finally, in the case of expert leaders, the application of skills becomes more driven by the internally held values of the leader. Lord and Hall (2005) further noted that the integration of leadership skills with leader identities is a critical aspect of the process of leadership development: The more salient a person's leader identity becomes, the more likely they will seek experiences that develop their leadership skills. Conversely, mastery of leadership skills will further strengthen the person's leader identity salience. In general, there appears to be a reciprocal relationship between all of the constructs reviewed in this section as underlying factors of leadership reluctance. Increased developmental readiness will increase mastery of leadership skills, which will positively influence leader efficacy. High levels of leader efficacy will increase MTL and leader identity salience. The process is likely to be cyclical and continuously unfolding throughout the span of a person's career.

Overcoming Leadership Reluctance: Development and Assessment Implications

Organizations can help promising individual contributors to overcome their leadership reluctance via a series of interventions such as coaching, leadership training, role modeling, feedback, and vicarious learning, among others (for example, Martin, Epitropaki, & O'Broin, 2018). DeRue, Nahrgang, Hollenbeck, and Workman (2012) examined how structured reflection through after-event reviews (AERs) promoted experience-based leadership development. They found that AERs consisting of three components – self-explanation, data verification, and feedback – had a positive effect on leadership development, and this effect was accentuated by conscientiousness, openness to experience, emotional stability, and prior developmental experiences. They further suggested that organizations should consider instituting AER processes as part of their broader leadership development strategies and executive coaching programs. Reichard and Johnson (2011) further pointed toward other leadership self-development strategies that individuals and organizations can utilize, such as periodic competency mapping, mind-stilling, and self-persuasion exercises. Because one size does *not* fit all, there is need for a wide portfolio of leadership development strategies on which organizations can capitalize to harness the potential of reluctant leaders. There are also implications for leadership selection processes, which need to expand beyond common selection criteria such as prior leadership experience. Stable traits that have been consistently shown to predict leadership effectiveness, such as conscientiousness and intelligence, should be targeted through the selection process. A systematic effort should be made during identification of high potentials to spot reluctant leaders whom common assessment processes may fail to detect. As Finkelstein, Costanza, and Goodwin (2018) note, in most organizations employees first have to be championed by their managers if they are to be designated "high potentials" (HiPo). Reluctant leaders may not make it to this stage of consideration because their managers may be less willing to fight for them and to be their advocates during the HiPo designation process. It may be easier to fall for the charm of self-selected leaders, who are eager, actively looking for opportunities, and consistently self-promoting. An even more alarming fact indicated by recent research is that even among companies known for their top talent management practices, less than one third were using assessment methods to actually identify HiPos (Church & Rotolo, 2013). Even in the case of those who used specific assessment methods, such as multisource ratings and personality inventories, it was unclear how assessment information was combined to make the designation decision. As Finkelstein and colleagues (2018, p. 6) note:

> Decision makers often believe they "know potential when they see it" . . . This belief in one's ability to spot potential can produce biases even in the face of contradictory assessment information, to the extent that some executives simply claim that the data are wrong if they do not match their decisions.

Thus, even in the presence of data pointing toward reluctant leaders' potential, decision makers may still choose eager, self-selected leaders because they "can *see* their potential," and once again the self-selection bias in leadership positions prevails. Organizations need to increase existing managers' awareness of this self-selection bias and other decision-making biases during leadership selection processes to widen the pool of HiPos beyond self-selected leaders to also include reluctant leaders. Further investment in leadership development programs to tackle the key sources of reluctance identified in the previous sections will potentially increase overall organizational leadership capability and effectiveness.

Conclusion

This chapter has tried to cast light on the individual factors that influence *claiming* leadership and to examine the possibility of a "self-selection bias" in existing leadership positions. Four factors were specifically presented that may explain why certain individuals are more attracted to leadership positions, including narcissism, gender, SES, and specific biological factors. On the opposite pole, a series of interconnected factors were examined that may underlie leadership reluctance, and particularly highlighted was the importance of leader identity salience. Individuals may refuse leadership because they lack MTL, leadership skills, developmental readiness, and/or leader efficacy, and they may have difficulty seeing themselves as leaders. Organizations need to systematically expand existing pools of HiPos to include reluctant leaders by utilizing data-driven assessment methods, because decision makers may be susceptible to biases that lead them to favor self-selected leaders. Organizations can further help reluctant leaders to overcome barriers by implementing a wide range of leadership development interventions.

References

Aron, E.N., & Aron, A. (1996). Love and expansion of the self: The state of the model. *Personal Relationships*, *3*(1), 45–58.

Arvey, R.D., Rotundo, M., Johnson, W., Zhang, Z., & McGue, M. (2006). The determinants of leadership role occupancy: Genetic and personality factors. *The Leadership Quarterly*, *17*(1), 1–20.

Ashforth, B.E., & Schinoff, B.S. (2016). Identity under construction: How individuals come to define themselves in organizations. *Annual Review of Organizational Psychology and Organizational Behavior*, *3*(1), 111–137.

Avolio, B., & Hannah, S.T. (2008). Developmental readiness: Accelerating leader development. *Consulting Psychology Journal: Practice and Research*, *60*(4), 331–347.

Ayman, R., & Korabik, K. (2010). Why gender and culture matter. *The American Psychologist*, *65*(3), 157–170.

Barling, J. (2014). *The science of leadership: Lessons from research for organizational leaders*. New York: Oxford University Press.

Barling, J., & Weatherhead, J.G. (2016). Persistent exposure to poverty during childhood limits later leader emergence. *Journal of Applied Psychology*, *101*(9), 1305–1318.

Bhanugopan, R., Wang, Y., Lockhart, P., & Farrell, M. (2017). Managerial skills shortages and the impending effects of organizational characteristics: Evidence from China. *Personnel Review*, *46*(8), 1689–1716.

Boyatzis, R.E., Smith, M.L., & Blaize, N. (2006). Developing sustainable leaders through compassion and coaching. *Academy of Management Learning & Education*, *5*(1), 8–24.

Bradley, R.H., & Corwyn, R.F. (2002). Socioeconomic status and child development. *Annual Review of Psychology*, *53*(1), 371–399.

Brunell, A.B., Gentry, W.A., Campbell, W.K., Hoffman, B.J., Kuhnert, K.W., & DeMarree, K.G. (2008). Leader emergence: The case of the narcissistic leader. *Personality and Social Psychology Bulletin*, *34*(12), 1663–1676.

Chan, K.Y., & Drasgow, F. (2001). Toward a theory of individual differences and leadership: Understanding the motivation to lead. *Journal of Applied Psychology*, *86*(3), 481–498.

Church, A.H., & Rotolo, C.T. (2013). How are top companies assessing their high-potentials and senior executives? A talent management benchmark study. *Consulting Psychology Journal*, *65*(3), 199–223.

Côté, S., Lopes, P.N., Salovey, P., & Miners, C.T.H. (2010). Emotional intelligence and leadership emergence in small groups. *The Leadership Quarterly*, *21*(3), 496–508.

Daly, M., Delaney, L., Egan, M., & Baumeister, R.F. (2015). Childhood self-control and unemployment throughout the life span: Evidence from two British cohort studies. *Psychological Science*, *26*(6), 709–723.

Davies, P.G., Spencer, S.J., & Steele, C.M. (2005). Clearing the air: Identity safety moderates the effects of stereotype threat on women's leadership aspirations. *Journal of Personality and Social Psychology*, *88*(2), 276–287.

Day, D.V., & Lance, C.E. (2004). Understanding the development of leadership complexity through latent growth modeling. In D.V. Day, S.J. Zaccaro, & S.M. Halpin (Eds.), *Leader development for transforming organizations: Growing leaders for tomorrow* (pp. 41–69). Mahwah, NJ: Lawrence Erlbaum.

Deloitte. (2017). *Rewriting the rules for the digital age: 2017 Deloitte global human capital trends report* [pdf]. Retrieved from www2.deloitte.com/content/dam/Deloitte/global/Documents/HumanCapital/hc-2017-global-human-capital-trends-gx.pdf

Deluga, R. (1997). Relationship among American presidential charismatic leadership, narcissism, and rated performance. *The Leadership Quarterly, 8*(1), 49–65.

De Neve, J.E., Mikhaylov, S., Dawes, C.T., Christakis, N.A., & Fowler, J.H. (2013). Born to lead? A twin design and genetic association study of leadership role occupancy. *The Leadership Quarterly, 24*(1), 45–60.

DeRue, D.S. & Ashford, S.J. (2010). Who will lead and who will follow? A social process of leadership identity construction in organizations, *Academy of Management Review, 35*(4), 627–647.

DeRue, D.S., Nahrgang, J.D., Hollenbeck, J.R., & Workman, K. (2012). A quasi-experimental study of after-event reviews and leadership development. *Journal of Applied Psychology, 97*(5), 997–1015.

Eagly, A.H., & Karau, S.J. (1991). Gender and the emergence of leaders: A meta-analysis. *Journal of Personality and Social Psychology, 60*(5), 685–710.

Eagly, A.H., & Karau, S.J. (2002). Role congruity theory of prejudice toward female leaders. *Psychological Review, 109*(3), 573–598.

Elprana, G., Felfe, J., Stiehl, S., & Gatzka, M. (2015). Exploring the sex difference in affective motivation to lead: Furthering the understanding of women's underrepresentation in leadership positions. *Journal of Personnel Psychology, 14*(3), 142–152.

Ely, K., Boyce, L.A., Nelson, J.K., Zaccaro, S.J., Hernez-Broome, G., & Whyman, W. (2010). Evaluating leadership coaching: A review and integrated framework. *The Leadership Quarterly, 21*(4), 585–599.

Ely, R., Ibarra, H., & Kolb, D. (2011). Taking gender into account: Theory and design for women's leadership development programs. *Academy of Management Learning & Education, 10*(3), 474–493.

Ensari, N., Riggio, R.E., Christian, J., & Carslaw, G. (2011). Who emerges as a leader? Meta-analyses of individual differences as predictors of leadership emergence. *Personality and Individual Differences, 51*(4), 532–536.

Epitropaki, O., Kark, R., Mainemelis, C., & Lord, R.G. (2017). Leadership and followership identity processes: A multilevel review. *The Leadership Quarterly, 28*(1), 104–129.

Epitropaki, O., Sy, T., Martin, R., Tram-Quon, S., & Topakas, A. (2013). Implicit leadership and followership theories "in the wild": Taking stock of information-processing approaches to leadership and followership in organizational settings. *The Leadership Quarterly, 24*(6), 858–881.

Felfe, J., & Schyns, B. (2014). Romance of leadership and motivation to lead. *Journal of Managerial Psychology, 29*(7), 850–865.

Finkelstein, L.M., Costanza, D.P., & Goodwin, G.F. (2018). Do your high potentials have potential? The impact of individual differences and designation on leader success. *Personnel Psychology, 71*(1), 3–22.

Fitzsimmons, T.W., Callan, V.J., & Paulsen, N. (2014). Gender disparity in the C-suite: Do male and female CEOs differ in how they reached the top? *The Leadership Quarterly, 25*(2), 245–266.

Foti, R.J., & Hauenstein, N.M.A. (2007). Pattern and variable approaches in leadership emergence and effectiveness. *Journal of Applied Psychology, 92*(2), 347–355.

Gentry, W.A., Logan, P., & Tonidandel, S. (2014). *Understanding the leadership challenges of first-time managers: Strengthening your leadership pipeline* [pdf]. Retrieved from http://insights.ccl.org/wp-content/uploads/2015/04/UnderstandingLeadershipChallenges.pdf

Grijalva, E., Harms, P.D., Newman, D.A., Gaddis, B.H., & Fraley, R.C. (2015). Narcissism and leadership: A meta-analytic review of linear and nonlinear relationships. *Personnel Psychology, 68*(1), 1–47.

Guillén, L., Mayo, M., & Korotov, K. (2015). Is leadership a part of me? A leader identity approach to understanding the motivation to lead. *The Leadership Quarterly, 26*(5), 802–820.

Hammond, M., Clapp-Smith, R., & Palanski, M. (2017). Beyond (just) the workplace: A theory of leader development across multiple domains. *Academy of Management Review, 42*(3), 481–498.

Hannah, S.T. (2006). Agentic leadership efficacy: Test of a new construct and model for development and performance. *Dissertation Abstracts International, Section A: Humanities and Social Sciences, 67*(2), 630.

Hannah, S.T., & Avolio, B. (2010). Ready or not: How do we accelerate the developmental readiness of leaders? *Journal of Organizational Behavior, 31*(8), 1181–1187.

Hannah, S.T., Avolio, B.J., Luthans, F., & Harms, P.D. (2008). Leadership efficacy: Review and future directions. *The Leadership Quarterly, 19*(6), 669–692.

Harms, P.D., Spain, S.M., & Hannah, S.T. (2011). Leader development and the dark side of personality. *The Leadership Quarterly, 22*(3), 495–509.

Heilman, M.E. (2001). Description and prescription: How gender stereotypes prevent women's ascent up the organizational ladder. *Journal of Social Issues, 57*(4), 657–674.

Higgins, E.T. (1987). Self-discrepancy: A theory relating self and affect. *Psychological Review, 94*(3), 319–340.

Hogg, M.A. (2000). Subjective uncertainty reduction through self-categorization: A motivational theory of social identity processes. *European Review of Social Psychology, 11*(1), 223–255.

Hoyt, C.L. (2005). The role of leadership efficacy and stereotype activation in women's identification with leadership. *Journal of Leadership and Organizational Studies, 11*(4), 2–14.

Judge, T.A., Bono, J.E., Ilies, R., & Gerhardt, M.W. (2002). Personality and leadership: A qualitative and quantitative review. *Journal of Applied Psychology, 87*(4), 765–780.

Judge, T.A., LePine, J.A., & Rich, B.L. (2006). Loving yourself abundantly: Relationship of the narcissistic personality to self- and other perceptions of workplace deviance, leadership, and task and contextual performance. *Journal of Applied Psychology, 91*(4), 762–776.

Kark, R., & Van Dijk, D. (2007). Motivation to lead, motivation to follow: The role of the self-regulatory focus in leadership processes. *Academy of Management Review, 32*(2), 500–528.

Kraus, M.W., Piff, P.K., & Keltner, D. (2009). Social class, sense of control, and social explanation. *Journal of Personality and Social Psychology, 97*(6), 992–1004.

Leary, M.R. (2007). Motivational and emotional aspects of the self. *Annual Review of Psychology, 58*(1), 317–344.

Lemoine, G.J., Aggarwal, I., & Steed, L.B. (2016). When women emerge as leaders: Effects of extraversion and gender composition in groups. *The Leadership Quarterly, 27*(3), 470–486.

Lent, R.W., & Brown, S.D. (2006). On conceptualizing and assessing social cognitive constructs in career research: A measurement guide. *Journal of Career Assessment, 14*(1), 12–35.

Levin, A. (2017, 21 June). Exclusive: Prince Harry on chaos after Diana's death and why the world needs "the magic" of the royal family. Retrieved from www.

newsweek.com/2017/06/30/prince-harry-depression-diana-death-why-world-needs-magic-627833.html

Li, W.D., Arvey, R.D., & Song, Z. (2011). The influence of general mental ability, self-esteem and family socio-economic status on leadership role occupancy and leader advancement: The moderating role of gender. *The Leadership Quarterly, 22*(3), 520–534.

Li, E.-D., Wang, N., Arvey, R.D., Soong, R., Saw, S.M., & Song, Z. (2015). A mixed blessing? Dual mediating mechanisms in the relationship between dopamine transporter gene DTA1 and leadership role occupancy. *The Leadership Quarterly, 26*(5), 671–686.

Lord, R.G., & Hall, R.J. (2005). Identity, deep structure and the development of leadership skill. *The Leadership Quarterly, 16*(4), 591–615.

Lord, R.G., & Maher, K.J. (1991). *Leadership and information processing: Linking perceptions and performance.* Boston, MA: Unwin Hyman.

Lord, R.G., Brown, D.J., Harvey, J.L., & Hall, R.J. (2001). Contextual constraints on prototype generation and their multilevel consequences for leadership perceptions. *The Leadership Quarterly, 12*(3), 311–338.

Martin, R., Epitropaki, O., & O'Broin, L. (2017). Methodological issues in leadership training: In pursuit of causality. In K.J. Sund, R.J. Galavan, & G.P. Hodgkinson (Eds.), *Methodological challenges and advances in managerial and organizational cognition* (pp. 73–94). Bingley: Emerald.

Mumford, M.D., Todd, E.M., Higgs, C., & McIntosh, T. (2017). Cognitive skills and leadership performance: The nine critical skills. *The Leadership Quarterly, 28*(1), 24–39.

Murphy, S.E. (1992). *The contribution of leadership experience and self-efficacy to group performance under evaluation apprehension* [Ph.D. dissertation]. University of Washington, Seattle, WA. Retrieved from https://digital.lib.washington.edu/researchworks/handle/1773/9167

Nevicka, B., De Hoogh, A.H.B., Van Vianen, A.E.M., Beersma, B., & McIlwain, D. (2011). All I need is a stage to shine: Narcissists' leader emergence and performance. *The Leadership Quarterly, 22*(5), 910–925.

Paulhus, D.L., & Williams, K.M. (2002). The dark triad of personality: Narcissism, Machiavellianism, and psychopathy. *Journal of Research in Personality, 36*(6), 556–563.

Polidano, C., Hanel, B., & Buddelmeyer, H. (2013). Explaining the socio-economic status school completion gap. *Education Economics, 21*(3), 230–247.

Popper, M., & Mayseless, O. (2007). The building blocks of leader development: A psychological conceptual framework. *Leadership and Organization Development Journal, 28*(7), 664–684.

Ramarajan, L. (2014). Past, present and future research on multiple identities: Toward an intrapersonal network approach. *Academy of Management Annals, 8*(1), 589–659.

Raskin, R., & Novacek, J. (2006). Narcissism and the use of fantasy. *Journal of Clinical Psychology, 47*(4), 490–499.

Raskin, R., Novacek, J., & Hogan, R. (1991). Narcissistic self-esteem management. *Journal of Personality and Social Psychology, 60*(6), 911–918.

Reichard, R.J., & Johnson, S.K. (2011). Leader self-development as organizational strategy. *The Leadership Quarterly, 22*(1), 33–42.

Riggio, R.E., Riggio, H.R., Salinas, C., & Cole, E.J. (2003). The role of social and emotional communication skills in leader emergence and effectiveness. *Group Dynamics: Theory, Research, and Practice, 7*(2), 83–103.

Rosette, A.S., & Tost, L.P. (2010). Agentic women and communal leadership: How role prescriptions confer advantage to top women leaders. *Journal of Applied Psychology, 95*(2), 221–235.

Rueb, J.D., Erskine, H.J., & Foti, R.J. (2008). Intelligence, dominance, masculinity, and self-monitoring: Predicting leadership emergence in a military setting. *Military Psychology, 20*(4), 237–252.

Rumberger, R.W., & Lamb, S.P. (2003). The early employment and further education experiences of high school dropouts: A comparative study of the United States and Australia. *Economics of Education Review, 22*(4), 353–366.

Schein, V.E. (1973). The relationship between sex role stereotypes and requisite management characteristics. *Journal of Applied Psychology, 57*(2), 95–100.

Schwartz, J., Bohdal-Spiegelhoff, U., Gretczko, M., & Sloan, N. (2016, February 16). *The gig economy: Distraction or disruption?* Retrieved from www2.deloitte.com/insights/us/en/focus/human-capital-trends/2016/gig-economy-freelance-workforce.html

Shondrick, S.J., & Lord, R.G. (2010). Implicit leadership and followership theories: Dynamic structures for leadership perceptions, memory, leader–follower processes. *International Review of Industrial and Organizational Psychology, 25*, 1–33.

Strang, S.E., & Kuhnert, K.W. (2009). Personality and leadership developmental levels as predictors of leader performance. *The Leadership Quarterly, 20*(3), 421–433.

Taggar, S., Hackett, R., & Saha, S. (1999). Leadership emergence in autonomous work teams: Antecedents and outcomes. *Personnel Psychology, 52*(4), 899–926.

Unsworth, K.L., Miscenko, D., & Johnston-Billings, A. (2016, August 5–9). Am I a leader or a friend? How new team leaders resolve their multiple identities. Paper presented at the Academy of Management Conference, Anaheim, CA.

Van Ewijk, R., & Sleegers, P. (2010). The effect of peer socioeconomic status on student achievement: A meta-analysis. *Educational Research Review, 5*(2), 134–150.

Wasylyshyn, K.M. (2005). The reluctant president. *Consulting Psychology Journal, 57*(1), 57–70.

PART II
Increasing the Scope of Leadership Research

5

LEADERSHIP AND ETHICS

You Can Run, but You Cannot Hide from the Humanities

Joanne B. Ciulla

As a philosopher, I never thought that I would be writing an essay on why we need the humanities, let alone one on why we need philosophy to do research on ethics, but here I am. In leadership studies, most research on ethics is done by social scientists, who usually work in business schools. For these researchers and their doctoral students, there is nothing like finding or designing a questionnaire and bestowing it on some unsuspecting group of employees in some organization. It is extraordinary how much of the literature in leadership studies is based on questionnaires, which makes me wonder why more philosophers have not gotten in on the act, since asking questions is what philosophers do. Perhaps it's because ethics is a peculiar topic. We all know about ethics, just like we all know about human behavior, because both subjects are part of our experiences as human beings. Nevertheless, one cannot get away with publishing a journal article on human behavior without acknowledging and citing the relevant literature in psychology, while you can publish an article on ethics and leadership without references to, or knowledge of, philosophy: Why is this? In what follows, I answer this question, and then I compare and contrast research methods in the social sciences and the humanities as a means of showing how research in both areas can work together to give us a deeper understanding of leadership studies in general, and of the nature of ethics in leadership in particular.

The Ascent of the Sciences

For perspective, let's start with a little history. From the ancient Greeks through the Enlightenment, the natural sciences were part of philosophy. The eighteenth-century Enlightenment and the triumph of Isaac Newton's discoveries led to the elevation of scientific method and the possibility of developing the moral sciences.

At that time, the ambitious *L'Encyclopédie*, edited by Denis Diderot and Jean le Rond d'Alembert (1751–80), did not distinguish between the humanities and the natural sciences (Diderot and Alembert, 1969). The encyclopedia intended to catalog and present a secularized account of knowledge, which the editors believed would change the way in which people think about the world. At that time, the line between the natural sciences and the humanities was drawn, but the line between the social sciences and the humanities was not. Even as late as the early 1900s, William James, one of America's most famous psychologists, held an appointment in Harvard's philosophy department.

It was not until the late eighteenth and early nineteenth centuries that there emerged unease with the growing differences between the humanities and the sciences. Biologist Thomas H.E. Huxley (1897) argued that the sciences were more important than the humanities for those pursuing careers in manufacturing and commerce, because the sciences offered meticulous mental training and promised to contribute to national well-being. Others, such as poet and critic Matthew Arnold (1974), worried that training in the sciences would produce a valuable specialist, but, without the humanities, not an educated person. Yet he also believed that the great texts in the sciences, such as Newton's *Principia* and Charles Darwin's *Origins of the Species*, should coexist with the classics in the humanities. The debate among these British scholars was really about what people needed to study to be educated members of society. As commentator Stephan Collini (2000, pp. x–xi) describes it:

> Romantic champions of the imagination were as likely to contrast the fullness of creative or emotional energy released by poetry with the impoverished conception of human life underlying the "dismal science" of political economy as to draw the line between the study of the human and the natural world.

Concern over the relationship between the humanities and the sciences continued to grow until 1959, when novelist and chemist C.P. Snow (2000) sounded the alarm in his famous Rede Lecture, "The Two Cultures." Snow argued that the growing communication and educational gap between two cultures of the sciences and the humanities was dangerous, because it hindered us from solving important social problems and left people poorly educated. For Snow, asking people to describe the second law of thermodynamics should be the same as asking them to describe the plot of a Shakespeare play: Citizens should be educated to know the answer to both. The lecture was largely a critique of the education system in the U.K., where the humanities were favored by the elites, who had the luxury of studying them because they did not need the "practical" knowledge required of those who went into business and the trades.

At the time, the two cultures were less of an issue in the United States because it had a liberal arts tradition in which students studied both the sciences *and* humanities. However, Snow's lecture was prescient because the gap between the sciences, social sciences, and humanities grew, and the ability of scholars in these domains of knowledge to talk to each other continued to shrink. Eventually, the debate about the two – now actually three – cultures seemed to morph into a debate over which were more useful and yielded better knowledge. This became especially true in the United States, where specialization and the divide between the natural sciences, social sciences, and humanities expanded even as educators and scholars embraced and touted the importance of interdisciplinary fields of study, research, and courses.

On Method

It is fascinating to see how elements of Snow's lecture and the debate leading up to it are especially relevant in fields like leadership studies. Most leadership scholars agree that leadership studies ought to be interdisciplinary. The problem is that, in the mainstream literature, the social sciences dominate. One could argue that this is because the largest portion of the literature still comes from academics who work in business schools. Business school faculties consist of mostly social scientists and rarely of scholars with humanities backgrounds – for the reasons described by Huxley in the 1880s. Like the debate that raged in Snow's time, there are those today who regard the humanities more as a luxury than s part of what one needs to get a job or contribute to society. In some U.S. states, legislators periodically suggest that the state universities get rid of courses in the humanities because they are impractical or extras that taxpayers cannot afford.

In higher education today, the social sciences tend to be regarded as epistemically superior to the humanities. By epistemically superior, I mean that the method and type of knowledge that social sciences produce is superior to the kind of knowledge that we get from the humanities. For instance, a well-designed survey study or lab study of ethics and leadership that employs the best scientific research methods is said to yield a kind of knowledge that is more useful, precise, and justifiable than the knowledge that you would get from reading a novel, a history book, or philosophical text. The perceived superiority of this knowledge comes from faith in the scientific method: If you get the method right, your results are significant or true, regardless of the topic under investigation.

This is a major tenet of positivism, which consists of the belief that the natural sciences set the standard for all other studies, including the humanities, that everything can be studied using scientific method, and that all explanation is causal and consists of subsuming particular cases under hypotheses. These tenets explain why most empirical papers in leadership studies spend more time explaining and justifying the methods of research than they do actually exploring or analyzing a problem. As *Leadership* editor Dennis Tourish (2017, p. 3) notes, leadership scholars tend to stick to "positivist methodologies and functionalist perspectives"; as a result, "the insights from this work seem increasingly trivial as method take precedence over substance." Of course, the problem with the social sciences is that, despite the best scientific methodology and statistical methods for accounting for error, the social sciences are different from the natural sciences. Unlike predicting the behavior of a chemical compound, predicting human behavior is less precise because human beings have free will.

The humanities do not have one method of research that promises that if you get the method right, you get true, relevant, or justifiable results. This does not mean that there is no such thing as research methods in the humanities: There are. They include historiography, literary theory, hermeneutics, and conceptual analysis. Like scientific method, they offer a systematic way of approaching research. Unlike scientific method, their approach offers no guarantee that using it will lead different researchers to come up with the same results or conclusion. The humanities do not claim to be predictive, but in some ways they can offer powerful insights into what people value, and into how they have behaved and might behave in the future. For instance, you can learn a great deal about market crashes by reading about tulip mania – a phenomenon that took place in Holland between 1634 and 1637, when speculators were willing to pay the price of an estate for one tulip bulb, and then they lost everything when the market bubble burst (MacKay, 2002). We may see the same behavior today in the Bitcoin market. Nonetheless, in regard to method, the humanities appear to be hopelessly subjective. To gain knowledge or be able to use it to predict things in the future, requires interpretation that may be hit or miss, whereas the scientific method dangles the seductive promise of objective truth.

In the leadership literature, it is more common to see humanities scholars making reference to social science literature than vice versa. Sometimes, social scientists try to do interdisciplinary work using the humanities, but they do it badly, because they fail to appreciate that there are certain standards as to how one uses sources and how to treat those sources (more on this later). The scientific approach to leadership studies relies on method and often avoids critical interpretation of sources, whereas interpretation is the bread and butter of the humanities. For example, if you look at most journal articles in *The Leadership Quarterly* or in other management journals, they have huge lists of references. As a reviewer, I find it astounding how many authors have clearly not read beyond the abstract or the titles of the articles they cite. They treat each study or assertion in an article as if it is a point of truth upon which they can support their paper. The problem with this is that simply stacking up citations is not a substitute for a good argument. To make an argument, you have to critically discuss and interpret the meaning and significance of the studies you cite – especially since few, if any, represent a finding that is broadly generalizable. The other problem with over-citation is that people hide behind citations as a way of not taking responsibility for information or ideas in a paper. For some researchers, citations are nothing more than name dropping.

I have been discussing the tension between the social sciences and the humanities, and some reasons why the gold standard in the leadership studies literature has been the social sciences rather than the humanities. I do not intend to disparage the social sciences, but rather to explain why the leadership studies literature has been dominated by the scientific approach. The priority of the social sciences over the humanities is prevalent across the academy and in the business schools where many leadership scholars work. Next, I tease out some differences between the social sciences and the humanities, so that we can get a better picture of how they contribute to our knowledge of human and social relationships, both of which are fundamental to the study of leadership in general, and of ethics in particular.

The Three Cultures

In his book *The Three Cultures*, psychologist Jerome Kagan (2009) revisits Snow's lecture and examines the natural sciences, social sciences, and humanities today. He says that there are several factors that have affected the status of humanities in universities. First, the humanities do not bring in large research grants. Second, the media and the public have become persuaded, as Huxley said, that the sciences and social sciences provide answers to social problems. Lastly, the attack of postmodernists such as Derrida and Foucault on the humanities shook the confidence of humanities scholars, whose work is not only inherently subjective, but whose research was so hopelessly biased by race, class, ethnicity, etc. that it was of little value. Despite the differences between the three cultures, Kagan (2009, p. 3) tells us that they all consist of these components:

1. A set of unquestioned premises that create preferences for particular questions and equally particular answers
2. A favored collection of analytical tools for gathering evidence
3. A preferred set of concepts that are at the core of explanations

He then goes on to compare and contrast the three cultures on nine dimensions. For our purposes, I will discuss only the comparison between the social sciences and the humanities to see where they differ and overlap (see Table 5.1), and then tease out what this would mean in leadership studies.

As you can see, the social sciences are in many ways quite close to the humanities in regard to dimension 1, their primary interests. Kagan says that the social sciences study human *behavior* and that the humanities study human *reactions*, but I think it is fair to say that, in a sense, both study both. By *reactions*, he means causal connections, but they might also be considered reasons. Neither of the disciplines alone is adequate for studying a complex human and social relationship such as leadership.

112 Joanne B. Ciulla

TABLE 5.1 Comparison of two cultures

Dimension	Social sciences	Humanities
1. Primary interests	Prediction and explanation of human behaviors and psychological states	An understanding of human reactions to events and the meanings humans impose on experience as a function of culture, historical era, and life history
2. Primary sources of evidence and control of conditions	Behaviors, verbal statements, gathered under conditions in which contexts cannot always be controlled	Written texts and human behaviors gathered under conditions of minimal control
3. Primary vocabulary	Constructs referring to psychological features, states, and behaviors of individuals or groups, with an acceptance of the constraints that the context of observation imposes on generality	Concepts referring to human behavior and the events that provoke them with serious contextual restrictions on inferences
4. Influence of historical conditions	Modest	Serious
5. Ethical influence	Major	Major
6. Dependence on outside support	Moderately dependent	Relatively independent
7. Work conditions	Small collaborations and solitary	Solitary
8. Contribution to the national economy	Modest	Minimal
9. Criteria for beauty	Conclusions that support a broad theoretical view of human behavior	Semantically coherent arguments described in elegant prose

Source: Kagan (2009, pp. 4–5)

Explanation and Understanding

The other two key ideas in Kagan's description of primary interests are that the social sciences aim to *explain* and the humanities aim to *understand*. One way of thinking of this distinction is as the difference between causal and a teleological accounts (Von Wright, 1971): Causal accounts tell us *how* we got here, and teleological accounts tell us *why* we are here. A causal account is linear or systemic, looking at how event A affects event B. A teleological explanation looks at why we have event A and what made event A possible. German philosopher and historian Wilhelm Dilthey (1996) said that history gives us understanding only if we can derive insights from it that are generalizable to elements of the human condition. Thus he pits scientific methods of explanation against hermeneutic methods of interpretation.

Hermeneutics is a method used in the humanities to understand texts. The ancient Greek rhetoricians developed it, and it was formalized in the Middle Ages. Medieval books contained what were called *accessus*, which were introductions or commentaries to a book and its author. They were sometimes anthologized as books of literary criticism and called *accessus ad auctores*. These books often stated the following questions as a means of interpreting the text (Quain, 1945).

Who (is the author)?

What (is the subject matter of the text)?

Why (was the text written)?

How (was the text composed)?

When (was the text written or published)?

Where (was the text written or published)?

By which means (was the text written or published)?

While these questions may seem quaint, they are in effect what most humanities scholars tend to do when they read a text. (Today, the "who, what, why, when, where, and how" are often associated with journalism.) Humanities scholars do not simply take what the author writes at face value; rather, they use these tools to interpret what to make of the text. The method does not promise objectivity, but it offers readers a way of interpreting the text in light of other works, and it gives a kind of insight into the subjectivity of the text. This allows them to explain the text in terms of what the author says and to understand the text in terms of what it means.

Sometimes, when leadership scholars attempt to use material from philosophy, history, or other areas of the humanities, they make the mistake of using the text as if it were a scientific study. They tell us what it says, but they fail to interpret what it means. In a sense, they do not seem to understand, or they fail to help their reader to understand, the narrative of their work and the citations that support it. For example, some leadership scholars cite philosopher Martin Heidegger when they write about authentic leadership, but they never explain to what part of Heidegger they are referring. Others do not seem to have read enough to notice that Heidegger does not mean the same thing they do when they talk about "authenticity." (For example, see Walumbwa, Avolio, Gardner, Wernsing, & Peterson, 2008.) This problem is exacerbated when authors do not read the philosophical text, but instead cite what someone else has said about it. By doing this, they lose the author's context and, sometimes, the argument behind the idea. As a result, they add a layer of subjectivity to what is already subjective about the work. Then, because leadership scholars cite each other, the result is that other articles on authentic leadership incorrectly cite Heidegger because their authors do not bother to read him either.

The lesson here is that, when you cite a humanities text, you must always go back to the original source and make sure that the source means what you or another author say it means. Another problem is that even if scholars do their homework when they cite a philosophical text, the use of in-text citations does not require them to give a page number, unless they quote from the text. Years ago, humanities scholars cited page numbers or other text references in footnotes even when they were not quoting a passage. Some philosophical texts contain numbers that are used for such citation. For example, the works of Plato have what are called *Stephanus pagination*: numbers and letters that tell the reader the exact spot in the text to which they may refer, regardless of the edition, translation, or even the language of the text.

Controlling Subjectivity

Kagan's second dimension concerns the sources of evidence and the degree of control that researchers have over the conditions of their research. Both the social sciences and the humanities study human nature, which is highly variable. The humanities not only are comfortable with this variability, but also sometimes celebrate it. Social scientists struggle because of the necessity to control the context and variables of their research. As explainers, they look for causal connections, or at least correlations. Social scientists simplify their vocabulary into somewhat narrow constructs that fit the context in which they are used. While works in the humanities have unlimited use of concepts, they are still required to use them consistently – for it would be illogical to change the meaning of a word without explanation.

Kagan points out, in his third dimension, that the context of the vocabulary in both areas determines the inferences we can make from them. So while the concepts used in the humanities are broad, the inferences that we can justifiably make from them are narrow – whereas the constructs in the social sciences are narrow and the inferences we can make from them are also quite narrow. For example, the results of a survey study about charisma in a company may be narrow in that they apply to the people studied, and perhaps open the door to being tested again and replicated in other groups in another study. The inferences one draws from the study of charismatic leaders in history could be useful in a different way, not because it has the potential to predict or be confirmed in subsequent studies, but because it has the potential to create hypotheses and constructs that could be used in designing such studies. In leadership studies, the theories are all too often grounded on other theories based on other limited empirical studies. This works well in the natural sciences, but when you are studying human relationships, the results gained in a lab or from a survey are still narrow and open to limited generalization.

Context

In his fourth dimension, Kagan says that social conditions produced by history do not play a significant role in the social sciences. This may be why some, but certainly not all, leadership researchers ignore context. For example, contingency theories hold what seems like the obvious position that leader effectiveness is determined by a mixture of context and other factors (Fiedler, 2008). The humanities offer leadership studies more than only context. They offer layers of understanding about human nature and human values. This is especially important in a field such as leadership studies because leadership is socially constructed and, as I have argued, morally constructed. By "morally constructed," I mean that the very idea of a leader has built-in moral assumptions about someone who ought to have utilitarian intentions, duties to stakeholders, responsibility of a group or organization, and care for followers and relevant stakeholders (Ciulla, 1995).

In a sense, the humanities offer a huge narrative "data set" about human nature and human behavior. Mining what philosophy, religion, literature, and art have to say about leadership, and then forming theories or testable hypotheses from it, adds a richness and depth to leadership studies that most of the current literature does not possess. The best example we have of this is James MacGregor Burns' (1978) book on transforming leadership, *Leadership*. Burns' theory is built on observations from history, not on social science studies. Researchers such as Bernard Bass (1985) then took Burns' theory and used it to build constructs and testable hypotheses, which then became his theory of transformational leadership.

The humanities can be used not only to help to formulate, but also to test, empirical constructs and to gain insights into leader behavior. For example, I did extensive archival research on Nelson Mandela and found that, contrary to descriptions of authentic leadership, Mandela did not fit the model of an authentic leader (Ciulla, 2013). The implications of my study were not only relevant for Mandela; they also raised new questions that could be turned into testable hypotheses about how iconic leaders like Mandela differ from other types of leader. Another important question in leadership studies concerns the relationship between a leader's public and private behavior. For this question, I studied U.S. presidents who committed adultery (Ciulla, 2016). My study discovered several areas for potential empirical research on how the desire to keep something like adultery secret tangibly affects a leader's ethical behavior on the job. These kinds of studies may seem merely anecdotal, but, with sufficient evidence and a strong argument, they certainly can be used to derive testable hypotheses. An ideal way of studying leadership might be to develop a hypothesis from one or more of the humanities, to test it in a lab or survey study, and then to see if it explains and adds to our understanding of current events and events in history, literature, religion, etc.

Ethics

Kagan's fifth dimension concerns the degree to which ethical values and questions are part of the questions asked and the inferences drawn in both types of research. He claims that ethics is a major part of the social sciences and the humanities, but it is not clear if this claim is that ethics *should* be a major part of both or whether it actually *is*. The old idea of a value-free, and hence more scientific, social science is still alive and kicking. There has been a growing literature on ethics in leadership studies that was in part inspired by the seminal research on ethical leadership by Michael Brown, Linda Treviño, and David Harrison (2005). Their study on ethical leadership uses a survey instrument to describe ethical leadership and to analyze its antecedents and consequences. They began research by interviewing people to find out what they thought an ethical leader was. The people whom they interviewed thought ethical leaders were honest, trustworthy, principled, fair, caring, and ethical in their personal lives (Brown and Treviño, 2006). They said that these virtues described the leader as a moral person. Other qualities they discovered had to do with whether managers tried to influence the ethical behavior of others. They called these qualities elements of the moral manager. Brown and colleagues developed a questionnaire to see if respondents had the same perceptions about what constituted an ethical leader. The study is not unlike some of the literature on traits in leadership studies: It describes people's perceptions of what qualities leaders should have.

The limitation of Brown and colleagues' findings is the fact that just because respondents perceive a leader to be ethical does not mean that a leader actually is ethical. For that, you need some sort of theory or conception of various ways in which the concept of "ethical" can be understood. So such studies take us only so far in terms of advancing our knowledge of what constitutes ethical leadership. Moreover, since the meaning of the moral vocabulary in their questionnaire is not defined – that is, it is not clear what people mean when the questionnaire asks them if they think their manager is ethical in their personal life. From a philosophical perspective, the use of moral language in this study is so vague that it is difficult to assess what the findings mean. Even if everyone has similar understandings of the moral terms, we still get a record only of their perceptions. If the experiment is replicated with different groups and in different settings with similar results, the information that it actually gives us about what people's perceptions of what constitutes ethical leaders is so general that its usefulness is quite modest.

Here is where I think that this sort of study would be better if it were built on a foundation of philosophical ethics. The argument for this is similar to the argument that I made for using humanities to develop hypotheses about other leader behaviors. The philosophical literature looks at ethics in terms of concepts and problems that have been critically analyzed and discussed for centuries. Like almost all of the humanities, when you enter into this literature, you enter into a conversation that spans the ages, which reveals that there is a surprising similarity to human nature and the ethical relationships and concerns that people have about leaders. An interdisciplinary study might still use interviews, but would also see how these perceptions of what is ethical measure up to various ethical theories. Wouldn't it be interesting to see how people's perceptions of ethics compared to moral theories that have been discussed from all angles for centuries, or to see how moral theories measure up to an ordinary person's perception of morality? However, perhaps the main reason why social scientists would benefit from using philosophy is to better analyze their findings and be able to use them as a means of understanding how leaders ought to act (see Flanigan, 2017). One of the main practical reasons for studying leadership is to learn how leaders can be better.

Kagan's Final Dimensions

In the sixth dimension, Kagan addresses some of the differences in funding that affect the status of the humanities and the social sciences that I discussed earlier. The seventh dimension describes how researchers in both fields work. Since humanities scholars tend to work alone, this can be a problem for interdisciplinary research, because the easiest way of spanning the divide in leadership studies and other areas is through collaboration. Another problem with how the humanists and social scientists work is *where* they work: Most university departments are fortified silos, and there is often little interaction between academics in the humanities and the social sciences.

Kagan's eighth dimension looks at how the social sciences and humanities contribute to the national economy. Here, he seems to mimic the prevailing thought in society today. The humanities may not directly contribute to the economy (unless you factor in the arts, movies, tourism to historical sights, and such). The humanities are not associated with making money, yet they are incredibly useful to the economy in terms of keeping it from losing money, abusing technology, perpetuating social injustice, and destroying the environment. In recent history, unethical behavior by leaders who operated without a sense of history, human nature, and moral values has crashed the global economy. More attention to history, literature, art, and other areas in education, and especially in regard to how we understand leadership, may not solve social problems, but they certainly help us to avoid them. Then again, this was part of the wariness that Snow and others had about overemphasis on the sciences. The other reason that the humanities are important is that they foster the critical skills and understanding of social values that are fundamental to the capacities that citizens need to maintain a healthy democracy. Philosopher Martha Nussbaum (1997) argues that the humanities cultivate three capacities: the ability to critically examine oneself; the ability to see oneself as a human being who is bound to all human beings; and narrative imagination, or the ability to understand the emotions and wishes of someone different from oneself.

Lastly, Kagan compares the criteria that social scientists and humanists use to judge whether a body of research or work is done well, or, as he says, is "elegant" or "beautiful." For the social scientist, beauty is fairly straightforward: It is the well-designed research that supports a broad theoretical view of human nature. Kagan is less clear on what humanists find beautiful. He says that they like arguments that are logically cogent and good writing. Yes, humanists admire good writing, but they aren't always good writers. One reason why social scientists do not read philosophy, literary theory, and some other areas of the humanities is that they are not always beautifully written. For social scientists, writing is more straightforward because it is simply the means of describing and analyzing their research. However, some socials scientists seem to delight in making up and using jargon, which is offputting to outsiders. One such term that is particularly annoying to philosophers who do ethics is the use of the word "ethicality" instead of "ethics." Since the two words can be used interchangeably, it is not clear why we would want another word – unless perhaps researchers think it makes them sound smarter. For social scientists, writing is how they describe their results and what they mean. For humanities scholars, writing is as important and, in some cases, more important than the research, because language and meaning are central to their work. Interdisciplinary work between the social sciences and humanities would be much easier if academics on both sides were to write better and try to be kind to their readers.

Conclusion

The social sciences are about – or are supposed to be about – *real* things that happen in the world, based on observation and data. Except for history, most of the humanities, such as the arts, literature, religion, and philosophy, are not about facts per se; rather, they concern themselves with fictions – creations of human imagination that are often drawn from perceptions of reality. Even history is a contested terrain because it can be fictionalized or selectively told by the powerful or some other group with an agenda. Yet, to some extent, leadership too is a creation of our imaginations – forged from human relationships that encompass the hopes, fears, dreams, passions, wants, and needs of our individual and collective experiences. A number of theories and experiments in the social sciences support the view that leadership is a perception, a romantic notion, and/or an implicit theory that people carry with them (Meindl, Ehrlich, & Dukerich, 1985). If this is so, why would the epistemic value of studying leadership in a novel, a painting, or a religious text be any less significant than an experiment done on undergraduates, or a survey given to people in a company? Whenever we study people, we aim at a moving target whose behavior is partly forged by perceptions, beliefs, free will, and imagination. Leadership studies scholars should do their best to be good social scientists – but, without the humanities, they are doomed to never fully understand leadership.

References

Arnold, M. (1974). Literature and science. In R.H. Super (Ed.), *The complete prose works of Matthew Arnold, vol. 10* (pp. 52–73). Ann Arbor, MI: University of Michigan Press.

Bass, B.M. (1985). *Leadership and performance beyond expectations*. New York: Free Press.

Brown, M.E., & Treviño, L.K. (2006). Ethical leadership: A review and future directions. *The Leadership Quarterly*, 17(6), 595–616.

Brown, M.E., Treviño, L.K., & Harrison, D. (2005). Ethical leadership: A social learning perspective for construct development and testing. *Organizational Behavior and Human Decision Processes*, 97(2), 117–134.

Ciulla, J.B. (1995). Leadership ethics: Mapping the territory. *Business Ethics Quarterly*, 5(1), 5–24.

Ciulla, J.B. (2013). Searching for Mandela: The saint as the sinner who keeps on trying. In D. Ladkin & C. Spiller (Eds.), *Authentic leadership: Clashes, convergences and coalescences* (pp. 152–175). Cheltenham: Edward Elgar.

Ciulla, J.B. (2016). Dangerous liaisons: Adultery and the ethics of presidential leadership. In G. Goethals & D. Bradburn (Eds.), *Politics, ethics and change: The legacy of James MacGregor Burns* (pp. 74–99). Cheltenham: Edward Elgar.

Collini, S. (2000). Introduction. In C.P. Snow (Ed.), *The two cultures* (2nd ed.) (pp. vii–lxxiii). New York: Cambridge University Press.

Diderot, D., & Alembert, M. (1969). *Encyclopedie, ou, Dictionnaire raisonne des sciences, des arts et des métiers*. Elmsford, NY: Pergamon Press.

Dilthey, W. (1996). *Hermeneutics and the study of history*. Eds. E.A. Makkreel & F. Rodi. Princeton, NJ: Princeton University Press.

Fiedler, F.E. (2008). The contingency model: A theory of leadership effectiveness. In J.M. Levine & R. Moreland (Eds.), *Small groups: Key readings* (pp. 369–382). New York: Psychology Press.

Flanigan, J. (2017, June 13). Philosophical methodology in leadership ethics. *Leadership*. Retrieved from http://journals.sagepub.com/doi/10.1177/1742715017711823

Huxley, T.H.E. (1897). Science and culture. In *Science and Education: Essays* (pp. 134–139). New York: Appleton.

Kagan, J. (2009). *The three cultures: Natural sciences, social sciences, and the humanities in the twenty-first century*. New York: Cambridge University Press.

MacGregor Burns, J. (1978). *Leadership*. New York: Harper Torchbooks.

MacKay, C. (2002). *Extraordinary popular delusions and the madness of crowds*. New York: Barnes & Noble Books.

Meindl, J.R., Ehrlich, S.B., & Dukerich, J.M. (1985). The romance of leadership. *Administrative Science Quarterly*, *30*(1), 78–102.

Nussbaum, M.C. (1997). *Cultivating humanity: A classical defense of reform in liberal education*. Cambridge, MA: Harvard University Press.

Quain, E.A. (1945). The medieval *accessus ad auctores*. *Traditio*, *13*, 215–264.

Snow, C.P. (2000). *The two cultures* (2nd ed.). New York: Cambridge University Press.

Tourish, D. (2017). Introduction: writing differently about leadership. *Leadership*, *13*(1), 3–4.

Von Wright, G.H. (1971). *Explanation and understanding*. Ithaca, NY: Cornell University Press.

Walumbwa, F.O., Avolio, B.J., Gardner, W.L., Wernsing, T.S., & Peterson, S.J. (2008). Authentic leadership: Development and validation of a theory-based measure. *Journal of Management*, *34*(1), 89–126.

6

LEADERSHIP IS MALE-CENTRIC

Gender Issues in the Study of Leadership

Stefanie K. Johnson and Christina N. Lacerenza

What if, when mentioning the word *leader*, a woman came to mind? When practicing and studying leadership, theories and recommendations are dominated by an androcentric (that is, male-centered) perspective. This is a critical issue to address when women comprise nearly 50 percent of the workforce – and, as of 2010, 50.8 percent of the population (Howden & Meyer, 2011) – but are often forgotten or overlooked when it comes to leadership because they do not fit the masculine prototype for leadership (for example, assertive, dominant, aggressive). When individuals think about the discovery of DNA by Watson and Crick, most are unaware that a female scientist, Rosalind Franklin, also contributed much to this scientific breakthrough (Klug, 1968). Similarly, many are unaware of the five female leaders who cooperated across parties to end a major U.S. government shutdown in 2013 (Bradley, 2016; Konner, 2015). Arguably, it is less easy to recall, or even to acknowledge, the role that women played in these events because it is more difficult to encode and recall counter-stereotypical information, and the stereotype for scientist and leader is male (Bordalo, Coffman, Gennaioli, & Shleifer, 2016). The societal contributions of female leaders may go unrecognized because the ways in which women lead do not always align with leadership stereotypes. We argue that the failure to account for leadership from a feminine perspective is a critical reason for the pervasive gender leadership gap, and that addressing this issue in leadership research will lead to more robust science and greater leadership effectiveness in practice.

The percentage of female executives within Fortune 100 companies increased from none in 1980 to 11 percent in 2001, but there has been a lack of progress over the last decade (Warner, 2015). Indeed, for the first time in eight years, the percentage of women on U.S. corporate boards declined in 2016, with women holding fewer than 20 percent of Fortune 500 board positions and only 4 percent of Fortune 500 chief executive officers (CEO) being women (McGregor, 2017). Further, more than two-thirds of Fortune 500 companies have no women of color on their boards at all (Warner & Corley, 2017). In fact, data suggest that it will take until the end of 2055 to reach gender parity on boards if we continue at the current rate (Jones, 2017). Although a reading of these data is concerning, the main point about women leaders on which we focus should not be the lack thereof; rather, let us attempt to learn something from women leaders and to shift our focus to the benefits they bring to the office.

Thus we begin this chapter with a brief review of evidence suggesting that those few companies with more women seem to outperform the rest. Specifically, women in top management (Dezsö & Ross, 2012) and holding C-suite positions (Noland, Moran, & Kotschwar, 2016) is linked to firm profitability. Likewise, companies with more women on their board are more profitable (Arguden, 2014) and are less likely to have to restate their earnings (Abbott, Parker, & Presley, 2012). Further, having more women board members can also create role models for talented women (Hewlett, 2014), result in increased women executives during the subsequent year (Matsa & Miller, 2011), and yield better investment returns (Lee, Marshall, Rallis, & Moscardi, 2015). In short, the data show that there is a business case for women in leadership. Moreover, it is quite perplexing to see the abundance of male leaders, with little to no female leaders, in which context the question becomes: "Why aren't women making it to the top?"

This question is not novel, and many have attempted to provide an answer. For instance, some have argued that this discrepancy is in part a result of women not seeking powerful positions at the same rate as men, or not "leaning in" (Sandberg, 2013). Others believe that traditional gender stereotypes continue to permeate the workforce (Lueptow, Garovich-Szabo, & Lueptow, 2001). For instance, men may be more attractive leader candidates because they are presumed to exhibit leader-like qualities, or agentic behaviors, such as dominance and assertiveness (Eagly & Johannesen-Schmidt, 2001). We believe that there is merit in these explanations, but also argue that, as a result of an abundance of opinions on this topic, several myths regarding gender and leadership have surfaced, limiting the impact of the current research. As such, the aim of this chapter is to address the issue of male-centric leadership practices by identifying and rebuking common myths associated with gender and leadership. Additionally, we provide several solutions (both research- and practice-oriented), designed to ameliorate the gender leadership gap and to stimulate future research.

Myth 1: Women and Men Lead Very Differently

From an early age, girls and boys are taught to adopt distinct mannerisms and behavioral patterns. For instance, men are socialized to be more aggressive (Eagly & Steffen, 1986), and they therefore exhibit higher levels of physical aggression than women (Archer, 2004). Another behavioral manifestation of gender differences relates to negotiating behavior, such that women are less likely to initiate negotiations than men (Kugler, Reif, Kaschner, & Brodbeck, 2017). Men also display higher levels of self-esteem and are more assertive, while women are more likely to be anxious, tender-minded, and trusting. Similarly, women tend to score higher on measures of emotional intelligence (Schutte et al., 1998). Despite these differences, as well as anecdotal evidence that would make it seem as if men and women lead differently, there is little research suggesting that gender plays a large role in predicting certain leadership styles and effectiveness. Further, most organizational scientists are in agreement that men and women lead and manage similarly (Eagly & Johnson, 1990).

Although some claim stark differences based on gender – in particular those whose audience includes the general public or practitioners (for example, Nelson, 2013) – scientific evidence continues to support earlier conclusions identifying similarities (Johnson, 2017). In 1990, Eagly and Johnson conducted a quantitative review of 162 studies to compare the leadership styles of men and women, and their results supported a more complex set of findings than the standard belief that men and women lead distinctively. Specifically, they found that, in organizational studies (studies conducted within a field setting), men and women did not differ in their interpersonally oriented style – that is, in "tending to the morale and welfare of the people in the setting" (Eagly & Johnson, 1990, p. 236). This stereotypical difference was found only in laboratory experiments and assessment studies, but the mean effect size was small. Further, across all settings (that is, organizational studies, laboratory experiments, and assessment studies), results suggested that women led more democratically and participatively, while men were more directive or autocratic – although the effect size was rather small (that is, mean weighted $d = .22$).

In addition to similarities across leadership styles, men and women are perceived similarly in regard to leadership effectiveness, but not emergence. In 1995, Eagly, Karau, and Makhijani conducted a meta-analysis of the relationship between gender and leadership effectiveness, and they found similar ratings in regard to this construct. In a later meta-analysis, there were no differences found in effectiveness ratings for men and women across all contexts (Paustian-Underdahl, Walker, & Woehr, 2014). In male-dominated industries, men are rated as more effective than women, and in high-level positions, no gender difference was found. Interestingly, men also tended to rate themselves higher than women (that is, there was a significant difference between male and female self-reported leadership effectiveness, with men reporting higher levels), but women tended to be rated higher on leadership effectiveness by others than men – particularly in more recent studies at the middle-manager level. Some researchers even argue that women have a leadership advantage (Rosette & Tost, 2010): It is alleged that successful women leaders are evaluated more favorably than their male counterparts as a result of their ability to overcome a double standard – that is, stricter requirements for a subordinate group (Foschi, 2000) – and to display excellence in a masculine position (Rosette & Tost, 2010).

These studies show that there really is little difference between women and men in terms of ability to lead and leadership style.

Myth 2: Women Are Not Motivated to Lead

A simple way of excusing the lack of women in leadership is to argue that women are simply not as driven to lead as are men. There is evidence that women are less motivated by power than men, and they may see more downsides to "reaching the top," such as greater conflict and having to make more tradeoffs in life (Gino, Wilmuth, & Brooks, 2015). A McKinsey *Wall Street Journal* study showed that 74 percent of male and 69 percent of female mid-level employees wanted to advance to the next level in their organizations; however, only 36 percent of male employees and 18 percent of female employees aspired to reach the C-suite (Barsh & Yee, 2012). Women may not aspire to reach the C-suite because those roles are perceived to be very masculine – that is, competitive, political, and aggressive (Cabrera, 2007). Women may be less motivated to reach positions when they perceive that they will not "fit in" (Peters, Ryan, Haslam, & Fernandes, 2012). Some of this may be a reflection of the backlash that women who do aspire to achieve or demonstrate power face, because of gender-role violations. This highlights the importance of taking a more gender-neutral approach to leadership. Organizations might be better served by those leaders who are the most honest, ethical, and service-oriented organizational members. Yet part of the reason why we maintain toxic leadership is to also maintain the masculine power structure, as suggested by the theory of hegemonic masculinity (Mavin, Williams, & Grandy, 2014). It is not leadership that women shy away from; it is power.

Myth 3: Biases against Women Are Extinct

Legally, women and men are one and the same, which has led to the demise of explicit discrimination towards women, or "blatant antipathy, beliefs that [members of stereotyped groups] are inherently inferior, [and] endorsement of pejorative stereotypes" (Cortina, 2008, p. 59). But *implicit* discrimination persists, and it leads to consequences similar to those of explicit discrimination (Jones, Peddie, Gilrane, King, & Gray, 2016). For example, benevolent sexism (the belief that women should be protected) can result in female managers receiving less-challenging developmental experiences and more positive (or unsubstantial) feedback, as compared to male counterparts (King et al., 2012). Likewise, letters of recommendation written about women tend to use more communal and less agentic adjectives as compared to those written about men, which results in a disadvantage for female applicants, because communal characteristics are negatively related to hiring decisions (Madera, Hebl, & Martin, 2009). Add to this the basic assumption that white men are more competent than other groups (for example, Fiske, Cuddy, Glick, & Xu, 2002), and it creates a difficult position for women.

Implicit discrimination towards women in the workplace can be partially explained by role congruity theory (Eagly et al., 2000), which suggests that gender roles shape the expectation that men should be agentic (for example, influential, assertive, self-confident), whereas women should be communal (for example, nurturing, empathetic, sensitive) (Eagly & Johannesen-Schmidt, 2001). Leadership roles are related to agentic attributes, triggering an automatic process of associating men with leadership positions to a greater degree than are women (Eagly & Karau, 2002). Meta-analytic evidence suggests that men are more likely to emerge as leaders than are women (Eagly & Karau, 1991). Further, as a result of traditional gender stereotypes created by a long-established societal norm that powerful positions are reserved for men, women continue to face implicit biases regarding their leadership abilities and, as described by Hollander (1992, p. 72), "begin with an initial hurdle to attaining legitimacy."

Women also face implicit discrimination, leading women to occupy only lower levels of leadership position, because if they adopt or display more masculine traits (that is, those typically identified with a leadership role), they can be penalized. When women display masculine traits, such as by adopting a direct leadership style, they are perceived more negatively (Eagly, Makhijani, & Klonsky, 1992) than men demonstrating the same behavior. For example, when evaluating real people (confederates) as partners for a game, or watching videos of interviews with targets, participants in a study rated women who self-promoted as less desirable teammates or candidates for a job (Rudman, 1998). Furthermore, when women speak in a direct, task-oriented manner, men see them as less likeable and less influential (Carli, LaFleur, & Loeber, 1995). Women need to both fit the leadership prototype *and* maintain feminine characteristics: a double bind (Eagly & Karau, 2002).

Negative reactions toward female leaders are particularly strong for women in top leadership roles, which tend to be the most masculine (Eagly & Karau, 2002; Martell, Parker, Emrich, & Crawford, 1998). In fact, women in these very top roles are seen as particularly negative, reflecting the stereotype of successful women as interpersonally cold, harsh, and belligerent (Heilman & Okimoto, 2007; Johnson, Sitzmann, & Nguyen, 2014). For example, Democratic presidential candidate Hilary Clinton was described as having "scrubbed out the femininity, vulnerability, and heart," and Yahoo! CEO Marissa Mayer was described as "unwilling to listen" (Chou, 2015). This characterization of high-profile female leaders as cold, harsh, and hostile (Dishman, 2012) can be described as "counter-communal" by gender-role theory (Heilman & Okimoto, 2007; Johnson et al., 2014).

To avoid being characterized as counter-communal, women need to demonstrate agentic behavior, yet still maintain a certain level of communal traits. For example, in a series of four studies (a qualitative study, an experiment, a survey, and a field study, comprising 405 participants), Johnson, Murphy, Zewdie, and Reichard (2008) found that both leader prototypes and gender stereotypes impact the evaluation of female leaders in conflicting ways. To meet both of these cognitive expectations, female leaders must fulfill the leader role by demonstrating high levels of masculine leadership qualities (that is, strength), while concurrently fulfilling their gender role by displaying feminine qualities (that is, sensitivity). In comparison, male leaders need only to demonstrate strength to be seen as effective. Fiske, Cuddy, and Glick, (2007) considered how factors signaling warmth alter subsequent judgments made in light of this first lens. Subsequent information can have an important effect. For example, when professional women, who are initially perceived as cold, talk about motherhood, it increases impressions of warmth (Cuddy, Fiske, & Glick, 2004).

Moving Forward: Solutions and Future Research

The previous section discussed and debunked several myths associated with the study of gender and leadership. Discerning the falsification of these myths is an initial step toward achieving equality within leadership (and the workplace), but, in addition to acknowledgment, other steps must be taken. In this section, we present a discussion of ways in which we can address these issues, categorized into research- and practice-based solutions.

Theoretical and Research-oriented Solutions

Create Gender-neutral Theories of Leadership

With a plethora of existing leadership theories (see Lord, Day, Zaccaro, Avolio, & Eagly, 2017, for a review) aligned with a multitude of empirical and meta-analytic evidence suggesting their utility (for example, Judge & Piccolo, 2004; Judge, Piccolo, & Ilies, 2004), it is easy to conclude that leadership effectiveness is, for the most part, understood. However, if we scrutinize the most prevalent leadership theories, not only do we see much overlap between the underlying concepts, from both a conceptual and methodological standpoint (Shaffer, DeGeest, & Li, 2016), but also a reliance on male-centric theories. Because of this, we argue that our current database of leadership theories – largely based on theories created by men about men – are inadequate. Specifically, current theories fail to adequately address women and, in essence, represent only male leadership theory. We have seen, in this chapter, that the extant research shows that there are few gender differences in the leadership styles of men and women – but does that mean that theories of leadership are gender-balanced? In a word, no.

If our theories of leadership are written about men by men, what might we be missing? Two recent reviews of the leadership literature (Lord et al., 2017; Meuser et al., 2016) highlight the most influential theories in leadership. Considering only those beyond trait, behavioral, and skills theory, the dominant theories include charismatic, transformational, strategic, leader–member exchange (LMX), implicit leadership theories, and diversity theories. Charismatic leadership theory, predominantly advanced by Jay Conger and Rabindra Kanungo (1994), focuses on how leaders create high levels of dedication in their followers by demonstrating behaviors that build trust and identification. James Kouzes and Barry Posner (2007), as well as Warren Bennis and Burton Nanus (1985), discuss charismatic leadership. The second major theory of our times is transformational leadership theory, championed by James McGregor Burns (2003), as well as by Bernard Bass and Bruce Avolio (1993). These theories focus on how leader behavior can transform follower identities. Next, there is strategic leadership, which focuses on leaders' ability to think strategically and to initiate change, as studied by Robert Ireland and Michael Hitt (2005), as well as Mathias Arrfelt, Robert Wiseman, and G. Thomas Hult (2013). All of these authors are men.

More diverse theories of leadership (in terms of primary theoreticians) include LMX theory and implicit leadership theory. Leader–member exchange had its roots in vertical dyad linkages, advanced by Fred Dansereau, George Graen, and William Haga (1975). However, the theory took a shift to focus more on the relationships between leaders and followers with the work of George Graen and Mary Uhl-Bien (1995). Similarly, early work on implicit leadership theories by Dov Eden and Uri Leviatan (1975) focused on four factors of leadership: support, work facilitation, interaction facilitation, and goal emphasis. This work continued under Robert Lord, Roseanne Foti, and Christy De Vader (1984), and the range of leader prototypes expanded greatly. Further work by Lynn Offermann, John Kennedy, and Philip Wirtz (1994), as well as Olga Epitropaki and Robin Martin (2005), also brought to light leader prototypes such as sensitivity. In these theories, there is more of a focus on communal leadership attributes – and there are more women authors.

In contrast, theory on diversity and leadership has primarily been led by women, such as Alice Eagly and Steven Karau (2002), and Alice Eagly and Linda Carli (2003), as well as Ashleigh Rosette and Robert Livingston (2012), and Ashleigh Rosette and Leigh Tost (2010). This raises the question of how leadership theories might be different if theories were to be created by women. Consider too the fact that many theories of leadership are based on the examination of, and interviews with, current leaders, such as the work of James Kouzes and Barry Posner (2007), as well as of Warren Bennis and Burton Nanus (1985), on charismatic leadership. In these studies, the authors interviewed mostly male leaders and inferred how to be an excellent leader from that research. Similarly, Thomas Peters and Robert Waterman's (1982) book *In Search of Excellence* looks at how the best companies are run (based mostly on male leaders), as does Jim

Collins' (2001) book *Good to Great*. If our theories of leadership are written by men about men, is it possible we are missing something? Perhaps this mismatch is keeping women out of leadership roles, and future leadership researchers should address this concern by developing more inclusive leadership theories. More scholarship is needed by women about both male *and* female leaders if we are to fully understand leadership in a gender-neutral way.

Change the Stereotype; Change Female Self-views

According to implicit leadership theory, individuals hold certain prototypes, or schemas, which they believe are indicative of leadership, and they evaluate others' leadership by comparing their leader prototypes to the behaviors demonstrated by others (Epitropaki & Martin, 2004). Schemas are activated automatically and subconsciously, and they serve as a filter by which information is processed, stored, and recalled. When information is consistent with one's schema for a certain group, it is more likely to be enacted and remembered. Within the leadership domain, it is argued that a common schema or prototype for a leader is that of a dominant, assertive, intelligent, and masculine individual (for example, Eagly, Wood, & Diekman, 2000). The prominence of this leadership schema not only affects our evaluations of others' leadership qualities, but it can also shape our own identity (that is, internal self-concept). In general, identities are important because they directly influence the cognitions, behaviors, and attitudes of others (for example, Ashforth, Harrison, & Corley, 2008). Individuals align their behaviors with the values and attitudes of their identities (Tajfel & Turner, 1979), and they behave in such a way as to elicit confirmation from others that secures their identities (Stryker & Burke, 2000). Thus an important part of being a leader is identifying with this role.

Not only do gender stereotypes color perceptions of female leaders (that is, by reducing the likelihood that others will look to a feminine individual as a leader), but also they can taint female leaders' perceptions of themselves and the degree to which they adopt a leader identity. Because the leadership role has traditionally been thought of as one that embodies stereotypical masculine characteristics (for example, aggression, power), a woman may not identify as a leader to the same extent as may a man because the woman has been socialized not to perceive herself as portraying these qualities. Thus her schema of the leadership role (which is influenced by gender stereotypes) may not align with her own tendencies, thereby reducing the onset of her leader identity. In support of this, Hoyt, Johnson, Murphy, and Skinnell (2010) conducted multiple laboratory experiments and found that, when gender stereotypes are salient to female leaders, women's confidence in their leadership abilities diminishes because fears that they will confirm a negative female stereotype are heightened.

Together, the potential negative evaluations of female leaders resulting from gender stereotypes, coupled with the fear of confirming a derogatory stereotype, can greatly diminish the onset of the leader identity within women. Having confidence in one's ability to develop and enact leadership is a prerequisite to seeing oneself as a leader and to engaging in a leadership role. As such, it is crucial that, as we progress with the study and practice of leadership, we begin to break down gender stereotypes related to this role to increase the chance that women will see themselves as leaders.

Practice-oriented Solutions

Hire Female Leaders

Similar to Nike Corporation's signature trademark, "Just Do It," we suggest that a critical and practical way of addressing the gender leadership gap is simple: Hire more female leaders. Companies perform similarly (Zhang & Qu, 2016) – if not better (for example, Davis, Babakus, Englis, & Pett, 2010; Khan & Vieito, 2013) – with women on the board, and we see the benefits of diversity really peak when women represent at least 25 percent of the executive team (Labaye, 2012; Roberson & Park, 2007). By introducing women to leadership positions, not only do benefits accumulate because of heightened diversity, but also, by having women represented in high-status positions, organizations can better serve their low-level female employees and increase the likelihood that they will also break the "glass ceiling," by providing them with female role models. Avery, McKay, and Wilson (2008) found that companies with gender-balanced work groups – that is, groups that contain less than 65 percent male members, gender-unbalanced groups having 65 percent male members or more – had significantly lower levels of perceived sex discrimination because when employees have colleagues with demographic similarities, they tend to report greater levels of support, trust, and inclusion. Specifically, in gender-balanced work groups, 5.1 percent of women perceived sex discrimination, whereas in unbalanced workgroups, 23.5 percent of women reported having experienced sex discrimination. Research also provides evidence for a role-model effect when it comes to female leadership. For example, in a randomized natural experiment conducted in India, Beaman, Duflo, Pande, and Topalova (2012) found that adolescent girls' career aspirations and educational attainment, as well as their parents' aspirations for them, increased in villages with leadership positions designated for women.

By increasing the number of female leaders (and therefore the number of examples that run counter to traditional stereotypes), the novelty of a woman in a position of power wears off, and biases can be eliminated. In fact, because seeing can mean believing, simply providing more examples of female leaders to an audience can make a difference. Iris Bohnet, director of the Women and Public Policy Program at the Harvard Kennedy School and co-chair of its Behavioral Insights Group, explained in an interview that a small change within

Kennedy School included adding portraits of female leaders to building walls that previously contained portraits of only male leaders (Morse, 2016). In sum, the call is simple: *Hire more female leaders.*

Why, then, are folks struggling with this agenda? As previously mentioned, science suggests that gender stereotypes are still at play. When evaluating and hiring a leader, it is likely that people rely on the representativeness heuristic, a process by which an individual evaluates the probability of "A" based on the degree to which it emulates (or is stereotypical of) "B" (Tversky & Kahneman, 1974). In other words, when the representativeness heuristic is employed, stereotypes are leveraged; thus men become more attractive leadership candidates because they are presumed to exhibit more leader-like qualities (for example, agentic behaviors such as dominance and assertiveness) (Eagly & Johannesen-Schmidt, 2001). In response, scientists and practitioners have begun to identify strategies that mitigate these biases, including increasing the number of women in hiring pools (Johnson, Hekman, & Chan, 2016) and using blind-hiring processes (Goldin & Rouse, 2000). We recommend the use of such strategies in the hope that they will lead to more female leaders being hired, and the underutilization of some 47 percent of the workforce will come to a halt.

Flip the Script and Hire the Best Person

Because of the lack of women in leadership roles, when women do make it to the top, they are seen as having achieved their positions because of their sex, rather than despite it. But what if we were to flip the script on leadership and talk about the affirmative action program for male leaders? For male-dominated jobs, there is in-group favoritism toward men (Tajfel, 1970) – sometimes spoken of as the "old (White) boys' network," or "the patriarchy" (for example, Marshall, 1984; Strober, 1984) – leading to homophily, or the tendency to promote individuals who are demographically similar to incumbents (Kanter, 1977). When women are hired, groups are harsher on female leaders whom they believe to have been selected based on their gender. In one study, researchers appointed the leader of a group based on one of three factors: gender, chance, or merit (Jacobson & Koch, 1977). After completing a task, these leaders and the other group members were given either positive or negative feedback; the other group members then evaluated the female leader. When the other group members received positive feedback, they did not attribute the success to the leader if she was selected based on gender; however, when receiving negative feedback, the other group members attributed their failure to the female leader if she was selected based on gender. Affirmative action programs can also hurt one's own self-views (Heilman, Simon, & Pepper, 1987). Implementing affirmative action policies may unfairly stigmatize women employees as "less competent," so, when framing an affirmative action program, it is beneficial to state that the most qualified candidate is being chosen.

Implement Plural Leadership Structures

A recent trend within organizations is the implementation of nontraditional leadership structures and teams, including flat hierarchies and self-managed teams (Kaplan et al., 2016). In comparison to traditional teams, self-managed teams do not have a formally designated leader at the beginning of the team's performance cycle; rather, an individual team member adopts (or multiple team members may adopt) the leadership role organically and over time (Humphrey, Hollenbeck, Meyer, & Ilgen, 2007). This team structure breeds shared leadership, or leadership in the plural (Denis, Langley, & Sergi, 2012), which is distributed and dynamic leadership. Because of this, the team might be more inclined to select and be influenced by individuals possessing qualities that are reflective of effective leadership and related to the task at hand, rather than to exhibit a bias associated with typical gender roles (for example, Bergman, Small, Bergman, & Bowling, 2014). In other words, the probability of a female leader emerging within this context may be higher than if an individual from outside of the team were to appoint a team leader (as is the case in more traditional team contexts).

Conclusion

At present, what is wrong with current leadership scholarship and practice is that it is too male-centric and not gender-neutral. The data used to derive most leadership theories and recommendations was collected by male researchers from male leaders, and it was analyzed and interpreted by mostly male scientists. Although Schein's (1973) early conclusion "think manager, think male" seems archaic, this claim continues to permeate leadership practice and theory, regardless of the fact that it is unethical, immoral, undesirable, and ineffective. Men seem to fit the bill of a leader to a greater degree than women only because constituents are blinded by antiquated gender stereotypes ("he is assertive, overbearing, and dominant, and therefore will make for a good leader"). Within this chapter, we have discussed such stereotypes and reviewed scientific evidence that debunks several myths associated with gender and leadership, providing conclusions that:

1. women and men lead similarly,
2. women are motivated to lead, and
3. biases against women still exist.

Acknowledging these conclusions represents an initial step towards gender parity in leadership; a second step is to implement several strategies that will assist with this goal. As such, we also identify several strategies, in the hope that readers will leverage these ideas for future research and practice.

References

Abbott, L.J., Parker, S., & Presley, T.J. (2012). Female board presence and the likelihood of financial restatement. *Accounting Horizons, 26*(4), 607–629.

Archer, J. (2004). Sex differences in aggression in real-world settings: A meta-analytic review. *Review of General Psychology, 8*(4), 291–322.

Arguden, Y. (2014, June 7). Why boards need more women. *Harvard Business Review*. Retrieved from https://hbr.org/2012/06/why-boards-need-more-women

Arrfelt, M., Wiseman, R.M., & Hult, G.T.M. (2013). Looking backward instead of forward: Aspiration-driven influences on the efficiency of the capital allocation process. *Academy of Management Journal, 56*(4), 1081–1103.

Ashforth, B.E., Harrison, S.H., & Corley, K.G. (2008). Identification in organizations: An examination of four fundamental questions. *Journal of Management, 34*(3), 325–374.

Avery, D.R., McKay, P.F., & Wilson, D.C. (2008). What are the odds? How demographic similarity affects the prevalence of perceived employment discrimination. *Journal of Applied Psychology, 93*(2), 235–249.

Barsh, J., & Yee, L. (2012). *Unlocking the full potential of women at work*. Retrieved from www.mckinsey.com/~/media/McKinsey/Business%20Functions/Organization/Our%20Insights/Unlocking%20the%20full%20potential%20of%20women%20at%20work/Unlocking%20the%20full%20potential%20of%20women%20at%20work.ashx

Bass, B.M., & Avolio, B.J. (1993). Transformational leadership and organizational culture. *Public Administration Quarterly, 17*(1), 112–121.

Beaman, L., Duflo, E., Pande, R., & Topalova, P. (2012). Female leadership raises aspirations and educational attainment for girls: A policy experiment in India. *Science, 335*(6068), 582–586.

Bennis, W., & Nanus, B. (1985). *Leaders: The strategies for taking charge*. New York: Harper & Row.

Bergman, S.M., Small, E.E., Bergman, J.Z., & Bowling, J.J. (2014). Leadership emergence and group development: A longitudinal examination of project teams. *Journal of Organizational Psychology, 14*(1), 111–126.

Bordalo, P., Coffman, K., Gennaioli, N., & Shleifer, A. (2016). Stereotypes. *Quarterly Journal of Economics, 131*(4), 1753–1794.

Bradley, E. (2016, May 4). Why women don't lead. *Huffington Post*. Retrieved from www.huffingtonpost.com/elizabeth-bradley-/why-women-dont-lead_b_9825286.html

Cabrera, E.F. (2007). Opting out and opting in: Understanding the complexities of women's career transitions. *Career Development International, 12*(3), 218–237.

Carli, L.L., LaFleur, S.J., & Loeber, C.C. (1995). Nonverbal behavior, gender, and influence. *Journal of Personality and Social Psychology, 68*(6), 1030–1041.

Chou, J. (2015, November 15). *Why assertive women aren't bitches: A scientific explainer*. Retrieved from www.refinery29.com/powerful-women-arent-bitches

Collins, J. (2001). *Good to great: Why some companies make the leap . . . and others don't*. London: Random House.

Conger, J.A., & Kanungo, R.N. (1994). Charismatic leadership in organizations: Perceived behavioral attributes and their measurement. *Journal of Organizational Behavior, 15*(5), 439–452.

Cortina, L.M. (2008). Unseen injustice: Incivility as modern discrimination in organizations. *Academy of Management Review, 33*(1), 55–75.

Cuddy, A.J., Fiske, S.T., & Glick, P. (2004). When professionals become mothers, warmth doesn't cut the ice. *Journal of Social Issues, 60*(4), 701–718.

Dansereau, F., Graen, G.B., & Haga, W. (1975). A vertical dyad linkage approach to leadership in formal organizations. *Organizational Behavior and Human Performance, 13*(1), 46–78.

Davis, P.S., Babakus, E., Englis, P.D., & Pett, T. (2010). The influence of CEO gender on market orientation and performance in service small and medium-sized service businesses. *Journal of Small Business Management, 48*(4), 475–496.

Denis, J.L., Langley, A., & Sergi, V. (2012). Leadership in the plural. *Academy of Management Annals, 6*(1), 211–283.

Dezsö, C.L., & Ross, D.G. (2012). Does female representation in top management improve firm performance? A panel data investigation. *Strategic Management Journal, 33*(9), 1072–1089.

Dishman, L. (2012, April 19). The *"bitch in the boardroom" stereotype: Women speak out about success and likability.* Retrieved from www.fastcompany.com/1834404/bitch-boardroom-stereotype-women-speak-out-about-success-and-likability

Eagly, A.H., & Carli, L.L. (2003). The female leadership advantage: An evaluation of the evidence. *The Leadership Quarterly, 14*(6), 807–834.

Eagly, A.H., & Johannesen-Schmidt, M.C. (2001). The leadership styles of women and men. *Journal of Social Issues, 57*(4), 781–797.

Eagly, A.H., & Johnson, B.T. (1990). Gender and leadership style: A meta-analysis. *Psychological Bulletin, 108*(2), 233–256.

Eagly, A.H., & Karau, S.J. (1991). Gender and the emergence of leaders: A meta-analysis. *Journal of Personality and Social Psychology, 60*(5), 685–710.

Eagly, A.H., & Karau, S.J. (2002). Role congruity theory of prejudice toward female leaders. *Psychological Review, 109*(3), 573–598.

Eagly, A.H., & Steffen, V. (1986). Gender and aggressive behavior: A meta-analytic review of the social psychological literature. *Psychological Bulletin, 100*(3), 309–330.

Eagly, A.H., Karau, S.J., & Makhijani, M.G. (1995). Gender and the effectiveness of leaders: A meta-analysis. *Psychological Bulletin, 117*(1), 125–145.

Eagly, A.H., Makhijani, M.G., & Klonsky, B.G. (1992). Gender and the evaluation of leaders: A meta-analysis. *Psychological Bulletin, 111*(1), 3–22.

Eagly, A.H., Wood, W., & Diekman, A.B. (2000). Social role theory of sex differences and similarities: A current appraisal. In T. Eckes & H.M. Trautner (Eds.), *The developmental social psychology of gender* (pp. 123–174). New York: Routledge.

Eden, D., & Leviatan, U. (1975). Implicit leadership theory as a determinant of the factor structure underlying supervisory behavior scales. *Journal of Applied Psychology, 60*(6), 736–741.

Epitropaki, O., & Martin, R. (2004). Implicit leadership theories in applied settings: Factor structure, generalizability, and stability over time. *Journal of Applied Psychology, 89*(2), 293–310.

Epitropaki, O., & Martin, R. (2005). From ideal to real: A longitudinal study of the role of implicit leadership theories on leader–member exchanges and employee outcomes. *Journal of Applied Psychology, 90*(4), 659–676.

Fiske, S.T., Cuddy, A.J., & Glick, P. (2007). Universal dimensions of social cognition: Warmth and competence. *Trends in Cognitive Sciences, 11*(2), 77–83.

Fiske, S.T., Cuddy, A.J., Glick, P., & Xu, J. (2002). A model of (often mixed) stereotype content: Competence and warmth respectively follow from perceived status and competition. *Journal of Personality and Social Psychology, 82*(6), 878–902.

Foschi, M. (2000). Double standards for competence: Theory and research. *Annual Review of Sociology, 26*(1), 21–42.

Gino, F., Wilmuth, C.A., & Brooks, A.W. (2015). Compared to men, women view professional advancement as equally attainable, but less desirable. *Proceedings of the National Academy of Sciences, 112*(40), 12354–12359.

Goldin, C., & Rouse, C. (2000). Orchestrating impartiality: The impact of" blind" auditions on female musicians. *American Economic Review, 90*(4), 715–741.

Graen, G.B., & Uhl-Bien, M. (1995). Relationship-based approach to leadership: Development of leader–member exchange (LMX) theory of leadership over 25 years – Applying a multi-level multi-domain perspective. *The Leadership Quarterly, 6*(2), 219–247.

Heilman, M.E., & Okimoto, T.G. (2007). Why are women penalized for success at male tasks? The implied communality deficit. *Journal of Applied Psychology, 92*(1), 81–92.

Heilman, M.E., Simon, M.C., & Pepper, D.P. (1987). Intentionally favored, unintentionally harmed? Impact of sex-based preferential selection on self-perceptions and self-evaluations. *Journal of Applied Psychology, 72*(1), 62–68.

Hewlett, S.A. (2014, March 13). What's holding women back in science and technology industries? *Harvard Business Review.* Retrieved from https://hbr.org/2014/03/whats-holding-women-back-in-science-and-technology-industries

Hollander, E.P. (1992). Leadership, followership, self, and others. *The Leadership Quarterly, 3*(1), 43–54.

Howden, L.M., & Meyer, J.A. (2011, May). *Age and sex composition, 2010: 2010 census briefs* [pdf]. Retrieved from www.census.gov/prod/cen2010/briefs/c2010br-03.pdf

Hoyt, C.L., Johnson, S.K., Murphy, S.E., & Skinnell, K.H. (2010). The impact of blatant stereotype activation and group sex-composition on female leaders. *The Leadership Quarterly, 21*(5), 716–732.

Humphrey, S.E., Hollenbeck, J.R., Meyer, C.J., & Ilgen, D.R. (2007). Trait configurations in self-managed teams: A conceptual examination of the use of seeding for maximizing and minimizing trait variance in teams. *Journal of Applied Psychology, 92*(3), 885–892.

Ireland, R.D., & Hitt, M.A. (2005). Achieving and maintaining strategic competitiveness in the twenty-first century: The role of strategic leadership. *The Academy of Management Perspectives, 19*(4), 63–77.

Jacobson, M.B., & Koch, W. (1977). Women as leaders: Performance evaluation as a function of method of leader selection. *Organizational Behavior and Human Performance, 20*(1), 149–157.

Johnson, S.K. (2017, August 17). What the science actually says about gender gaps in the workplace. *Harvard Business Review.* Retrieved from https://hbr.org/2017/08/what-the-science-actually-says-about-gender-gaps-in-the-workplace

Johnson, S.K., Hekman, D.R., & Chan, E.T. (2016, April 26). If there's only one woman in your candidate pool, there's statistically no chance she'll be hired. *Harvard Business Review.* Retrieved from https://hbr.org/2016/04/if-theres-only-one-woman-in-your-candidate-pool-theres-statistically-no-chance-shell-be-hired

Johnson, S.K., Murphy, S.E., Zewdie, S., & Reichard, R.J. (2008). The strong, sensitive type: Effects of gender stereotypes and leadership prototypes on the evaluation of male and female leaders. *Organizational Behavior and Human Decision Processes, 106*(1), 39–60.

Johnson, S.K., Sitzmann, T., & Nguyen, A.T. (2014). Don't hate me because I'm beautiful: Acknowledging appearance mitigates the "beauty is beastly" effect. *Organizational Behavior and Human Decision Processes, 125*(2), 184–192.

Jones, C. (2017, March 7). State Street using investment power to get more women on boards. *USA Today*. Retrieved from https://eu.usatoday.com/story/money/2017/03/07/state-street-using-investment-power-get-more-women-boards/98846306/

Jones, K.P., Peddie, C.I., Gilrane, V.L., King, E.B., & Gray, A.L. (2016). Not so subtle: A meta-analytic investigation of the correlates of subtle and overt discrimination. *Journal of Management, 42*(6), 1588–1613.

Judge, T.A., & Piccolo, R.F. (2004). Transformational and transactional leadership: A meta-analytic test of their relative validity. *Journal of Applied Psychology, 89*(5), 755–768.

Judge, T.A., Piccolo, R.F., & Ilies, R. (2004). The forgotten ones? The validity of consideration and initiating structure in leadership research. *Journal of Applied Psychology, 89*(1), 36–51.

Kanter, R.M. (1977). Some effects of proportions on group life: Skewed sex ratios and responses to token women. *American Journal of Sociology, 82*(5), 965–990.

Kaplan, M., Dollar, B., Melian, V., Van Durme, Y., & Wong, J. (2016). Shape culture: Drive strategy. In Deloitte, *Global human capital trends 2016: The new organization – Different by design* [pdf] (pp. 37–46). Retrieved from www2.deloitte.com/content/dam/Deloitte/global/Documents/HumanCapital/gx-dup-global-human-capital-trends-2016.pdf

Khan, W.A., & Vieito, J.P. (2013). CEO gender and firm performance. *Journal of Economics and Business, 67*, 55–66.

King, E.B., Botsford, W., Hebl, M.R., Kazama, S., Dawson, J.F., & Perkins, A. (2012). Benevolent sexism at work: Gender differences in the distribution of challenging developmental experiences. *Journal of Management, 38*(6), 1835–1866.

Klug, A. (1968). Rosalind Franklin and the discovery of the structure of DNA. *Nature, 219*(5156), 808–810.

Konner, M. (2015, March 6). A better world, run by women. *Wall Street Journal*. Retrieved from www.wsj.com/articles/a-better-world-run-by-women-1425657910

Kouzes, J.M., & Posner, B.Z. (2007). Leadership is in the eye of the follower. In J. Gordon (Ed.), *The Pfeiffer book of successful leadership development tools* (pp. 3–10). New York: John Wiley & Sons.

Kugler, K.G., Reif, J.A.M., Kaschner, T., & Brodbeck, F.C. (2017). Gender differences in the initiation of negotiations: A meta-analysis. *Psychological Bulletin, 144*(2), 198–222.

Labaye, E. (2012). *Women matter 2012: Making the breakthrough* [pdf]. Retrieved from www.mckinsey.com/~/media/McKinsey/dotcom/client_service/Organization/PDFs/Women_matter_mar2012_english.ashx

Lee, L.E., Marshall, R., Rallis, D., & Moscardi, M. (2015). *Women on boards: Global trends in gender diversity on corporate boards* [pdf]. Retrieved from www.msci.com/documents/10199/04b6f646-d638-4878-9c61-4eb91748a82b

Lord, R.G., Day, D.V., Zaccaro, S.J., Avolio, B.J., & Eagly, A.H. (2017). Leadership in applied psychology: Three waves of theory and research. *Journal of Applied Psychology, 102*(3), 434–451.

Lord, R.G., Foti, R.J., & De Vader, C.L. (1984). A test of leadership categorization theory: Internal structure, information processing, and leadership perceptions. *Organizational Behavior and Human Performance, 34*(3), 343–378.

Lueptow, L.B., Garovich-Szabo, L., & Lueptow, M.B. (2001). Social change and the persistence of sex typing, 1974–1997. *Social Forces*, *80*(1), 1–36.

Madera, J.M., Hebl, M.R., & Martin, R.C. (2009). Gender and letters of recommendation for academia: Agentic and communal differences. *Journal of Applied Psychology*, *94*(6), 1591–1599.

Marshall, J. (1984). *Women managers: Travelers in a male world*. New York: John Wiley & Sons Ltd.

Martell, R.F., Parker, C., Emrich, C.G., & Crawford, M.S. (1998). Sex stereotyping in the executive suite: "Much ado about something." *Journal of Social Behavior and Personality*, *13*(1), 127–138.

Matsa, D.A., & Miller, A.R. (2011, January). *Chipping away at the glass ceiling: Gender spillovers in corporate leadership* [Working paper]. Retrieved from www.rand.org/content/dam/rand/pubs/working_papers/2011/RAND_WR842.pdf

Mavin, S., Williams, J., & Grandy, G. (2014). Negative intra-gender relations between women: Friendship, competition, and female misogyny. In S. Kumra, R. Simpson, & R.J. Burke (Eds.), *The Oxford handbook of gender in organizations* (pp. 223–248). Oxford: Oxford University Press.

McGregor, J. (2017, June 23). The number of new female board members dropped last year. *LA Times*. Retrieved from www.latimes.com/business/la-fi-on-leadership-female-boards-20170622-story.html

McGregor Burns, J. (2003). *Transforming leadership: A new pursuit of happiness*. New York: Grove Press.

Meuser, J.D., Gardner, W.L., Dinh, J.E., Hu, J., Liden, R.C., & Lord, R.G. (2016). A network analysis of leadership theory: The infancy of integration. *Journal of Management*, *42*(5), 1374–1403.

Morse, G. (2016, July 1). Designing a bias-free organization. *Harvard Business Review*. Retrieved from https://hbr.org/2016/07/designing-a-bias-free-organization

Nelson, A. (2013, August 9). *How women lead differently, and why it matters*. Retrieved from www.fastcompany.com/3000249/how-women-lead-differently-and-why-it-matters

Noland, M., Moran, T., & Kotschwar, B.R. (2016). *Is gender diversity profitable? Evidence from a global survey* [Working paper]. Retrieved from https://piie.com/publications/working-papers/gender-diversity-profitable-evidence-global-survey

Offermann, L.R., Kennedy, J.K., & Wirtz, P.W. (1994). Implicit leadership theories: Content, structure, and generalizability. *The Leadership Quarterly*, *5*(1), 43–58.

Paustian-Underdahl, S.C., Walker, L.S., & Woehr, D.J. (2014). Gender and perceptions of leadership effectiveness: A meta-analysis of contextual moderators. *Journal of Applied Psychology*, *99*(6), 1129–1145.

Peters, K., Ryan, M., Haslam, S.A., & Fernandes, H. (2012). To belong or not to belong: Evidence that women's occupational disidentification is promoted by lack of fit with masculine occupational prototypes. *Journal of Personnel Psychology*, *11*(3), 148–158.

Peters, T.J., & Waterman Jr, R.H. (1982). *In search of excellence: Lessons from America's best-run companies*. New York: Collins.

Roberson, Q.M., & Park, H.J. (2007). Examining the link between diversity and firm performance: The effects of diversity reputation and leader racial diversity. *Group & Organization Management*, *32*(5), 548–568.

Rosette, A.S., & Livingston, R.W. (2012). Failure is not an option for black women: Effects of organizational performance on leaders with single versus dual-subordinate identities. *Journal of Experimental Social Psychology*, *48*(5), 1162–1167.

Rosette, A.S., & Tost, L.P. (2010). Agentic women and communal leadership: How role prescriptions confer advantage to top women leaders. *Journal of Applied Psychology*, *95*(2), 221–235.

Rudman, L.A. (1998). Self-promotion as a risk factor for women: The costs and benefits of counter-stereotypical impression management. *Journal of Personality and Social Psychology*, *74*(3), 629–645.

Sandberg, S. (2013). *Lean in: Women, work, and the will to lead*. London: Random House.

Schein, V.E. (1973). The relationship between sex role stereotypes and requisite management characteristics. *Journal of Applied Psychology*, *57*(2), 95–100.

Schutte, N.S., Malouff, J.M., Hall, L.E., Haggerty, D.J., Cooper, J.T., Golden, C.J., & Dornheim, L. (1998). Development and validation of a measure of emotional intelligence. *Personality and Individual Differences*, *25*(2), 167–177.

Shaffer, J.A., DeGeest, D., & Li, A. (2016). Tackling the problem of construct proliferation: A guide to assessing the discriminant validity of conceptually related constructs. *Organizational Research Methods*, *19*(1), 80–110.

Strober, M.H. (1984). Toward a general theory of occupational sex segregation: The case of public school teaching. In B.F. Reskin (Ed.), *Sex segregation in the workplace: Trends, explanations, remedies* (pp. 144–156). Washington, D.C.: National Academy Press.

Stryker, S., & Burke, P.J. (2000). The past, present, and future of an identity theory. *Social Psychology Quarterly*, *63*(4), 284–297.

Tajfel, H. (1970). Experiments in intergroup discrimination. *Scientific American*, *223*(5), 96–103.

Tajfel, H., & Turner, J.C. (1979). An integrative theory of intergroup conflict. In *The Social Psychology of Intergroup Relations* (pp. 33–47). Monterey, CA: Brooks/Cole.

Tversky, A., & Kahneman, D. (1974). Judgment under uncertainty: Heuristics and biases. *Science*, *185*(4157), 1124–1131.

Warner, J. (2015, August 4). *The women's leadership gap: Women's leadership by the numbers*. Retrieved from www.americanprogress.org/issues/women/reports/2015/08/04/118743/the-womens-leadership-gap/

Warner, J., & Corley, D. (2017, May 21). *The women's leadership gap: Women's leadership by the numbers*. Retrieved from www.americanprogress.org/issues/women/reports/2017/05/21/432758/womens-leadership-gap/

Zhang, Y., & Qu, H. (2016). The impact of CEO succession with gender change on firm performance and successor early departure: Evidence from China's publicly listed companies in 1997–2010. *Academy of Management Journal*, *59*(5), 1845–1868.

7

ARE LEADERSHIP THEORIES WESTERN-CENTRIC?

Transcending Cognitive Differences between the East and the West

Kenta Hino

Mainstream leadership literature, created and developed by researchers who have grown up or been educated in the West, has tended to focus on the measurement of, and suggestions for, the effective behavior of leaders. This emphasis on behavior may be as a result of cognitive differences between the West and East (see Nisbett, 2003, for an overview). Westerners are likely to focus on an individual's behavior, characteristics, and features, rather than on their context and relationships. Since the mainstream literature was developed in Western culture, especially in North America, Western-centric leadership studies abound. This chapter argues that an East Asian cognitive style will be helpful to better understand leadership as a relationship between a leader and followers.

The East Asian cognitive style has two main characteristics not shared with the Western style: It is holistic, and it thinks long term. Nisbett, Peng, Choi, and Norenzayan (2001) showed that Westerners are more likely to pay attention to an object and its category when inferring causality, while East Asians are likely to use a more holistic, relational, and dialectic view. Stemming from this cognitive tendency and the Confucian tradition, East Asians view all interpersonal relationships, including leadership, as long-lasting, mutually beneficial obligations that cannot be seen from a short-term perspective. While Westerners are likely to understand leadership as an individual's traits and behavior, their East Asian counterparts instead consider it as a mutually influential relationship depending not only on the leader's characteristics, but also on those of the followers and the context. The pursuit of the idea that different people view leadership differently will bring new insight to leadership studies and practice, unlike studies such as the GLOBE Project (House, Hanges, Javidan, Dorfman, & Gupta 2004). While this comprehensive international comparison revealed that the extent to which certain leadership styles are favored differs from culture to culture, this chapter shows that what people consider to be leadership differs between the East and the West. This chapter will contend that the mainstream literature is too leader-centric and propose an alternative view based on a non-Western – more specifically, East Asian – cognitive style. As described in this chapter, this East Asian view shares some important points with emerging leadership studies.

This chapter flows as follows: First, we review some international comparisons of cognitive style between the East and West (for example, Nisbett, 2003), to show how East Asians tend to view the world as holistic, long term, and circulating, in contrast with Westerners' category-based and single-way causality. Next, relying on comprehensive reviews (Lord, Day, Zaccaro, Avolio, & Eagly, 2017; Takahashi, Ishikawa, & Kanai 2012), we will briefly summarize the mainstream literature, such as work on behavioral, transformational/charismatic, and contingent approaches, all of which focus primarily on an individual leader. The GLOBE Project (House et al., 2004) is also mentioned to emphasize the unique feature of this chapter. In other words, this chapter focuses not on the cultural differences or similarities in favored leadership style, but on the differences in cognitive style between cultures.

Next, to emphasize the advantages offered by East Asian's cognitive style, we note some faults in recent studies on paternalistic leadership. Paternalism is a value, policy, or practice whereby the people in authority treat those who are expected to be obedient with warmth and severity. The leadership behavior based on this value has received attention from researchers recently and is thought to be effective across cultures. Although studies of paternalistic leadership have not yet come to a clear definition of paternalistic behavior (see Pellegrini & Scandura, 2008, for an overview), East Asians' views can introduce a different perspective and understanding. In the long-term perspective, East Asians often think that the relationship between parents and children can be understood as a cycle in which good and bad times come repeatedly, and they believe that self-concept is developed through this cycle. Parents and children also become aware of and deepen their mutual obligation and trust through this cycle. In a similar vein, East Asians are likely to regard paternalistic leadership as a cycle of good and bad times, through which the relationship advances. For them, leadership cannot be understood as simply a set of behaviors.

Finally, we will argue that new leadership perspectives focusing on followers and contexts in the long term can be helpful for understanding leadership across East and West. Some reviews of the history of leadership studies (for example, Lord et al., 2017; Lord, Gatti, & Chui, 2016) have suggested that the research focus in the literature has shifted away from the individual leader towards an examination of the relationships, exchanges, and social identities that are shared by leader and follower. We have not, however, found evidence supporting the notion that these perspectives are influenced by an Eastern cognitive style. We believe that East Asians' views on leadership will contribute to a more extensive advancement of this profound literature.

Cognitive Differences between East Asian and Western Cultures

Western society emphasizes the individual. This section begins with anecdotal examples to support this notion. For example, Western culture prefers to name things after great leaders more than do Eastern cultures. For example, it sounds strange to Japanese that the U.S. Navy names its aircraft carriers after former U.S. presidents; in China and Japan, such vessels are usually named after places and weather phenomena. While individuals' names are used in Korea, these are usually the names of historical heroes. The naming of large vessels after recent leaders, such as Ronald Reagan and George H.W. Bush, is beyond the Japanese imagination. When traveling in Western cities, an Eastern traveler will find that there are statues of great leaders everywhere, including in marketplaces, outside the front of the city hall, and even on an ordinary street corner. Statues of leaders will be less common in the traveler's home country. In fact, before modernization, East Asian culture had no tradition of building statues of great leaders in public places to celebrate or memorialize a leader's achievements.

As these anecdotes indicate, it seems that Western culture is likely to honor individuals when something has been achieved; people attribute remarkable achievements to individuals' behaviors and term these behaviors "leadership." In other words, Westerners are more likely to pay attention to individual leaders when explaining the causality of achievements are their Eastern counterparts. These phenomena can be understood as cognitive differences rooted in culture – that is, that the way we see the world is different from culture to culture.

There is theoretical evidence to support the idea that people within different cultures see the world differently. More specifically, East Asians are more likely to explain events with reference to the context. Reviewing various studies ranging from experiments to literature reviews, Nisbett (2003, p. 109) concluded that:

> Asians . . . view the world in holistic terms: They see a great deal of the field, especially the background event; they are skilled in observing relationships between events; they regard the world as complex and highly changeable and its components as interrelated; they see events as moving in cycles between extremes.

People often attribute a behavior to an actor's characteristics and personality, while ignoring other possible causes. Ross (1977) termed this tendency "fundamental attribution error," and Gilbert and Malone (1995) termed it "cognitive bias." Miller (1984) found that sampled American adults were more likely to make reference to general dispositions and less to the specific context as causal explanations than were Indian adults. In other words, Americans are more likely to commit a fundamental attribution error or to partake in cognitive bias than are their Eastern counterparts. This may be the reason why the leader-centric perspective is dominant in the research literature developed in North America.

In contrast with Westerners, Easterners, including East Asians, are thought to regard leadership as constituting dynamic mutual relationships that depend not only on an individual leader's traits and behavior, but also on their followers and the context. In other words, East Asians think that it is necessary to pay attention to followers and context, as well as to the leader, to distinguish whether a certain instance of leadership is effective or not.

Views on how change occurs also differ. Westerners are likely to believe that future change will continue in the same direction, whereas people in Confucian and Buddhist cultures are likely to believe that the world is always changing, as in a moving cycle, and that it is filled with contradictions. This belief, called naive dialecticism (Spencer-Rodgers, Williams, & Peng, 2010), also influences the view of leadership in East Asia. To East Asians, the relationship between a leader and their followers develops over time through many stages, during the course of which the two may clash. East Asians believe such clashes to be beneficial, or even necessary, to building better relationships in the future. In a clash, leaders and followers can understand each other more deeply owing to the expression of their true feelings. East Asians are likely to think that leadership cannot be described as time-sliced dimensions of leaders' behaviors, as the literature suggests.

Self-concept is another key indicator that there are cognitive differences in leadership between East and West. Because of their collectivist culture, East Asians consider the self-concept also to be influenced by relationship with others and by context. Reviewing anthropological and psychological studies, including empirical works, Markus and Kitayama (1991) argued that Asians' self-concept is based on fundamental relatedness to others, or a sense of belongingness to the group, while Americans consider the self to be more individualistic. However, we call attention to the fact that all Asians do not always and automatically define themselves as members of a group or collective who should contribute to the objects of the larger whole. East Asians sometimes consciously consider what their relationships and contexts mean, and decide to identify with it or not, just as do Westerners. However, the tendency to define the self based on relationships with others is generally seen in East Asian cultures: It is natural for people to behave in a manner that accords with their self-images, as defined and influenced by the relationship and context. In other words, as recent leadership studies on the social identity perspective have suggested (see DeRue & Ashford, 2010, for an overview), the effectiveness of leadership depends on the activation of the leader's and followers' self-concepts. While East Asians are likely to believe that the self-concepts of leaders and followers might influence each other and change in a nonlinear manner, a social identity perspective might be a possible way of understanding the East Asian cognitive style, or the way in which East Asians see the world.

To summarize, East Asians view the world more holistically, focus on contextual factors rather than individual characteristics, believe that change is not linear, but cyclical, and consider the self-concept to be influenced by others. Taking these cognitive differences into consideration, this chapter argues that the mainstream leadership literature, which is generated in the West (especially North America), appears excessively leader-centric. In fact, the next section will indicate that the main focus of leadership studies has been the individual leader – that is, that these studies have tried to understand leadership by measuring a leader's behavioral style, under the assumption that it is static and independent of relationship and context.

The Focus of Leadership Studies is Historically on an Individual "Leader"

Relying on comprehensive reviews of leadership studies (Lord et al., 2017; Takahashi et al., 2012), this section shows that the mainstream literature focuses on individual leaders and explains effective leadership as driven by the traits and behaviors of the individual. Because of their inclination toward individual leaders, these approaches could be regarded as leader-centric. The behavioral approach flourished at U.S. universities, including the University of Michigan (for example, Likert, 1961), Ohio State University (for example, Fleishman & Harris, 1962), and elsewhere. The tendency to focus on an individual leader might not be separated from the birthplace of this approach.

The meaningful finding of this early research is the identification of two broad categories, task-oriented, and people- or society-oriented behavior – although different researchers used different terms (for instance, researchers at Ohio University used "initiating structure" and "consideration"). A leader influences the attitudes, decision making, and behavior of their followers, but we could not find evidence in this literature of the idea that leadership is co-created by the leader and followers, or that the influence of the leader's behavior is affected by the followers' cognitions.

Following the behavioral approach, researchers have conducted various studies sharing the leader-centric perspective that focuses on leaders' traits and behaviors. For instance, transformational or charismatic leadership has been receiving attention from many researchers around the world for more than 40 years, and the main focus of this approach is the identification of effective leadership as the leader's individual behavior. This research stream has developed behavioral scales such as the Multifactor Leadership Questionnaire (MLQ) (Bass, 1985) and the Conger and Kanungo Scale (Conger, Kanungo, Menon, & Mathur, 1997), and it has tried to confirm relationships among these leadership behaviors and outcome variables. Most of these approaches – especially the transformational approach – could therefore be regarded as an extension of the behavioral approach, although some remarkable exceptions can be found, including Shamir, House, and Arthur (1993), who proposed a theoretical model in which followers are motivated by charismatic behavior to uncover their own cognitive process.

Of course, not all studies have focused solely on leaders. Studies among those categorized as contingency approaches have used followers' attitudes (Fiedler, 1967) and knowledge (Vroom & Yetton 1973) as situational factors. However, in those models, the follower is only one of the situational factors affecting which leadership style is effective. These researchers were not interested in how leader's behavior would be perceived, what type of relationship would develop between a leader and followers, or how the researchers could depict this relationship. The studies mentioned are both leader-centric approaches, as well as behavioral approaches.

Mainstream literature has paid attention to culture as a contingency factor that influences the effectiveness of leadership. Researchers have tried to clarify which leadership style is favored or effective in certain cultures. Of these studies, the GLOBE project (House et al., 2004) provided the most comprehensive results, using data gathered from 62 countries. Identifying cultures according to nine dimensions and classifying them into ten clusters, the authors investigated participants' implicit leadership theories – that is, their implicit understanding of individual leaders' effective attributes and behaviors. In all, 112 leader attribute and behavior items were rated, and subsequent factor analyses yielded six leadership dimensions, such as charismatic/value-based, team-oriented, and participative, among others. This set of procedures showed that different cultures favored different leadership styles. For example, charismatic/value-based leadership is not as well supported in Confucian Asia as it is in Anglo culture.

Although the GLOBE project certainly clarified that the style favored in Western culture – especially in North America – is not common around the world, this study did not show that people think differently about leadership in the East and the West. Culture influences how the world is seen, as well as which values are favored – that is, it generates cognitive differences. In the leadership context, following Den Hartog and Dickson (2003), we can conclude that culture should influence the cognitive prototypes of leadership and culture-specific enactments of leadership. In non-Western cultures, people might not think of leadership as belonging to an individual's attributes and behaviors. The following sections will show how we can apply East Asian cognitive style to leadership studies and what existing approaches are possible ways of using this cognitive style.

How Should Paternalistic Leadership Be Understood?

We should acknowledge the difference between studying prevalent leadership style in Western society and studying leadership from the non-Western viewpoint. To emphasize this difference and to express how the adoption of a non-leader-centric, more holistic, view can prove a fruitful way of studying leadership, we will note a set of studies on paternalistic leadership, thought to be the prevalent leadership style in non-Western society, including East Asia. These studies have clarified the paternalistic behavioral style and offered varied descriptions of the phenomena (see Pellegrini & Scandura, 2008, for an overview). While many studies (for example, Chen, Eberly, Chiang, Farh, & Chen, 2014; Cheng et al., 2014) have assumed a relationship of social exchange between leader and follower, they have attempted to measure behavioral styles defined as authoritarian, benevolent, and moral, and to confirm a positive relationship between a leader's behavior and followers' performance.

Those studies that assume a social exchange relationship certainly show a remarkably different cognitive point of view from that of the mainstream literature. However, these studies nevertheless focus on the leader's behavior to explore effective leadership. Even if these studies do reach the conclusion that paternalistic leadership can be explained as characterized by authoritarian and benevolent behavior, this would simply replicate the findings of earlier work, which found task-oriented and people-oriented behavior to be effective styles. In this section, we will propose what advantages there might be for paternalistic leadership to be explored from an Eastern cognitive style.

One direction for understanding paternalistic leadership is to view it from a more longitudinal perspective, as East Asians do. East Asians view paternalistic leadership as a process and a relationship that changes over time, while recent paternalistic leadership studies typically define it as "a style that combines strong discipline and authority with fatherly benevolence" (Farh & Cheng, 2000, p. 91). However, a leader's hidden intentions may escape sight at first glance: Followers might hate the toughness of their leader, but, after a long period, they might recognize the leader's true intentions for them and the hidden prudence in the series of actions they have witnessed. Recalling that many stories of fathers and sons involve the stages of conflict, settlement, and forgiveness, Westerners are able to understand that paternalistic leadership cannot be understood through the measurement of time-sliced behavior. We argue that if researchers wish to produce more fruitful conclusions about paternalistic leadership, they should adopt a view oriented toward the long term, which explores the effects of leadership over time.

Another direction would be to pay attention to the self-concept. Although most social exchanges are characterized by mutual unspecified obligation (Blau, 1964), parent–child relationships are exceptional. Parents do not always take care of their children with the expectation of a return. Children do not always accept what their parents say because of their fear of being scolded or the expectation of being rewarded. Rather, their self-concepts as "the child's parents" and "the parents' child" play an important role in the parent–child relationship. Parents express a strict and affective attitude for their child; the child accepts or opposes what its parents say. Viewed in a more longitudinal perspective, the relationship and self-concept of each is likely to be undistinguished. Parents and children develop their self-concepts in a relationship constructed by their mutually influenced behaviors. Like parent-child relationships, East Asians are likely to think that relationships, self-concepts, and behaviors influence each other and can be separated only with difficulty.

In a similar vein, focusing on the leader's and followers' self-concepts will provide more fruitful insights for understanding the paternalistic leadership literature. The exchange of benevolence and loyalty assumed in paternalistic leadership is not based on a psychological contract or an unobligated debt–credit relationship, but is based on long-term mutual trust and the self-concept developed within the relationship. In sum, the exploration of paternalistic leadership simply as the behavior of the leader entails a fundamental limitation. A more longitudinal view based on self-concept, like that adopted from the Eastern cognitive style, would clarify how and why the paternalistic relationship develops. This argument can be applied to paternalistic leadership studies no matter the culture.

Future Avenues for Research

As argued in this chapter, mainstream literature rooted in North America has viewed the concept of leadership as stemming from individuals' traits and behaviors. The basis of this view is in Westerners' atomistic and analytical cognitive style. In contrast to this view, some cognitive psychologists have found that East Asians view the world as more holistic and relational; self-concepts are, in this view, likely to be defined by relatedness to others rather than as personally differentiated characteristics. Leadership studies influenced by the Eastern cognitive style would therefore regard leadership as a relationship between a leader and followers, influenced by their context and self-concepts. As our review of paternalistic leadership has indicated, non-Western approaches are not necessarily studies on leadership styles prevalent in non-Western culture or studies conducted by non-Western researchers; rather, it is the cognitive style, or the way of seeing the world, on which the study is based that is in question.

This chapter indicates that East Asians see "leadership" differently from their Western counterparts. What will be gained by a more holistic, relational, and context-dependent view on leadership? We note two possible approaches to non-Western-centric leadership studies, paving the way for a more holistic, relational, and self-concept-based understanding of leadership. The first would be to advance the existing literature based on the follower- and context-oriented view. As other chapters in this volume suggest, some research originating from the West has shown the importance of followers and context, and has adopted those variables within its models. Although we could not find evidence that shows that these researchers learned from, or are influenced by, East Asians' cognitive style, these approaches will bring further theoretical and practical implications into the leadership studies field. This section will mention these approaches briefly.

The second approach would be to draw some hints from actual non-Western leaders. If non-Western leaders were to be qualitatively investigated, scholars might find that the roles played by followers and contexts are essential to explaining leadership. Many stories told by leaders and followers speak of the processes through which they experience mutual obligation, conflict, and subsequent settlement or deeper mutual trust. In this regard, a study of Konosuke Matsushita, founder of Panasonic, is a remarkable example (Kotter, 1997). Studying non-Western leaders will open researchers' eyes to relationship, context, and events as a moving cycle without intention. However, as a result of space limitations, we will focus here on the first approach alone.

Some Western precursors can be found of the first approach. In this chapter, an emphasis is placed on the advantages offered by the East Asians' way of seeing the world. However, because no possible theoretical approach born in East Asia was found, existing theories incorporating relationship, context, and self-concept into their theoretical framework could be used.

One possible way forward is to focus on the relationship between a leader and followers. One of the first studies to focus on this relationship was that conducted by Hollander (1958). His work introduced the "idiosyncrasy credit" model, which postulated a dynamic interpersonal evaluation relationship, in which followers judged whether they would give their leader latitude beyond the appointed legitimacy of authority. Before enjoying wide latitude, a leader must conform to the group's common expectancies to accumulate idiosyncrasy credit. Hollander's work pointed out that this relationship must develop over a long period, so it is clearly differentiated from conventional mainstream Western leadership research.

Another research line can be found in a series of studies exploring what was termed the vertical dyadic linkage (VDL) approach, which evolved into leader–member exchange (LMX) theory. These works focus on the social relationship between the leader and followers (members), rather than the behavioral style of the individual leader. Among the early works of this group published in the 1970s, Dansereau, Graen, and Haga, (1975) paid attention to how the social-exchange relationship developed over time. Graen and Uhl-Bien (1995), in their historical review of this stream of research, argued that the literature had shown that the leader and individual followers came to feel a mutual obligation and influence through the development of a longitudinal relationship, from stranger, via acquaintance, to maturity. In addition, certain studies postulated that this dyadic relationship expands to the organizational level – that is, a set of dyadic relationships influencing each other. Although Lord and colleagues (2017, p. 442) pointed out that "most LMX research measures exchange quality in a static and absolute manner rather than in dynamic and relative terms," the idea of developing a relationship is certainly attractive. With reference to the argument of this chapter, we can propose that relationships can be examined for circulation from good to bad and bad back to good. The relationship should not be assumed to develop in only one direction.

The social-identity perspective is a current prevalent research stream based on the social-cognitive and relational view. When a follower identifies with their group or leader, they behave in a group- or leader-oriented manner. Whether to identify with the group/leader relates to the follower's self-concept; thus this approach postulates that leadership and its results depend not only on the leader, but also on the followers and context. Although earlier works (for example, Van Knippenberg & Hogg, 2003) maintained that followers who were identified with their groups attached the most group-prototypical member to "leadership," this approach came to argue that followers' self-concepts are dynamic and context-embedded (for example, Oyserman, Elmore, & Smith, 2012).

Compared with the idiosyncratic model and LMX theory, recent social-identity approaches that consider the dynamic and changeable self have advantages for exploring leadership from an East Asian holistic and relational viewpoint. As a literature review by Lord and colleagues (2016) indicated, we can postulate three different levels of identity: individual, relational, and collective. The behavior of individuals is assumed to depend on what level of identity is activated. For instance, followers with individual level identity behave in an individual-oriented manner, and those with collective level identity behave in a group- or organization-oriented manner. A leader and their followers would influence each other's' identity levels. As stated earlier in relation paternalistic leadership, relationships can be understood in light of mutually influenced self-concepts, as well as social exchanges. While it is obvious that researchers are increasingly paying attention to the social-identity approach in Western society, it will also be helpful to study the seemingly prevalent leadership style in non-Western society.

With a view to the historical development of leadership literature, it may be the right time to move away from the leader-centric view toward a more relational, identity-based view. This would mean that Western researchers might incorporate the non-Western cognitive style into leadership studies without intending to do so – that a non-Western cognitive style may already have begun to compete with the conventional Western cognitive style. This will establish a new mainstream that transcends the differences between East and West.

References

Bass, B.M. (1985). *Leadership and performance beyond expectations*. New York: Free Press.
Blau, P.M. (1964). *Exchange and power in social life*. New York: John Wiley & Sons.
Chen, X.P., Eberly, M.B., Chiang, T.J., Farh, J.L., & Cheng, B.S. (2014). Affective trust in Chinese leaders: Linking paternalistic leadership to employee performance. *Journal of Management*, 40(3), 796–819.

Cheng, B.S., Boer, D., Chou, L.F., Huang, M.P., Yoneyama, S., Shim, D., . . . Tsai, C.Y. (2014). Paternalistic leadership in four East Asian societies: Generalizability and cultural differences of the triad model. *Journal of Cross-cultural Psychology*, 45(1), 82–90.

Conger, J.A., Kanungo, R.N., Menon, S.T., & Mathur, P. (1997). Measuring charisma: dimensionality and validity of the Conger–Kanungo scale of charismatic leadership. *Canadian Journal of Administrative Sciences*, 14(3), 290–301.

Dansereau, F., Graen, G., & Haga, W.J. (1975). A vertical dyad linkage approach to leadership within formal organizations: A longitudinal investigation of the role making process. *Organizational Behavior and Human Performance*, 13(1), 46–78.

Den Hartog D.N., & Dickson, M.W. (2003). Leadership and culture. In J. Antonakis, A.T. Cianciolo, & R.J. Sternberg (Eds.), *The nature of leadership* (pp. 249–278). Thousand Oaks, CA: Sage.

DeRue, D.S., & Ashford, S.J. (2010). Who will lead and who will follow? A social process of leadership identity construction in organizations. *Academy of Management Review*, 35(4), 627–647.

Farh, J.L., & Cheng, B.S. (2000). A cultural analysis of paternalistic leadership in Chinese organizations. In J. Li, A. Tusi, & E. Waldon (Eds.), *Management and organizations in the Chinese context* (pp. 84–127). Basingstoke: Palgrave Macmillan.

Fiedler, F.E. (1967). *A theory of leadership effectiveness.* New York: McGraw-Hill.

Fleishman, E.A., & Harris, E.F. (1962). Patterns of leadership behavior related to employee grievances and turnover. *Personnel Psychology*, 15(1), 43–56.

Gilbert, D.T., & Malone, P.S. (1995). The correspondence bias. *Psychological Bulletin*, 117(1), 21–38.

Graen, G.B., & Uhl-Bien, M. (1995). Relationship-based approach to leadership: Development of leader–member exchange (LMX) theory of leadership over 25 years – Applying a multi-level multi-domain perspective. *The Leadership Quarterly*, 6(2), 219–247.

Hollander, E.P. (1958). Conformity, status, and idiosyncrasy credit. *Psychological Review*, 65(2), 117–127.

House, R.J., Hanges, P.J., Javidan, M., Dorfman, P.W., & Gupta, V. (Eds.). (2004). *Culture, leadership, and organizations: The GLOBE study of 62 societies.* Thousand Oaks, CA: Sage.

Kotter, J.P. (1997). *Matsushita leadership: Lessons from the twentieth century's most remarkable entrepreneur.* New York: Free Press.

Likert, R. (1961). *New patterns of management.* New York: McGraw-Hill.

Lord, R.G., Day, D.V., Zaccaro, S.J., Avolio, B.J., & Eagly, A.H. (2017). Leadership in applied psychology: Three waves of theory and research. *Journal of Applied Psychology*, 102(3), 434–451.

Lord, R.G., Gatti, P., & Chui, S.L. (2016). Social-cognitive, relational, and identity-based approaches to leadership. *Organizational Behavior and Human Decision Processes*, 136, 119–134.

Markus, H.R., & Kitayama, S. (1991). Culture and the self: Implications for cognitive style, emotion, and motivation. *Psychological Review*, 98(2), 224–253.

Miller, J.G. (1984). Culture and the development of everyday social explanation. *Journal of Personality and Social Psychology*, 46(5), 961–978.

Nisbett, R.E. (2003). *The geography of thought: Why we think the way we do.* New York: Free Press.

Nisbett, R.E., Peng, K., Choi, I., & Norenzayan, A. (2001). Culture and systems of thought: Holistic versus analytic cognition. *Psychological Review, 108*(2), 291–310.

Oyserman, D., Elmore, K., & Smith, G. (2012). Self, self-concept, and identity. In M.R. Leary & J.P. Tangney (Eds.), *Handbook of self and identity* (pp. 69–104). New York: Guilford Press.

Pellegrini, E.K., & Scandura, T.A. (2008). Paternalistic leadership: A review and agenda for future research. *Journal of Management, 34*(3), 566–593.

Ross, L. (1977). The intuitive psychologist and his shortcomings: Distortions in the attribution process. *Advances in Experimental Social Psychology, 10*, 173–220.

Shamir, B., House, R.J., & Arthur, M.B. (1993). The motivational effects of charismatic leadership: A self-concept based theory. *Organization Science, 4*(4), 577–594.

Spencer-Rodgers, J., Williams, M.J., & Peng, K. (2010). Cultural differences in expectations of change and tolerance for contradiction: A decade of empirical research. *Personality and Social Psychology Review, 14*(3), 296–312.

Takahashi, K., Ishikawa, J., & Kanai, T. (2012). Qualitative and quantitative studies of leadership in multinational settings: Meta-analytic and cross-cultural reviews. *Journal of World Business, 47*(4), 530–538.

Van Knippenberg, D., & Hogg, M.A. (2003). A social identity model of leadership effectiveness in organizations. *Research in Organizational Behavior, 25*, 243–295.

Vroom, V.H., & Yetton, P.W. (1973). *Leadership and decision-making*. Pittsburg, PA: University of Pittsburgh Press.

8
LEADERSHIP AND THE MEDIUM OF TIME

Robert G. Lord

In his book *The Time Paradox*, social psychologist Philip Zimbardo notes that most visitors treat the Crypt of the Capuchin Monks in Rome as a "sight to be seen" rather than as a prompt for serious contemplation (Zimbardo & Boyd, 2008, p. 5). Yet he notes that, at this site, a deeper meaning related to time unites the past, the present, and the future. This meaning was made salient by a pile of bones and the following inscription on the floor: "What you are, they once were. What they are, you will be."

Like the visitors to the crypt, most leadership researchers miss the deeper importance of time. It is not that, eventually, nations, organizations, groups, and individuals all share the same fate; rather, according to Zimbardo and Boyd (2008), it is that *time is the medium in which these entities live*. Time underlies many important processes and behaviors related to leadership, including the development of leadership skills, coordination in groups, sense-making that is grounded in the past, expectations for the future, and attempts to act on the present so as to change the future. Without a full understanding of this temporal medium, essential aspects of leadership may be missed. As Marshal McLuhan noted near the middle of the last century, "The medium is the massage" (McLuhan & Fiore, 1967). By this, he meant that each medium has multiple and often unrecognized effects on how humans perceive and process the information carried by the medium. Similarly, we expect that each facet of time has multiple effects on organizational processes and related leadership activities that often are unrecognized.

Recently, the role of time has gained increasing attention as scholars attempt to better understand organizational processes (Ancona, Goodman, Lawrence, & Tushman, 2001; Bluedorn & Jaussi, 2008; Castillo & Trinh, 2018; Sonnentag, 2012). In the leadership studies field, prior research related to time has focused on a number of specific issues, such as the trajectories followed by developing leaders (Day & Sin, 2011; Miscenko, Guenter, & Day, 2017), visionary leadership (van Knippenberg & Stam, 2014), proactive behaviors (Parker & Wu, 2014), or the effects of temporal leadership on team coordination and performance (Alipour, Mohammed, & Martinez, 2017; Mohammed & Nadkarni, 2011; Santos, Passos, Uitdewilligen, & Nubold, 2016). Yet even these approaches have not adequately acknowledged that time is a deep construct that varies according to: one's past, present, or future orientation (Shipp, Edwards, & Lambert, 2009); the consideration of near versus far futures (Trope & Liberman, 2003; Kivetz & Tyler, 2007); the direction in which actions and potential flow across time (Lord, Dinh, & Hoffman, 2015); the amount of time needed for change to take place (Day & Lord, 1988; Spisak, O'Brien, Nicholson, & van Vugt, 2015); and whether the focus is on perceptions of past leadership or prediction of future outcomes (Agle, Nagarajan, Sonnenfeld, & Srinivasan, 2006; Hansbrough & Lord, 2018). Even though many studies have recognized the importance of time, the methods used by empirical studies do not capture many of its fundamental aspects (Castillo & Trinh, 2018).

As one can see, these multiple aspects of time imply that it is a medium with many facets that are likely to influence leadership processes. This chapter attempts to take a deeper look at several aspects of time, with the hope of helping leadership researchers to see the implications of this medium in which we all live. More specifically, we will focus on five domains or issues that unite the topic of leadership with time. The first is that leaders (and followers) are parts of evolving dynamic systems in which leadership structures are continually changing; hence one must understand the nature of dynamic changes that occur as time progresses, rather than only conceptualize leadership at a given point in time.

The second issue is a need to explicitly acknowledge that the present is but a moment in time that reflects the convergence of happenstance, past choices, and planned or hoped-for outcomes – that is, the present, as we experience it, occurs as a result of a filtering of many potentialities that could have happened, but did not. At one time, these other potentials may have been as likely as the alternatives that actually did occur, but they were eliminated as the future marched toward the present. Consequently, unless we think carefully about time and leadership processes, we can be deceived. For example, attempting to understand and explain leadership in the future by looking backwards at prior events creates an illusion of certainty and sensible evolution towards a specific outcome that occurs because we only see that part of what could have happened which actually did happen. Yet the future holds uncertain potentials and many surprises, and some of these will fundamentally shift leadership and organizational processes in new, unpredictable directions (Taleb, 2007).

A third issue is that people can time travel virtually, and they spend considerable time thinking about and planning for the future. They also act in the present in ways that draw on this virtual vision and thereby change the possibilities that may await them. Similarly, groups and organizations take collective actions based on future-oriented expectations.

Fourth, as one moves from a consideration of the present to the future, the range of possible outcomes expands, but so does uncertainty and associated anxiety. Consequently, a critical aspect of effective leadership is sense-giving, through visions that engage the identities of groups and individuals (Stam, Lord, van Knippenberg, & Wisse, 2014), and which help them to manage the anxiety associated with uncertainty about the future (Hirsh, Mar, & Peterson, 2012; Hogg, 2014). Leaders can help with this issue in a number of ways, as we will see subsequently.

Fifth and finally, much of the effect of leaders on performance is indirect – that is, leader effects often involve a delayed impact on procedures and structures that takes time to develop, such as into ethical or safety cultures. For example, leaders may be critical in creating environments, such as ethical or safety cultures, which support important work goals, yet those cultures do not develop and change quickly. Understanding the impact of leadership thus requires identifying the appropriate time lag, which may be shorter for some kinds of individual level effects and may increase with levels in an organizational or government hierarchy. At higher levels of organizations, these lags may be substantial: The full effects of chief executive officers (CEOs) may take years to materialize (Day & Lord, 1988).

We turn now to elaborating these specific issues, which will be addressed in order, and will be followed by a general discussion of leadership and time.

Issue 1: Leadership, Dynamic Systems, and Time

Researchers are beginning to recognize that leadership is an important part of complex, dynamic systems and that understanding how a complex system functions across time is necessary to understand leadership effects. Uhl-Bien and colleagues (Hazy & Uhl-Bien, 2014; Marion & Uhl-Bien, 2001) popularized the examination of complex, dynamic systems in the leadership field, although the idea of a systems approach has its origins in a number of prior theories, including Katz and Kahn's (1978) influential work on open systems theory, theories that extend outwardly from an organization to its external environment (Hooijberg, 1996), and theories that reach inwardly to include followers (Shamir, 2007; Uhl-Bien, Riggio, Lowe, & Carsten, 2014) and groups (Grand, Braun, Kuljanin, Kozlowski, & Chao, 2016).

The hallmark of complexity is that the interaction of diverse system parts produces complexity (Page, 2007), and this interaction can unfold over time at multiple levels of an organization (Simon, 1962). Furthermore, interactions may be produced by feedback processes in which one part of a system accepts or modifies an input originating from a different system component or the environment. As such processes reverberate across system units, new structures and constructs can emerge without any central direction – perhaps even without leadership. To illustrate how this interaction process works, consider that complexity resulting from a conscious integration of many local processes within the human brain often creates an entirely new construct (Dehaene, 2014) – a process called compilational aggregation (Dinh et al., 2014; Kozlowski & Klein, 2000). This entire process takes only a few hundred milliseconds. At the other end of the time spectrum, the emergence of new organizational strategies or identities from interactions within a complex dynamic system can take a decade (Hazy, 2008). Yet leadership does have an impact on complex systems, albeit often indirectly and through its influence on the rules or processes that guide interactions in the system (Hazy & Uhl-Bien, 2014).

It is helpful to recognize that dynamic systems adapt to changes in the external or internal environments by moving through time to a new point of stability that is called an attractor. This movement, however, can be erratic, as the system changes and explores a new landscape. Thus movement over time is not necessarily linear, and the movement to a new point of stability is often preceded by a period of high variability or high entropy (Stephen, Dixon, & Isenhower, 2009). Leaders should recognize and perhaps contribute to this process, even though we might classically think that a leader's goal would be to decrease variability and the uncertainty that often accompanies it. At times, high variability may be needed to allow a system to find new solutions, but such variability can come from any level or part of a system, and it may involve processes that operate on many timescales. Typically, emergence from lower levels creates this variability and allows systems to explore, and eventually move to, new attractors.

In short, complex adaptive systems comprise a cacophony of processes and time-dependent cycles, each influencing a part of the system, but often within different time frames. These time-dependent processes all aggregate to affect the way in which a system functions. This richness is missed when researchers take a retrospective approach to understanding leadership, such as by asking about leadership traits or styles in surveys, because surveys typically reflect combined perceptions across unspecified periods of time. Even longitudinal research that captures information about specific points in time often also misses much of this picture because the data collection often will pick up only those processes whose cycles have certain time lags (for example, with measurements at 3, 6, and 9 months) and will miss processes with longer or shorter cycles.

To move from leadership theories focused on entities and antecedents to a more process-oriented understanding, a more comprehensive approach to thinking about how to treat time in the study of leadership processes is needed. Table 8.1 identifies multiple domains that have been investigated as dynamic systems in the past, and it indicates a relevant time frame for processes to unfold within each domain. The nature of leadership processes may be quite different across these domains, operating automatically at faster time frames ($<$ 500ms), or more slowly at conscious levels ($\geq$ 500ms).

As Dinh, Lord, and Hoffman (2014) noted, the very fastest processing speeds depend on the type of architecture that is guiding information processing, with embodied architectures operating as fast as 5ms; emotional architectures, as fast as 10ms; connectionist architectures completing processing within 200–500ms; and symbolic architectures requiring at least 500ms. What this means is that because leaders or leadership researchers are often focused on a single level in Table 8.1, they can miss many unrecognized and unintended effects that operate at lower levels, and perhaps also at levels that are much higher and operate much more slowly. For example, when theory is focused at the level of goal emergence, perhaps being concerned with a leader's effects on the regulatory focus of goals (that is, promotion versus prevention goals), then the effects of much faster-acting emotions or the effects of much slower group processes may be missed.

How leadership occurs, then, naturally depends on the domain in which influences are operating and the time frame of interest. When focusing on intrapersonal processes, leaders can prime various automatic processes to create an influence that seems instantaneous. For example, leaders, either intentionally or unintentionally, can infect others via emotional contagion processes that operate in a few hundred milliseconds, and they can prime different levels of follower self-concepts by their choices of pronouns (Lord & Brown, 2004).

TABLE 8.1 Dynamic systems domains and characteristic time frames

Domain	Time frame	Researchers
Emotion	5–50ms	Metcalf & Mischel (1999); Kuppins, Oravecz, & Tuerlinckx (2010)
Information access	10–30ms	Newell (1990)
Person construal	200ms	Freeman & Ambady (2011)
Consciousness	300ms	Dehaene (2014)
Information processing	5ms–10sec	Bassett & Gazzaniga (2011); Dinh, Lord, & Hoffman (2014)
Goal emergence	250–500ms	Carver & Scheier (2002)
Goal orientation	250–500ms	DeShon & Gillespie (2005)
Leadership emergence	Minutes–hours	Acton, Foti, Lord, & Gladfelter (2018); DeRue (2011)
Identity construction	Minutes–weeks	Ashforth & Schinoff (2016); Lord, Gatti, & Chui (2016)
Group process	Minutes–days	Grand et al. (2016)
Personality	Months–years	Read et al. (2010); Mischel & Shoda (1998)
Organizational complexity	Months–decades	Marion (1999); Hazy (2008)
Leadership niches	Centuries–millennia	Spisak et al. (2015)

Interaction processes and time frames are quite different at the dyadic and group levels. For example, social processes such as claiming and granting leadership (DeRue & Ashford, 2010) may provide the building blocks of dyadic interactions. Leadership acts become part of the communication–behavior cycles that Weick (1979) terms "double-interacts," as an individual's leadership actions are accepted or rejected by dyadic partners, which in turn feeds back to the original actor, who might adjust their behavior accordingly. The effects of these double-interacts can aggregate, as various dyadic structures influence each other, allowing group-level structures to emerge (Acton et al., 2018; DeRue, 2011). Typically, such processes can occur within a few hours, or perhaps over a few days, but they could develop over longer periods of time – although research suggests that dyadic relations tend to form quickly in newly acquainted leader–follower dyads (Liden, Wayne, & Stilwell, 1993), and we would expect group structures also to stabilize relatively quickly.

When the company hierarchical level is the focus, leadership processes can take much longer than days or weeks – sometimes even requiring years or decades, as was the case with Intel, for example. As described by Hazy (2008), leadership processes at Intel were less obvious because they involved the catalyzing of adaptive, dynamic processes, rather than the imposition of organizational strategies in a top-down manner. Specifically, management at Intel created an organizational structure that encouraged and rewarded new products and strategies in a bottom-up way. They did this by allocating resources to products based on their success in the marketplace (profit margins), allowing successful products to flourish, while less-successful products gradually declined. Further, because this strategy was outwardly focused, there were many cycles of products and market feedback involved in this decade-long change process, which moved Intel from a memory chip to a microprocessor company. Thus the effects of leadership on system functioning were diffuse and distributed over time. For research purposes, a formal computational system is often used to represent such processes, because they may take years to actually observe (Hazy, 2008; Hazy & Uhl-Bien, 2014).

Leadership processes at each of the levels in Table 8.1 require unique theories and methodologies, yet there is also a fractal quality in that, at each level, one system component influences another, and this influence plays out through actions and feedback that occur over time. But such process may be opaque to leadership researchers, unless they learn the theories and methodologies appropriate to each level. This is a daunting task, and many researchers may merely see leadership as a personal, trait-like quality, rather than as part of more complex, time-dependent, hierarchical systems. Although such trait views can have merit, they may miss the dynamics that produce effective system outcomes. Thus a theory of leadership that fully explains phenomena must move beyond person-centered leadership perceptions to embrace the multilevel, multi-time, process-oriented approach of complexity theory.

One heuristic strategy, which is based on an insight from levels-of-analysis research offered by Yammarino, Dionne, Chun, and Dansereau (2005), is to also examine the time frames and leadership processes immediately above and below one's theoretical focus. As they suggest, this may spur scientific advancement. The reason why this strategy makes sense in a dynamic system is that there are exchanges of information and resources across many hierarchical levels in dynamic systems. In general, higher levels set constraints on lower-level systems, such that group cultures or climates may constrain individual group members' behaviors, while it is the aggregation of lower level inputs that often combines to create a group outcome, such as the individual inputs that occur when a group is problem solving. Similarly, a higher-level structure from companies or divisions may constrain group processes and structures, yet the company level may depend on the combined products from multiple groups. A critical question in understanding leadership at the group level, then, is whether it is the upward or the downward exchange of information and resources that is most critical. This question cannot be answered without examining three levels at once. This can be done without much trouble in terms of statistical analysis (see Schaubroeck et al., 2012, for an example), but, as we have suggested, it is more challenging from a processing perspective, because individual, group, and organizational levels often involve different time spans. Thus, when aggregating from individuals to groups, it is not only aggregation across individuals that is important, but also aggregation across time.

What is needed to advance our understanding is a theoretical system that maps how time, cycles, social and organizational processes, and leadership processes change at various hierarchical levels. Jaques (1989) discussed such differences in terms of "the time span of discretion," which means the amount of time it takes workers at various hierarchical levels to have effects, but this work is rarely cited by contemporary leadership research, even though it has continued to have an impact on system design and consulting. In contrast, most multilevel leadership theory applies statistical approaches to examine how a particular process varies across hierarchical levels. This is a good start, but the recommendation here goes beyond that by recognizing that the nature of dynamic systems functioning varies with hierarchical levels (see Table 8.1). Moreover, these factors may interact with other aspects of the medium of time that were noted at the start of the chapter. One approach to addressing this complexity may be to incorporate time as a focal variable in agent-based modeling (Castillo & Trinh, 2018).

Issue 2: The Present as Happenstance and the Nonlinear Effects of Time

Organizations must prepare for many futures, as is illustrated by the common use of multiple scenarios in the forecasting area – yet expectations regarding the future are often quite wrong (Taleb, 2007), and they may miss fundamental shifts that dramatically change the nature of an organization's future. Stapp (2009) calls these shifts "quantum collapses," to reflect the fact that the wave of future possibilities has been reduced to a single instance (that is, the present) and that other possibilities for the present, which once existed, have been annihilated. Thus change in future states sometimes reflects a normal gradual development, but occasionally organizations are confronted with radically different environments, which reflect quantum collapses that fundamentally change reality. Consequently, the path to the future is much more than a linear evolution along an anticipated scenario; it might better be characterized as a number of quantum jumps among disconnected threads leading to the future, many of which are unknown when viewed from the present.

This juxtaposition of linear and radical change, which may be associated with jumps among disconnected threads into the future, is not new to the leadership field. For example, Tushman and Romanelli (1985) distinguished between convergent and reorientation phases in organizational evolution, and they noted that convergent periods require mainly symbolic leadership that supports current conceptualizations, whereas reorientations require both symbolic activity and substantive activities that initiate and implement changes.

There is substantial merit in that perspective, but, as we noted already, many dramatic changes in dynamic systems may occur without much guidance from leaders, despite the attention that leadership vision has gained in the past few decades. Van Knippenburg and Stam (2014) confront this issue, noting that we know surprisingly little about visionary leadership and the processes by which leaders motivate others to contribute to their vision. Their arguments are extended by recognizing that vision involves followers, as well as leaders (Stam, van Knippenberg, & Wisse, 2010). Both followers and leaders are part of a multilevel dynamic system in which individual and collective identifications are enacted as the visions are pursued (Stam et al., 2014). Occasionally, this bottom-up enactment of a vision can create new identities for organizational members and outcomes that were not envisioned by leaders. In other words, a leader's vision may primarily be a catalyst that changes both people and organizations – sometimes dramatically. Nevertheless, I argue that there is much more beneath the surface of such change, and that we need to revise our notions of time and future potentials to more fully understand the process and the role of leadership.

In an article drawing on concepts from quantum theory, Jessica Dinh, Ernest Hoffman, and I suggested that we miss an important aspect of organizational events if we think of time only as flowing from the present into the future (Lord et al., 2015). We argued that, to develop a fuller understanding, it was necessary to "reverse the arrow of time" and to think of *potentials* as flowing from the future back to the present. Furthermore, it is helpful to represent this process as a probability wave in which many potentials are present in the more distant future, but in which, as it flows towards the present, potentials are winnowed by constraints, until one of the many potentials that had previously existed is translated into the present we experience. The advantage of this perspective is that it recognizes that there were many alternative "presents" that were possible at one time and which were perhaps as likely as the present that actually materialized, but which are now gone and perhaps were never even consciously considered.

To see how this process can operate, consider the case of Amy, a history major from Glasgow, Scotland, who is currently a tour guide in Berlin. Although this potential was always there in Amy's distant future, Amy discovered it only after a friend convinced her to move to Berlin, where she met and married a tour guide, who then convinced Amy that she could do this job as well. In short, constraints associated with friends, location, and partners changed, allowing Amy to explore an alternative career that she had never previously considered, but which she now absolutely loves. And, while this was happening, the alternatives that Amy had considered, such as moving to London, became very unlikely. The many potentials that such a move might have offered were winnowed out and remain largely unknown to Amy.

In short, the present we experience is somewhat arbitrary, reflecting happenstance and enactment, as well as vision, and often it is radically different than what we or our leaders had anticipated it to be. Moreover, this present can be defined at multiple levels, from an organization's profitability, to a group's affective state, to an individual's situated identity, to the activation of a particular thought or feeling. Leadership processes can have influence on the presents that are created at all of these levels, albeit within different time frames.

The critical point in this line of reasoning is that these multiple potentialities exist in the future simultaneously, but in an indefinite or unformed state, until they become entangled with a sufficient number of constraints to create the present that we experience. In other words, the present emerges from the set of many potentials, while other potentials are simultaneously obliterated, and this is a continual process, although we experience only its outcome. For example, there once were many potential versions of this chapter (and this book) that could have been written, but were not. This view of time suggests that the emergence of a radically new and previously unexpected present is not so surprising, because the present emerges from future potentials, rather than evolves from the past. But the constraints that winnow potential futures do evolve from the past to the future; hence the present is the juncture of a two-way flow across time: Constraints move in a present-to-future direction and potentials, in a future-to-present direction. In this way, the medium in which we breathe and act – the present – unites both the past and the future.

Lord and colleagues (2015) theorize that linear change occurs when past constraints are maintained, and nonlinear change occurs when new patterns of constraints occur and become entangled with potentials flowing from the future. For example, limits on human information processing (a constraint) were radically changed by the invention of computers, and this change became scalable with the invention of microprocessors, laptops, and smartphones. Changes in these constraints then allowed many very different potentials to be created by human activity, and the world we experience is far different than it would have been had these information-processing constraints not changed. At an organizational level, changes in CEOs often change many constraints, which allows new potentials to be discovered, such as new organizational strategies, although effects on organizational performance are not always positive (Schepker, Kim, Patel, Thatcher, & Campion, 2017). At the individual level, changes in constraints deriving from occupations, locations, or social relations often allow new possibilities to occur, although our argument is that these possibilities had previously existed in a partially formed manner.

Many people now suggest that an even more profound change will occur when the constraint created by limited human intelligence is exceeded by artificial intelligences – but, from the perspective of the present, one cannot predict exactly how such change will affect society. One may understand the potential evolution of the new constraint associated with artificial intelligence rather than more limited human intelligence, but its effect on the present reflects a quantum collapse caused by the entanglement of many system properties that cannot be understood until the quantum collapse occurs. Consequently, making sense of this change may be possible only in retrospect. As Steve Jobs is reputed to have said, one can connect the dots only looking backwards. This is because the medium of time often hides the emerging future. Nevertheless, people spend considerable time and effort considering the future, and they act in ways that attempt to control the future – an issue addressed in the next section.

Issue 3: Time Travel, Exploration of Time, and Pragmatic Prospecting

The quantum theory view of reality creation described in this chapter fits with the arguments raised by Stapp (2009), a Nobel-prize-winning physicist, who also views the present as a quantum collapse. A view of reality as something that is created also fits with insights from Weick (1995), who argued that sense-making has a strong enactment component, and it also fits with the emphasis of complexity theorists (for example, March, 1991; Page, 2007) on exploration as a way of discovering potentials that remain hidden without action. Exploration extends the notion of vision as involving cognitions related to taking action (for example, Stam et al., 2014) and discovering what might be possible – that is, exploration is a way of moving to a different region of the probability wave that an individual, group, or organization will eventually inhabit.

A critical mode of exploration may be virtual, involving cognitive time travel to the past, and perhaps even to the future. For example, Obodaru (2012) has investigated the role of counterfactual thinking in people's constructions of their professional self-concepts. This is a process in which people look backward, asking what would have happened if they had pursued different alternatives.

In doing so, people transcend reality to construct alternative paths through time that could have been taken in their lives. People also imagine alternative futures, and most people spend far more time thinking about the future than the past (Baumeister & Vohs, 2016). Their concern is what the future will be and what can they do in the present to change the likelihood of future outcomes: a phenomenon that Baumeister, Vohs, and Oettingen (2016) label "pragmatic prospection." Pragmatic prospecting involves translating wishes and ideal selves into actions by considering potential obstacles and how to deal with them (Baumeister et al., 2016; Kivetz & Tyler, 2007). It is through these thoughts and actions that people can alter the probability waves of potentials that flow from the future towards the present.

As theories of prospection describe, people can time travel to the future, anticipating (often incorrectly) what their future will be and how the future relates to the present. As they do this, two very important factors change. First, as people consider the distant future, they move from a system grounded in the concrete reality they experience (the embodied, situated me), to a more abstract representation that is freed from specific details (a hypothetical me). Trope and Liberman (2003) describe this change in terms of temporal construal theory. They maintain that a higher-level construal (that is, a broader, more abstract representation) occurs for the same information when it pertains to the distant future compared to the near future. For example, goals and categories tend to be at the superordinate level (for example, "be kind to others") when describing the distant future, but at the subordinate level in describing near-futures (for example, "help the neighbor whose car is stuck in a snowdrift"). In addition, people's preferences are more dependent on the *desirability* of an outcome in the distant future; in the near future, the *feasibility* of attaining an outcome becomes more important.

Second, building on temporal construal theory, Kivetz and Tyler (2007) demonstrated that thinking of the distant future activates an ideal self that emphasizes principles, values, and one's true self, whereas thinking of the near future activates a pragmatic, action-oriented self, guided by practical concerns and constraints. Moreover, these different selves help to explain the effects of temporal orientation on idealistic versus pragmatic preferences. Thus temporal distance changes the way in which people think and their emphasis on a self that is grounded internally in ideals versus externally in pragmatic concerns.

In short, when people travel to the distant future, their language, mental models, and preferences change. Nevertheless, people can draw conclusions from such time travel, and they can use that information to alter their behavior in the present (Baumeister et al., 2016). Part of the reason for this effect is that futures seem less situationally constrained than the present, so that considering the self in the future may create a sense of empowerment or authenticity that is carried back to the present. Based on this reasoning, leaders may want to communicate a vision involving a distant future that allows others to create a personal meaning in the present. Effective leadership may require that leaders *and followers* jointly construct a personally and collectively meaningful "bridge" between the distant future and the present.

Because pragmatic prospection may be crucial for a leader to manage, it is helpful to take a closer look at this process. Seligman, Railton, Baumeister, and Sripada (2013) emphasize that representations of future possibilities are ubiquitous in humans, but such pragmatic prospection does not involve backward causation from the future to the present; rather, it is based on the evaluative assessments of representations of possible future states. This future–present linkage is why the notion of elaborating potential work selves (Straus, Griffin, & Parker, 2012) can have such a powerful effect on identity development by making them less abstract.

But how do people construct a representation of the future as is done in pragmatic prospection? Schacter and colleagues (2012) argue that people use episodic memory and default networks to support complex goal-oriented simulations. Episodic memory involves the retrieval of vivid specific instances from the past, typically in the hippocampal region of the brain, and default networks are neural networks that situate the self in context and construct autobiographical episodes. Simulating the future using these cognitive structures takes advantage of the constructive nature of the hippocampus, whether remembering the past or imagining the future (Addis & Schacter, 2012). In other words, fragments of past experience are reconfigured with new information to create an imagined scenario that is personally relevant, and people then draw inferences from this scenario to adjust their behavior in the present. For example, one might use memories regarding a particular alley to imagine being mugged if one were to walk through it late at night, and, as a consequence, they might alter their present behavior by finding a safer route. In a similar way, leaders could draw on elements from common experience to create a relevant vision that they tie to action goals in the present. And they may learn about one of their many possible futures as these action goals are implemented in the present.

Gilbert and Wilson (2007) also discuss the neurological basis of pragmatic prospection, pointing to the role of default networks and the frontal regions of the brain in supporting such processes. They also note that people use embodied reactions as a way of evaluating their reactions to simulated future events. Thus pragmatic prospection combines information from architectures (that is, embodied and symbolic) with different time parameters (see Table 8.1). Interestingly, simulations and predictions are often wrong, according to Gilbert and Wilson (2007), because they are decontextualized and cannot incorporate actual enactment processes. Enactment smoothly integrates various time spans and levels of analysis as we behave in context – but this is difficult to do in simulations, which may overemphasize a particular hierarchical level.

There are many ways in which leadership processes could relate to this use of time in pragmatic prospection. For example, leaders could emphasize to followers a prevention regulatory focus and fear, or alternatively a promotion regulatory focus and positive emotions (Kark & van Dijk, 2007). Similarly, they could draw on common experiences from past episodes (Morgeson, 2005) as elements in constructing images of the future. They could use counterfactual thinking (Obodaru, 2012) to consider the consequences of having acted differently in the past as part of a teaching or learning emphasis. Or they could combine such information with knowledge of how important external constraints are likely to change (for example, population growth, climate change, peak oil production) to help to create a virtual vision of the future that incorporates important aspects of context. They could also use elements from the past as a way of building a linkage between abstract, uncertain futures and a more constrained, pragmatic present as a way of creating a meaning with broad appeal.

Yet leaders need to keep in mind that the time medium in which these thoughts and potential actions occur is multidimensional. For example, one can focus on the cognitive aspects of vision and meaning creation, but there is also an analogous emotional dimension that may exist on another timescale, as was illustrated in Table 8.1, and which may emphasize embodied, rather than symbolic, processing. Leaders and followers must also address the uncertainty and associated anxiety that considering the distant future elicits – an issue addressed in the following section.

Issue 4: Uncertainty, Emotions, and the Distant Future

It is important to stress that because a distant future is more abstract, hypothetical, and decontextualized, it is has many fewer constraints than the present. Consequently, the distant future has many more possibilities, but they have lower probabilities of occurring (Lord et al., 2015), and they may exist in a form that cannot be known until they become entangled with constraints in the present. In other words, the distant future has high entropy and is more uncertain than the near future or present. This uncertainty creates tension and anxiety (Hirsch et al., 2012) and negative emotions (Baumeister et al., 2016), which people attempt to limit.

In addition, to fully understand the implications of this process, one needs to understand that emotions operate on a timescale that is much faster than conscious cognitions. Thus typical individual and leadership attempts to directly regulate the emotional processes are unlikely to work, because cognitive and behavioral processes are too slow. Other, more indirect, means may be more effective. For example, Gross and Thompson (2014) indicate that antecedent processes, such as selecting or modifying situations, complement emotion regulation processes that occur after an affective event is experienced, such as redeploying attention or changing one's cognitive interpretation. Focusing attention and changing cognitive interpretations may be particularly useful strategies for leaders to mitigate the anxiety associated with distant visions.

Helping others to cope with the emotional aspects of uncertainty also may empower them to act differently.

There are several ways of limiting uncertainty that can reduce follower's negative emotions. One way is to set goals that narrow attention and elicit information that prepares one for action (Kanfer, Frese, & Johnson, 2017). Another is to rely on schematic understanding and stereotypes, rather than recognizing the nuanced differences among situations and people (Hirsch et al., 2012). But reducing uncertainty in these ways also limits potentials. Another way, which may enhance flexibility, is to emphasize learning and self-improvement motivation, which is associated with future work selves (Anseel, Strauss, & Lievens, 2018).

Time traveling to the distant future also has implications for how one conceptualizes leadership, with the distant future emphasizing higher-level construals comprising the central features of a leadership prototype, rather than peripheral features or more concrete behavior (Anseel et al., 2018). Hogg (2014) also argues that high uncertainty is aversive for most individuals and that, to reduce uncertainty, people are motivated to identify with groups that have clear prototypes. He also suggests that uncertainty provokes a search for meaning. Thus identity processes that pertain to the future may need to be formulated at abstract levels and perhaps then may be linked with actions that may be directly related to the present. For example, the city of Amsterdam has a program to be carbon-neutral by 2050, but, like almost all European cities, it has specific, concrete goals for 2015, 2020, 2030, and 2035 (Michell, 2016).

Leaders who want to expand potential by mental time travel to the distant future must also address the high uncertainty and lack of meaning of this decontextualized time perspective. Paradoxically, motivational factors that promote uncertainty reduction may counteract the expanded horizons that such time travel affords. The responses of leaders to such emotions must fit with the different timescale for emotions compared to that for cognitions or social behavior.

Issue 5: Depth of Time and Leadership

"Depth of time" refers to the shortness or length of a particular time period, and it is relevant to leadership because some aspects of leadership, such as executive leadership, take considerable time to mature (Day & Lord, 1988; Jaques, 1989). Emphasizing a time frame that is too short may underestimate such effects. Delayed or lagged effects occur, in part, because the indirect effects of leaders on system structures, procedures, and culture take time to develop. As one moves down the hierarchy from organization culture to a group culture or climate, one might expect faster effects that involve weeks or months. To illustrate, Dragoni's (2005) work on goal orientation indicates that leaders can influence both a work group climate and an individual psychological climate, and that both of these factors affect an individual's goal orientation state (that is, learn, prove, or avoid) and their resulting motivation and task behaviors. Dragoni (2005) notes that consistency in a leader's achievement-oriented behaviors will produce stronger effects – and often effects that occur more rapidly.

Dragoni's work also notes the advantages of thinking about triplets of hierarchical levels. Specifically, she found that, in understanding the relation of group goal-orientation climate, one needed to distinguish between mechanistic and organic organizations (Dragoni & Kuenzi, 2012). Similarly, Schaubroeck and colleagues (2012) found that ethical leadership created an ethical culture, which in turn affected ethical behavior. Further, the effects of ethical behavior cascaded down three levels in military organizational hierarchies (that is, company, platoon, and squad levels) – a process that takes additional time, but which was essential in understanding the origins of ethical culture.

Table 8.2 indicates many areas in which indirect structures are important and in which leadership processes can have delayed effects. This can happen at many different levels in an organization, and such structures can be a useful way of seeing how levels are linked. In general, higher-level units, which have slower dynamics, can operate as constraints on lower-level system functioning

TABLE 8.2 Domains in which leaders can have both direct and indirect effects on processes

Domain	Direct mechanism	Indirect mechanism	Researchers
Goal orientation	Individual goal-orientation climate	Group goal-orientation climate	Dragoni (2005)
Regulatory focus	Hope versus anxiety	Innovation/efficiency	Kark & van Dijk (2007)
Affect	Emotional contagion	Group emotional contagion	Barsade (2002)
Identity	Priming, justice	Group inclusion/exclusion	Lord & Brown (2004); Lind (2000)
Servant leadership	Group identification	Serving culture	Liden, Wayne, Liao, & Meuser (2014)
Social justice	Interpersonal justice	Procedural justice climate	Cho & Dansereau (2010)
Ethical behavior	Modeling/social learning theory	Ethical climate	Mayer, Kuenzi, Greenbaum, Bardes, & Salvador (2009); Schaubroeck et al. (2012)
Innovation	Opening/closing (explore/exploitation)	Exploration/exploitation climate	Rosing, Frese, & Bausch (2011)
Vision	Individual possible self	Group possible self	Stam et al. (2014)

(Lord et al., 2015), and their effects may cascade down hierarchies from organizational, to group, to individual, to intra-individual processes. The time frame for processes at these levels varies substantially (see Table 8.1), suggesting that both the time signature of leadership effects and the nature of leadership processes will vary with hierarchical level. For example, emotional contagion may happen automatically and in only a few seconds as one individual mimics a leader's facial expression and begins to feel a similar emotion – and if this process then spreads through group members, a momentary emotional climate may occur. However, it may take many repetitions of this process to create an enduring group affective climate (Barsade, 2002).

Time is an important factor in understanding such multilevel effects. Leadership research or practice that deals only with a narrow slice of time may capture the dynamics at individual levels, but will likely miss the dynamics at other levels, which may be more enduring and have greater overall effects. Again, we see the advantages of a multilevel time perspective that parallels the multilevel thinking associated with statistical analysis. Equally important, in longitudinal studies, one needs a clear theoretical basis for specifying appropriate time lags (Castillo & Trinh, 2018), but that may be a multilevel issue. Linking the sources specified in Tables 8.1 and 8.2 can offer insights regarding appropriate lags. To illustrate, although the processes producing subordinate behavior may be rapid, such as goal orientation (DeShon & Gillespie, 2005), the way in which leadership influences these processes may be very slow and indirect, involving both individual- and group-level effects that develop over time, such as goal-orientation climate (Dragoni, 2005). Thus theoretical precision is needed in specifying appropriate time lags.

Implications: Temporal Medium for Research and Practice

Research cited in both Tables 8.1 and 8.2 indicates that there are many time frames within which leadership effects may occur. This has both practical and methodological implications for leadership. In both application and theory development, we need to specify the relevant time frame within which effects occur. However, the medium of time involves more than an issue of how fast processes are. As noted at the outset of this chapter, it also involves orientations toward the past, present, or future; near versus distant futures (or pasts); the direction in which events flow, which may be the opposite for behaviors and potentials; depth of time associated with particular leadership processes; and whether one's concern is with understanding the past or predicting the future. These concerns were addressed as separate issues in this chapter for expositional purposes, but the medium of time that leadership and other individual, social, or organizational processes inhabit involves the simultaneous effects of all of these temporal features. Moreover, these aspects of time may interact and may need to be understood as a whole – that is, there may be specific types of pattern in the temporal medium that have very different implications for understanding leadership (or other social-organizational processes). One future challenge for the leadership field is to chart some of these patterns. Table 8.1 may be helpful, but it involves only one aspect of the temporal medium (speed).

In the absence of such a typology for leadership and a temporal medium, what advice might be offered to a leadership theorist or practitioner? One possibility is to evaluate any theory, or proposed practice or intervention, in terms of a series of questions tied to the five issues addressed in this chapter.

1. Thinking in terms of dynamic systems, what is the key level of concern, how quickly do processes at this level work, what is the nature of task and social feedback, and what is likely to be going on at adjacent system levels?
2. Thinking in terms of happenstance, which is more important: evolving trajectories projecting into the future, or the potentials for unanticipated surprises? In other words, should the focus be on exploiting the potentials that can be understood from one's present perspective, or should it be on exploring and creating new potentials? Turning this issue towards the leadership field, should our concern be with understanding and applying known leadership processes (for example, styles of leadership) based on looking backwards, or should it be with discovering and encouraging new types of leadership?
3. Turning to the issue of prospecting, what types of prospecting are guiding individuals as they imagine the future and consider its implications for the present? Is prospecting guided by the right regulatory focus, by the right construal of past events, or by the projecting of constraints into the future? How might ambidextrous leadership that encourages both exploration and exploitation (Rosing et al., 2011) or complexity theory be applied to this issue?
4. What is the human reaction to considering distant futures, and how does it limit potential? How can leaders help to manage the emotions associated with a highly uncertain future and the cognitive implications of abstractly representing the future? How can leaders facilitate the development of meaning that links the future to the present?
5. At what temporal depth are leadership processes operating? Are there multiple depths that need to be considered? How can integration across many temporal depths occur, and what are the leadership implications of this process?

Although each question is challenging and interesting, a rich view of the temporal medium we inhabit suggests that leaders and leadership theory needs to deal with multiple aspects of time, often simultaneously. One way of doing this may be to use agent-based modeling techniques (Castillo & Trinh, 2018) to simulate complex systems and to inform experimental or longitudinal studies. Addressing two additional questions may also be helpful.

6. Is there value in expanding a theoretical focus to consider the levels adjacent to the focal level? Related to this, to what extent can representations and processes that are meaningful at one level generalize to another level?
7. Is our concern mainly with understanding the past or predicting the future, and how far backward or forward should we go?

As leadership researchers, we can also ask how well our field has managed the medium of time in the theories we construct or the methods we use. Do we have an implicit continuum from the past to the future that justifies retrospectively oriented research on the grounds that it will predict future leadership processes? And is such a continuum reasonable if we take a more comprehensive view of the medium of time? Research on charismatic leadership by Agle and colleagues (2006) suggests that it is not. They conducted a survey of top-management teams' perceptions of their CEO's charisma, and they correlated this combined rating with both past and future performance. Reflecting retrospective sense-making based on known performance, there were strong relations between many indicators of prior organizational performance and perceptions of a CEO's charisma, but the relations between charisma and future performance indices were very small and not significant. The implication of this finding may be that leadership is most meaningful when looking backward and when socially constructing explanations for outcomes (Meindl, 1995).

Developing a theory of leadership that has causal implications for the future is more challenging. It may require an emphasis on predictive, rather than retrospective, research designs, and it may require that we understand enactment processes that occur at multiple hierarchical levels and with multiple groups of individuals. It may also require that we pay as much attention to how leaders manage constraints as we do to how they interact with others (typically, followers). Finally, for such approaches to be effective, we need to more thoroughly ground leadership research in the medium of time.

References

Acton, B.P., Foti, R.J., Lord, R.G., & Gladfelter, J.A. (2018). *Putting emergence back in leadership emergence: A dynamic, multilevel, process-oriented framework.* ~*The Leadership Quarterly* (in press).

Addis, D.R., & Schacter, D.L. (2012). The hippocampus and imagining the future: Where do we stand? *Frontiers in Human Neuroscience, 5*(4), 1–14.

Agle, B.R., Nagarajan, N.J., Sonnenfeld, J.A., & Srinivasan, D. (2006). Does CEO charisma matter? An empirical analysis of the relationships among organizational performance, environmental uncertainty, and top management team perceptions of CEO charisma. *Academy of Management Journal, 49*(1), 161–174.

Alipour, K.K., Mohammed, S., & Martinez, P.N. (2017). Incorporating temporality into implicit leadership and followership theories: Exploring inconsistencies between time-based expectations and actual behaviors. *The Leadership Quarterly, 28*(2), 300–316.

Ancona, D.G., Goodman, P.S., Lawrence, B.S., & Tushman, M.L. (2001). Time: A new research lens. *Academy of Management Review, 26*(4), 645–663.

Anseel, F., Strauss, K., & Lievens, F. (2018). How future work selves guide feedback seeking and feedback responding at work. In D.L. Ferris, R.E. Johnson, & C. Sedikides (Eds.), *The self at work* (pp. 295–318). New York: Routledge

Ashforth, B.E., & Schinoff, B.S. (2016). Identity under construction: How individuals come to define themselves in organizations. *Annual Review of Organizational Psychology and Organizational Behavior, 3*, 111–137.

Barsade, S.G. (2002). The ripple effect: Emotional contagion and its influence on group behavior. *Administrative Science Quarterly, 47*(4), 644–675.

Bassett, D.S., & Gazzaniga, M.S. (2011). Understanding complexity in the human brain. *Trends in Cognitive Science, 15*(5), 200–209.

Baumeister, R.F., & Vohs, K.D. (2016). Introduction to the special issue: The science of prospection. *Review of General Psychology, 20*(1), 1–2.

Baumeister, R.F., Vohs, K.D., & Oettingen, G. (2016). Pragmatic prospection: How and why people think about the future. *Review of General Psychology, 20*(1), 3–16.

Bluedorn, A.C., & Jaussi, K.S. (2008). Leaders, followers, and time. *The Leadership Quarterly, 19*(6), 654–668.

Carver, C.S., & Scheier, M.F. (2002). Control processes and self-organization as complementary principles underlying behavior. *Personality and Social Psychology Review, 6*(4), 304–3015.

Castillo, E.A., & Trinh, M.P. (2018). In search of missing time: A review of the study of time in leadership research. *The Leadership Quarterly, 29*(1), 165–178.

Cho, J., & Dansereau, F. (2010). Are transformational leaders fair? A multi-level study of transformational leadership, justice perceptions, and organizational citizenship behaviors. *The Leadership Quarterly, 21*(3), 409–421.

Day, D.V., & Lord, R.G. (1988). Executive leadership and organizational performance: A critical review of current data and theory. *Journal of Management, 14*(3), 111–122.

Day, D.V., & Sin, H.-P. (2011). Longitudinal tests of an integrative model of leader development: Charting and understanding developmental trajectories. *The Leadership Quarterly, 22*(3), 545–560.

Dehaene, S. (2014). *Consciousness and the brain: Deciphering how the brain codes our thoughts.* New York: Penguin.

DeRue, D.S. (2011). Adaptive leadership theory: Leading and following as a complex adaptive process. *Research in Organizational Behavior, 31*, 125–150.

DeRue, D.S., & Ashford, S.J. (2010). Who will lead and who will follow? A social process of leadership identity construction in organizations. *Academy of Management Review, 35*(4), 627–647.

DeShon, R.P., & Gillespie, J.Z. (2005). A motivated action theory account of goal orientation. *Journal of Applied Psychology, 90*(6), 1096–1027.

Dinh, J.E., Lord, R.G., & Hoffman, E. (2014). Leadership perception and information processing: Influences of symbolic, connectionist, emotion, and embodied architectures. In D.V. Day (Ed.), *The Oxford handbook of leadership and organizations* (pp. 305–330). New York: Oxford University Press.

Dinh, J.E., Lord, R.G., Gardner, W., Meuser, J.D., Liden, R., & Hu, J. (2014). Leadership theory and research in the new millennium: Current theoretical trends and changing perspectives. *The Leadership Quarterly, 25*(1), 36–62.

Dragoni, L. (2005). Understanding the emergence of state goal orientation in organizational work groups: The role of leadership and multilevel climate perceptions. *Journal of Applied Psychology, 90*(6), 1084–1095.

Dragoni, L., & Kuenzi, M. (2012). Better understanding work unit goal orientation: Its emergence and impact under different types of work unit structure. *Journal of Applied Psychology, 97*(5), 1032–1048.

Freeman, J.B., & Ambady, N. (2011). A dynamic interactive theory of person construal. *Psychological Review, 118*(2), 247–279.

Gilbert, D.T., & Wilson, T.D. (2007). Prospection: Experiencing the future. *Science, 317*(5843), 1351–1354.

Grand, J.A., Braun, M.T., Kuljanin, G., Kozlowski, S.W.J., & Chao, G.T. (2016). The dynamics of team cognition: A process-oriented theory of knowledge emergence in teams. *Journal of Applied Psychology, 101*(10), 1353–1385.

Gross, J.J., & Thompson, R.A. (2014). Emotional regulation: Conceptual and empirical foundations. In J.J. Gross (Ed.). *Handbook of emotional regulation* (pp. 3–20). New York: Guilford Press.

Hansbrough, T.K., & Lord, R.G. (2018). *The double dissociation between leadership perceptions and leadership performance* [Working paper].

Hazy, J.K. (2008). Leadership or luck? The system dynamics of Intel's shift to microprocessors in the 1970s and 1980s. In M. Uhl-Bien & R. Marion (Eds.), *Complexity and leadership, Part I: Conceptual foundations* (pp. 379–415). Charlotte, NC: Information Age.

Hazy, J.K. & Uhl-Bien, M. (2014). Changing the rules: The implications of complexity science for leadership research and practice. In D.V. Day (Ed.), *The Oxford handbook of leadership and organizations* (pp. 709–732). Oxford: Oxford University Press.

Hirsh, J.B., Mar, R.A., & Peterson, J.B. (2012). Psychological entropy: A framework for understanding uncertainty-related anxiety. *Psychological Review, 119*(2), 304–320.

Hogg, M.A. (2014). From uncertainty to extremism: Social categorization and identity processes. *Current Directions in Psychological Science, 23*(5), 338–342.

Hooijberg, R. (1996). A multidirectional approach towards leadership: An extension of the concept of behavioral complexity. *Human Relations, 49*(7), 917–946.

Jaques, E. (1989). *Requisite organization: The CEO's guide to creative structure and leadership*. Arlington, VA: Carson Hall & Co.

Kanfer, R., Frese, M., & Johnson, R.E. (2017). Motivation related to work: A century of progress. *Journal of Applied Psychology, 102*(3), 338–355.

Kark, R., & van Dijk, D. (2007). Motivation to lead, motivation to follow: The role of the self-regulatory focus in leadership processes. *Academy of Management Review, 32*(2), 500–528.

Katz, D., & Kahn, R.L. (1978). *The social psychology of organizations* (2nd ed.) New York: John Wiley & Sons.

Kivetz, Y., & Tyler, T.R. (2007). Tomorrow I'll be me: The effects of time perspectives on the activation of idealistic versus pragmatic selves. *Organizational Behavior and Human Decision Processes, 102*(2), 193–211.

Kozlowski, S.W.J., & Klein, K.J. (2000). A multilevel approach to theory and research in organizations: Contextual, temporal, and emergent processes. In K.J. Klein & S.W.J. Kozlowski (Eds.), *Multilevel theory, research, and methods in organizations: Foundations, extensions, and new directions* (pp. 3–90). San Francisco, CA: Jossey-Bass.

Kuppins, P., Oravecz, Z., & Tuerlinckx, F. (2010). Feelings change: Accounting for individual differences in the temporal dynamics of affect. *Journal of Personality and Social Psychology, 99*(6), 1042–1060.

Liden, R.C., Wayne, S.J., & Stilwell, D. (1993). A longitudinal study on the early development of leader-member exchanges. *Journal of Applied Psychology, 78*(4), 662–674.

Liden, R.C., Wayne, S.J., Liao, C., & Meuser, J.D. (2014). Servant leadership and serving culture: Influence on individual and unit performance. *Academy of Management Journal, 57*(5), 1434–1452.

Lind, E.A. (2000). Fairness heuristic theory: Justice judgments as pivotal cognitions in organizational relations. In J. Greenberg & R. Cropanzano (Eds.), *Advances in organizational justice* (pp. 56–88). San Francisco, CA: New Lexington Press.

Lord, R.G., & Brown, D.J. (2004). *Leadership processes and follower self-identity*. Mahwah, NJ: Lawrence Erlbaum.

Lord, R.G., Dinh, J.E., & Hoffman, E.L. (2015). A quantum approach to time and organizational change. *Academy of Management Review, 40*(2), 263–290.

Lord, R.G., Gatti, P., & Chui, S.L.M. (2016) Social-cognitive, relational, and identity-based approaches to leadership. *Organizational Behavior and Human Decision Processes, 136*, 119–134.

March, J.G. (1991). Exploration and exploitation in organizational learning. *Organizational Science, 2*(1), 71–87.

Marion, R. (1999). *The edge of organization: Chaos and complexity theories of formal social systems*. Thousand Oaks, CA: Sage.

Marion, R., & Uhl-Bien, M. (2001). Leadership in complex organizations. *The Leadership Quarterly, 12*(4), 389–418.

Mayer, D.M., Kuenzi, M., Greenbaum, R., Bardes, M., & Salvador, R. (2009). How low does ethical leadership flow? Test of a trickle-down model. *Organizational Behavior and Human Decision Processes, 108*(1), 1–13.

McLuhan, M., & Fiore, Q. (1967). *The medium is the massage: An inventory of effects*. Harmondsworth: Penguin.

Meindl, J.R. (1995). The romance of leadership as a follower-centric theory: A social constructionist approach. *The Leadership Quarterly, 6*(3), 329–341.

Metcalf, J., & Mischel, W. (1999). A hot/cool-system analysis of delay of gratification: Dynamics of willpower. *Psychological Review, 106*(1), 3–19.

Michell, N. (2016, September 6). *How Amsterdam is building a zero-emission city*. Retrieved from https://cities-today.com/how-amsterdam-is-building-a-zero-emissions-city/

Miscenko, D., Guenter, H., & Day, D.V. (2017). Am I a leader? Examining leader identity development over time. *The Leadership Quarterly, 28*(5), 605–620.

Mischel, W., & Shoda, Y. (1998). Reconciling processing dynamics and personality dispositions. *Annual Review of Psychology, 49*, 229–258.

Mohammed, S., & Nadkarni, S. (2011). Temporal diversity and team performance: The moderating role of team temporal leadership. *Academy of Management Journal, 54*(3), 489–508.

Morgeson, F.P. (2005). The external leadership of self-managing teams: Intervening in the context of novel and disruptive events. *Journal of Applied Psychology, 90*(3), 497–508.

Newell, A. (1990). *Unified theories of cognition*. Cambridge, MA: Harvard University Press.

Obodaru, O. (2012). The self not taken: How alternative selves develop and how they influence our professional lives. *Academy of Management Review, 37*(1), 34–57.

Page, S.W. (2007). *The difference: How the power of diversity creates better groups, firms, schools, and societies*. Princeton, NJ: Princeton University Press.

Parker, S.K., & Wu, C-H. (2014). Leading for proactivity: How leaders cultivate staff who make things happen. In D.V. Day (Ed.), T*he Oxford handbook of leadership and organizations* (pp. 380–403). Oxford: Oxford University Press.

Read, S.J., Monroe, B.M., Brownstein, A.L., Yang, Y., Chopra, G., & Miller, L.C. (2010). A neural network model of the structure and dynamics of human personality. *Psychological Review, 117*(1), 61–92.

Rosing, K., Frese, M., & Bausch, A. (2011). Explaining the heterogeneity of the leadership–innovation relationship: Ambidextrous leadership. *The Leadership Quarterly, 22*(5), 956–974.

Santos, C.M., Passos, A.M., Uitdewilligen, S., & Nubold, A. (2016). Shared temporal cognitions as substitute for temporal leadership: An analysis of their effects on temporal conflict and team performance. *The Leadership Quarterly, 27*(4), 574–587.

Schacter, D.L., Addis, D.R., Hassabis, D., Martin, V.C. Spreng, R.N., & Szpunar, K.K. (2012). The future of memory: Remembering, imagining, and the brain. *Neuron, 76*(4), 677–694.

Schaubroeck, J.M., Hannah, S.T., Avolio, B.J., Kozlowski, S.W.J., Lord, R.G., Trevino, L.K., Dimotakis, N., & Peng, A.C. (2012). Embedding ethical leadership within and across organizational levels. *Academy of Management Journal, 55*(5), 1053–1078.

Schepker, D.J., Kim, Y., Patel, P.C., Thatcher, S.M.B., & Campion, M.C. (2017). CEO succession, strategic change, and post-succession performance: A meta-analysis. *The Leadership Quarterly, 28*(6), 701–720.

Seligman, M.E.P., Railton, P., Baumeister, R.F., & Sripada, C. (2013). Navigating into the future or driven by the past. *Perspectives on Psychological Science, 8*(2), 119–141.

Shamir, B. (2007). From passive recipients to active co-producers: Follower's roles in the leadership process. In B. Shamir, R. Pillai, M. Bligh, & M. Uhl-Bien (Eds.), *Follower-centered perspectives on leadership: A tribute to the memory of James R. Meindl* (pp. ix–xxxix). Charlotte, NC: Information Age.

Shipp, A.J., Edwards, J.R., & Lambert, L.S. (2009). Conceptualization and measurement of temporal focus: The subjective experience of the past, present, and future. *Organizational Behavior and Human Decision Processes, 110*(1), 1–22.

Simon, H.A. (1962). The architecture of complexity. *Proceedings of the American Philosophical Society, 106*(6), 467–482.

Sonnentag, S. (2012). Time in organizational research: Catching up on a long neglected topic in order to improve theory. *Organizational Psychology Review, 2*(4), 361–368.

Spisak, B.R., O'Brien, M.J., Nicholson, N., & van Vugt, M. (2015). Niche construction and the evolution of leadership. *Academy of Management Review, 40*(2), 291–306.

Stam, D., Lord, R.G., van Knippenberg, D., & Wisse, B. (2014). An image of who we might become: Vision communication, possible selves, and vision pursuit. *Organization Science, 25*(4), 1172–1194.

Stam, D., van Knippenberg, D., & Wisse, B. (2010). Focusing on followers: The role of regulatory focus and possible selves in explaining the effectiveness of vision statements. *The Leadership Quarterly, 21*(3), 457–468.

Stapp, H.P. (2009). *Mind, matter and quantum mechanics*. Berlin: Springer.

Stephen, D.G., Dixon, J.A., & Isenhower, R.W. (2009). Dynamics of representational change: Entropy, action, and cognition. *Journal of Experimental Psychology: Human Perception and Performance, 35*(6), 1811–1832.

Strauss, K., Griffin, M.A., & Parker, S.K. (2012). Future work selves: How salient hoped-for identities motivate proactive career behaviors. *Journal of Applied Psychology*, 97(3), 580–598.

Taleb, N.N. (2010). *The black swan*. London: Penguin.

Trope, Y., & Liberman, N. (2003). Temporal construal. *Psychological Review*, 110(3), 403–421.

Tushman, M.L., & Romanelli, E. (1985). Organizational evolution: A metamorphosis model of convergence and reorientation. *Research in Organizational Behavior*, 7, 171–222.

Uhl-Bien, M., Riggio, R.E., Lowe, K.B., & Carsten, M.K. (2014). Followership theory: A review and research agenda. *The Leadership Quarterly*, 25(1), 83–104.

Van Knippenberg, D., & Stam, D. (2014). Visionary leadership. In D.V. Day (Ed.), *The Oxford handbook of leadership and organizations* (pp. 241–259). Oxford: Oxford University Press.

Weick, K.E. (1979 [1969]). Enactment and organizing. In *The social psychology of organizing* (pp. 147–166). New York: Random House.

Weick, K.E. (1995). *Sensemaking in organizations*. Thousand Oaks, CA: Sage.

Yammarino, F.J., Dionne, S.D., Chun, J.U., & Dansereau, F. (2005). Leadership and levels of analysis: A state-of-the-science review. *The Leadership Quarterly*, 16(6), 879–919.

Zimbardo, P., & Boyd, J. (2008). *The time paradox: The new psychology of time*. New York: Free Press.

9

LEADERS ARE COMPLEX

Expanding Our Understanding of Leader Identity

Stefanie P. Shaughnessy and Meredith R. Coats

Decades of research have focused on how individuals develop into leaders. What began as a question of whether leaders are born versus made has evolved into an interest in how stable traits (what an individual is "born" with) interact with training and experiences (how an individual is "made"). Questions, though, have largely remained focused on how an individual develops *into* a leader and whether they initially identify as a leader. These are certainly important questions, and great strides have been made in answering them. An unintended consequence of placing such emphasis on these questions, however, is that how leaders *continue* to develop is often overlooked. Leaders are not static individuals who stop developing once they become leaders; they are much more complex. Experiences that happen early after an individual adopts a leader identity, either formally or informally, can alter their sense of self and approach to leading. It is therefore necessary to expand our understanding of leader development to encompass how leader identities continue to morph and change over time.

An individual's identity provides important information. Through identities, individuals remember who they were previously, know who they are currently, and decide who they want to be in the future. Identities provide the lens through which experiences are understood and internalized. Research suggests that how individuals view themselves is a narrative process in which leaders rely on past experiences to aid their sense-making efforts (Gergen, 1999; Hall, 2004; Kegan, 1982) – that is, individuals construct a coherent narrative of who they are by tying recent and past experiences together to create a unified story of self within a role, such as a leader role. Importantly, this sense-making process implies that identity may be subject to change as more experiences and information are drawn upon.

Leader Identity

Identities are salient features of individuals that shape goals, behaviors, and cognitions. Scholars suggest that individuals hold multiple identities that vary as a function of context and time (for example, Ashforth & Johnson, 2001; Gergen, 1999), and which impact behaviors in myriad settings (for example, Burke & Reitzes, 1981; van Knippenberg, van Knippenberg, De Cremer, & Hogg, 2004). Within an organizational context, researchers have focused on the claiming and granting of identities (Carroll & Simpson, 2012; DeRue & Ashford, 2010), as well as how specific identities, such as leader identities, develop and form (Chan & Drasgow, 2001; Day, Fleenor, Atwater, Sturm, & McKee, 2014; Lord & Hall, 2005). Often, the claiming and granting process occurs around relational roles, such as who is a follower and who is a leader, because identities are in part related to the way in which individuals perceive their role in relation to the roles of others within their environment (Hall, 2004). Whether an individual identifies as a leader, and how they identify as a leader, provides an important explanatory mechanism for workplace behaviors and outcomes.

Identity extends beyond the self, to influence how individuals perceive and relate to others (Baumeister, 1999; Gergen, 1999). Leader identities provide the lens through which an individual views a subordinate's behavior and ultimately responds to that subordinate. Importantly, each identity may result in different strategies and tactics of influence, as identities are used to define relationships (Ashton-James, Baaren, Chartrand, Decety, & Karremans, 2007). Through disentangling and studying the complexities of leader identities, we can begin to understand and predict the linkages between the identities and behaviors of leaders in the workplace.

Leadership is commonly defined as a process between leaders and their followers (Day & Harrison, 2007). The nature of this process suggests that there is a continual feedback loop between how a leader identifies and how they interact with their subordinates. Continuous interactions act as a source of feedback that not only leads to constant refinement, but constantly changes the nature and interplay of a leader and their subordinates.

Ultimately, leader identity underlies essential workplace interactions, which impacts performance and relationships. Identities are relational constructs (Gergen, 1999) that provide a motivating force for role performance (Burke & Reitzes, 1981). Performance and relationships between leaders and followers are arguably the most important outcomes in the leadership literature. Expanding leader identity theory such that it can better predict and explain key outcomes is thus a critical step to advancing the study of leadership. In particular, there is a need to understand the complexity of leader identity, including how it evolves once developed.

The leadership literature has focused, to this point, largely on the question of *whether* an individual identifies as a leader (Chan & Drasgow, 2001; Lord &

Hall, 2005). Those who do identify as leaders and have strong leader identities tend to have higher motivation to lead (Guillén, Mayo, & Korotov, 2015), to be more likely to see themselves as capable and effective leaders (Day & Sin, 2011), to be more self-aware (Emery, Daniloski, & Hamby, 2011), and to be more likely to change ineffective behaviors (Day, Harrison, & Halpin, 2009). Research largely demonstrates the positive outcomes in work and relational processes that result from an individual identifying as a leader, improving individual leadership processes. Our understanding of these relationships, however, is driven by static conceptualizations of leader identity that are assumed to generalize throughout an individual's career. To improve understanding of the relationships, they must be examined from a perspective that allows development and organizationally relevant outcomes to vary dynamically over time.

Studying identity in general, and specifically leader identity, is essential for understanding *how* and *why* leaders behave as they do rather than simply *if* they do. Identities drive thought, affect, motivation, and action (Day & Harrison, 2007; Gardner & Avolio, 1998; Shamir, House, & Arthur, 1993). They also change over time, as will be elaborated next. Expanding theory and application of leader identity to be as complex and dynamic as leaders themselves will therefore lead to stronger ties between leader identity and key outcomes of identities.

Developing a Leader Identity

A critical first step in understanding how an individual identifies as a leader is understanding the development of identity. Leader identity is an individual's self-perception that encompasses their needs, motivations, abilities, values, interests, and other aspects inherent to how they define themselves as a leader (Hall, 2004). Over time, and throughout varied developmental leader experiences, an individual's leader identity changes and becomes more refined and complex (Day & Lance, 2004). There are many factors that influence leader identity; experiences early in life and those throughout different career stages change and refine how an individual perceives themselves.

Identifying as a leader encourages an individual to seek further developmental opportunities, with successful opportunities solidly establishing an identity of "leader." Internalizing the identity of leader can lead to a spiraling effect, facilitating the individual's leader development (Burke & Reitzes, 1981; Lord & Hall, 2005). Work experiences prove critical to the continued development and refinement of a leader identity, yet are not the only way in which leader identity develops. While leaders are often thought of as being in supervisory positions in organizations, development of leader identities often begins before individuals enter the workforce. Childhood and early developmental experiences begin to shape these identities well before the start of an individual's career. Leadership experiences across the lifespan, from early childhood through late adulthood, contribute to the ever-changing nature of identity.

Childhood and Adolescent Experiences

Developing as a leader is an unfolding process that begins early in childhood for some and extends throughout an individuals' career and lifespan (Day et al., 2009). Intrinsic motivation to lead can begin early in life (Gottfried et al., 2011). Individuals begin to form identities and thoughts about leadership by observing role models, such as parents, and incorporating family history and values into their sense of self (Adler, 2011; Popper, Mayseless, & Castelnovo, 2000). In adolescence, peers and organized social systems impact the development of identity (Damon & Hart, 1982; Koepke & Denissen, 2012; Siegler & Alibali, 2005), and participation in sports can foster leader development (Chelladurai, 2011). For example, being the captain of a football team or the president of a school club appears to be formative in how many individuals identify as a leader (Plemmons, Srinivasan, & Plourde, 2016). These early childhood and adolescent experiences with parents and other role models, as well as experiences in organized sports and clubs, lay the foundation for implicit understandings of what it means to be a leader.

In a recent study of leader identities in the U.S. Army, experiences encountered while growing up were critical in initially shaping participants into leaders (Plemmons et al., 2016). Family members served as role models who guided behavior, setting the stage for the leader the individual would become. Parental models were often mentioned in relation to how participants believed they became a leader. Participants noted that, as they reflected back on parental models, they extracted the overarching messages and incorporated them into their leader roles and, subsequently, leader identities.

Involvement with sports teams as a child was another experience that promoted development of a leader identity. Participating in sports provided an opportunity to develop and practice leadership skills. Sports provided an outlet to influence others, to push teammates to perform, helping participants to realize their potential to be a leader. This became more apparent when participants held a position as a team captain, because this was often their first experience of leading others. Much of a participant's development into a leader was found to stem from applying leadership lessons learned while growing up to later actions as a leader in an Army setting.

Adulthood Experiences

Adult experiences also impact development of a leader identity. As individuals continue to develop, relationships with peers become important learning opportunities that further leader development and identity (Day, 2000). For example, as individuals and their peers continue to move into more supervisory roles, they learn not only from their own experiences, but also from observing the successes and mistakes of their peers in similar positions. Peer interactions offer opportunities for individuals to emerge as leaders in various social situations (Day et al., 2014). During adulthood, individuals are exposed to a wide variety of situations and interactions that provide the opportunity to know themselves better – an inherent aspect of leader development (Boyce, Zaccaro, & Wisecarver, 2010; Carroll & Simpson, 2012).

Entering the workplace exposes individuals to both informal and formal leadership roles that continue to define and reshape self-concept, and encourage the identity of leader. What often begins as an individual contributor role can evolve into informal leadership within teams, and then into more formal leadership through promotions over time. Skills gained as an individual contributor can result in leadership perceptions among others (Lord & Hall, 2005), reinforcing and strengthening a newly formed leader identity (Wisse & Rus, 2012). Importantly, aspects of both the individual and the context can influence the type of leader skills that they develop (Lord & Hall, 2005), and ultimately the type of leader identity formed.

Interviews with U.S. Army soldiers about how they identify as leaders led to the creation of a taxonomy of common identity types (see Table 9.1) (Shaughnessy, Coats, Karalus, & Srinivasan, 2017). Qualitative coding revealed that leaders view themselves in an assortment of ways, with specific behaviors, cognitions, and motivations associated with different leader identities. Interestingly, findings demonstrated that the behaviors and cognitions of leaders across the various identities were similar, but the underlying motivations differed. For example, leaders who identified as managers and parents both aimed to provide professional development to subordinates, yet their motivations for doing so were in stark contrast. Managers were often motivated to provide development so that subordinates would do their jobs well, reflecting positively on the leader. Conversely, leaders who identified primarily as parents were often motivated to provide professional development to help their subordinates to grow and improve as people, providing subordinates with lifelong success. In short, the manager was motivated to benefit the organization and the supervisor; the parent was motivated to benefit the subordinate.

It is important to note that leader identities discussed by participants were largely discussed as stable identities. This is consistent with the literature: Individuals tend to view who they are as a coherent sense of self (Kegan, 1982). As DeRue and Ashford (2010, p. 628) aptly stated: "Most research on leadership and identity acknowledge that identities develop over time, but then goes on to theorize about a leader identity that, once internalized, becomes a static and enduring feature of the person." While participants spoke of stable identities, they alluded to a more complex development trajectory whereby their leader identity morphed over time. This can be seen in how participants at different levels – or ranks, in a military setting – described leader identities. The junior ranks tended to have less complex identities: Who they were as leaders was directly related to simplistic implicit theories of

TABLE 9.1 A taxonomy of leader identities

Identity	Definition
Buddy	Acting as a friend and peer; engaging with subordinates as a teammate instead of in a supervisory capacity
Buffer	Providing a defense between the team and the outside world; ensuring subordinates are protected from unnecessary information and influence, so they may focus on their jobs
Coach	Preparing subordinates for their next role; teaching, demonstrating, encouraging practice; wanting subordinates to improve in their jobs; training subordinates
Empowerer	Enabling subordinates to grow and learn; providing safe situations for trial and error, and allowing subordinates to make mistakes to promote learning; encouraging subordinate ownership of situations and tasks
Facilitator	Providing emphasis and purpose to the tasks at hand; supporting subordinates by ensuring they have the knowledge and resources to complete their jobs and develop
Guide	Communicating the organizational vision and setting clear expectations; teaching subordinates to think and plan; helping subordinates to find the right path; encouraging self-reflection
Manager	Supervising subordinates and viewing self primarily as boss; ensuring organizational goals and tasks are met; providing opportunities for professional development
Mentor	Providing a developmental road map to subordinates; being available; challenging subordinates through difficult tasks and providing opportunity to learn from mistakes
Parent	Providing care and support to subordinates; responsible for subordinate well-being; teaching subordinates and passing down knowledge; acting as role model to whom subordinates look up
Parental figure	Completing "parent" tasks, such as teaching subordinates, passing down knowledge, and providing career counseling; playing role of "parent" expected by subordinates
Role model	Setting example of appropriate behavior; showing subordinates how to complete tasks by doing tasks with them; leading by example
Servant	Emphasizing setting up subordinates for success; putting subordinates' development and needs before own; taking time to explain why, to provide direction and guidance, so subordinates may excel
Standard-bearer	Setting example of appropriate organizational behavior and enforcing that standard to ensure compliance through a strong presence; leading by example
Teacher	Providing knowledge and wisdom to subordinates; encouraging critical thinking skills; includes training aspects and showing subordinates how to perform tasks
Team builder	Creating units in which individual subordinates' strengths are leveraged to create effective group; encouraging subordinates to work together for maximum effect; drawing people together

leadership based on formal leadership education or their prior role as a peer to their now-subordinates. Leaders with more experience noted lessons learned as they developed, and had more elaborate concepts and definitions of themselves as leaders, implying learning over time. For example, many junior leaders identified as a "big brother" to their subordinates, viewing themselves as a role model who could help to guide the soldiers and pass down knowledge they had gathered from their past experiences. As these leaders gained more experience and matured, they transitioned from identifying as a "big brother" to identifying as a parent to their subordinates. While both identities encompass a close familial relationship with subordinates, the maturity and complexity of the role, as well as the extent of the responsibilities the leader felt towards their subordinates, strengthened the longer they were in leadership positions and the more responsibility their formal position entailed.

The evolution of identity demonstrates that development does not stop once an individual becomes a leader. Again, leaders are much more complex. Continuous exposure to new situations, both in and out of the workplace, affords a continued opportunity to experiment and apply new knowledge, skills, and experiences. Opportunities to experiment and test new skills and knowledge, as well as to incorporate feedback both from the environment and from others, provides leaders with information about their actions and behaviors. This ongoing process allows leaders to develop and refine how they identify. Leadership research must account for the complexity that exists within leader identities.

Refining a Leader Identity

Being a leader is ideally a process of growth that occurs over time. Individuals develop and change, applying new knowledge and experiences as they learn. As they develop as a leader, they try new activities, learn new skills, and further develop their leader identity (Lord & Hall, 2005). Leadership styles and tactics that were successful at one point may fail at a different time or in a different context. Leaders adapt. They refine their approaches and revise strategies that do not work, discard identities that are uncomfortable, and incorporate new experiences and outcomes into their personal narrative of who they are and why they act. Yet the existing literature depicts identity as relatively stable once an individual enters adulthood.

It is thus necessary to expand our conceptualization of leader identity to include growth and development over time, taking into consideration the dynamism and complexity that exists in individuals. Given that identity is socially constructed through interpersonal transactions and the fact that an individual can have multiple personal identities, the literature suggests that identity is not actually static (Demo, 1992). In organizational contexts, an individual's identity may undergo change as they shift roles in the organization

(Ibarra, Snook, & Guillén Ramo, 2010). As Day and Sin (2011, p. 547) note: "Leader identity may not be particularly stable, especially among those who are relatively early into the leader development process." In other words, an individual's identity that was shaped by early roles may change as new roles require different knowledge, skills, and perceptions about the organization.

To advance the study of leader identity, it is critical to address how leaders not only *form*, but also *change* their identities over time. As an individual gains new experiences and continues to develop in both their work and personal lives, the information is incorporated into their existing leader identity, often slightly modifying their self-narrative (Erez & Earley, 1993). The majority of research recognizes that identity develops, but then research approaches to identity become static. Context and interactions change, however, and hence so do identities (DeRue & Ashford, 2010). Identities are not stagnant nor are leader identities.

Change may occur through momentary processes, such as emotions and cognitions (Dinh et al., 2014) or through lengthier experiences, such as job assignments or training schools, which build new skill sets and knowledge bases (Chan & Drasgow, 2001; Day, Harrison, & Halpin, 2009; Wisse & Rus, 2012). Hall (2004) notes that both critical events and role transitions may lead to changes in an individual's personal identity by triggering reflection and self-awareness. Reflection on experiences is a critical process in leadership development, because it allows leaders to draw insights, learning, and meaning from experiences (Maurer, Leheta, & Conklin, 2017).

Reflecting on experiences contributes to development and growth as a leader. Professionals test out various personas, or provisional selves, during work transitions (Ibarra, 1999), and they take into consideration the reactions of others to their trial styles. As new leaders engage in feedback-seeking behaviors (Ashford, 1989) and reflect on others' perspectives (Ashley & Reiter-Palmon, 2012), they may gain, alter, or shed identities. Significant negative feedback from others may be an especially relevant experience that can lead an individual to reflect on what led to the reaction, to come to understand how they are being perceived, and to modify their identity as a result.

Experiences across various contexts and roles contribute to identity refinement and impact the way in which leaders view themselves. Because various interactions and experiences are continually incorporated into identities, individuals are able to maintain a consistent and coherent sense of self (Erez & Earley, 1993). Home and work experiences and interactions are two areas of life that can profoundly influence the way in which individuals identify, and they allow for the testing of various aspects of leader identities and provisional selves.

Home Experiences

Home life undoubtedly impacts work life. The family-to-work spillover literature has evolved to examine and assess such impacts. While early work focused on how work and family domains could negatively impact one another, more recent conceptualizations have expanded to encompass the positive synergies that can result from experiences in both work and home environments (Grzywacz & Marks, 2000). The theory of work–family enrichment posits that experiences in one role can positively impact experiences in another role by means of both performance and affect (Greenhaus & Powell, 2006). Home experiences can result in positive changes in an individual's work sphere by means of their impact on leader identity development.

As stated previously, childhood experiences in the home led to the development of a leader identity. Home life continued to impact leader identity in adulthood, as well. Among leaders in the U.S. Army, home experiences were commonly mentioned as impacts for work leader roles (Plemmons et al., 2016). Soldiers reported development and change as leaders as a result of marriage, divorce, and children. These experiences directly impacted an individual's leader self-concept.

Spouses led leaders to re-examine how they interacted with subordinates, and to modify their behaviors and their approach to leadership. Participants credited their spouses with "calling them out" on behaviors, encouraging leaders to become more compassionate towards subordinates. Spouses were also credited with helping soldiers to become more mature as leaders, providing them with the ability to better consider others while making decisions. While taking others into consideration began in the home, it was transferred to the workplace; Army leaders remarked that they were better able to take their soldiers' needs into consideration. This feedback from spouses helped leaders to become more aware and, through these experiences, learn more about who they wanted to be as leaders. Ultimately, these changes led to more mature Army leaders, who identified as leaders in more complex ways.

Divorce proved a critical life experience for some, resulting in introspection and re-evaluation of how an individual interacted with others. The divorce process forced participants to reflect on shortcomings in relationships, consequently leading to growth as a leader. Army leaders reported being better able to communicate with subordinates as a result of self-reflection post-divorce. They also felt that they were better able to relate to their subordinates, allowing the leaders to better connect with their soldiers and to more strongly impact their development.

Parenthood perhaps had the largest reported impact on leader identity development. Parents tested leadership styles and provisional leader identities on their children. This testing – this trial and error – allowed leaders to figure out what tactics felt most comfortable and to modify ineffective strategies. It also led to changes in how leaders identified, with some shifting their work leader identity role to that of a parent and others emphasizing the importance of appropriately modeling behaviors as a result of interactions with their children. Actions and identities at home directly impacted actions and identities at work.

Work Experiences

Professionals who experience a role shift may create provisional selves, or possible, but not yet fully formed, professional identities that will be tested and revised or discarded (Ibarra, 1999). Leadership styles and tactics that were successful at one point may fail at a different time or in a different context. Subordinates differ, including in what they expect from leaders, which may impact the interactions between leader identity and follower identities (Erez & Earley, 1993).

How individuals perceive themselves is often shaped by comparison to other individuals. Individuals are exposed to leaders whom they like and dislike, and they then intentionally incorporate or exclude those leaders' behaviors into their own sense of leadership and identity. Role modeling previous leaders is a common way in which leaders develop (Bass, Waldman, Avolio, & Bebb, 1987; Day et al., 2009; Wofford & Goodwin, 1994). U.S. Army leaders described developing leader identities based on prior leaders (Shaughnessy, Lanzo, & Coats, 2018). Successful, "good," leaders were emulated. These prior "good" leaders were said to have shown a high degree of care for their subordinates. Soldiers also described developing leadership styles, tactics, and identities that were the antithesis of previous "bad" leaders for whom they had worked. Participants noted the emotions and overall climate associated with negative leaders. These experiences drove participants to vow never to behave in a similar manner and to develop leader identities that they wished their prior leaders had adopted. Motivations among Army leaders for adopting specific leader identities were largely to protect their subordinates from bad leadership, so that their subordinates would never have to experience what they had.

Acquiring and modifying specific leader identities as a result of prior leaders is consistent with broader existing work on identity. These conclusions are similar to findings by Burke and Reitzes (1981, p. 90), who frame their research in terms of identities and counter-identities: "In order to be (some identity), one must act like (some identity). In order to not be (some other identity), one must not act like (that other identity)." Erez and Earley (1993) note that managers are often evaluated by employees in terms of how they impact employees' self-worth and well-being. Subordinates thus develop and modify their own leader identities at least partially based on negative work events and a desire for others to never have similar experiences.

As noted previously, participants alluded to leader identity trajectories whereby their leader identity changed as they progressed through their career (Shaughnessy et al., 2017). Identifying as a buffer – that is, a leader who keeps things out of the unit so that subordinates can focus on work – appears to transition into identifying as a facilitator – that is, a leader who not only keeps distractions out of the unit, but also provides the resources necessary for subordinates to complete their jobs well. Both identities focus on enabling subordinates to perform their jobs, but facilitators have moved past simply removing obstacles to also providing resources. Participants did not appear to shed the buffer leader identity, but to add to it, to arrive at a facilitator leader identity (see Figure 9.1).

The buffer and facilitator identities are two identities that emerged from the interviews alongside multiple other leader identities. They ranged from simpler, newly formed leader identities to more complex identities. As Hall (2004, p. 154) stated: "Identity is a complex and multifaceted construct, which relates to the way an individual perceives himself or herself in relation to 'others' in the environment." Young leaders identified as buddies – that is, friends with their subordinates – and buffers – that is, a formal force keeping work distractions away. Intermediate leaders identified as mentors, focused on developing their subordinates, and guides, who communicate a vision and direct subordinates. The most experienced leaders identified in the most complex ways, as parents, providing support and well-being, and as servants, placing their subordinates' needs and development above their own.

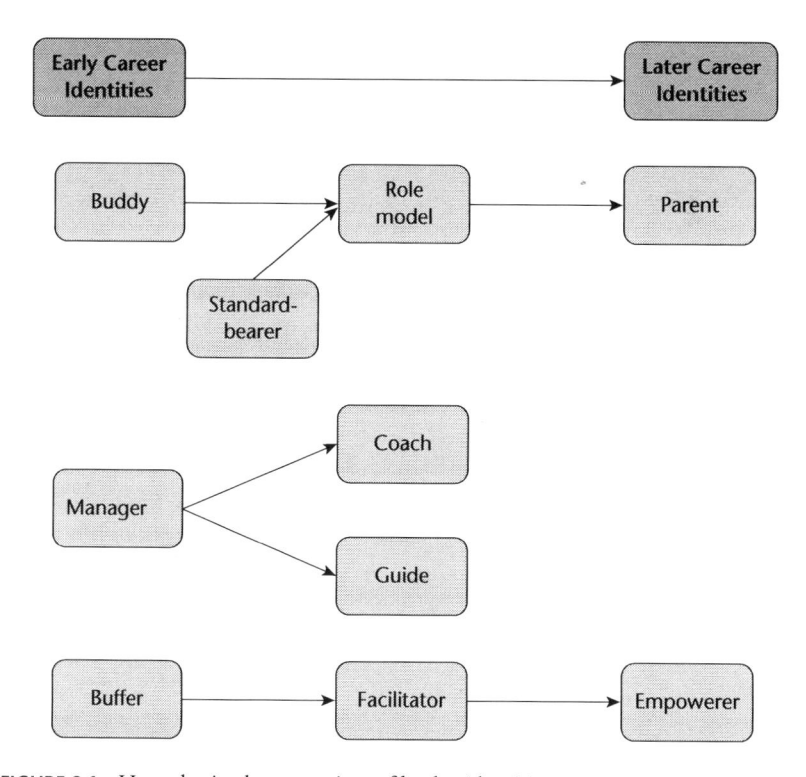

FIGURE 9.1 Hypothesized progression of leader identities.

Similarly, the transitional leader identity of buddy appears to develop into a leader identity of parent. Buddies were commonly found in young enlisted soldiers who had recently been promoted into their first leadership role. As such, these young noncommissioned officers (NCOs) tended to identify as leaders focused on maintaining friendships with their subordinates. The highest ranked NCOs often identified as parents, focused on protecting subordinates and ensuring that they were set to succeed as individuals, not simply as soldiers. While the interview data is undoubtedly cross-sectional in design, participants implied that leader identity changes had occurred, especially when questioned as to how they had changed over time. Buddies gained maturity through additional leader experiences, which led to their adopting parent leader identities later in their careers. They moved from viewing their subordinates as peers and friends to viewing them as children. Both leader identities are highly focused on relationships with their subordinates, but the focus of the relationship changed: Those who identified as parents took ownership of their subordinates' actions, while those who identified as buddies did not.

Importantly, leader identities are not typically discarded for entirely different ones; what is more common is for participants to report tweaking aspects of how they view themselves as leaders. It appears that the motivations of a leader stay the same over time, but, through experiences and refinement of their identity, the cognitions and behaviors enacted change. This suggests that individuals form an initial leader identity based on previous life experiences and modify it as they progress as leaders. Early transitional leader identities appear to set a leader on a path to develop into a set of specific identities that evolve from their original leader identity.

Future Research

A better understanding of the various identities that exist in leadership roles, and of how those identities may shift over time, opens multiple, more nuanced, avenues for research, including the exploration of leader–subordinate dyadic relationships and the examination of the impact of type of leader identity on team outcomes. Once more knowledge is gained on the types of leader identity that exist, better prediction of leader decisions and priorities can ensue. Knowing how leader identities may change can assist in understanding how to create context to activate specific leader identities.

Importantly, furthering understanding of leader identity as a part of the leadership process paves the way toward knowing more about leadership over time. (For a more detailed look at leadership and time, see Chapter 8 in this volume.) In particular, understanding how identity develops over a leader's career can aid in understanding the developmental trajectories of leaders and how experiences both in and out of the workplace contribute to these career trajectories. Previous research indicates the importance of life experiences in the development of leader identity, but these studies are largely retrospective in nature. To expand and confirm theories of identity formation throughout life experiences, longitudinal studies are necessary. Incorporating such complexity in processes of leadership allows the field to better measure and model the life cycle of leader development.

To move toward measuring and modeling the life cycle of leader development, it will be imperative for future research studies to recognize the dynamism that exists in identity, and to actively seek to capture and measure that dynamism and change. Rather than asking if an individual identifies as a leader, or even how they identify as a leader at a single time point, researchers should aim to capture what experiences, events, and interactions influence identity and when these changes occur. By measuring and modeling identity development in a way that is more consistent with theorized processes of development, a richer and more comprehensive understanding of leader life cycles will emerge.

Ultimately, better knowledge of leader identities, and the match between leader identities and follower needs, may lead to improved performance by the leader, subordinates, and team as a whole. Because identity influences behaviors and interactions between leaders and subordinates, it is likely that how an individual identifies as a leader has significant impacts on team climate. Future research should seek to integrate the formation, development, and outcomes of leader identity with other key outcomes, such as team dynamics and team emergent states, informing the relational processes of leadership and influences on those with whom leaders interact.

Conclusion

Ultimately, understanding not only whether an individual identifies as a leader, but also how they identify and how their identity changes over time will strengthen leader development paradigms. Leader identity is a complex and continually evolving process that impacts how individuals behave and interact with others. Research has demonstrated that the process of leader identity is an important component in understanding social relationships and performance outcomes in the workplace. To improve knowledge of this process, there is a need to delve further into the complexities that underlie how an individual identifies as a leader. Further investigation into the myriad ways in which leaders identify, as well as how those identities change and develop over time, will improve understanding of leader identity and ultimately improve leader development. Leaders are complex individuals. Theories and research must account for such complexity if they are to further the study of leadership.

References

Adler, N. (2011). I am my mother's daughter: Early developmental influences on leadership. In S.E. Murphy & R.J. Reichard (Eds.), *Early development and leadership: Building the next generation of leaders* (pp. 159–178). New York: Routledge.

Ashford, S.J. (1989). Self-assessments in organizations: A literature-review and integrative model. *Research in Organizational Behavior, 11*, 133–174.

Ashforth, B.E., & Johnson, S.A. (2001). Which hat to wear? The relative salience of multiple identities in organizational contexts. In M.A. Hogg & D.J. Terry (Eds.), *Social identity processes in organizational contexts* (pp. 31–48). Philadelphia, PA: Psychology Press.

Ashley, G.C., & Reiter-Palmon, R. (2012). Self-awareness and the evolution of leaders: The need for a better measure of self-awareness. *Journal of Behavioral and Applied Management, 14*(1), 2–17.

Ashton-James, C., Van Baaren, R.B., Chartrand, T.L., Decety, J., & Karremans, J. (2007). Mimicry and me: The impact of mimicry on self-construal. *Social Cognition, 25*(4), 518–535.

Bass, B.M., Waldman, D.A., Avolio, B.J., & Bebb, M. (1987). Transformational leadership and the falling dominoes effect. *Group and Organization Studies, 12*(1), 73–87.

Baumeister, R.F. (1999). The nature and structure of the self: An overview. In R.F. Baumeister (Ed.), *The self in social psychology* (pp. 1–24). Philadelphia, PA: Psychology Press.

Boyce, L.A., Zaccaro, S.J., & Wisecarver, M.Z. (2010). Propensity for self-development of leadership attributes: Understanding, predicting, and supporting performance of leader self-development. *The Leadership Quarterly, 21*(1), 159–178.

Burke, P.J., & Reitzes, D.C. (1981) The link between identity and role performance. *Social Psychology Quarterly, 44*(2), 83–92.

Carroll, B., & Simpson, B. (2012). Capturing sociality in the movement between frames: An illustration from leadership development. *Human Relations, 65*(10), 1283–1309.

Chan, K.Y., & Drasgow, F. (2001). Toward a theory of individual differences and leadership: Understanding the motivation to lead. *Journal of Applied Psychology, 86*(3), 481–498.

Chelladurai, P. (2011). Participation in sport and leader development. In S.E. Murphy & R.J. Reichard (Eds.), *Early development and leadership: Building the next generation of leaders* (pp. 95–114). New York: Routledge.

Damon, W., & Hart, D. (1982). The development of self-understanding from infancy through adolescence. *Child Development, 53*(4), 841–864.

Day, D.V. (2000). Leadership development: A review in context. *The Leadership Quarterly, 11*(4), 581–613.

Day, D.V., & Harrison, M. (2007). A multilevel, identity-based approach to leadership development. *Human Resource Management Review, 17*(4), 360–373.

Day, D.V., & Lance, C.E. (2004). Understanding the development of leadership complexity through latent growth modeling. In D.V. Day, S.J. Zaccaro, & S.M. Halpin (Eds.), *Leader development for transforming organizations: Growing leaders for tomorrow* (pp. 41–70). Mahwah, NJ: Lawrence Erlbaum.

Day, D.V., & Sin, H.P. (2011). Longitudinal tests of an integrative model of leader development: Charting and understanding developmental trajectories. *The Leadership Quarterly, 22*(3), 545–560.

Day, D.V., Fleenor, J.W., Atwater, L.E., Sturm, R.E., & McKee, R.A. (2014). Advances in leaders and leadership development: A review of 25 years of research and theory. *The Leadership Quarterly*, 25(1), 63–82.

Day, D.V., Harrison, M.M., & Halpin, S.M. (2009). *An integrative approach to leader development: Connecting adult development, identity, and expertise*. New York: Routledge.

Demo, D.H. (1992). The self-concept over time: Research issues and directions. *Annual Review of Sociology*, 18(1), 303–326.

DeRue, D.S., & Ashford, S.J. (2010). Who will lead and who will follow? A social process of leadership identity construction in organizations. *Academy of Management Review*, 35(4), 627–647.

Dinh, J.E., Lord, R.G., Gardner, W.L., Meuser, J.D., Liden, R.C., & Hu, J. (2014). Leadership theory and research in the new millennium: Current theoretical trends and changing perspectives. *The Leadership Quarterly*, 25(1), 36–62.

Emery, C., Daniloski, K., & Hamby, A. (2011). The reciprocal effects of self-view as a leader and leadership emergence. *Small Group Research*, 42(2), 199–224.

Erez, M., & Earley, P.C. (1993). *Culture, self-identity, and work*. New York: Oxford University Press.

Gardner, W.L., & Avolio, B.J. (1998). The charismatic relationship: A dramaturgical perspective. *Academy of Management Review*, 23(1), 32–58.

Gergen, K.J. (1999). *The saturated self: Dilemmas of identity in contemporary life*. New York: Basic Books.

Gottfried, A.E., Gottfried, A.W., Reichard, R.J., Guerin, D.W., Oliver, P.H., & Riggio, R.E. (2011). Motivational roots of leadership: A longitudinal study from childhood through adulthood. *The Leadership Quarterly*, 22(3), 510–519.

Greenhaus, J.H., & Powell, G.N. (2006). When work and family are allies: A theory of work–family enrichment. *Academy of Management Review*, 31(1), 72–92.

Grzywacz, J.G., & Marks, N.F. (2000). Reconceptualizing the work–family interface: An ecological perspective on the correlates of positive and negative spillover between work and family. *Journal of Occupational Health Psychology*, 5(1), 111–126.

Guillén, L., Mayo, M., & Korotov, K. (2015). Is leadership a part of me? A leader identity approach to understanding the motivation to lead. *The Leadership Quarterly*, 26(5), 802–820.

Hall, D.T. (2004). Self-awareness, identity, and leader development. In D.V. Day, S.J. Zaccaro, & S.M. Halpin (Eds.), *Leader development for transforming organizations: Growing leaders for tomorrow* (pp. 153–176). Mahwah, NJ: Lawrence Erlbaum.

Ibarra, H. (1999). Provisional selves: Experimenting with image and identity in professional adaptation. *Administrative Science Quarterly*, 44(4), 764–791.

Ibarra, H., Snook, S., & Guillén Ramo, L. (2010). Identity-based leader development. In N. Nohria & R. Khurana (Eds.), *Handbook of leadership theory and practice* (pp. 657–678). Boston, MA: Harvard Business School Press.

Kegan, R. (1982). *The evolving self: Problem and process in human development*. Cambridge, MA: Harvard University Press.

Koepke, S., & Denissen, J.J. (2012). Dynamics of identity development and separation–individuation in parent–child relationships during adolescence and emerging adulthood: A conceptual integration. *Developmental Review*, 32(1), 67–88.

Lord, R.G., & Hall, R.J. (2005). Identity, deep structure and the development of leadership skill. *The Leadership Quarterly*, 16(4), 591–615.

Maurer, T.J., Leheta, D.M., & Conklin, T.A. (2017). An exploration of differences in content and processes underlying reflection on challenging experiences at work. *Human Resource Development Quarterly, 28*(3), 337–368.

Plemmons, S.A., Srinivasan, R., & Plourde, S. (2016, April). Becoming less reactive and more mature as a leader. In S.A. Plemmons (Chair), *Leader development: Developing self and developing others*. Symposium conducted at the 31st annual conference of the Society for Industrial and Organizational Psychology, Anaheim, CA.

Popper, M., Mayseless, O., & Castelnovo, O. (2000). Transformational leadership and attachment. *The Leadership Quarterly, 11*(2), 267–289.

Shamir, B., House, R.J., & Arthur, M.B. (1993). The motivational effects of charismatic leadership: A self-concept based theory. *Organization Science, 4*(4), 577–594.

Shaughnessy, S.P., Coats, M.R., Karalus, S.P., & Srinivasan, R. (2017, April). Development and metamorphosis of leader identities. In S.P. Shaughnessy & M.R. Coats (Co-Chairs) *Identities at work: Self-concept in organizational settings*. Symposium conducted at the 32nd annual conference of the Society for Industrial and Organizational Psychology, Orlando, FL.

Shaughnessy, S.P., Lanzo, L.A., & Coats, M.R. (2018, August). The good, the bad, and the complex: Learning to lead through role models. Poster session presented at the 78th annual conference of the Academy of Management, Chicago, IL.

Siegler, R.S., & Alibali, M.W. (2005). Information-processing theories of development. In R.S. Siegler (Ed.), *Children's thinking* (4th ed.) (pp. 65–106). Upper Saddle River, NJ: Prentice Hall.

Van Knippenberg, D., van Knippenberg, B., De Cremer, D., & Hogg, M.A. (2004). Leadership, self, and identity: A review and research agenda. *The Leadership Quarterly, 15*(6), 825–856.

Wisse, B., & Rus, D. (2012). Leader self-concept and self-interested behavior: The moderating role of power. *Journal of Personnel Psychology, 11*(1), 40–48.

Wofford, J.C., & Goodwin, V.L. (1994). A cognitive interpretation of transactional and transformational leadership theories. *The Leadership Quarterly, 5*(2), 161–186.

10
TURNING A BLIND EYE TO DESTRUCTIVE LEADERSHIP

The Forgotten Destructive Leaders

Birgit Schyns, Pedro Neves, Barbara Wisse, and Michael Knoll

Traditionally, leadership research – and also leadership practice – has focused on the positive characteristics and behaviors of leaders or leadership (for example, Lord, Day, Zaccaro, Avolio, & Eagly, 2017). Selection processes, for instance, usually focus on testing candidates for leadership positions on qualities such as their skills, their positive traits, and their intelligence, from the perspective that candidates who have more of these characteristics would probably be more likely to be successful and effective leaders. Attention to the possession of negative traits (for example, psychopathy, narcissism), or to having an overabundance of traits and characteristics that are, in principle, considered to be positive (for example, ambition, extraversion), is relatively scarce. (For an exception, see Judge, Piccolo, & Kosalka, 2009, who elaborated upon the potential dark sides of bright leader traits, the bright sides of dark traits, and nonlinear relationships between bright traits and leader effectiveness.)

Likewise, leadership development programs often seem to focus on strengthening the positive behaviors of leaders instead of recognizing and curbing the negative ones (Harms, Spain, & Hannah, 2011). The emphasis is put on who organizations want to hire, develop, and promote, rather than on who organizations should avoid. This lopsided consideration of the positive sides of leadership is mirrored in leadership research. Indeed, research focuses predominantly on explaining what makes leaders or leadership successful and not so much on understanding the phenomenon of destructive or negative leadership as an everyday occurrence (rather than a political exception). Interestingly, a recent historical overview of leadership research (Lord et al., 2017) mentions abusive leadership research only very briefly, underlining the focus of leadership research in the past on positive aspects of leadership.

Of course, this focus on the positive side of leadership has contributed tremendously to the development of the field. However, the one-sided attention to the positive side of leadership also seems to have had costs: The destructive leader has been forgotten. This may have had three consequences, as follows.

1. It may have opened the door for people with negative traits and characteristics (or with a surplus of positive ones) to enter the leadership arena.
2. It may have distracted from developing interventions aimed at decreasing negative leader behaviors or leadership processes.
3. It may have led to a general lack of understanding of the phenomenon of destructive or negative leaders and leadership.

Fortunately, recent research is now attempting to fill this gap, but more work needs to be done.

The Issue with Destructive Leadership

While research in organizations often finds relatively low mean values of, for example, abusive supervision at any one time (for example, Schyns, Felfe, & Schilling, 2018; Tepper, 2000), many employees (between 10 and 16 percent of the U.S. workforce) report having worked under a supervisor who was offensive, hostile, or obstructive at some point during their career (Namie & Namie, 2000; Tepper, Duffy, Henle, & Lambert, 2006). This means that the experience of destructive leadership is not uncommon. Notably, at least to some extent, this experience of destructive leadership seems to be linked to actual negative leaders' traits and behavior. For instance, it has been argued that about 26 percent of bullying incidents are caused by the presence of leaders with psychopathic traits (Boddy, 2011). Apart from the fact that destructive leadership is prevalent, it also has myriad negative effects on followers, organizations, and even society as a whole (for example, Schyns & Schilling, 2013).

Destructive leadership is, without a doubt, an important field of research. The lack of attention that it has received, compared to its positive counterpart, is fairly visible, to the point at which it sparks discussions on whether the "dark side" should actually be considered a facet of leadership, or it merely belongs to the realm of poor managerial practices. If we take a closer look at the most recent reviews on the topic (Krasikova, Green, & LeBreton, 2013; Thoroughgood, Sawyer, Padilla, & Lunsford, 2016), we notice that a significant proportion of the concepts associated with destructive leadership actually avoid using the word "leadership" (for example, abusive supervision, petty/managerial tyranny, supervisor undermining, strategic bullying). As a consequence, many questions still remain. Some are parallel to those posed in the research into positive leadership; some are unique to this area. Specifically, we argue that the field could be furthered by answers to the following four questions – on perspectives, intention, type of intention, and context.

1. In terms of *perspectives* (Martinko, Harvey, Brees, & Mackey, 2013): Do all followers perceive the same leader as destructive, or are there differences based on, for example, personality, implicit leadership theories, and affect? Do leaders see their behavior similarly to how employees see it? How do other stakeholders interpret the leaders' behavior?
2. In terms of *intention* and linked to the question of perspectives: Do (some) leaders use destructive leadership intentionally or only because of incompetence and/or indifference? Do different followers attribute intentions differently to the same leader, again based on their own backgrounds, personalities, experiences, and so on?
3. Next, *type of intention*: Tepper (2007) differentiates the intention to hurt the follower from the intention to increase performance (see also Boddy, 2011). Tepper (2007) also differentiates the intention of the perpetrator from the intention attributed by the target, the latter of which may make a difference for the targets' reactions (see Liu, Liao, & Loi, 2012).
4. Finally, we should ask how *context* influences the perception of, and actual behavior relating to, destructive leadership – that is, recognize that some contexts might be more permissive towards destructive leadership, and some contexts might reduce or facilitate the perception of destructive leadership.

We raise these questions with a nod towards research into positive leadership, in which some of these issues remain under-researched (in terms of context, see Liden & Antonakis, 2009). We argue here that destructive leadership research, as a younger field, should avoid those issues from early on, to speed up our understanding of the nuances of the destructive leadership process and to provide a more comprehensive perspective of leadership.

Therefore, in this chapter, we argue that what is wrong with leadership is the relative neglect of destructive leadership, leaving organizations with too little support in how to deal with this issue. In addition, we will argue that the current research in to destructive leadership suffers from some pitfalls – namely, a lack of differentiation between leaders' and followers' perspectives of destructive leadership (behavior versus perception), and a lack of understanding of the complexities behind (perceived) intentions, as well as contextual influences.

Before we address these four questions in turn, we will first discuss the most researched concepts in the field of destructive leadership and explain their differences. Moreover, we will showcase some empirical results to outline the importance of research into destructive leadership. We will then turn to the questions we raised (regarding perception, intention, and context) and offer some suggestions for how they may inform future research in this emerging field.

Subsequently, we will include recommendations for organizational practice, such as in terms of leader development (see Chapters 11 and 12 in this volume), as well as the teaching of future leaders (see Chapter 13), and for human resources managers.

Destructive Leadership: A Brief Overview of Concepts and Results

Definition and Concepts

The definition of destructive leadership that we use here is:

> . . . a process in which over a longer period of time the activities, experiences and/or relationships of an individual or the members of a group are repeatedly influenced by their supervisor in a way that is perceived as hostile and/or obstructive.
>
> *(Schyns & Schilling, 2013, p. 141)*

Notably, a differentiation can be made between destructive leader behavior and destructive leadership (Schyns & Schilling, 2013). Destructive leader behavior can be any behavior by a leader, but does not necessarily have to relate to influencing followers (for example, being careless with company goods and materials, lying to clients and external stakeholders, etc.), while destructive leadership explicitly takes into account the direction of the behavior towards one or more follower(s). In other words, destructive leader behavior can include harmful actions that do not necessarily involve leading others, whereas destructive leadership, by definition, involves the perception of antagonistic actions performed by leaders in the process of leading followers (or a single follower) toward certain organizational goals. Here, we focus on follower-directed behavior rather than leader behavior more generally.

Also important to note is that our definition of destructive leadership is slightly different from another oft-used definition. Einarsen, Aasland, and Skogstad (2007, p. 207) defined destructive leadership as:

> . . . the systematic and repeated behavior by a leader, supervisor or manager that violates the legitimate interest of the organization by undermining and/or sabotaging the organization's goals, tasks, resources, and effectiveness and/or the motivation, well-being or job satisfaction of his/her subordinates.

They differentiate two dimensions of leadership behavior – subordinate- and organization-oriented behaviors – both of which can be negative (or anti) or positive (or pro). Based on their conceptualization, Einarsen and colleagues

(2007) differentiate four categories of leadership (depending on whether the leadership is anti- or pro-organization and anti- or pro-follower) – namely, tyrannical, derailed, supportive-disloyal, and constructive. Three of those categories pertain to destructive leadership. First, tyrannical leaders act in line with organizational goals, but "humiliate, belittle, and manipulate subordinates in order to get the job done" (Einarsen et al., 2007, p. 212). In doing so, they significantly undermine the motivation, well-being, or job satisfaction of subordinates. Second, derailed leaders "display anti-subordinate behaviors like bullying, humiliation, manipulation, deception or harassment, while simultaneously performing anti-organizational behaviors like absenteeism, shirking, fraud, or theft" (Einarsen et al., 2007, pp. 212–213). Both types of destructive leader would fall within the scope of our chapter. However, the third type of destructive leader, the supportive-disloyal leader, who "shows consideration for the welfare of subordinates while violating the legitimate interest of the organization by undermining task and goal attainment" (Einarsen et al., 2007, p. 213), would not be covered here, because the behavior towards their followers is positive.

Apart from different conceptualizations of the construct, the literature also hosts a discussion of phenomena relating to destructive leadership, the most prevalent being abusive supervision and petty tyranny (see Krasikova et al., 2013, and Thoroughgood et al., 2016, for additional concepts). The concept that has received the most attention in this field is abusive supervision, which is defined as "the sustained display of hostile verbal and nonverbal behaviors, excluding physical contact" (Tepper, 2000, p. 178). This concept explicitly refers to follower-directed behavior and the perception of this behavior, and as a consequence studies on abusive supervision are relevant to this chapter.

Ashforth (1994, p. 757) introduced petty tyranny, which is defined as someone who "lorded his or her power." He describes six dimensions of petty tyranny – namely, arbitrariness and self-aggrandizement, belittling subordinates, lack of consideration, forcing style of conflict resolution, discouraging initiative, and noncontingent punishment. All of those are directed to the follower and thus fall within the scope of this chapter.

Outcomes

In terms of outcomes, research consistently finds that destructive leadership is problematic for both followers and organizations, and to some extent even for society. Schyns and Schilling (2013) recently conducted a meta-analysis of the relationship between destructive leadership and a variety of outcome variables (see also Zhang & Liao, 2015, for another recent meta-analysis). Results indicate the expected negative correlations between destructive leadership and positive followers' outcomes and behaviors (for example, attitudes towards the leader, well-being, and individual performance), and positive correlations between destructive leadership and negative outcomes (for example, turnover intention, resistance towards the leader, follower stress, and counter-productive work behavior). As Schyns and Schilling (2013) expected, they found the highest correlation between destructive leadership and attitudes towards the leader (for example, trust and liking). Organizations who have destructive leaders might consequently have issues relating to performance, as well as turnover, but also relating to reputation and potentially lawsuits – issues that amount to more than US$23.8 billion annually in the United States alone (Tepper et al., 2006).

On a societal level, there may be substantial damages as a consequence of long-term incapacity of employees subjected to abusive supervision – namely, as a result of the physical health problems it creates and exacerbates (Liang, Hanig, Evans, Brown, & Lian, 2017). In addition, several studies illustrate the adverse effects of destructive leadership on spouses and other family members (Hoobler & Brass, 2006; Tepper, 2000). For instance, Carlson, Ferguson, Perrewé, and Whitten (2011) found that abusive supervision ultimately influences subordinate family function and satisfaction through relationship tension. This body of research demonstrates the effects of destructive leadership to extend beyond the subordinate and organizational context. Based on these findings, it is obvious that destructive leadership is an important area on which leadership research needs to focus, but also to which organizational practice needs to pay attention. In the next section, we will turn to the question of perception of, versus behavior relating to, destructive leadership.

Perception versus Behavior

While most leadership research equates follower ratings with actual leadership behavior (see Martinko et al., 2013, for a critique on destructive leadership), this assumption has been increasingly questioned. Indeed, if we are to rely on follower ratings of leader behavior as a key measure of leadership processes, we would like to have some certainty about the extent to which these ratings are accurate. Over the last several years, research has shown that behavioral ratings not only reflect recall of actual behaviors, but also are influenced by individual differences among followers, contextual factors, and even research methods (for a recent review, see Hansbrough, Lord, & Schyns, 2015). Follower ratings of leader behavior are thus often biased, and these biases are also likely to be present when destructive leadership is assessed.

Martinko and colleagues (2013) can be credited with a substantial amount of research into the perceptions and attributions relevant to the assessment of abusive supervision. They argue that it is important to take into account the followers' points of view regarding abusive supervision, to the extent that certain follower characteristics influence perception of abusive supervision. For example, they found that followers' hostile attribution style relates to their perception of abusive supervision. Likewise, it has been suggested that followers with low self-esteem may be more likely to report more negative leader behavior. This may be because followers with low self-esteem are more aware of, or sensitive to, negative behaviors of leaders, or because their perception of the negative behaviors of leaders is more negative than the perception of the same by those with high self-esteem (Wisse, Sanders, Barelds, & Laurijssen, 2018).

In a quest to further address this question, Schyns and colleagues (2018) conducted several experimental studies using descriptions of leaders. They found that perception of abusive supervision partly, but not fully, mediates the relationship between abusive behaviors and follower reactions. They also found stronger perception effects in a field study, highlighting that actual leadership is often ambiguous in terms of follower interpretation. As such, and although both leader behavior and subordinates' perceptions of those behaviors contribute to the destructive leadership process, findings like this clearly indicate that it is important to investigate which part of the behavior is actual and which part is perception.

Consequently, to avoid the same issues that the more general leadership research domain has suffered from over a long span of time, it is important that research into destructive leadership explicitly addresses issues related to accuracy, bias, and the measurement of behavior versus the perception of that behavior. It is, however, noteworthy in this respect that the most prominent concept of destructive leadership – that is, abusive supervision – explicitly refers to follower perception (Tepper, 2000). Of course, if we are interested in followers' perceptions of leader behavior, the issue of bias is less relevant, because, in this case, each follower assessment can be seen as an individual's perspective or unique experience (see Hansbrough et al., 2015). However, research on abusive supervision has also shown these perceptions to be shared within a team to some extent (which may vary between teams), creating an "ambient" (Farh & Chen, 2014) in which the shared element is precisely the behavior of the supervisor. Moreover, most measurements of destructive leadership refer to more concrete leader behaviors and use frequency ratings. Such ratings should give a more reliable account of actual behavior than, for instance, ratings of the perceived intensity of a described behavior (see Hansbrough, Lord, Schyns, & Foti, 2018).

Tackling the behavior-versus-perceptions issues is also very important for organizational practice relating to destructive leadership, so that appropriate measures can be taken to address destructive leadership as a leader behavior, but also to understand why some followers might perceive more, and suffer more under, destructive leadership. Insight into factors that could prevent employees from becoming the victims of those willing to harm others is key to help those employees in need of ways of coping more effectively with perceived destructive behaviors of their leaders (Velez & Neves, 2016; Wisse et al., 2018). We argue that, specifically in terms of the relationship between destructive leadership and follower reactions, (attributed) intentions will be a key issue. We turn to intentions in the next section of this chapter.

Intentions and Type of Intentions

Leader Intentions

Another question relating to destructive leadership is whether or not the leader is intentionally destructive –that is, sets out to harm or to obstruct followers – and how this is perceived by followers. For example, leaders high in the "dark triad" personality traits (for example, Paulhus, 2014; Paulhus & Williams, 2002) – notably, narcissists and psychopaths – will intentionally use abusive supervision to hurt their followers. Other leaders might simply be incompetent or unable to see the destructiveness of their behavior because, for example, they believe it will prompt a response, such as increased effort (Tepper, 2007). This differentiation is important in terms of how leaders' destructive leadership is addressed. Arguably, unintentional destructive leaders should be more open to training and development that helps them to shift their behaviors. Here, 360-degree feedback might help them to understand how their behavior is perceived at different levels of the organization.

However, leaders who intentionally use destructive behavior – especially those who are high in negative traits – might be more resistant to (the idea of) training and development. The dark triad traits of narcissism, psychopathy, and Machiavellianism have all been linked to a lack of empathy for others (Paulhus, 2014). This means that leaders high in these traits are unlikely to be very concerned with their followers' (affective) reactions to their leadership.

As an example of the difficulties relating to dark triad leaders and possible training, we can point to narcissists. Here, research has shown that narcissists do not react well to feedback. They can get aggressive following negative feedback (for example, Barry, Chaplin, & Grafeman, 2006), and they can devalue the source of the feedback (Kausel, Culbertson, Leiva, Slaughter, & Jackson, 2015). Consequently, organizational interventions relating to these types of leader will have to be carefully considered because training might not be very successful. For leaders high in dark triad traits, it is consequently more important to create a context (for example, Cohen, 2016; Neves & Schyns, 2018) that reins in their behavior (at which we will look more closely later in the chapter). In other words, for the development of effective organizational interventions and recommendations, it is important to understand the types of intention that leaders have when using destructive leadership.

Follower-attributed Intention

Followers can attribute different intentions to a leader's behavior, similarly to what they do when they attribute intentions to the organization (Costa & Neves, 2017). For example, the reactions of employees to perceived breaches of the psychological contract vary substantially depending on whether or not they blame the organization (that is, attribute intention in the nonfulfillment of its obligations) or the economic context (that is, attribute no intention and thus assign no responsibility). Similarly, followers might attribute their leader's behavior to internal stable characteristics, such as the leader's personality, or circumstances such as stress or pressure from senior leadership. Presumably, the first attribution would lead to more negative reactions than the latter because, in the first case, the behavior is unlikely to change, while, in the second case, it might pass (for a similar argument see Schyns et al., 2018).

Theoretical considerations and empirical studies relating to perceived intention and abusive supervision have argued and found that attribution is relevant for the relationship between abusive supervision and follower reactions (for example, Martinko et al., 2013). For example, Schyns and colleagues (2018) examined the moderating effect of intention between the perception of abusive supervision and reactions. They found that when abusive supervision was manipulated, attribution of intention played a role only at low levels of abusive supervision, probably because the effect of the manipulation was so strong that attribution did not add anything. In the field study, attribution to the supervisor increased some of the effects of abusive supervision. Consequently, follower-attributed intentions are relevant in terms of their reactions and can potentially explain why some followers react differently to destructive leadership than do others.

Attribution of Types of Intention

Tepper (2007) differentiates between two types of intention from the leader's perspective when "using" abusive supervision: the intention to improve performance, and the intention to hurt. Here, Tepper (2007) also differentiates between the objectives of the leader and the attribution of the follower. An example of leaders who are likely to intend to improve performance through their destructive behaviors towards their followers are, arguably, Einarsen and colleagues' (2007) tyrannical leaders. The definition does not explicitly refer to objectives versus attribution, but this could be an interesting path for further examination.

Liu and colleagues (2012) empirically tested the impact of the differentiation between these types of intention on the relationship between abusive supervision and creativity. They found that performance attribution can mitigate some of the effects of abusive supervision. Specifically, they found that attributed performance-promotion motives moderated the relationship between abusive supervision and creativity, so that the relationship between abusive supervision and creativity was less negative when attributed performance motives were high. In contrast, attributed injury-initiation motives moderated the relationship between abusive supervision and creativity, so that abusive supervision was more negatively related to creativity when attributed injury motives were high.

This means that, to better predict the consequences of abusive supervision, examining how followers attribute abusive supervision is relevant.

Nonetheless, whether we are discussing different perspectives of destructive leadership or the underlying or attributed intentions of such behaviors, the story is not complete without a careful consideration of the context in which it occurs. We therefore turn to the role of context in the next section of this chapter.

The Barrel and the Apple: Contextual Factors in Destructive Leadership

As Tepper (2000, p.178) acknowledged in his seminal paper on abusive supervision, "the same individual could view a supervisor's behavior as abusive in one context and as non-abusive in another context," thus highlighting the importance of the setting in which these events and processes are examined. Indeed, it appears that destructive leadership often results from systemic, rather than only individual, factors (Erickson, Shaw, Murray, & Branch, 2015). However, the lack of studies that examine these systemic issues – namely, environmental and institutional factors – is evident (Mulvey & Padilla, 2010). A deeper understanding of the contexts in which the destructive leadership process occurs – as well as context factors that help to break the negative spiral stemming out of the experience of destructive leadership – is fundamental for the development of more comprehensive models and more effective strategies to deal with its impact.

Despite the scarce empirical research on the contextual conditions that affect the destructive leadership process, its relevance has been widely recognized. Quite recently, Thoroughgood and colleagues (2016, p. 6) criticized leader-centric approaches because of their disregard for contextual factors, claiming that "it is difficult to link 'bad' leader behaviors clearly with destructive leadership outcomes across all contexts." Similarly, the toxic triangle model developed by Padilla, Hogan, and Kaiser (2007) argues that destructive leadership results from the confluence of three aspects: destructive leaders, susceptible followers, and conducive environments. The model of destructive leadership proposed by Krasikova and colleagues (2013) also specifies the contribution of contextual factors – namely, how scarcity of resources and a cultural orientation towards the endorsement of such behaviors enhance their occurrence.

From a national cultural perspective, different authors have presented findings supporting the importance of context. Comparing samples from the United States and South Korea, Kernan, Watson, Chen, and Kim (2011) found that, in cultures high on achievement (that is, those that emphasize personal success through competence) and benevolence (that is, those that demonstrate concern for the welfare of others) values, employees reacted more strongly (and negatively) to abusive supervision. In a study that compared Anglo and Confucian Asian cultures, Vogel and colleagues (2015) also found evidence that culture matters for the interpretation of abusive supervision, in that employees from the Anglo cluster found their supervisors to be less fair as a result of abusive supervision, with consequences for trust in the supervisor and work effort, than did their Asian counterparts.

However, and although the evidence suggests that national culture plays an important role, the organizational context in which these behaviors occur probably has an even stronger effect. Thus we will now discuss organizational contexts that either aggravate or minimize the destructive leadership process.

According to Padilla and colleagues (2007), conducive environments are those characterized by four facets: instability; perceived threat; "negative" cultural values (high power distance, uncertainty avoidance, and collectivism); and an absence of checks and balances and institutionalization. The idea that some environments foster abuse was further developed by Hu and Liu (2017), and Ferris, Zinko, Brouer, Buckley, and Harvey (2007). While the former proposed that environments with a mechanistic structure and a hostile climate enhance the relationship between the leader's predisposition to, and actual, abusive behaviors, the latter highlighted the role played by perceived organizational politics in the creation of uncertainty where there is little control over the environment and thus where strategic bullying thrives.

Although empirical tests of these ideas are still scarce, the studies so far have consistently supported the previous propositions. For example, Mawritz and colleagues (Mawritz, Dust, & Resick, 2014; Mawritz, Mayer, Hoobler, Wayne, & Marinova, 2012) found that hostile climates not only predict the frequency of abusive supervision, but also exacerbate interpersonal deviance as a response to abuse. Kiewitz, Restubog, Shoss, Garcia, and Tang (2016) focused on the impact of abusive supervision on defensive silence and found evidence supporting the role of a climate of fear in exacerbating the abusive supervision–fear–defensive silence relationship. In a similar direction, Neves (2014) found that, in organizations that had undergone downsizing, submissive employees (that is, those with low core self-evaluations and low co-worker support) reported significantly more abuse from their supervisors than those working for organizations that did not implement downsizing.

Research on environments that hinder the emergence, or minimize the impact, of destructive leadership is even scarcer than that on conducive/hostile environments, but, once again, the findings tend to be consistent. Such a distinction is important, because preventing a conducive climate from growing might be less effective than developing a climate in which it is actively signaled that such behaviors are not tolerated. Creating an abuse-intolerant climate in which management does not tolerate rude and abusive behaviors, and punishes perpetrators, establishes clear policies and standards, reduces perceptions of supervisor abuse, and, at the same time, aggravates the felt violation associated with abuse (Kernan, Racicot, & Fisher, 2016). Curiously, Frazier and Bowler (2015) found that destructive leaders (operationalized as supervisors undermining followers) also contributed to the development of a climate that helps to sustain destructive behaviors – namely, by suggesting that employee voice is not encouraged and is risky.

Taken together, the existing evidence suggests that the relationship between destructive leaders and the environments in which they live and work is complex, and if we are to deal effectively with destructive leadership, the interconnections between leaders, followers, and context deserve more attention.

Followers as the Context of Leadership

In addition to organizational or cultural context, followers can be part of a context that facilitates or hinders destructive leadership. Leaders might even rely on the contribution of followers to fulfill their destructive aims (Krasikova et al., 2013). The new domain of followership produced a number of conceptual and empirical studies that show the many ways in which followers may contribute to destructive leadership (for example, Carsten & Uhl-Bien, 2013; Knoll, Schyns, & Petersen, 2017; Lipman-Blumen, 2004). Drawing on this previous research and the conceptual contributions made by Thoroughgood and colleagues (Thoroughgood, Padilla, Hunter, & Tate, 2012; Thoroughgood et al., 2016), we propose to distinguish five types of follower, depending on their involvement in destructive leadership.

- *Victims* suffer from tyrants and leaders who engage in destructive acts. Cynically, victims are part of the process of destructive leadership, because their suffering spreads fear, and their apparent weakness lets the destructive leader appear powerful.
- *Bystanders* observe the unethical or illegal acts conducted by destructive leaders. In tolerating destructive acts, bystanders contribute to destructive leadership by discouraging victims and concealing destructive conditions from outsiders.
- *Conformers* execute orders from destructive leaders, and thus they actively contribute to destructive outcomes. They comply, because they try to minimize the consequences of not going along (Padilla et al., 2007), which may be direct punishment or a loss of status and privileges.
- *Colluders* associate with destructive leaders to achieve personal gain (Padilla et al., 2007). They find colluding instrumental in achieving their own aims. They may share the worldview of the destructive leader, or they may simply be selfish and opportunistic (Barbuto, 2000; Lipman-Blumen, 2005; Kellerman, 2004; Thoroughgood et al., 2012).
- Finally, the *puppet master* refers to followers who manipulate a leader into conducting or commanding destructive acts. Research on upward influence and organizational politics has shown that followers can influence leaders, for example by ingratiation, inspirational and personal appeal, granting

leadership, and legitimization (DeRue & Ashford, 2010; Yukl & Tracey, 1992). These could, for example, be followers high in dark triad personality traits themselves, who engage in strategic follower behavior (Schyns, Wisse, & Sanders, 2018).

Summary and Outlook

Throughout this chapter, we have built the case for destructive leadership. A one-sided, positivistic, approach to leadership clearly ignores a significant part of the leaders' behavioral repertoire, and it has unintended consequences for our knowledge of leadership and for organizational practice. We constructed our arguments around four major points: different perspectives over destructive actions, its underlying intentions, the type of intentions, and the context in which it occurs.

Implications for Theory and Research

As previously stated, we argued in this chapter that four questions are relevant to research into destructive leadership. These questions have strong implications for theory and research. First, researchers need to build theoretical models that take into account the perspective of destructive behavior that is relevant for their specific assumptions. For example, when including leader personality in the prediction of destructive behavior, actual behavior, rather than follower perceptions, might be more relevant. In contrast, when follower reactions are considered an outcome, then follower perceptions of destructive behavior are crucial. Either way, better models need to clarify the perspective that researchers take and, most importantly, appropriately test the assumptions. (For example, perception is not the same as behavior and should therefore not be used as a measurement of objective behavior.)

More research is needed on both attributed and actual (types of) intention of destructive leadership. This is the case both to understand the processes involved in why leaders use destructive behavior and how destructive leadership shapes the reactions towards destructive leadership (for example, Schyns et al., 2018). An important step forward for research into destructive leadership would thus be the inclusion of intentions within process models.

Further attention should also be given to the role played by different contexts. Most immediately, our thoughts go to the need to conduct further research on climates that effectively prevent aggression and how to institutionalize them to develop strong destructive-intolerant cultures. The broader environment, including elements such as the role played by external institutions like the media, government agencies, and other actors and observers, as well as the degree of complexity, instability, and perceived threat (Mulvey & Padilla, 2010), should also be taken into account.

Practical Implications

The recognition of destructive leadership as a relevant organizational phenomenon also has important practical implications. The most obvious implication has to do with the need to pay more attention to the "dark side" of leadership. Individuals at multiple levels of the organization should be trained to identify and act when they see colleagues or leaders engaging in destructive behaviors, or when they see the conditions for the emergence of such behaviors arise. Similarly, and given the human and financial toll that destructive leadership takes, managers should spend resources developing policies that signal that the organization does not tolerate such behaviors and channels through which organizational members can report such actions, in the event that they occur (Kernan et al., 2016). Organizations should also take into account that destructive leadership problems can have different origins and interpretations (that is, perceptual versus behavioral, intentional versus unintentional, aiming to harm versus aiming to improve performance), and therefore the effectiveness of strategies to deal with them might differ.

Implications for Teaching Leadership

It appears, when looking at higher education, that the focus is still on positive leadership. This has several implications for students of leadership. First, students leave higher education unprepared for the occurrence of destructive leadership and hence are unable to cope with its fallout. This applies to their role as followers, leaders, and human resource managers. We call on educators to prepare students for the possibility that they might be subjected to destructive leadership in their working lives. In their roles as followers, students need to understand how to cope with destructive leadership, and where and when to ask for help – and even when it is time to leave a leader to prevent severe consequences for themselves. In their own roles as leaders, they need to be able to see the signs of (future) destructive leadership, ideally before one of their subordinates gains a leadership position (see also Schyns et al., 2018). As human resource managers, students need to be able to apply tools to manage destructive leaders, either through leader development (for example, when there is simply a question of a leader's ignorance of the effects of their leadership or where destructive leadership arises because of role stress) or through careful management of the consequences for followers.

Conclusion

All in all, research into destructive leadership has made a lot of progress over the last two decades. We especially know how detrimental it can be to followers, organizations, and society as a whole. In this chapter, we have outlined issues regarding perspectives, intentions, and context that can further improve our knowledge about destructive leadership, can inform practitioners, and can support students of leadership.

References

Ashforth, B.E. (1994). Petty tyranny in organizations. *Human Relations, 47*(7), 755–778.

Barbuto, J.E. (2000). Influence triggers: A framework for understanding follower compliance. *The Leadership Quarterly, 11*(3), 365–387.

Barry, C.T., Chaplin, W.F., & Grafeman, S.J. (2006). Aggression following performance feedback: The influences of narcissism, feedback valence, and comparative standard. *Personality and Individual Differences, 41*(1), 177–187.

Boddy, C.R. (2011). Corporate psychopaths, bullying and unfair supervision in the workplace. *Journal of Business Ethics, 100*(3), 367–379.

Carlson, D.S., Ferguson, M., Perrewé, P.L., & Whitten, D. (2011). The fallout from abusive supervision: An examination of subordinates and their partners. *Personnel Psychology, 64*(4), 937–961.

Carsten, M.K., & Uhl-Bien, M. (2013). Ethical followership: An examination of followership beliefs and crimes of obedience. *Journal of Leadership and Organizational Studies, 20*(1), 45–57.

Cohen, A. (2016). Are they among us? A conceptual framework of the relationship between the dark triad personality and counterproductive work behaviors (CWBs). *Human Resource Management Review, 26*, 69–85.

Costa, S., & Neves, P. (2017). It is your fault! How blame attributions of breach predict employees' reactions. *Journal of Managerial Psychology, 32*(7), 470–483.

DeRue, S., & Ashford, S. (2010). Who will lead and who will follow? A social process of leadership identity construction in organizations. *Academy of Management Review, 35*(4), 627–647.

Einarsen, S., Aasland, M.S., & Skogstad, A. (2007). Destructive leadership behavior: A definition and conceptual model. *The Leadership Quarterly, 18*(3), 207–216.

Erickson, A., Shaw, B., Murray, J., & Branch, S. (2015). Destructive leadership: Causes, consequences and countermeasures. *Organizational Dynamics, 44*(4), 266–272.

Farh, C., & Chen, Z. (2014). Beyond the individual victim: Multilevel consequences of abusive supervision in teams. *Journal of Applied Psychology, 99*(6), 1074–1095.

Ferris, G.R., Zinko, R., Brouer, R.L., Buckley, M.R., & Harvey, M.G. (2007). Strategic bullying as a supplementary, balanced perspective on destructive leadership. *The Leadership Quarterly, 18*(3), 195–206.

Frazier, M.L., & Bowler, M. (2015). Voice climate, supervisor undermining, and work outcomes: A group-level examination. *Journal of Management, 41*(3), 841–863.

Hansbrough, T.K., Lord, R.G., & Schyns, B. (2015). Reconsidering the accuracy of follower leadership ratings. *The Leadership Quarterly, 26*(2), 220–237.

Hansbrough, T.K., Lord, R.G., Schyns, B., & Foti, R. (2018). Separating episodic and semantic memory to improve the validity of leadership scales [Manuscript in preparation].

Harms, P.D., Spain, S., & Hannah, S. (2011). Leader development and the dark side of personality. *The Leadership Quarterly, 22*, 495–509.

Hoobler, J.M., & Brass, D.J. (2006). Abusive supervision and family undermining as displaced aggression. *Journal of Applied Psychology, 91*(5), 1125–1133.

Hu, L., & Liu, Y. (2017). Abuse for status: A social dominance perspective of abusive supervision. *Human Resource Management Review*, *27*(2), 328–337.

Judge, T.A., Piccolo, R.F., & Kosalka, T., 2009. The bright and dark sides of leader traits: A review and theoretical extension of the leader trait paradigm. *The Leadership Quarterly*, *20*(6), 855–875.

Kausel, E.E., Culbertson, S.S., Leiva, P.I., Slaughter, J., & Jackson, A.T. (2015). Too arrogant for their own good? Why and when narcissists dismiss advice. *Organizational Behavior and Human Decision Processes*, *131*, 33–50.

Kellerman, B. (2004). *Bad leadership*. Cambridge, MA: Harvard Business School Press.

Kernan, M.C., Racicot, B.M., & Fisher, A.M. (2016). Effects of abusive supervision, psychological climate, and felt violation on work outcomes: A moderated mediated model. *Journal of Leadership and Organizational Studies*, *23*(3), 309–321.

Kernan, M.C., Watson, S., Chen, F.F., & Kim, T.G. (2011). How cultural values affect the impact of abusive supervision on worker attitudes. *Cross-cultural Management: An International Journal*, *18*(4), 464–484.

Kiewitz, C., Restubog, S.L., Shoss, M.K., Garcia, P.R., & Tang, R.L. (2016). Suffering in silence: Investigating the role of fear in the relationship between abusive supervision and defensive silence. *Journal of Applied Psychology*, *101*(5), 731–742.

Knoll, M., Schyns, B., & Petersen, L.-E. (2017). How the influence of unethical leaders on followers is affected by their implicit followership theories. *Journal of Leadership and Organizational Studies*, *24*(4), 450–465.

Krasikova, D.V., Green, S.G., & LeBreton, J.M. (2013). Destructive leadership: A theoretical review, integration, and future research agenda. *Journal of Management*, *39*(5), 1308–1338.

Liang, L.H., Hanig, S., Evans, R., Brown, D.J., & Lian, H. (2017, November 27). Why is your boss making you sick? A longitudinal investigation modeling time-lagged relations between abusive supervision and employee physical health. *Journal of Organizational Behavior*. Advance online publication. Retrieved from https://onlinelibrary.wiley.com/doi/abs/10.1002/job.2248

Liden, R.C., & Antonakis, J. (2009). Considering context in psychological leadership research. *Human Relations*, *62*(11), 1587–1605.

Lipman-Blumen, J. (2004). *The allure of toxic leaders: Why we follow destructive bosses and corrupt politicians and how we can survive them*. Oxford: Oxford University Press.

Lipman-Blumen, J. (2005). *The allure of toxic leaders*. New York: Oxford University Press.

Liu, D., Liao, H., & Loi, R. (2012). The dark side of leadership: A three-level investigation of the cascading effect of abusive supervision on employee creativity. *Academy of Management Journal*, *55*(5), 1187–1212.

Lord, R.G., Day, D.V., Zaccaro, S.J., Avolio, B.J., & Eagly, A.H. (2017). Leadership in applied psychology: Three waves of theory and research. *Journal of Applied Psychology*, *102*(3), 434–451.

Martinko, M.J., Harvey, P., Brees, J., & Mackey, J. (2013). Abusive supervision: A review and alternative perspective. *Journal of Organizational Behavior*, *34*, S120–S137.

Mawritz, M.B., Dust, S.B., & Resick, C.J. (2014). Hostile climate, abusive supervision, and employee coping: Does conscientiousness matter? *Journal of Applied Psychology*, *99*(4), 737–747.

Mawritz, M.B., Mayer, D.M., Hoobler, J.M., Wayne, S.J., & Marinova, S.J. (2012). A trickle-down model of abusive supervision. *Personnel Psychology*, *65*(2), 325–357.

Mulvey, P.W., & Padilla, A. (2010). The environment of destructive leadership. In B. Schyns & T. Hansbrough (Eds.), *When leadership goes wrong: Destructive leadership, mistakes, and ethical failures* (pp. 49–71). Greenwich, CT: Information Age.

Namie G., & Namie R. (2000). *The bully at work*. Naperville, IL: Sourcebooks.

Neves, P. (2014). Taking it out on survivors: Submissive employees, downsizing, and abusive supervision. *Journal of Occupational and Organizational Psychology*, *87*(3), 507–534.

Neves, P., & Schyns, B. (2018). Destructive uncertainty: The toxic triangle, implicit theories and leadership identity during organizational change. In M. Vakola & P. Petrou (Eds.), *Organizational change: Psychological effects and strategies for coping* (pp. 131–141). London: Routledge.

Padilla, A., Hogan, R., & Kaiser, R.B. (2007). The toxic triangle: Destructive leaders, susceptible followers, and conducive environments. *The Leadership Quarterly*, *18*(3), 176–194.

Paulhus, D.L. (2014). Toward a taxonomy of dark personalities. *Current Directions in Psychological Science*, *23*(6), 421–426.

Paulhus, D.L., & Williams, K. (2002). The dark triad of personality: Narcissism, Machiavellianism, and psychopathy. *Journal of Research in Personality*, *36*(6), 556–568.

Schyns, B., & Schilling, J. (2013). How bad are the effects of bad leaders? A meta-analysis of destructive leadership and its outcomes. *The Leadership Quarterly*, *24*(1), 138–158.

Schyns, B., Felfe, J., & Schilling, J. (in press). Is it me or you? How reactions to abusive supervision are shaped by leader behavior and follower perceptions *Frontiers in Psychology-Organizational Psychology*.

Schyns, B., Wisse, B.M., & Sanders, S. (2018). Shady strategic behavior: Recognizing strategic behavior of dark triad followers. *Academy of Management Perspectives*. In press.

Tepper, B.J. (2000). Consequences of abusive supervision. *Academy of Management Journal*, *43*(2), 178–190.

Tepper, B.J. (2007). Abusive supervision in work organizations: Review, synthesis, and research agenda. *Journal of Management*, *33*(3), 261–289.

Tepper, B.J., Duffy, M.K., Henle, C.A., & Lambert, L.S. (2006). Procedural injustice, victim precipitation, and abusive supervision. *Personnel Psychology*, *59*(1), 101–123.

Thoroughgood, C.N., Padilla, A., Hunter, S.T., & Tate, B.W. (2012). The susceptible circle: A taxonomy of followers associated with destructive leadership. *The Leadership Quarterly*, *23*(5), 897–917.

Thoroughgood, C.N., Sawyer, K.B., Padilla, A., & Lunsford, L. (2016). Destructive leadership: A critique of leader-centric perspectives and toward a more holistic definition. *Journal of Business Ethics*. Advance online publication. Retrieved from https://arizona.pure.elsevier.com/en/publications/destructive-leadership-a-critique-of-leader-centric-perspectives-

Velez, M.J., & Neves, P. (2016). Abusive supervision, psychosomatic symptoms, and deviance: Can job autonomy make a difference? *Journal of Occupational Health Psychology*, *21*(3), 322–333.

Vogel, R.M., Mitchell, M.S., Tepper, B.J., Restubog, S.L.D., Hu, C., Hua, W., & Huang, J. (2015). A cross-cultural examination of subordinates' perceptions of and reactions to abusive supervision. *Journal of Organizational Behavior*, *36*(5), 720–745.

Wisse, B., Sanders, S., Barelds, D.P.H., & Laurijssen, L.M. (2018). No regard for those who need it: The moderating role of follower self-esteem in the relationship between leader psychopathy and leader self-serving behavior [Manuscript under review].

Yukl, G., & Tracey, J.B. (1992). Consequences of influence tactics used with subordinates, peers, and the boss. *Journal of Applied Psychology, 77*(4), 525–535.

Zhang, Y., & Liao, Z. (2015). Consequences of abusive supervision: A meta-analytic review. *Asia Pacific Journal of Management, 32*(4), 959–987.

PART III
Improving Leadership Practice and Expanding Our Thinking about Leadership

11

LEADERSHIP DEVELOPMENT STARTS EARLIER THAN WE THINK

Capturing the Capacity of New Leaders to Address the Leader Talent Shortage

Susan E. Murphy

Every year, in late October, we witness droves of young children taking over neighborhoods, aiming to secure fistfuls of candy while clad in muscle-padded, superhero costumes and role-playing powerful, strong, and larger-than-life superheroes. In fact, the National Retail Federation estimates that 3.7 million children costumes are sold each year in the United States (Salay, 2017). The popularity of dressing up as superheroes almost all year around and watching the actions of real-life leaders (parents, teachers, authority figures, etc.) gives children various insights into the effects of power and influence. These important lessons leave children with specific tactics to lead playground games or to impose structure on the loose social order of early childhood. Research has shown that, as a form of influence, leadership occurs in the preschool years when children work to mobilize their peers (Murphy & Reichard, 2011; Recchia, 2011). Throughout childhood, children take on formal leadership roles in activities, sports, and clubs, as well informal roles in friendship groups both inside and outside of school. Most youth programs, such as Guides and Scouts, focus on developing these young leadership skills and character attributes. Once students enroll in college and university, young leaders have an increasingly large array of leadership development opportunities available to them on campuses. College and university curriculums and specific programs focusing on leadership have been shown to enhance students' motivation to lead and to increase their self-awareness for further leadership development (Riggio, Ciulla, & Sorensen, 2003; Zimmerman-Oster, 2003), as well as to increase their future earning capacity (Kuhn & Weinberger, 2005).

Why, then, if children, adolescents, and college students have experience of leading others and being led by others, and have been involved in leader development activities, do organizations and their human resource directors still scramble to find those who can fill leadership roles in their organizations? In the United States, human resource professionals claim that only 30 percent of their organization's leadership are of high quality, with only 44 percent reporting that they think their organizations have the internal talent to fill leadership roles (Wellin, 2018). In this chapter, I propose that understanding leadership development at earlier stages of life can help to reduce future leadership skill shortages for three reasons.

1. The way in which leadership is offered by learning and development staff must increasingly capitalize on the leadership experience of new managers by incorporating previous youth leadership development and by responding to the development needs of new leaders.
2. Organizations must focus on positioning the practice of leadership to appeal to emerging adults' way of connecting and leading. Many are globally connected, competitive, independent, and are accustomed to high levels of feedback (Patel, 2017). At an early age, adolescents and emerging adults can become YouTube stars with the potential to influence 50 million people, and they are rapidly mastering all of the necessary tools of innovation, networking, and tech to succeed as young entrepreneurs.
3. The shortages of leadership talent demonstrate a failure to fully capitalize on the potential of diverse leaders. Future leadership positions will be filled by those with less traditionally defined leadership potential and will therefore require new human resource talent metrics.

By understanding more about leadership at an early age and the role that societal definitions have on fostering, and in some cases hindering, leadership development across individuals, organizations can take advantage of a rich leadership bench.

I begin this chapter with a brief review of the changing tasks of leaders in for-profit and not-for-profit contexts, followed by a review of the building blocks for youth leadership development, including the importance of leader identity, leadership self-efficacy, and role models, and finally I discuss ways in which both schools and organizations can continue the development of diverse, sometimes overlooked, leaders.

The Context: New Ways of Leading for New Leaders

In many ways, today's organizations look vastly different than those of just 20 years ago, yet surprisingly the content of current leadership development activities has remained focused on many of the same concepts and techniques used as far back as 40 years ago (Hogan & Warrenfeltz, 2003). The growth of the service, tech, and healthcare sectors, along with the commensurate decline in the manufacturing sector, has resulted in a fundamental change in the tasks of leadership and the skills required to facilitate workplace innovation, to support high levels of customer service and teamwork, and to enhance productivity. Concepts such as service leadership, innovation leadership, and global leadership appear in popular business publications and training webinars, highlighting these changing requirements. There are calls for leaders to think differently, to lead differently, and to balance work and life differently than their predecessors. Tomorrow's emerging leaders are currently developing essential leadership skills by leading informal groups, sports teams, and friendship networks. Many of these experiences put these future leaders in good stead for working within entrepreneurial ventures and startups characterized by informal power structures, which require interpersonal influence and effective communication, and in which the future leaders experience quick goal feedback (Myers & Sadaghiani, 2010). Young people's extensive use of technology-enabled networking also prepares them to one day participate fully in the loose confederations of "gig workers," who freelance on project-based work. Emerging adults are also poised to tackle issues of global and local leadership with their extensive use of worldwide social media platforms such as WeChat (a Chinese messenger and social media app with almost 1 billion daily users). As noted by Lee and Olszewski-Kubilius (2014), both technology and greater mobility have served to reduce the distance between countries. Students who take advantage of college/university study-abroad programs benefit by developing their leadership skills and building a global worldview (Samardžija, Walker, & Bazdan, 2017).

Although adolescents and emerging adults appear to have mastered social media and global connection, there remains concerns that these "true digital natives" (that is, those who have never lived without smartphones or the Internet, born between 1995 and 2010) lack some of the interpersonal and face-to-face skills that remain important for the leadership role (PayScale, 2016). Generation Z, however, has shown itself to be savvy with respect to new methods of leadership. Well-known student- and youth-led movements, often described as "digital democracy," began with the Arab Spring, in which young people leveraged their social media skills to mobilize large numbers of followers (Stieglitz & Dang-Xuan, 2012), and has more recently been evidenced in the strong collective student response to mass school shooting at Marjory Stoneman Douglas High School, in Parkland, FL. The students at the forefront of the movement were also well equipped to rally others and demanded legislation to keep young people safe in their schools, using expertise they had gained from classroom debate skills learned as part of a district-wide extemporaneous speaking program (Gurney, 2018).

In addition to the positive new forms of leadership, Generation Z may be disrupting the workplace with demands for working methods and programs that cater to their individual needs (Patel, 2017). This is a generation that has been allowed to design every element of their own Nikes online and even to garnish their own frozen yogurt with hand-selected toppings. These demands for individualized solutions across a wide range of products and services increase the potential for technology to play an expanded role in new forms of leadership development. For example, Rolls Royce has partnered with a tech firm to provide individualized leader development content through specialized apps that take into account new leaders' developmental goals. One large southwest U.S. medical center uses an aggressive high-level shadowing program for brand new hires who have recently completed a Masters' degree in health administration, satisfying individual ambition. Other companies do not waste time on generic leadership training, but instead build upon the leader development techniques pioneered at General Electric to provide new leaders with experience in solving pressing corporate problems. Although companies are gearing up to accommodate the preferences of the newest wave of Generation Z employees, they should keep in mind that their past concern for Millennial employees' shortcomings emerged as overblown, with that generation found not only to be team-oriented, knowledgeable about tech, motivated, and eager to communicate with their supervisors, but also to have taken up leadership roles, with Millennials now occupying 83 percent of management positions (Myers & Sadaghiani, 2010).

Promoting and understanding leadership development among young people is becoming more commonplace (Karagianni & Montgomery, 2017; Lee & Olszewski-Kubilius, 2014), and it may provide organizational human resource talent managers with additional methods for identifying those early high-potentials with the right constellation of traits and experience to grow into leadership positions. A thorough understanding of the range of previous leadership experiences of young leaders can help organizations to compete more effectively in an increasingly global, interconnected, and digital world.

Background to Understanding Youth Leader Development: Leader Identity Formation in Children and Adolescents

Whether it be the prestige of leading a line of classmates to lunch or having special classroom duties, those chosen to serve in influential roles fully recognize the importance of these situations early in life. By the time an individual reaches high school, college, or even their first job, ideas about what leaders do and how well an individual performs as a leader are often well informed. A broad-based understanding of youth leadership development takes into account both contributing developmental factors and underlying cognitive processes. For example, research showed that adolescent traits, measured at age 17 by the "Big Five" dimensions (McCrae & Costa, 1989), predicted later leader emergence and transformational behavior at age 29 (Reichard et al., 2011). These data from the Fullerton Longitudinal Study showed that extraversion, openness to experience, and conscientiousness were positively related to leader emergence, while neuroticism was negatively related. In addition, those adolescents who were more extraverted and less neurotic were more likely to also later exhibit transformational leadership behaviors. These traits for leadership have been shown to have a genetic basis as well (De Neve, Mikhaylov, Dawes, Christakis, & Fowler, 2013). Environmental influences such as parenting style and attachment style have been investigated in youth leadership. One study, for instance, showed that authoritative parenting style and taking part in modest rule breaking were related to later leader emergence and number of leadership roles attained (Avolio, Rotundo, & Walumbwa, 2009).

Leader identity – that is, the extent to which a leader identifies with the leadership role and sees themselves as a competent leader – serves as an underlying explanatory process for leader development in much of the work on adult leadership development (Carroll & Levy, 2010; Day, Harrison, & Halpin, 2009; Carroll & Levy, 2010; Epitropaki, Kark, Mainemelis, & Lord, 2017; Ibarra, Snook, & Guillén-Ramo, 2010; Lord & Hall, 2005; see also Chapter 9, in this volume). Through leadership development activities, leader identity strengthens (Day & Sin, 2011) and changes focus from the individual leader themselves to higher levels of collective focus (Lord & Hall, 2005). Although leader identity has also been a central theme in much of the college leadership development research (Komives, Longerbeam, Owen, Mainella, & Osteen, 2006), little work has been done on examining the role of leader identity in youth development, with the exception of Murphy and Johnson's (2011) lifespan approach to leader development (see Figure 11.1). The model incorporates the impact of developmental factors of early experiences, parental influences, and traits and characteristics on the processes of leader identity and

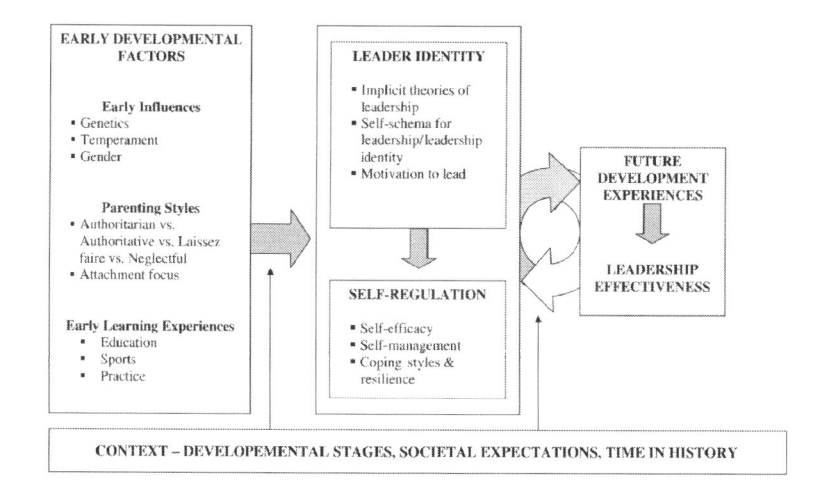

FIGURE 11.1 A lifespan approach to leader development.

leadership efficacy development (Murphy, 2002). Within this section, I review some of the major elements of leader identity formation that have implications for later leader development, as well as for recognizing and developing untapped leadership potential.

Key Ingredients for Early Leadership Development: Leader Identity, Leadership Self-efficacy, and the Process of Self-regulation

Leader identity is defined formally as "a sub-component of one's working self-concept that includes leadership schemas, leadership experiences and future representations of oneself as a leader" (Epitropaki et al., 2017, p. 107). For youth, future representations of themselves as leaders serve as a basis for their "identity work" in the early stages of leader identity formation and later in further developing their motivation to lead (Chan & Drasgow, 2001; Stiehl, Felfe, Elprana, & Gatzka, 2015). Identity work is defined as "people being engaged in forming, repairing, maintaining, strengthening or revising the constructions that are productive of a sense of coherence and distinctiveness" (Sveningsson & Alvesson, 2003, p. 1165). Throughout childhood and adolescence, a major developmental task is identity formation (Santrock, 2015), and crucial transition points in school are associated with cultural milestones that provide important developmental trigger points, which extend to leader identity (Murphy & Johnson, 2011). Even more important for youth leadership is the impact that idealized leader characteristics have on children's and adolescents' identification with the leadership role. Research shows that, for working-age individuals, the leadership characteristics that are seen as most prototypical of effective leaders include a high level of intelligence, dominance, assertiveness, confidence, and independence, which are considered to be typically agentic qualities. Implicit leadership theory (Lord, Foti, & DeVader, 1984; Phillips & Lord, 1982) and the leader categorization theory (Lord & Maher, 1991) focused on the ways in which individuals use prototypic dimensions to characterize another as an effective leader, but these same processes play a role when an individual considers their own leader identity. The extent to which their identity content matches their implicit theory of effective leaders may determine the strength of the individual's leader identity and play an important role in early leadership development. However, the research thus far has exclusively focused on adult leadership. For example, self-to-prototype comparisons tended to predict leader behavior with respect to affiliation (Guillén, Mayo, & Korotov, 2015) and efficacy for leadership (Murphy, Jansson, & Hoyt, 2017), while another study showed that the content of leader identity matched demonstrated leader behaviors (Johnson, Venus, Lanaj, Mao, & Chang, 2012). In my own development work with young leaders over the last 20 years, I have asked them to draw a leader, or to pull together words and images that demonstrate leader characteristics, and I then ask that they assess to what extent they possess those leadership characteristics. For many young leaders, this exercise allows them to talk about the responsibilities and behaviors of leaders as a precursor to deeper reflection about where their leadership skills fit their image of effective leaders.

In addition to understanding how prototypic leader ideals play a role in leader identity formation, other components of leader identity are also important to consider in youth leadership development. There is some research that suggests individuals who have more experience with different types of leaders are less likely to rely on more stereotyped or simplistic views of the leadership of others (Foti & Lord, 1987) or of their own leadership (Lord & Hall, 2005). One recent study seemed to bear that out: In a sample of 665 individuals from the United States, younger individuals with less leadership experience held a more agentic view of leadership than did older workers with more experience in organizations (Murphy, 2017). This may be a result not only of their lack of experience with leaders in the forms of bosses and team leaders, but also of their overreliance on fictional portrayals of powerful heroes and inept bosses. We sometimes refer to this as "The Office" effect: Whether it is the British version or American version of the television series, in each the boss was largely incompetent. These "novice" leaders may also hold a leader identity that contains a predominate focus on the individual leader, as opposed to a focus on the group or the larger collective within the organization (Lord & Hall, 2005).

Finally, leader identity is also part of a broader process explained by self-regulation of leader behavior. Self-regulation refers to the process by which people use appropriate goals or standards to align their behaviors and self-concepts (Brockner & Higgens, 2001). According to self-regulatory views of leadership, if an individual is to see themselves as a leader, there must be a self-matching process that occurs, which produces a motivation to lead and which may or may not work in tandem to exhibit leader behaviors. The performance of the leader then reinforces or weakens a previous appraisal of their self-efficacy for the leadership role through negative or positive efficacy spirals (Murphy, 1992, 2002; Murphy & Johnson, 2016). It is important to remember that seeing oneself as a leader or being seen by others as a leader does not occur independently of one's context because leadership is socially constructed. As mentioned previously, trait theories of leadership suggest that these children filling leadership roles would show dominance in the form of extraversion, conscientiousness, and other such traits, which allows them to fulfill the role of leader in the eyes of followers, allowing them to appear more "leader-like." DeRue and Ashford's (2010) work builds upon social identity theory of leadership (Hogg, 2001) to discuss the process of assuming leadership roles: Whether the individual is granted or engages in taking the leader identity is based on the extent that their leader behaviors are prototypical to the group. And childhood context and social rules give cues early on as to who will be seen as prototypical with respect to group-level behaviors. Whether it is the young girl trying out leadership and being told that she is "too bossy" or "too loud," or the shy newcomer from another part of the country who is teased for his unusual accent, cliques of adolescents who determine popularity could serve as a sorting mechanism for determining leader prototypicality. Recent research on popularity suggests that there are two kinds: We may think of status and influence (perceived popularity) as typical popularity, but it is exercised by bringing fear to others, while popularity based on likability involves the use of social influence to encourage people to want to be around the person (Prinstein, 2017). Popularity as prototypicality would also dictate which group members are allowed to reach leader status and has implications for their taking on future leadership roles.

Role Modeling and Application to Youth Leadership Model

One of the last keys to youth leader development that works in concert with both leader identity and leader self-regulatory processes is role modeling. The primary mechanism behind role modeling is that when the individual views other successful leaders and thinks about what they themselves might become in the future, it provides examples of *possible selves* (Markus & Norius, 1986), and it can provide an impetus for trying on *provisional selves* (Ibarra, Wittman, Petriglieri, & Day, 2014) by taking on leadership tasks inside and outside of school. A recent qualitative study developed a framework for examining role-modeling effectiveness specifically for emerging leaders (Bowers, Rosch, & Collier, 2016). First, the role model provided insight into the qualities of effective leaders and may have served to displace more naive implicit theories of effective leadership. Broad exposure to an actual successful leader could also help to develop the young person's leader identity by strengthening the congruence between their implicit theory and their own qualifications. Interestingly, in Bowers and colleagues' (2016) study, these emerging leaders were less likely to report learning from role models who struggled or who had less desirable characteristics. Specifically, the emerging leaders learned about the contribution of a professional work ethic and effective interpersonal skills. Role models in this study also helped to increase the youth's motivation to lead, but, interestingly, this increase seemed to occur only among those youth who had developed a personal relationship with the role model. Although this increase in motivation to lead could be the result of reducing the discrepancy between ideal leader and the young leader's own identity, it appears that this role modeling occurred within more of a social cognitive framework in which emerging adults learned vicariously through others about leadership (Bandura, 1997). A final gain, then, was an increase in current leadership self-efficacy for the emerging adult.

Leadership role models are said to be lacking for women and people of color. At the time of writing of this chapter, Marvel franchise movie *Black Panther* showed black men and women as powerful leaders in a technologically advanced civilization. The response among the African American community to the movie and message has been overwhelmingly positive, and it has represented a source of pride given the community's typical portrayal in film. Women and people of color spend less time as central characters, and have less dialog, than white men (Anderson & Daniels, 2016). Individuals who fail to see people who look like them in leadership roles either in real life or as portrayed in the media can end up disidentifying with the leadership role (Arminio et al., 2000). Unfortunately, school curriculums provide limited exposure to role models who are women or people of color. Moreover, a recent study showed that if a child's teacher looks like them, they do better in school, they report feeling more cared for, they are more interested in their schoolwork, and they have more confidence in their teachers' abilities to communicate with them (Gershenson, Lindsay, Hart, & Papageorge, 2017). U.S. schools have mostly white teachers, with only 18 percent being nonwhite (U.S. Department of Education, 2016).

In summary, there are a number of factors affecting later leadership effectiveness that occur in early childhood and continue throughout emerging adulthood. Seeing oneself as a leader and being seen as a leader by others is the result of a number of leader identity development and self-regulation processes that either reinforce or discourage us to exercise leadership. The next section discusses ways of incorporating past leadership development into on-the-job leader development.

Leveraging Youth Leadership Experience in Organizational Leader Development Programs

With the vast resources directed toward leadership training in organizations, is there evidence that it works? As mentioned previously, the shortage of organizational leaders reported by many human resource managers seems to indicate that leader development efforts are not hugely successful. However, meta-analyses of leadership development research show positive effects, albeit varying in strength across a range of factors (Avolio, Reichard, Hannah, Walumbwa, & Chan, 2009; Lacerenza et al., 2017). Hence a better question is: *Where and when is leadership development effective?* Lacerenza and colleagues (2017) identified a number of moderating conditions that would improve the impact of leadership development, including the presence of a needs analysis, feedback, multiple delivery methods, spaced training sessions, an on-site location, and face-to-face delivery. Building upon some of these findings and incorporating an understanding of youth leadership development, this section explores additional practical ways of further increasing the effectiveness of adult leader development.

Incorporate "New" Leaders into "New" Leadership Models

Leadership models in organizations can be more explicit regarding the specific types of leadership that are being cultivated. Often, there is a disconnect between those forms of leadership that are espoused and those forms that are rewarded. More extensive studies of effective leadership relevant to a particular organization and industry can help to focus attention on leadership for innovation and customer focus. A company's existing leadership models should also be examined for bias. For example, companies have worked to edit their selection and recruiting, as well as performance appraisals, for words that promote one category of leader over another (see, for example, with respect to gender, Gaucher, Friesen, & Kay, 2011). Even in the discourse on leadership development, the words used to describe program goals and outcomes, and the activities used, can telegraph to individuals their level of fit for leadership within the company.

Considering more inclusive leadership models would also improve on how individuals are selected to participate in leadership development. To identify leadership potential, the use of talent grids, 360-degree assessments, and validated measures of potential are the coin of the realm. Unfortunately, these assessments may be perpetuating previous models about who leaders are and what leaders do, based on the success of current incumbents. Talent managers are looking for bright and capable leaders, but they are also somewhat risk-averse and want to make sure that these individuals fit the espoused organizational values and culture. Google, for example, has collected large quantities of data for assessing effective leader characteristics and effective teams, and for identifying best methods for selecting employees, but there remains an overreliance on the word "fit" to the existing culture. This tendency can have even more severe ramifications beyond hiring similar employees based on general ideological fit. In her book *Weapons of Math Destruction*, Cathy O'Neil (2016) demonstrates how building algorithms to select successful news anchors builds on existing biases. If you were to run an algorithm to pick successful a news anchor, you would include gender and race as an attribute, but, because the most successful and highest paid news anchors are white men, women and people of color would be disqualified, because they are less likely to hold those positions now (are "less successful"), and hence why would we select people who do not currently succeed in these jobs? Therefore, the way in which we identify talent currently may not bring in diverse voices and backgrounds to build a competitive leadership pipeline. Utilizing thorough needs analysis for training that reduces bias and forms appropriate leadership models will be the key, as well as making sure that there are adequate role models for these new leaders.

Take into Account Learners' Past Leadership Experience and Developmental Stage, and Leverage Their Growth Mindset

The introduction of the idea of growth mindset is currently popular in schools across the United States (Dweck, 2006). Rather than viewing student ability as fixed, pupils and teachers are encouraged to view ability as skills that can be grown and developed. The youth leadership development model presented earlier is predicated on the belief that leadership skills can be developed. Building efficacy and building identity have at their core the fact that one can change and develop these leadership skills. Research has shown that, for other identities, subtle manipulations can increase an individual's belief in their abilities. For example, only when individuals were told that entrepreneurship was an ability that could be developed (a growth mindset) were participants in a study more likely to see entrepreneurship positively and as a part of their own identity (Pollack, Burnette, & Hoyt, 2012). Although a growth mindset is a positive and powerful strategy for acquiring ability, you cannot merely tell people to change their mindset. With children, the malleability of the brain works to underscore why effort, the right strategies, and good advice can lead to earning more course credits, higher grades, and higher standardized test scores (Yeager et al., 2016). Microsoft is using this idea to change the way in which it approaches leader development for its managers (Dweck & Hogan, 2016). The focus of Microsoft's efforts is not only on broadening its definition of talent, but also on setting up high-risk projects in which participants can fail hard and fail quickly as a way of learning new abilities. This risk taking and fast learning were rewarded. Employers also encourage the sharing of "hacks," whereby individuals are encouraged to work company-wide to solve a particular issue. They develop business plans and teams. This leadership development is invaluable and often leads to permanent leadership positions carrying the project forward.

Currently, research in leadership development provides a focus on mindset more broadly defined as developmental readiness (Avolio & Hannah, 2008) – that is, it asks: What are the characteristics of those ready to further develop their leadership skills? New leaders come to the workplace with a history and with a range of skills. Building upon past experiences in leadership roles that date back before adults entered the workforce may be a way of pointing toward the types of experience that prepare them for their next developmental goals. This involves looking not only at years of experience, but also at the types of experience that have led to the individual's current leadership efficacy and leader developmental efficacy. Murphy and Johnson (2016, p. 76) suggested that understanding both the individual's level of confidence in their own leadership ability and their belief in their ability to develop leadership is important for positive leader development:

> Leader developmental efficacy is defined as the belief in oneself to continually develop leadership knowledge and skills and, therefore, increases motivation to develop and the self-regulatory resources needed to work on difficult assignments and assume responsibility for one's own development.

An individual can set up ways of exploring leader developmental efficacy through developmental activities that look at long-standing philosophies of leadership, or through projective exercises such as drawing leaders or developing metaphors for leadership to uncover the content of ingrained implicit prototypes for leadership. These activities would also encourage self-awareness to facilitate the understanding of the growth mindset and being clear about the ways in which individuals develop as leaders.

Acknowledge and Give Space for Leader Development as Identity Work

As mentioned previously, much of what we do in relation to work can be explained by identity work. Who we are as professionals, as workers, co-workers, bosses, or team members is part of how we execute our work. Ibarra, Snook, and Guillén-Ramo (2010) specifically argue that leadership development is ultimately about facilitating an identity transition from particular ideas about leadership, which may be more simplistic, to more complex and higher-level leadership skill sets. This process of identity work was first identified by Alvesson and Willmott (2002). More specifically for leadership identity development work, Carroll and Levy (2010) distinguish the need for a construction of identity rather than merely behavioral regulation of a previous identity. Regulation would suggest a formed leader identity with some room for accommodations, whereas this ongoing construction provides a rich view of how leader development activities actively work on building new leader identities in the context of the self and others. In other words, a leadership identity is not merely an intra-individual, personal identity, but is a socially constructed and negotiated relationship in the context of others (Marchiondo, Myers, & Kopelman, 2015). The implications of both this individual and social process require that organizations do what they can to facilitate identity transformations that perhaps exchange one form of leadership for another. It becomes important to give learners a clear understanding of role-specific leader behaviors set against the backdrop of organizational values and strategic objectives. Barriers to these transitions can arise when newly appointed leaders do not see themselves in the leadership role because they over-identify with their past role as professional or as an individual contributor. Promotion to "manager," in some organizations, is not well received by all employees because many can worry about giving up their former relationships with their peers. Acknowledging these barriers and developing methods for supporting these identity transitions becomes crucial, as does utilizing assessments of leader identity (strength and level), leadership self-efficacy, and developmental efficacy to help to target appropriate types of leader development in the context of leader purpose and self-awareness.

Nontraditional leaders (defined as those not typically represented in the leadership ranks in an organization) may require more leadership opportunities, more role models, and more optional ways to work on leadership identity than those traditionally filling leadership roles. Women-only leadership programs

(Ely, Ibarra, & Kolb, 2011) focus on the particular challenges one might face as a woman in an organization, including exercising power, dealing with bias (conscious or unconscious), and discussions of identity conflict that can occur for women in high-level leadership roles. Other programs exclusively for Asian Americans, African Americans, or other underrepresented groups would underscore issues of developmental efficacy and identity, as well as issues of identity conflict, within organization leadership models (Johnson & Sy, 2016).

Summary

Leadership development is a lifelong process that is intimately intertwined with one's long-standing self-concept. Seeing oneself as a leader and being seen as a leader is the culmination of many years of positive and negative leadership experiences. A good understanding of the contributors to early childhood and emerging adulthood leadership can help to widen the net for emerging leaders and may stem the leadership shortage faced by many organizations. Leadership development professionals can start by designing leadership development programs that build upon previous leadership experiences and which focus a good portion of leader development on important leader identity work to help individuals to make successful leadership transitions.

References

Alvesson, M., & Willmott, H. (2002). Identity regulation as organizational control: Producing the appropriate individual. *Journal of Management Studies, 39*(5), 619–644.

Anderson, H., & Daniels, M. (2016, April). Film dialogue in 2000 screenplays broken down by gender and age. Retrieved from https://pudding.cool/2017/03/film-dialogue/index.html

Arminio, J., Carter, S., Jones, S.E., Kruger, K., Lucas, N., Washington, J., . . . & Scott, A. (2000). Leadership experiences of students of color. *NASPA Journal, 37*(3), 406–510.

Avolio, B.J., & Hannah, S.T. (2008). Developmental readiness: Accelerating leader development. *Consulting Psychology Journal: Practice and Research, 60*(4), 331–347.

Avolio, B.J., Reichard, R.J., Hannah, S.T., Walumbwa, F.O., & Chan, A. (2009). A meta-analytic review of leadership impact research: Experimental and quasi-experimental studies. *The Leadership Quarterly, 20*(5), 764–784.

Avolio, B.J., Rotundo, M., & Walumbwa, F.O. (2009). Early life experiences and environmental factors as determinants of leadership emergence: The role of parental influence and rule breaking behavior. *The Leadership Quarterly, 20*(3), 329–342.

Bandura, A. (1997). *Self-efficacy: The exercise of control.* New York: Freeman.

Bowers, J.R., Rosch, D.M., & Collier, D.A., (2016). Examining the relationship between role models and leadership growth during the transition to adulthood. *Journal of Adolescent Research, 31*(1), 96–118.

Brockner, J., & Higgens, T. (2001). Regulatory focus theory: Implications for the study of emotions at work. *Organizational Behavior and Human Decision Processes, 86*(1), 35–66.

Carroll, B., & Levy, L. (2010). Leadership development as identity construction. *Management Communication Quarterly, 24*(2), 211–231.

Chan, K., & Drasgow, F. (2001). Toward a theory of individual differences and leadership: Understanding the motivation to lead. *Journal of Applied Psychology, 86*(3), 481–498.

Day, D.V., & Sin, H.P. (2011). Longitudinal tests of an integrative model of leader development: Charting and understanding developmental trajectories. *The Leadership Quarterly, 22*(3), 545–560.

Day, D.V., Harrison, M.M., & Halpin, S.M. (2009). *An integrative approach to leader development: Connecting adult development, identity, and expertise.* New York: Psychology Press.

De Neve, J., Mikhaylov, S., Dawes, C.T., Christakis, N.A., & Fowler, J.H. (2013). Born to lead? A twin design and genetic association study of leadership role occupancy. *The Leadership Quarterly, 24*(1), 45–60.

DeRue, S.D., & Ashford, S.J. (2010). Who will lead and who will follow? A social process of leadership identity construction in organizations. *Academy of Management Review, 35*(4), 627–647.

Dweck, C.S. (2006). *Mindset: The new psychology of success.* New York: Random House.

Dweck, C.S., & Hogan, K. (2016, October 6) How Microsoft uses growth mindset to develop leaders. *Harvard Business Review.* Retrieved from https://hbr.org/2016/10/how-microsoft-uses-a-growth-mindset-to-develop-leaders

Ely, R. Ibarra, H., & Kolb, D. (2011). Taking gender into account: Theory and design for women's leadership development programs. *Academy of Management Learning and Education, 10*(3), 474–493.

Epitropaki, O., Kark, R., Mainemelis, C., & Lord, R.G. (2017). Leadership and followership identity processes: A multilevel review. *The Leadership Quarterly, 28*(1), 104–129.

Foti, R., & Lord, R. (1987). Prototypes and scripts: The effects of alternative methods of processing information. *Organization Behaviour and Human Decision Processes, 39*(3), 318–341.

Gaucher, D., Friesen, J., & Kay, A.C. (2011). Evidence that gendered wording in job advertisements exists and sustains gender inequality. *Journal of Personality and Social Psychology, 101*(1), 109–128.

Gershenson, S., Lindsay, C.A., Hart, C.M.D., & Papageorge, N. (2017, March). *The long-run impacts of same-race teachers* [pdf]. Retrieved from http://ftp.iza.org/dp10630.pdf

Guillén, L., Mayo, M., & Korotov, K. (2015). Is leadership part of me? A leader identity approach to understanding motivation to lead. *The Leadership Quarterly, 26*(5), 802–820.

Gurney, K. (2018, February 23). Last fall, they debated gun control in class. Now, they debate lawmakers on TV. *Miami Herald.* Retrieved from www.miamiherald.com/news/local/education/article201678544.html

Hogan R., & Warrenfeltz, R. (2003). Educating the modern manager. *Academy of Management Learning and Education, 2*(1), 74–84.

Hogg, M.A. (2001). A social identity theory of leadership. *Personality and Social Psychology Review, 5*(3), 184–200.

Ibarra, H., Snook, S., & Guillén-Ramo, L. (2010). Identity-based leader development. In n. Nohria & R. Khurana (Eds.), *Handbook of leadership theory and practice* (pp. 657–667). Cambridge, MA: Harvard Business School.

Ibarra, H., Wittman, S., Petriglieri, G., & Day, D. (2014). Leadership and identity: An Examination of three theories and new research directions. In D. Day (Ed.), *Handbook of leadership and organizations* (pp. 285–302). Oxford: Oxford University Press.

Johnson, R.E., Venus, M., Lanaj, K., Mao, C., & Chang, C.H. (2012). Leader identity as an antecedent of the frequency and consistency of transformational, consideration, and abusive leadership behaviors. *Journal of Applied Psychology, 97*(6), 1262–1272.

Johnson, S.K., & Sy, T. (2016, December 19). Why aren't there more Asian Americans in leadership positions? *Harvard Business Review.* Retrieved from https://hbr.org/2016/12/why-arent-there-more-asian-americans-in-leadership-positions

Karagianni, D., & Montgomery, A.J. (2017). Developing leadership skills among adolescents and young adults: a review of leadership programmes, *International Journal of Adolescence and Youth, 23*(1), 86–98.

Komives, S.R., Longerbeam, S.D., Owen, J.E., Mainella, F.C., & Osteen, L. (2006). A leadership identity development model: Applications from a grounded theory. *Journal of College Student Development, 47*(4), 401–418.

Kuhn, P., & Weinberger, C. (2005). Leadership skills and wages. *Journal of Labor Economics, 23*(3), 395–436.

Lacerenza, C.N., Reyes, D.L., Marlow, S.L., Joseph, D.L., & Salas, E. (2017). Leadership training design, delivery, and implementation: A meta-analysis. *Journal of Applied Psychology, 102*(12), 1686–1718.

Lee, S.-Y., & Olszewski-Kubilius, P. (2014). Leadership development and gifted students. In R.J.R. Levesque (Ed.), *Encyclopedia of adolescence* (pp. 1557–1565). New York: Springer.

Lord, R.G., & Hall, R.J. (2005). Identity, deep structure and the development of leadership skills. *The Leadership Quarterly, 16*(4), 591–615.

Lord, R.G., & Maher, K.J. (1991). *Leadership and information processing: Linking perceptions and performance.* New York: Routledge.

Lord, R.G., Foti, R.J., & DeVader, C.L. (1984). A test of leadership categorization theory: Internal structure, information processing, and leadership perceptions. *Organizational Behavior and Human Performance, 34*(3), 343–378.

Marchiondo, L.A., Myers, C.G., & Kopelman, S. (2015). The relational nature of leadership identity construction: How and when it influences perceived leadership and decision-making. *The Leadership Quarterly, 26*(5), 892–908.

Markus, H., & Norius, P. (1986). Possible selves. *American Psychologist, 41*(9), 954–969.

McCrae, R., & Costa, P. (1989). The structure of interpersonal traits: Wiggins' circumplex and the five-factor model. *Journal of Personality and Social Psychology, 56*(4), 586–595.

Murphy, S.E. (1992). *The contribution of leadership experience and self-efficacy to group performance under evaluation apprehension* (Ph.D. dissertation). University of Washington, Seattle, WA.

Murphy, S.E. (2002). Leader self-regulation: The role of self-efficacy and "multiple intelligences." In R. Riggio, S. Murphy, & F. Pirozzolo, (Eds.), *Multiple intelligences and leadership* (pp. 163–186). Mahwah, NJ: Lawrence Erlbaum.

Murphy, S.E. (2017, June). *Holding out for a hero: The mismatch between larger than life implicit leadership theories and today's leadership requirements.* Keynote speech made at the sixth annual European School of Management and Technology Conference on Organisational Behaviour, Berlin.

Murphy, S.E., & Johnson, S.K. (2011). The benefits of a long-lens approach to leader development: Understanding the seeds of leadership. *The Leadership Quarterly, 22*(3), 459–470.

Murphy, S.E., & Johnson, S.K. (2016). Leadership and leader developmental self-efficacy: Their role in enhancing leader development efforts. *New Directions in Student Leadership, 149*, 73–84.

Murphy, S.E., & Reichard, R.J. (Eds.). (2011). *Early development and leadership: Building the next generation of leaders.* New York: Routledge.

Murphy, S.E., Jansson, M.P., & Hoyt, C. (2017, August). *Implicit theories and leader identity congruence: Leadership self-efficacy effects for men and women under stereotype threat.* Paper presented at Academy of Management annual meeting, Atlanta, GA.

Myers, K.K., & Sadaghiani, K. (2010). Millennials in the workplace: A communication perspective on millennials' organizational relationships and performance. *Journal of Business and Psychology, 25*(2), 225–238.

O'Neil, C. (2016). *Weapons of math destruction.* New York: Crown Books.

Patel, D. (2017, September 21) 8 ways generation Z will differ from millennials in the workplace. *Forbes.* Retrieved from www.forbes.com/sites/deeppatel/2017/09/21/8-ways-generation-z-will-differ-from-millennials-in-the-workplace/#7dd0147c76e5

PayScale. (2016). *2016 workforce-skills preparedness report.* Retrieved https://www.payscale.com/data-packages/job-skills

Phillips, J.S., & Lord, R.G. (1982). Schematic information processing and perceptions of leadership in problem-solving groups. *Journal of Applied Psychology, 67*(4), 486–492.

Pollack, J., Burnette, J., & Hoyt, C.L. (2012). Self-efficacy in the face of threats to entrepreneurial success: Mindsets matter. *Basic and Applied Social Psychology, 34*(3), 287–294.

Prinstein, M. (2017). *Popular: The power of likeability in a status-obsessed world.* New York: Viking.

Recchia, S. (2011). Preschool leaders in the early childhood classroom. In S.E. Murphy & R.J. Reichard (Eds.), *Early development and leadership: Building the next generation of leaders* (pp. 39–58). New York: Psychology Press/Routledge.

Reichard, R.J., Riggio, R.E., Guerin, D.W., Oliver, P.H., Gottfried, A.W., & Gottfried, A.E. (2011). A longitudinal analysis of relationships between adolescent personality and intelligence with adult leader emergence and transformational leadership. *The Leadership Quarterly, 23*(3), 471–481.

Riggio, R.E., Ciulla, J.B., & Sorensen, G.J. (2003). Leadership education at the undergraduate level: A liberal arts approach to leadership development. In S.E. Murphy & R.E. Riggio (Eds.), *The future of leadership development* (pp. 223–236). Mahwah, NJ: Lawrence Erlbaum.

Salay, M. (2017, October 9). *Let's do the numbers: Halloween edition.* Retrieved from www.marketplace.org/2017/10/09/economy/lets-do-numbers-halloween-edition

Samardžija, J., Walker, J.K., & Bazdan, V. (2017). Career development and personal success profile of students–followers and students–potential future leaders: The case of RIT Croatia. *Management: Journal of Contemporary Management Issues, 22*, 85–107.

Santrock, J. (2015). *Adolescence* (16th ed.). New York: McGraw Hill.

Stieglitz, S., & Dang-Xuan, L. (2013). Social media and political communication: A social media analytics framework. *Social Network Analysis and Mining, 3*(4), 1277–1291.

Stiehl, S.K., Felfe, J., Elprana, G., & Gatzka, M.B. (2015). The role of MtL for leadership training effectiveness. *International Journal of Training and Development, 19*(2), 81–97.

Sveningsson, S., & Alvesson, M. (2003). Managing managerial identities: Organizational fragmentation, discourse and identity struggle. *Human Relations, 56*(10), 1163–1193.

U.S. Department of Education. (2016). *The state of racial diversity in the educator workforce* [pdf]. Retrieved from www2.ed.gov/rschstat/eval/highered/racial-diversity/state-racial-diversity-workforce.pdf

Wellin, R. (2018). Leader capability stalled again: It's time to close the gaps. Retrieved from www.ddiworld.com/glf2018/leadership-capability

Yeager, D.S., Romero, C., Paunesku, D., Hulleman, C.S., Schneider, B., Hinojosa, C., . . . & Dweck, C.S. (2016). Using design thinking to improve psychological interventions: The case of the growth mindset during the transition to high school. *Journal of Educational Psychology, 108*(3), 374–391.

Zimmerman-Oster, K. (2003). How can I tell if it's working? Ten strategies for evaluating leadership development programs in higher education. *Concepts and Connections, 11*, 511.

12

WHAT IS WRONG WITH LEADERSHIP DEVELOPMENT AND WHAT MIGHT BE DONE ABOUT IT?

David V. Day and Zhengguang Liu

When first approached about writing a chapter on what's wrong with leadership development and how potentially to fix it, our response was: *Just a chapter?* We would need an entire book! Maybe even a book series! Sarcasm and cynicism aside, it is a daunting task to try to concisely summarize what are the major obstacles preventing the field of leadership development from having more impact, because there are so many limitations currently in the field.

How do we know that leadership development systems are having a less-than-ideal impact? Recent survey findings suggest that only around 13 percent of respondents thought that they had done a "quality job" in terms of leadership training (Lacerenza, Reyes, Marlow, Joseph, & Salas, 2017, p. 1686). The figures are no better when it comes to the success rate of leaders who are "filling the leadership pipeline" in their respective organizations (Kaiser, 2005).

It is no news flash that many believe their leadership development systems to lack demonstrable impact. The bigger and more important question is: Why is that still the case? One plausible answer is that there has been an enduring tendency to find the "magic bullet" program or practice that will cure all leadership development ills. A corollary to this tendency is that there is no barrier to entry for someone to call themselves a leadership development consultant or leadership specialist. If you can find someone to pay you for providing leadership development interventions, then you are a leadership development consultant regardless of the evidence (if any) behind your practices. Researchers are not blame-free in terms of this problem, either. For far too long, academic researchers have argued about what is the "right" leadership theory – something that will never be decided unequivocally. But academics are exceptional at fomenting territorial disputes, and, as a result, there is still a collective spinning of the wheels on this front.

What we will argue (see also Day, 2000) is that there is a lack of both theoretical grounding and deep stores of evidence on which to base leadership development practices. Part of the issue is the lag times involved: It takes time for theories of leadership development to be vetted in peer-reviewed journals. The same can be said for published, peer-reviewed research evidence on the topic. It is heartening to see scholars – especially younger ones – taking on the challenges of contributing to the science of leadership development theoretically and empirically. But even if we have a broader base of sound scholarship to draw from, there will be a lag before we can integrate it into practice. At least this has been the excuse historically – but it is time to say enough is enough and to take action. In that spirit, we will summarize some of what we see as the most pressing issues facing the field of leadership development, organized around gaps in theory, research, and practice. After reviewing these gaps or shortcomings, we will conclude with a brief section identifying ways in which we might move to remedy them.

Leadership Development Theory

One of the most fundamental limitations, historically, within the leadership development field is a lack of theory. Whereas there is more than 100 years of empirical research devoted to understanding leadership and finding the right leadership theory, relatively little effort has been devoted to understanding leadership development as a separate process. The underlying assumption may have been that if the best theory of leadership were to be finally discovered or proven through scientific research, then it would merely be a matter of training people in that theory. Needless to say, leadership development is a lot more complex than that.

One of the underlying complexities is that leader development (that is, the development of individual leaders) is different from leadership development (Day, 2000). Developing individual leaders does not inherently ensure that effective leadership will result. This is because leadership is a social and interpersonal process. Thus we might be able to develop the capacity for individuals to be effective in leadership roles and processes, but that development does not necessarily mean that the capacity will be applied or applied effectively. In addition, leader development is embedded in ongoing adult development (Day, Harrison, & Halpin, 2009). Attempting to understand and study leader development devoid of its connections with adult development is pretty shortsighted, if not downright ridiculous. Why is that the case? For one thing, we know that, as adults age, there is a loss of cognitive resource and processing capacity. What then differentiates high-functioning older adults from those whose functioning deteriorates dramatically as they age? One explanation provided by lifespan psychologists is the ongoing use of compensatory processes and mechanisms. Some adults learn to compensate for these age-related declines such that their functioning may even be superior to that of younger adults. It depends on how well they have also leveraged their life experiences.

More recently, theoretical perspectives have been offered that integrate various related fields of leader development. Specifically, one focus has been on integrating the areas of expertise and expert performance, self-regulation and identity, and adult development (Day et al., 2009). What such an approach recognizes is that leader development is shaped by a number of related processes, each with its own literature and scientific base of empirical research findings. Thus, unlike the leadership literature, the literature on leader development needs to be more integrative in terms of its approach, to more fully capture the richness associated with the development of adults and leaders.

It has been noted elsewhere that the field of leadership development is dominated by an episodic, event-driven focus in which development of leaders and leadership is thought to occur through periodic participation. Unfortunately, that is not how development is motivated. What motivates development (that is, the allocation of resources to learning, growth, and personal change) over extended periods of time is the internalization of self-views related to the self as a leader (Day & Dragoni, 2015). These self-views include identity, self-efficacy, and self-awareness as a leader. People engage in activities that are important to their core identities, whether it is social identities or more role-based identities (Miscenko & Day, 2016). This is critically important to motivate practice over time periods spanning years, decades, or even the entire lifespan. In short, developmental activities need to be engaged in as a matter of course in the ongoing experience of the focal target. This is why more and better theory is needed integrating leader development with adult development. Specifically, we need to better understand conceptually what motivates the extended periods of practice (besides identity) that are required to develop as an expert in any field, including as an expert leader.

Another missing piece when it comes to theory and leadership development involves identifying the proper outcomes. There is an implicit assumption that the most appropriate outcome for studying leader development – or leadership development – is improvements in job performance. That is unrealistic for several reasons. We know that people struggle during development such that there are initial drops in performance before there are established gains. As lifespan developmental psychologists have noted, development is typically not a perfectly positive or linear phenomenon (Baltes, 1997); rather, development inherently involves a process of gains and losses such that the trajectory of development is often curvilinear. Another limitation to adopting job performance as the outcome of interest in leadership development theory is that it replaces development with performance. Theories of leader development should focus on *development* as the outcome of interest and not performance. Gains in performance may eventually occur, but it is through the application of developmental gains (that is, job performance) that this happens. In other words, performance is a more distal outcome associated with the application of skills and competencies, and mindsets and worldviews, that are shaped through developmental processes. It is not that job performance is irrelevant; rather, it is a more distal outcome that depends, to some degree, on enhanced development.

Leadership Development Research

Leader and leadership development research has emerged in recent years as an active field separate from traditional leadership research. Throughout these years, researchers have been devoting their efforts to understanding the nature of development and gathering robust empirical evidence for the efficacy of development of leaders and leadership, which has resulted in a growing number of publications on this topic. At the same time, however, along with the proliferation of research in leadership development, scholars have been struggling with challenges and key concerns. As discussed previously in this chapter, the most prominent challenge is the lack of established theory in this field. More specifically, leadership development researchers have been confronted with challenges stemming from the complexity associated with conceptualizing and modeling time (Day, 2014), various types of variable that may or may not be amenable to change over time, and understanding what is available in the form of support. In this section, we briefly discuss these and other challenges, and we examine potential means of addressing such challenges.

Time and Development

As discussed by Day (2014), Lord (see Chapter 8, in this volume), and others, time has played an essential – albeit it mainly an implicit – role in leadership theory and research. For leadership development, in particular, time is an indispensable consideration. Some in the field have argued that leader development is a process that is likely to unfold across the entire adult lifespan (Day et al., 2009), which compounds the challenge of studying it rigorously. A pressing challenge for researchers is to try to accommodate such long-term perspectives in any single study, considering all of the various resource challenges in terms of labor invested and money. The longitudinal nature of leader development requires extra effort and consideration in research designs. Researchers need to consider when to measure, how often to measure, the appropriate tools to use to measure, and the methods with which to evaluate the effects of interventions at various points in time (Day, 2014). Furthermore, it is difficult to chart trajectories of development in empirical studies based on a discrete event, or even a series of discrete events. One reason is that there will probably be influences from other unexpected factors, such as the individual's natural development and maturation.

Because of the serious nature of such challenges, it is encouraging to see research projects such as the Fullerton Longitudinal Study (Gottfried et al.,

2011; Guerin et al., 2011) adopting a lifespan developmental perspective in addressing the time issues related to leader development. A few additional studies (Miscenko, Guenter, & Day, 2017; see also Day & Dragoni, 2015) have explored leader and leadership development using multilevel analysis (within-person and between-person). Furthermore, we are sanguine about the application of advanced methodologies, including growth modeling, time series analysis, latent class modeling, experience sampling methods, and hierarchical linear modeling, to help researchers to better understand the processes of development. In recent years, studies have also been conducted from an interdisciplinary perspective (for example, psychology, education, biology, and neuroscience) to provide more insight into the development of individual leaders and collective forms of leadership. The use of newly developed methodologies, as well as trends in embracing other disciplines, will help to advance a more holistic understanding of leader and leadership development, and will serve as the foundation for improving related practices.

Variables in Leadership Development

The process of leadership development is complicated and is affected by multiple factors in various ways. In previous decades, researchers in this area paid much attention to the individual differences that influence leadership development, such as heredity (for example, genes), demographic features (for example, gender, birth order, height, facial attractiveness), and personal traits (for example, temperament, personality, intelligence). These variables are important in helping researchers to better understand the underlying characteristics (that is, motives) of leader and leadership development. For example, Chan and Drasgow (2001) found support for the assertion that individual differences in personality predict the relative level of an individual's motivation to lead. In subsequent research, Hong, Catano, and Liao (2011) found that different aspects of motivation to lead (that is, affective/identity, social-normative, and noncalculation) predicted more distal outcomes related to leader emergence and effectiveness.

On a more challenging note, such variables are relatively distal and unchangeable, and they usually have limited scope for development. Simply put, they do not change much over the lifespan. For example, a long-standing focus linking personality with leadership added questionable value in terms of understanding leadership development processes (that is, change), since personality tends to be a relatively enduring dispositional factor (House, Shane, & Herold, 1996). As a result of these challenges, the next generation of leader development studies are moving in the direction of exploring more proximal and malleable variables or attributes, such as motivation to lead, lessons learned from challenging experiences, changes in leader self-views (for example, leader self-identity, self-efficacy, and self-awareness), and systematic changes in individual or collective capabilities (that is, knowledge, skills, and abilities), which shape individual and collective capabilities into developmental outcomes through the implementation of relevant interventions. As such, developmental interventions might be better conceptualized as moderators rather than as predictors or mediators in the developmental process.

We are in the early days with regard to understanding potentially malleable variables associated with leader or leadership development. Researchers in the field need to keep focusing on those more proximal and malleable factors associated with changes in individual leader development or more collective leadership development. The development in qualitative (for example, case studies, grounded theory research) and quantitative (for example, latent growth modeling) methods provides opportunities for us to identify and model those constructs with the greatest potential for understanding long-term changes (that is, development) in individuals and collectives engaged in shared work.

Support for Long-term Development

Researchers in the field of leadership development (broadly construed to include leader development) have paid more attention to the outcome of changes in individuals (that is, leader development) and collectives than to the facilitative factors (that is, available support) that ensure that the changes occur and are maintained over time. In other words, current studies tend to be too leader-centric in focusing on the person(s) at the expense of the externally supportive conditions needed for development. It is abundantly clear that development does not occur in a vacuum, and it is necessary to take into account those external forces that motivate and support developmental changes. Leadership and its development is inherently embedded in context, and that development is a function of both internal and external factors. Available support variables can be significant moderators of changes that can strengthen or weaken the relationship between those malleable variables and relevant developmental outcomes. In addition, these supportive factors can help to describe boundary conditions associated with changes. It is essential to include the supporting interpersonal contextual effects of organizations and teams, while also considering individual factors.

Encouragingly, recent researchers have recognized the importance of providing support and have begun to explore various forms of support in facilitating leader development. Two studies demonstrated considerable variance in the type of support variables, such as structured reflection by means of after-event review and supervisor support by means of role modeling, as well as setting high standards for performance (DeRue, Nahrgang, Hollenbeck, & Workman, 2012; McCall & McHenry, 2014). Nonetheless, there is a great need to explore other forms of available support (for example, organization culture, interpersonal interaction atmosphere, and interpersonal relationship quality) and to more thoughtfully consider the conditions under which different forms of support are most helpful, to whom, and when.

Leadership development is inherently a multilevel process (Avolio, 2004; Day & Dragoni, 2015), and the support variables usually arise from higher levels associated with the team level or organization. Hence we will need to be very clear as to the appropriate level(s) at which we are studying support variables, and to choose the type of research design, measures, and analyses that are most appropriate for the respective focus. In particular, it appears that cross-level approaches (for example, effects of organizations and teams on individuals) provide great promise for furthering our understanding of developmental processes. Moreover, as discussed by Yammarino and Dionne (see Chapter 2, in this volume), multilevel methods and analyses have been advancing rapidly in recent years, including techniques such as multilevel modeling and multi-level mediation or moderation, as well as various types of change analysis (for example, latent change score modeling). Such advances make it possible to simultaneously consider the variables at various levels and their interaction, as well as potential reciprocal effects. Finally, the modern analysis technology of Big Data and social network analysis also provide access to real, but complicated, contextual factors in which leadership development is embedded.

Ultimately, these three challenges highlighted require researchers to raise their individual and collective standards in their respective research efforts, but they have the potential to provide huge dividends in term of better understanding of the forces for, and support of, leadership development – potentially across most of the lifespan. This will involve constructing more comprehensive theory, designing insightful longitudinal research projects, and using state-of-the-science analytic techniques that could lead to ways of accelerating the underlying processes in practice.

Practice in Leadership Development

The ever-increasing demand for effective leadership shines a spotlight on the importance of leadership development practices in contemporary organizations. For this and other reasons, organizations have been designating leadership as a top strategic priority and potential source of their competitive advantage, and they have been investing in its development accordingly. In the United States alone, an estimated US$60 billion is spent annually on various leadership development programs, and that amount is growing rapidly each year (O'Leonard, 2014; Zenger, 2012). Despite the perceived strategic importance and increasing investments, however, it is not an easy task to find demonstrably effective leadership development initiatives that clearly provide return on the typically considerable investments. Making estimating return on development investments (Avolio, Avey, & Quisenberry, 2010) even more challenging is the general trend away from discrete, event-based programs toward ongoing, embedded developmental practices.

Claims for the long-term effectiveness of leadership development initiatives are suspect. Results of surveys by the Corporate Executive Board (CEB) of more than 3,500 leaders across 50 organizations indicated that approximately two-thirds of sampled senior leaders thought that the leadership development practices in their organizations were, to a large degree, broken (see Day & Dragoni, 2015). In this section, we discuss the key issues that are associated with the effectiveness of leadership development practices – especially factors that detract from providing expected levels of return on investment. These topics include the continuous nature of development, and individual and collective leadership, as well as the issue of implementation and evaluation.

Continuous Nature of Development

From a practitioner perspective, leadership tends to be more about the position than the process. An overarching concern is preparing individuals to assume leadership positions and to fill the leadership pipeline (Charan, Drotter, & Noel, 2011). Accordingly, leadership development is often subsumed within the broader objective of succession management. Another frequent use of leadership development programs is to fulfill a type of role socialization function – that is, once an individual is promoted into a leadership position, they will attend a series of intensive and dedicated developmental programs, at various time intervals, the topics of which vary across time (for example, delegation this time, strategic vision another time). In formal leadership development programs, participants engage in sessions aiming to help them to be more effective in terms of their knowledge, skills, abilities, and broader leadership competence. In addition, according to the hierarchical nature of organizations, leadership development programs are usually categorized into several types, such as high-potential employee programs, mid-level leader programs, and senior executive programs, to cater to the needs of different corporate constituencies.

Despite the diversity of such programs, they are often isolated, with almost no connection to each other. Each discrete program or event serves as a stand-alone offering, with little or no attempt to link things in any meaningful way. The current way of identifying needs and implementing leadership development programs implies a widespread misperception that development is episodic in nature and that dramatic breakthroughs can be achieved through several intensive, short-term programs. In other words, organizations hold the naive and unrealistic view that effective leadership can be obtained through participating in a series of unconnected, discrete initiatives. This assumption is at odds with what is known about adult development.

Partly as a result of the illusion of rapid pace of development and the related issue of overestimating the developmental impact of leadership development programs, the management of many organizations believes, at least implicitly, that investments in such programs will bring near-immediate improvement to the practice of leadership at both the individual and collective levels. In contrast to this short-sighted practitioner perspective, researchers into the dynamics of leadership development have surmised that leader development is a continuous and ongoing process, possibly spanning the entire adult lifespan (Day et al., 2009). What matters most in this developmental process is not so much the program or event per se nor providing a variety of experiences, but what is learned from the experience regardless of from where that experience emanates. Learning is most often realized as a disciplined process in which certain tools and practices, such as structured reflection, can be highly useful in facilitating learning from experience. Organizations should therefore take into account the developmental nature of leadership and place the emphasis on activating the occurrence of ongoing learning when designing and implementing leadership development initiatives, rather than keep fumbling around with implementing sessions of discrete training, as well as designing (and redesigning) various curriculums. What often matters the most for learning are a few relatively simple features, such as reflection, feedback, and support. Encouragingly, some organizations have recognized the long-term nature of leader or leadership development and have designed these types of ongoing, continuous program (see Vicere & Fulmer, 1997). For instance, equipping leaders with coaches or mentors in their daily work can help them to learn and develop effectively in real time, over an extended period.

Individual Leader and Collective Leadership

Current leadership development initiatives are mainly targeted at individuals, with the aim of developing participants' leadership attributes and changing their behavior so as to better fit a predefined competence model of what an effective leader should be and do (Ford & Harding, 2007). Unfortunately, this individual competence approach is unlikely to bring about major changes in leader behavior or mindsets. There is no guarantee of better leadership as a result of implementing this approach because it ignores the typically collective and contextual nature of leadership and development. On the one hand, the increasing complexity and challenges that contemporary organizations are facing often require more inclusive and collective forms of leadership (Day, Gronn, & Salas, 2006). Leadership inherently involves a dynamic social interaction within a specific situational context. In other words, leadership development should not be treated as a process along which individual leaders are considered to be isolated and relatively unconnected units; rather, leadership is a more systematic and networked function that is integrated across follower, team, and organizational levels. Current developmental initiatives often fail to consider the collective dynamic between leaders and followers, as well as the wider context within which leadership occurs. Thus the effectiveness of such programs is difficult to transfer back to real workplace settings. As noted previously in this chapter, researchers have worked theoretically and empirically over the past couple of decades to distinguish leader development from leadership development (for example, Day, 2000). In practice, leader development is about the acquisition of individual knowledge, skills, abilities, and broader competencies (that is, human capital) to enhance the capacity of individuals to be effective in leadership roles and processes, formal or informal. Conversely, leadership development is mainly concerned with developing a collective's capacity to produce leadership. This relies more on the connections of relationships (that is, social capital) between people – so-called leaders and followers – engaged in shared work.

Both sets of developmental practices are essential to organizations, despite differences in terms of goal setting, training content, implementation strategies, and anticipated benefits. The overarching point is that it is not an "either/or" proposition, but more like "and/both," to effectively link individual leader development with more collective forms of leadership development. The good news is that most organizations have gained extensive experience in developing individual leaders through coaching, job assignments, action learning, formal classroom training, and other practices (Lacerenza et al., 2017). Nonetheless, there is still much less known about how to develop more collective organizational forms of leadership. More work is needed to deepen our understanding of this topic.

To develop collective leadership, we need to first consider that leadership functions and develops interpersonally as a mutual influence process among relationships, rather than as an intrapersonal phenomenon within separate and independent beings. Research has suggested that the quality of leader–follower relations is related to the alignment and commitment among followers, and thus is instrumental for leadership effectiveness (Dulebohn, Bommer, Liden, Brouer, & Ferris, 2012). In addition, we need to view leadership as a process within a team and organization. Leadership can be treated as a distributed structure that is shared among team members, and hence leadership role rotation among team members and various types of teamwork (for example, team learning) can facilitate greater leadership capacity in a team or organization (Day, Gronn, & Salas, 2004). Overall, this suggests that we need to shift our perspectives from "self" to "self-in-relation," and from "act on" (that is, leaders acting on followers) to "act with" (that is, leaders acting with followers). We also need to incorporate perspectives from group dynamics, and to consider organization contexts when designing and implementing leadership development initiatives. It is recommended that, to transcend many of the current limitations with leadership development, we seek ways of linking individual leader development with collective leadership development to enhance overall levels of leadership capacity in teams and organizations (Day & Dragoni, 2015).

Implementation and Evaluation

A wide variety of leadership interventions, such as training, 360-degree feedback, executive coaching, mentoring, networking, global job assignments, and action learning, have been used as ways of developing leaders and leadership. Although a few innovative methods have been developed and put into practice in recent years (for example, multimedia simulations), formal training is still the method most commonly used by organizations that invest in leadership development (Lacerenza et al., 2017). Training differs across myriad features, but one of the most important is whether the training is focused on providing information, demonstration, or practice (or some combination of these). Although training scientists tend to agree that practice-based training is perhaps the most efficacious delivery approach, information-based and demonstration-based methods are still common in organizations, mainly because of their relatively lower costs and the ease of their delivery.

This assertion regarding training delivery was supported by the meta-analytic findings of Lacerenza and colleagues (2017). Under traditional training approaches, trainers tend to operate under the assumption that there is a "one best way" of developing leaders and that they can teach leaders how to behave in ways that match the so-called ideal leader profile (that is, prototype). This is inconsistent with what we know from research evidence, which suggests that individuals – and individual leaders – start at different places and change in different ways. In short, those individuals developing as leaders do not demonstrate identical trajectories (Day & Sin, 2011). This is because of many factors, including previous experience and the individual's level of developmental readiness, as well as how they respond to a presenting experience or intervention (Day & Thornton, 2017). The individualized nature of development challenges the potential impact of training and development interventions that operate under assumptions of artificial similarity among participants.

A related challenge stems from the widely embraced (but not empirically validated) 70–20–10 rule of leadership development, which suggests that, to ensure the effectiveness of leadership interventions:70 percent of the efforts should come from challenging work experiences; 20 percent, from others in the form of feedback, coaching, and support; and only 10 percent of developmental efforts should be derived from formal training programs (McCall, Lombardo, & Morrison, 1988). In practice, however, current organizations are putting a lot of resources into approaches that might not be the most impactful. For example, some prominent organizations have created and branded their own "corporate universities" to provide classes and leadership training in-house. Most of these efforts are either unevaluated or their evaluation results are proprietary. Another key and long-standing issue is that evaluation of the effectiveness of leadership development programs remains a challenge. It is not an easy task to find an appropriate evaluation method, not to mention to obtain appropriate evidence of the effectiveness of leadership development interventions. As a result, it is probably safe to conclude that any of these practices *could be* effective for leadership development, but it is unclear whether they actually *are* (Avolio et al., 2010). We need more and better evidence for these claims.

In the end, the development of leadership is often espoused by organizations as a strategic priority, but these same organizations struggle to figure out what is the best way of implementing programs, processes, and practices to help them to achieve their goals of filling the so-called leadership pipeline. One underlying reason for this state of affairs is the deep gap between theory and practice in leader or leadership development. Thus it is the right time for practitioners in organizations to strengthen partnerships with researchers in developing practically useful and theoretically rigorous approaches to developing individual and collective leadership. Indeed, this was one of the recommendations of researchers who recently reviewed the empirical evidence on leadership training (Lacerenza et al., 2017). Certainly, leadership development theory and research should also inform leadership development practice. The rewards of such efforts lie in their potential to produce innovative advances in the science and practice of leadership development.

Where to from Here?

It is a comparatively easy job to point out all of the flaws, shortcomings, and limitations of leadership development; it is another matter to offer constructive suggestions on how to fix these issues. Despite such challenges, we will present a few of the most pressing issues that need to be addressed to make leadership development more rigorous and impactful. These represent the proverbial tip of the iceberg, but they are a start.

If there is an overarching issue in terms of "fixing" leadership development – which is probably an overstatement – it is taking a systemic perspective on development. Present research and practices focus on mainly discrete episodes and relatively short time frames. How do various experiences link together to provide for meaningful development, including individual motivation to develop? Any individual leader is part of a broader system that needs to be leveraged to motivate development over the long term.

Theory is important in terms of providing a sound roadmap for leader and leadership development. In particular, more theory is needed that incorporates a longitudinal perspective focusing on development over longer time periods (decades or the entire lifespan). Also needed are more theoretical perspectives on the multilevel nature of development. There are intra- and interpersonal issues to understand in terms of development, as well as the nesting of individuals in broader collectives. This gets at the distinction described in the chapter between leader and leadership development: How can we capitalize on the "and/both" nature of development, which includes developing leaders while also developing collective forms of leadership capacity? Both individual and collective forms of leadership require developmental investments if organizations are to maximize their potential capacity to engage in effective leadership when needed.

At the interface of theory and research is the role of time in development. At a theoretical level, we need more disciplined thinking about what changes and when (not to also mention why). Without more clearly articulated theory on these concerns, researchers have no guide to identifying the most appropriate measurement periods. The typical approach is to divide the intervention into equal parts, but that risks missing the hypothesized changes in whatever outcomes are being measured (see Day, 2014). At present, the best advice for researchers is to measure as many time waves as possible, but that is pretty much like using a blunt instrument to do brain surgery. We can – and should – do better.

At the interface of theory and practice, we are reminded of a quote from Peter Drucker that suggests that every practice rests on theory, even if the practitioners are unaware of that theory. Understanding and applying theory to design interventions that will bring about the desired changes in the allocated time frame seems like it would be a fairly basic task – but interventions typically expand to fill the amount of time that is allocated to whomever is delivering the intervention. A related concern is how long are the effects of a leadership development intervention intended to last: Forever? That seems pretty unrealistic, but what is the alternative? We have not heard any practitioners talk about something like the "half-life" of their interventions.

It is also the case that there are plenty of opportunities for greater integration between research and practice. For example, how many leadership development programs still use the Myers-Briggs Type Indicator (MBTI) to measure and provide feedback on personality? That is pretty depressing, to consider given that the criterion-related validity of the MBTI is pretty much nonexistent. And then there is the whole emotional intelligence [sic] industry: another set of practices lacking robust predictive validity. What is really needed, however, is more longitudinal evidence of the effectiveness of leadership development systems in the form of integrated practices, rather than separate, stand-alone practices or interventions.

Related to all of the above recommendations is the need to conceptualize development as a highly individualized phenomenon. People start at different places and change in different ways, based on different sets of knowledge, skills, and abilities that are bundled as leadership competencies. Getting beyond all of the various issues about change over time, there is a scalability concern: How can we scale our interventions in such a way that can also tailor things for a given individual? What does this imply in terms of theory and research if development truly is an inherently individualized endeavor? At the risk of stating the obvious, we need some hard thinking around our theory and research if we are to be helpful in informing somewhat idiosyncratic, individual-centric practice.

In closing, John Gardner (1990) has said that we have barely scratched the surface in our efforts toward leadership development – that, in the near future (that is, in the middle of the twenty-first century), people will look back on current practices as primitive. If that's true, that will be progress!

References

Avolio, B.J. (2004). Examining the full range model of leadership: Looking back to transform forward. In D.V. Day, S.J. Zaccaro, & S.M. Halpin (Eds.), *Leader development for transforming organizations: Growing leaders for tomorrow* (pp. 71–98). Mahwah, NJ: Lawrence Erlbaum.

Avolio, B.J., Avey, J.B., & Quisenberry, D. (2010). Estimating return on leadership development investment. *The Leadership Quarterly, 21*(4), 633–644.

Baltes, P.B. (1997). On the incomplete architecture of human ontogeny: Selection, optimization, and compensation as foundation of developmental theory. *American Psychologist, 52*(4), 366–380.

Chan, K.Y., & Drasgow, F. (2001). Toward a theory of individual differences and leadership: Understanding the motivation to lead. *Journal of Applied Psychology, 86*(3), 481–498.

Charan, R., Drotter, S., & Noel, J. (2011). *The leadership pipeline: How to build the leadership powered company* (2nd ed.). San Francisco, CA: Jossey-Bass.

Day, D.V. (2000). Leadership development: A review in context. *The Leadership Quarterly, 11*(4), 581–613.

Day, D.V. (2014). Time and leadership. In A.J. Shipp & Y. Fried (Eds.), *Time and work: How time impacts groups, organizations and methodological choices, vol. 2* (pp. 30–52). New York: Psychology Press.

Day, D.V., & Dragoni, L. (2015). Leadership development: An outcome-oriented review based on time and levels of analyses. *Annual Review of Organizational Psychology and Organizational Behavior, 2*, 133–156.

Day, D.V., & Sin, H.P. (2011). Longitudinal tests of an integrative model of leader development: Charting and understanding developmental trajectories. *The Leadership Quarterly, 22*(3), 545–560.

Day, D.V., & Thornton, A.M.A. (2017). Leadership development. In J. Antonakis & D.V. Day (Eds.), *The nature of leadership* (3rd ed.) (pp. 354–381). Thousand Oaks, CA: Sage.

Day, D.V., Gronn, P., & Salas, E. (2004). Leadership capacity in teams. *The Leadership Quarterly, 15*(6), 857–880.

Day, D.V., Gronn, P., & Salas, E. (2006). Leadership in team-based organizations: On the threshold of a new era. *The Leadership Quarterly, 17*(3), 211–216.

Day, D.V., Harrison, M.M., & Halpin, S.M. (2009). *An integrative approach to leader development: Connecting adult development, identity, and expertise*. New York: Routledge.

DeRue, D.S., Nahrgang, J.D., Hollenbeck, J.R., & Workman, K. (2012). A quasi-experimental study of after-event reviews and leadership development. *Journal of Applied Psychology, 97*(5), 997–1015.

Dulebohn, J.H., Bommer, W.H., Liden, R.C., Brouer, R.L., & Ferris, G.R. (2012). A meta-analysis of antecedents and consequences of leader–member exchange: Integrating the past with an eye toward the future. *Journal of Management, 38*(6), 1715–1759.

Ford, J., & Harding, N. (2007). Move over management: We are all leaders now. *Management Learning, 38*(5), 475–493.

Gardner, J.W. (1990). *On leadership.* New York: Free Press.
Gottfried, A.E., Gottfried, A.W., Reichard, R.J., Guerin, D.W., Oliver, P.H., & Riggio, R.E. (2011). Motivational roots of leadership: A longitudinal study from childhood through adulthood. *The Leadership Quarterly, 22*(3), 510–519.
Guerin, D.W., Oliver, P.H., Gottfried, A.W., Gottfried, A.E., Reichard, R.J., & Riggio, R.E. (2011). Childhood and adolescent antecedents of social skills and leadership potential in adulthood: Temperamental approach/withdrawal and extraversion. *The Leadership Quarterly, 22*(3), 482–494.
Hong, Y., Catano, V.M., & Liao, H. (2011). Leader emergence: The role of emotional intelligence and motivation to lead. *Leadership and Organization Development Journal, 32*(4), 320–343.
House, R.J., Shane, S.A., & Herold, D.M. (1996). Rumors of the death of dispositional research are vastly exaggerated. *Academy of Management Review, 21*(1), 203–224.
Kaiser, R.B. (Ed.) (2005). *Filling the leadership pipeline.* Greensboro, NC: Center for Creative Leadership.
Lacerenza, C.N., Reyes, D.L., Marlow, S.L., Joseph, D.L., & Salas, E. (2017). Leadership training design, delivery, and implementation: A meta-analysis. *Journal of Applied Psychology, 102*(12), 1686–1718.
McCall, J.M.W., Lombardo, M.M., & Morrison, A.M. (1988). *The lessons of experience: How successful executives develop on the job.* New York: Lexington Books.
McCall, M.W., & McHenry, J.J. (2014). Catalytic converters. In C.D. McCauley & M.W. McCall (Eds.), *Using experience to develop leadership talent* (pp. 396–421). San Francisco, CA: Jossey-Bass.
Miscenko, D., & Day, D.V. (2016). Identity and identification at work. *Organizational Psychology Review, 6*(3), 215–247.
Miscenko, D., Guenter, H., & Day, D.V. (2017). Am I a leader? Examining leader identity development over time. *The Leadership Quarterly, 28*(5), 605–620.
O'Leonard, K. (2014, January). *The corporate learning factbook 2014: Benchmarks, trends, and analysis of the U.S. training market* [pdf]. Retrieved from https://legacy.bersin.com/uploadedfiles/012714WWBCLF.pdf
Vicere, A.A., & Fulmer, R.M. (1997). *Leadership by design: How benchmark companies sustain success through investment in continuous learning.* Boston, MA: Harvard Business School Press.
Zenger, J. (2012, May 2). Does leadership development really work? *Forbes.* Retrieved from www.forbes.com/sites/jackzenger/2012/05/02/does-leadership-development-really-work-2/#6863152a45a9

13

SOLVING THE PROBLEM WITH LEADERSHIP TRAINING

Aligning Contemporary Behavior-based Training with Mindset Conditioning

Alex Leung and Thomas Sy

Leadership is highly valued because it plays an important role in individual, group, and organizational success (Yammarino, 2013). Accordingly, organizations have developed various forms of training programs, with the aim of transforming employees into better leaders. Such training programs are designed to enhance individuals' requisite knowledge, skills, and abilities for formal leadership roles (Day, 2000). Among such programs, the top-spending area is management and leadership, taking up 35 percent of the US$70 billion spent each year on training and development in the United States (Bersin, 2014). Despite the amount of resources devoted to leadership training and development, the effectiveness of leadership training programs is commonly viewed as problematic.

Organizations are dissatisfied with their current leadership training programs. A recent survey found that only 38 percent of leaders and 25 percent of human resource professionals rate the leadership quality across their organization as "very good" or "excellent" (Boatman & Wellins, 2011). Only 14 percent of surveyed organizations believe that they have done an excellent job of training their leaders (Schwartz, Bersin, & Pelster, 2014). Furthermore, only 32 percent of leaders and 18 percent of human resource professionals reported "strong" or "very strong" agreement that their leaders are prepared to meet future business needs (Schwartz et al., 2014). Despite allocating more funds to leadership training programs in recent years, these results suggest that leadership training remains largely unsuccessful; hence merely spending more money each year is unlikely to be sufficient or effective (Wakefield, Abbatiello, Agarwal, Pastakia, & van Berkel, 2016). In contrast to the view of practitioners, however, scientific reviews of the effectiveness of leadership training programs have found largely positive effects (Avolio, Reichard, Hannah, Walumbwa, & Chan, 2009). In the most recent and perhaps most extensive review, Lacerenza, Reyes, Marlow,

Joseph, and Salas (2017) found positive effects across four primary criteria (Kirkpatrick, 1959): reactions (satisfaction with training), learning (acquisition of knowledge and skill), transfer (behavioral enactment of trained content), and results (achievement of organizational goals). Leadership training programs are estimated to account for increases of 25 percent in learning, 28 percent in behavior enactment of leadership, 20 percent in job performance, and 25 percent in organizational outcomes.

The discrepancy between practitioner views and findings from academic research on the effectiveness of leadership training may be explained by the scientist–practitioner gap (House & Aditya, 1997), whereby practitioner-based training programs are largely designed without referencing science-based findings. Such atheoretical approaches, without empirical support, are likely to result in an array of training programs that may not be effective (Boatman & Wellins, 2011; Schwartz et al., 2014). In contrast, meta-analyses of leadership training programs in the social science literature yield largely positive effects for leadership training. The studies reviewed in these meta-analyses may reflect a selection bias toward the best-designed leadership training programs (Lacerenza et al., 2017). Even the common practice of including unpublished studies in such reviews may be biased because these studies are often carefully designed and implemented to fulfill the higher standards required for publication. As such, results from meta-analyses may not accurately reflect the types and efficacy of leadership training programs generally found in industry. Beyond the possibility of publication bias, most organizations develop training programs under the constraints of practicality (for example, difficulty of program implementation, budgetary restrictions, competing program initiatives, etc.) In short, academics' findings may not reflect the realities experienced by practitioners in industry, where the effectiveness of leadership training programs have been shown to be problematic. Having said that, both practitioners and academics echo similar questions that must be addressed to advance the efficacy of leadership training programs: What is missing in current leadership training programs? How can training efficacy be improved? We address these questions by highlighting the importance of cultivating a leader mindset, focusing on the core components of leader identity and implicit theories of leadership and followership.

Leadership Mindset

An important consideration for leadership training programs is the content for leader development (Day, Fleenor, Atwater, Sturm, & McKee, 2014). Specifically, what leader attributes should be developed? Leading scholars note the importance of distinguishing training that targets leader development or leadership development (for example, Day, 2000). Leader development is focused on developing individual leaders, which is distinct from leader*ship* development, which involves the multiple individuals (for example, leaders and followers), as well as contextual factors (for example, organizational structure and norms), which may influence the process of leadership. Our focus is on leader development.

It remains unclear which knowledge, skills, or attitudes should be targeted to yield maximum effectiveness in leadership training programs, although most training programs seemingly focus on the two former (that is, knowledge and skills) at the expense of the latter (that is, attitudes) (Lacerenza et al., 2017). As such, we focus our discussion on the attitudinal component involved in the development of a *leader mindset*, which reflects beliefs related to leadership. Although leader mindset can encompass a range of topics, we hone in on the core components of leader identity (Day et al., 2014; Epitropaki, Kark, Mainemelis, & Lord, 2017) and implicit theories of leadership and followership (Epitropaki, Sy, Martin, Tram-Quon, & Topakas, 2013; Sy, 2010). These core components have been largely neglected in leadership training programs, and yet they offer potential avenues for improving leadership training effectiveness. We now provide a brief overview of these core components and describe their relevance as a key aspect of leader development, along with practical strategies for training design and implementation.

Leader Identity

Leader identity is an integral component of leader development (Day & Harrison, 2007). Leader identity is a deep-rooted knowledge structure that serves as the basis for individuals' enactment of leadership behaviors (Lord & Hall, 2005) – that is, leaders and the behavioral enactments of leadership arise from the formation of a leader identity. Moreover, the "content" of leader identity shapes individuals' leadership style, which has implications for organizational outcomes (Sy et al., 2018). Leader identity is defined as the individual's self-definition based on meanings associated with being a leader or how the individual thinks of themselves as a leader (Miscenko, Guenter, & Day, 2017). Leader identity is a form of self-schema that is nested within the broader construct of self-concept. Self-concept is a relatively stable and enduring cognitive structure that can encompass the content, attitudes, or evaluations that serve the purpose of sense-making and motivation, and which provide a sense of self-worth (Oyserman & Markus, 1998). In contrast, self-schemas are more dynamic and active working structures (situated identities) that shape current perceptions, emotions, and behaviors, often automatically (Markus & Wurf, 1987). Thus specific self schemas (for example, implicit theories of leadership and followership) can change in a given context (Epitropaki et al., 2013), but not necessarily the whole self-concept. Accordingly, leader identity is relatively dynamic, governed by a homeostasis process that allows for deviations from the set point and yet self-adjusts to revert to homeostasis (Sy et al., 2018). Homeostasis is determined by the salient (activated) identity that is central to the individual's self-concept.

Thus some individuals have a homeostasis for leadership (or followership) if leader (follower) identity is more central to their self-concept (Epitropaki et al., 2017). For example, a manager may, on occasion, follow the lead of a subordinate, but the manager will default to the central homeostasis identity of leader.

Research has highlighted the importance and interplay of leader identity in the development of leadership skills and behaviors (Lord & Hall, 2005). Leader identity is the foundation for developing oneself as a leader (Epitropaki et al., 2017). Employees who do not possess a leader identity are not likely to pursue leader development opportunities. Moreover, trainee readiness is critical for training to succeed (Salas, Tannenbaum, Kraiger, & Smith-Jentsch, 2012). An employee may not be ready for leadership training if the employee does not self-identify as a leader, and any training provided is likely to be unsuccessful because training transfer will be minimal. Leader identity and behavioral skills develop in parallel, and the development of each advances in parallel fashion. Miscenko and colleagues (2017) investigated the codevelopment of leader identity and behavioral skills in a longitudinal study with postgraduate students on a seven-week leadership course at a Dutch business school. Measures of leader identity and behavioral skills (that is, initiating structure and consideration behaviors) were assessed across seven time points. Using latent growth curve modeling and latent change score analyses, they found that changes in leader identity are associated with changes in leader behavioral skills across time. The results highlight the importance of jointly developing leader identity in conjunction with leader behavioral skills.

Implicit Theories of Leadership and Followership

Implicit leadership theories (ILTs) are individuals' schemas of leaders (Lord & Maher, 1991). They reflect the images held about the traits and behaviors of leaders (Schyns & Meindl, 2005), and they are organized into hierarchical categories (Lord, Foti, & De Vader, 1984), as follows.

1. Superordinate (leaders vs. non-leaders)
2. Basic (different domains of leadership, such as military vs. political)
3. Subordinate (different leader types within domains of leadership, such as Democratic vs. Republican political leaders)

Implicit leadership theories are socially shared among members of society, and key prototypic dimensions include Sensitivity, Dedication, Tyranny, Charisma, Attractiveness, Masculinity, Intelligence, and Strength (Epitropaki & Martin, 2004).

Similarly, implicit followership theories (IFTs) are defined as schemas about the traits and behaviors that characterize followers (Sy, 2010). Paralleling the categorical structure of ILTs, IFTs are also organized hierarchically and socially shared, with key prototypical dimensions including Industry, Enthusiasm, Good Citizen, Conformity, Insubordination, and Incompetence (Sy, 2010).

Implicit theories serve an important function as an interpretative lens through which information is processed (Chiu, Hong, & Dweck, 1997). Implicit leadership and followership theories are used by individuals as a sense-making function (Weick, 1995) to understand and respond to leaders and followers (Sy, 2010). Regardless of their accuracy, individuals rely on implicit theories to form impression of others, and they continue to make use of their implicit theories despite the presence of overwhelming contradictory scientific evidence (Lewandowsky, Oberauer, & Gignac, 2013).

The potency of ILTs and IFTs as an interpretative lens is realized in its influence on behaviors. People use ILTs and IFTs as the basis for interpreting others' behaviors and as the foundation for generating their own behaviors. Accordingly, people use ILTs to ascribe the status of leader to others via recognition-based processes and based on a perceived match between the behavior of others and the attributes of pre-existing ILT prototypes (Lord & Maher, 1991). This has implications for a wide range of organizational outcomes, including leadership advancement. For example, ILTs may explain the disproportionally low representation of minorities in leadership positions (Sy et al., 2010).

Relatedly, implicit theories serve as the foundation for generating behaviors, such as leadership styles. Sy (2010) developed the notion of the "predisposition proposition," positing that, over time, individuals may internalize and endorse certain IFTs that predispose them to perceive and manage others in a consistent manner. Accordingly, this results in a stable management style that reflects people's assumptions about the underlying nature of followers (Bass & Bass, 2008; Eden, 1990; McGregor, 1960). The predisposition proposition is supported by empirical research showing that the leadership behaviors of transformational leaders are a function of their IFTs, which comprise largely positive conceptions of followers (Goodwin, Wofford, & Boyd, 2000).

The Perception–Behavior Link

Research has demonstrated a close connection between implicit theories and behavioral enactment, such as in the predisposition proposition (Bargh, Chen, & Burrows, 1996). This connection, or perception–behavior link, posits that the perception or activation of a schema (for example, IFTs) evokes corresponding behaviors consistent with that cognition, given that both are mentally represented and linked within the same cognitive network. Accordingly, the activation of one results in the co-activation of the other (Dijksterhuis & van Knippenberg, 1998). The perception–behavior link is created based on repeated observations of highly correlated representations in our environments (Feldman, 1981). The co-activation of perception and behavior strengthens over time to become a habitual action tendency that is triggered in the presence of relevant stimuli (Bargh, 1989). Empirical support for the perception–behavior link is well established in the social psychological literature (Chartrand & Bargh, 1999; Payne,

Brown-Iannuzzi, & Loersch, 2016). For example, activating conceptions of a "professor" and "hooligan" influenced participants' cognitive task performance positively and negatively, respectively (Dijksterhuis & van Knippenberg, 1998). Moreover, research in neuroscience provides evidence (for example, mirror neurons) for the hard-wired nature of the perception–behavior link (Rizzolatti, Fogassi, & Gallese, 2001), showing that the same set of neurons are activated whether one thinks about an action (perception) or actually performs the behavior. In addition, research support is found in the leadership literature showing that positive perceptions of followers result in corresponding positive behaviors (for example, Goodwin et al., 2000; Whiteley, Sy, & Johnson, 2012). In short, leadership style or behaviors can be explained by the perception–behavior link because leaders develop habitual response tendencies based on perceived or activated schema (for example, IFTs) (Engle & Lord, 1997; Sy, 2010).

To summarize, leader mindset training is an important aspect of leader development. First, implicit theories may play an important role in shaping leader identity, which will be further elaborated shortly. Second, possessing the right mindset (that is, leader identity) is foundational for the pursuit of leader development opportunities. Third, mindset and skill development are mutually reinforcing and impact learning, as well as training transfer. Finally, people's mindsets serve as the interpretive lens for understanding others and as the foundation for generating their own behavior. As such, people's mindsets have ubiquitous influence on organizational behavior because the proclivity for the co-activation of mindset and behavior strengthens over time to create habitual action tendencies (for example, leadership style). This rationale highlights the importance of jointly developing leader mindset and behavioral skills – yet few training programs take such a balanced approach to leader development, with the imbalance favoring behavioral-based training. Next, we review common training approaches, after which we turn the focus to mindset training to bring balance to leader development efforts.

Training Methods Overview

The prevailing focus of leadership training programs is on developing behavioral skills (Day et al., 2014), with little or no consideration of the corresponding need to train and align individuals' mindsets. Leadership training programs are delivered in many forms, but may be broken into three broad categories: information-based, demonstration-based, and practice-based (Salas & Cannon-Bowers, 2001). The purpose of information-based methods is to provide insightful information related to leadership, which may include lectures, presentations, and books. Demonstration-based methods provide employees with contextually correct or incorrect examples of leadership behaviors through media such as simulations and videos. Lastly, training programs that entail role-playing and guided practice are considered practice-based.

Among all leadership training program delivery methods, the instructor-led lecture (information-based) is the most common, beating the use of other methods by at least 21 percent (Wentworth, 2016). Organizations such as Twitter, IBM, and Dale Carnegie utilize such methods to provide information and insights for their employees to better understand the underlying leadership concepts endorsed by the organization.

Researchers have posited that, among the three broad categories of training delivery methods, practice-based training may be the most critical because it enables trainees to implement what they learned in a realistic environment (Weaver, Rosen, Salas, Baum, & King, 2010). Such a claim is also supported by neuroscience (for example, Brown & Brown, 2012), in that the activation of individuals' emotional circuits is triggered by their real-life experiences, allowing individuals to transfer what they have learned into behaviors more easily. On-the-job exercises, for instance, allow employees to put knowledge into action through a series of interactions with other employees, making it more salient (Arthur, Bennett, Edens, & Bell, 2003).

Coaching and mentoring is also effective in affording individuals practice under realistic conditions, with the guidance of others (Higgins & Kram, 2001). Researchers have found that having a mentor benefits individuals' personal and professional development (for example, Kram & Isabella, 1985). Specifically, research has found that the relationship quality between a mentor and mentee is important, in which mentors provide mentees with advice, support, and feedback, while mentees reciprocate with cooperation and commitment – that is, leader–member exchange (LMX) theory (Graen & Uhl-Bien, 1995). Higher quality relationships between mentors and mentees allow for more positive outcomes, such as improved job performance, satisfaction, and organizational commitment (Dulebohn, Bommer, Liden, Brouer, & Ferris, 2012).

Organizations often combine these training methods to improve training effectiveness. Indeed, organizational researchers assert that training programs are most effective when all three delivery methods are incorporated (for example, Salas et al., 2012). Such a multiple-method approach may allow the strengths of each training method to complement the weaknesses of another. For example, although lectures (that is, information-based) may provide a better conceptual understanding of the ideal leader, they may not allow trainees to put that knowledge into action. However, demonstrated-based training may use simulations to show examples of poor and excellent leadership behaviors, but its efficacy rests upon trainees gaining informational insights into the conditions and rationale regarding (in)appropriate behaviors. Although practice-based training allows trainees to gain practical experience, the efficacy of this approach may hinge on an understanding of how behaviors are related to leadership effectiveness. The use of a multiple-method approach may therefore maximize the overall effectiveness of leadership training programs (Arthur et al., 2003).

Aligning Leader Behavior and Mindset

A key tenet of the science of training is the need to align behavioral change with a corresponding shift in mindset (Salas et al., 2012). As noted, contemporary training approaches do little to train and align an individual's mindset with their behavior. For instance, information-based training, such as classroom-style lectures and presentations, may solely provide trainees with a "to-do list" of desirable leadership behaviors. Demonstration-based training suffers from the same issue, in that trainees are informed only what behaviors are considered appropriate, and they thereby underestimate the difficulty of behavioral change without identity change. Although practice-based training is considered the most effective (Weaver et al., 2010), it targets behavioral skills while potentially overlooking the importance of identity alignment. Indeed, training effectiveness may not be optimized if behavioral skills and identity are not aligned (Miscenko et al., 2017).

Consequences of Misaligned Leader Behavior and Mindset

When an individual's behaviors are contradicted by a set of beliefs, the individual may experience psychological discomfort. Leon Festinger (1957) described this phenomenon as "cognitive dissonance." Within the leadership training context, cognitive dissonance may occur when new information or prescribed behavioral skills contradicts trainees' pre-existing mindsets (for example, identity). To overcome the psychological discomfort caused by this contradiction, individuals may either change their behaviors to match their mindset, or change their mindset to match their behaviors. Given the emphasis on behavioral-based training, it seems that contemporary leadership training programs – whether intentionally or otherwise – rely on the notion that changing employee behaviors may result in a corresponding shift in mindset. For example, information-based training programs may educate trainees on some set of prescribed leadership behaviors, such as the four key behaviors of transformational leadership (Avolio et al., 2009), while demonstration-based training programs provide opportunities for trainees to observe examples of targeted competencies, such as behaviors associated with charisma (Antonakis, Fenley, & Liechti, 2011).

The success of these behavioral-based training approaches depends on a corresponding change in leader mindset brought about by cognitive dissonance (that is, changing identity to match behaviors). Although behavioral-based leadership training can result in a corresponding change in leader mindset (for example, identity), the net effect of the change is minimal (Miscenko et al., 2017). Moreover, this process requires trainees to endure the psychological discomfort of mindset change during the transition. Such discomfort may be a barrier that makes it difficult for trainees to complete the entire behavioral change process, which may affect the effectiveness of behavioral-based training approaches. As noted, the other alternative to resolving cognitive dissonance is that trainees may align their behaviors to their existing mindset (that is, no behavioral change because trainees maintain existing behaviors to ensure alignment with existing mindset). In other words, transfer of training for behavior change may be hampered to the extent that behaviors conflict with trainees' existing mindset. Thus it is critical to develop leadership training programs that target and align behavioral and mindset change. The reliance on behaviors to create a corresponding change in mindset may be insufficient to bring about alignment.

Developing Leader Mindset

Organizations are advised to directly cultivate leader mindset as an integral part of leadership training programs. Although a variety of approaches may be employed, we focus on two that we have experience of implementing with a diverse range of organizations and leaders (for example, students and executives) and which are supported by empirical evidence: cultivating leader identity, and inducing Pygmalion leadership.

Cultivating Leader Identity

The process of developing a leader identity has been described primarily as an unplanned process based on the accumulation of socialization and organizational experiences over time (Day, 2000). As such, fortuitous childhood experiences and parental upbringing (Keller, 1999, 2003) can shape leader identity, as can environmental factors such as culture (House, Javidan, Hanges, & Dorfman, 2002). Although organizations may attempt to incorporate planned leadership experiences (for example, job assignments to develop leadership skills or capabilities), such efforts target behavioral change and are not designed to cultivate identity development. The scientific study of leader identity is a nascent field, with little guidance on how best to cultivate leader identity. Here, we describe a purposeful approach to cultivating leader identity. Moreover, this approach allows for the targeting of specific attributes to incorporate as part of one's leader identity (that is, types of leader identity).

One of the coauthors developed the "leadership logo" exercise as a method of cultivating leader identity. As with all training, this method is most effective when implemented as part of a broader systemic leader development effort (Salas et al., 2012). Just as company logos tend to reflect idealized and aspirational attributes, individuals' leadership logos reflect idealized attributes to which they aspire as leaders. The leadership logo is a symbolic graphical representation of the future leader with which individuals are self-identified. This notion of a future leader identity is consistent with research showing that people construct past, present, and future identities (Roberts, 2002). These future-oriented representations have been called possible selves, which are defined as personalized enactive conceptions of the self "one is striving to become" (Markus & Nurius, 1986). Empirical research shows that people develop into senior leadership roles by performing "identity work" via experimenting with "provisional selves" as trials for leadership identities (Ibarra, 1999, 2004).

The leadership logo activity consists of a sequence of multiple training sessions that consecutively build on knowledge and insights discovered in each step. Participants are initially given contextual background and rationale for the leadership logo, as described above. Next, participants assess their current and desired future states. To facilitate the assessment, participants are guided through a series of questions about:

- their community, such as "How would you describe your current/ideal community (for example, profession, region, family, friends, nonprofit, religious, etc.)?";
- their company, such as "What are the core beliefs and values of your current/ideal company?"; and
- themselves, such as "What are your strengths and weaknesses?" and "Which of your attributes can be developed further as strengths?"

These questions were developed to capture the different levels of leader identity development (Day et al., 2014). Participants then analyze their responses for core value themes (for example, service to a minority community as a role model, emphasis on egalitarian values or shared power, etc.). Based on these core value themes, participants write their mission (for example, "To champion change and inspire the political passion of a new generation") and vision (for example, "An innovative healthcare leader fostering social awareness through creativity and empowerment in the community") statements after receiving a workshop on their meaning, purpose, and characteristics, along with examples. With their heightened self-knowledge and awareness, participants then create their leadership logo: a symbolic graphical representation reflecting their mission, vision, and core value themes (see Figure 13.1 for examples). Participants create the logos at the conceptual level, and these are then digitally produced by a professional graphic designer.

The leadership logo activity achieves several goals for cultivating leader mindset. First, the knowledge and reflection gained through this series of activities are designed to enhance self-awareness, which has been posited as foundational for leader development (Epitropaki et al., 2017).

Second, the sequence of activities across multiple training sessions that consecutively build on knowledge and insights reflects forms of identity work

FIGURE 13.1 Examples of leadership logos.

(Ibarra, 1999, 2004) that afford participants opportunities to intentionally shape their leader identity, rather than leaving its formation to unplanned events.

Third, the leadership logo is a symbolic artifact that serves as a training aid, which reinforces learning post-training. In doing so, the leadership logo enhances the transfer of training goals to the workplace. Many participants utilize their leadership logo in their daily work lives. For example, one manager created a brooch in the likeness of her leadership logo and wears it daily as a reminder of her values and goals as a leader. Another manager framed a large poster of his leadership logo, which serves as a visual daily induction that urges him toward realizing his leadership vision. These examples illustrate the fourth goal of the leadership logo: nudging leaders toward the enactment of their idealized leader identity (Thaler & Sunstein, 2008).

Inducing Pygmalion Leadership

The leadership logo activity illustrates how leader mindsets can be shaped and cultivated in organizations, which also has implications for influencing leadership behaviors – that is, visual cues can have a reflexive influence on behavior, as explained in our previous discussion on the perception–behavior link (Engle & Lord, 1997; Sy, 2010). Here, we extend this notion further by illustrating how mindsets can be induced in a manner that influences leadership behaviors. We provide a grounding on the tenets of "Pygmalion leadership," and illustrate practical implementation strategies via ILTs and IFTs.

Ample evidence demonstrates that a positive mindset can be induced to improve individual performance across various settings (for example, Eden, 1990; Rosenthal & Jacobson, 1968). This phenomenon is known as the Pygmalion effect (Rosenthal & Jacobson, 1968), which is a special case of the self-fulfilling prophecy, whereby inducing individuals' positive expectations of others results in a corresponding increase in others' performance. Rosenthal and Jacobson (1968) first discovered that teachers' expectations are highly related to students' performance. Similarly, Eden and colleagues (for example, Eden & Ravid, 1982) discovered that leaders' expectations have a significant influence on followers' performances. Besides performance, research on the Pygmalion effect has found a positive relationship between leader expectations and their affect toward followers (Rosenthal, 1993), which results in greater leader support and guidance.

Indeed, a recent meta-analysis shows that Pygmalion leadership interventions had the largest impact in comparison to other leadership styles (Avolio et al., 2009). Specifically, Pygmalion leadership interventions showed the greatest success rate (79 percent) in comparison with other leadership interventions (65 percent). Moreover, beyond having the greatest overall impact, Pygmalion leadership also had the largest effects on both behavioral (for example, performance, leader emergence) and cognitive (for example, idea generation, confidence) outcomes, and had similar effects to other leadership styles on affective outcomes (for example, liking, satisfaction).

The vast majority of Pygmalion leadership interventions involve the artificial manipulation of leaders' performance expectations for their followers, such as providing leaders with false performance information (Eden et al., 2000). This limitation poses a problem for implementing Pygmalion leadership interventions in organizational settings because of ethical concerns about manipulations involving false information, or where leaders' performance expectations cannot easily be manipulated because leaders' expectations for their followers' performance occur naturally based on prior knowledge of performance history. As such, prior limitation for implementing Pygmalion leadership interventions can be addressed by focusing on naturally occurring Pygmalion effects via IFTs (Sy, 2010). Empirical research has shown that the positive dimensions of IFTs (that is, Industry, Enthusiasm, and Good Citizen) are positively related to the Pygmalion effect. Specifically, Whiteley and colleagues (2012) tested the naturally occurring Pygmalion leadership model with 151 workplace leader–follower dyads. Their results provided support for naturally occurring Pygmalion leadership, and they found that the positive dimensions of leaders' IFTs (or LIFTs) triggered the Pygmalion effect. Specifically, LIFTs led to higher performance expectations, liking, and relationship quality, which positively impacted follower performance. Additional support for the naturally occurring Pygmalion leadership model comes from research showing that the positive effects and behaviors of transformational leaders can be explained by their positive IFTs (Goodwin et al., 2000). These results show the promise of inducing mindsets, such as LIFTs, to bring about positive leadership outcomes.

The notion of inducing positive mindsets can be extended to the domain of ILTs. Implicit leadership theories consists of eight dimensions: Sensitivity, Dedication, Tyranny, Charisma, Attractiveness, Masculinity, Intelligence, and Strength. To develop an effective leadership intervention integrating ILTs, organizations should first identify their idealized leader prototype because ILTs vary across different groups (for example, Den Hartog et al., 1999). For example, Festekjian, Tram, Murray, Sy, and Huynh (2013) found that preferences for ILTs differed across different ethnic groups within the same country: Specifically, Asian Americans were judged based on a competent leader prototype (that is, intelligence and dedication), whereas Caucasian Americans were judged based on an agentic leader prototype (that is, masculinity, dynamism, and tyranny). Organizations can uncover endorsed leadership prototypes with the leadership logo activity.

When positive ILTs are induced, the activated mindset may elicit the Galatea effect. Like the Pygmalion effect (Eden, 1984), the Galatea effect is a special case of self-fulfilling prophecy in which leaders' *self-expectations* lead to positive outcomes (Babad, Inbar, & Rosenthal, 1982). For example, if leaders believe that they are dedicated and dynamic, they are more likely to engage in behaviors that correspond to these attributes. Research provides support for the Galatea effect in work settings. For instance, Eden and Zuk (1995) conducted one of the first studies investigating the Galatea effect. They experimentally induced mindset in a group of military cadets by suggesting that the cadets were unlikely to experience seasickness and that, even if they did experience it, seasickness would not influence their overall performance. Their results showed that cadets who were part of the mindset induction group experienced less seasickness and performed better compared to those who were in the control group. Furthermore, McNatt and Judge (2004) conducted an experiment to examine the Galatea effect using a sample from a Big Four accountancy firm. Some participants received a positive mindset induction to believe that their achievements were the result of their abilities and effort, whereas participants in the control group received no mindset induction. Results showed that participants who received the positive mindset induction showed a substantial increase in work performance, whereas participants in the control condition showed no performance differences.

Hundreds of empirical studies have demonstrated the validity and impact of mindset induction (for example, McNatt and Judge, 2004). Organizations may include ILTs and IFTs in their mindset leadership interventions because not only are individuals' behaviors guided by their mindset (Dweck, 1986, 1999, 2012), but also the connection between mindset and behaviors can be strengthened over time (the perception–behavior link) to become a habitual action tendency that is triggered in the presence of relevant stimuli (Bargh, 1989). When leaders think more positively of their followers, they are more likely to behave and lead more positively. Similarly, when the desirable attributes of their idealized leader identity are consistently induced, they are more likely to realize that transformation.

This transformation can be facilitated by consistently activating leader identity, which can be accomplished with the leadership logo exercise. As described, leaders have used their leadership logo to serve as a consistent daily induction that nudges them toward their leadership vision. Because the leadership logo is the embodiment of the leader's values, expectations, and behaviors, these attributes are triggered upon perceiving the graphical symbol. Preliminary research supports the use of graphical symbols as a means of mindset induction. Sy and Eden (2014) proposed that organizational aesthetics can be leveraged as a form of leadership intervention based on the perception–behavior link where graphic symbols serve as cues that trigger the initial perceptual processes. Indeed, researchers have recognized organizational aesthetics as a form of social influence because it shapes social meaning. Organizational aesthetics can take the form of paintings, photographs, sculptures, pictures, color, and such visual artifacts as company logos and websites. These graphical symbols are created and manipulated in organizational life to shape social reality, which can be extended to shaping individuals' perceptions about leaders (ILTs) and followers (IFTs). To test this notion, Sy and Eden (2014) used word-art posters to induce positive and negative IFTs in an experimental study. The 4ft × 6ft posters were embedded with positive words (for example, industry, enthusiasm, good citizen, etc.) and negative words (for example, conformity, insubordination, incompetence, etc.) describing the attributes of followers that are socially shared by members of society (Sy, 2010). The posters were placed at eye level, inconspicuously, on a wall 8 feet in front of seated participants, to reflect the typical positioning of artwork in any organizational setting. Although visible, participants were not aware of the intended purpose of the posters. Moreover, they were given a bogus cover story, and they believed that the study concerned perceptions of others. As such, they were instructed to read a vignette about a follower and then to form an impression of the person. Consistent with the perception–behavior link, participants exposed to the positive word-art poster, in comparison to those exposed to the negative word-art poster, formed more positive impressions of the follower, as well as judged the follower to be higher-performing and to be more deserving of a promotion. In short, these results illustrate that leader mindset can be induced via the activation of ILTs and IFTs, which then influence leader behaviors.

Conclusion

Effective leadership training programs require the holistic development of knowledge, behavioral skills, and attitudinal mindsets (Salas et al., 2012). However, contemporary programs emphasize the knowledge and behavioral components, while giving little attention to mindset development. This imbalanced approach can dampen the effectiveness of even the best programs and may account for the poor evaluation of leadership training effectiveness widely shared by practitioners. We offer a solution to correct this imbalance by focusing on the core mindset components of leader identity, ILTs, and IFTs. A key goal was to offer insights into the theoretical nature linking mindsets and behaviors; perhaps just as importantly, we have illustrated and provided practical strategies regarding how leadership mindset training and interventions may be implemented in organizational settings. We hope that our discussion sparks insights and enthusiasm. Individuals are transformed into leaders when balanced training programs effectively align behavior and mindset.

References

Antonakis, J., Fenley, M., & Liechti, S. (2011). Can charisma be taught? Tests of two interventions. *Academy of Management Learning and Education*, *10*(3), 374–396.

Arthur, W., Jr., Bennett, W., Jr., Edens, P.S., & Bell, S.T. (2003). Effectiveness of training in organizations: A meta-analysis of design and evaluation features. *Journal of Applied Psychology*, *88*(2), 234–245.

Avolio, B.J., Reichard, R.J., Hannah, S.T., Walumbwa, F.O., & Chan, A. (2009). A meta-analytic review of leadership impact research: Experimental and quasi-experimental studies. *The Leadership Quarterly*, *20*(5), 764–784.

Babad, E.Y., Inbar, J., & Rosenthal, R. (1982). Pygmalion, Galatea, and the Golem: Investigations of biased and unbiased teachers. *Journal of Educational Psychology*, *74*(4), 459–474.

Bargh, J.A. (1989). Conditional automaticity: Varieties of automatic influence in social perception and cognition. In J. Uleman & J. Bargh (Eds.), *Unintended thought* (pp. 3–51). New York: Guilford Press.

Bargh, J.A., Chen, M., & Burrows, L. (1996). Automaticity of social behavior: Direct effects of trait construct and stereotype activation on action. *Journal of Personality and Social Psychology*, *71*(2), 230–244.

Bass, B.M., & Bass, R. (2008). *The Bass handbook of leadership: Theory, research, and managerial applications*. New York: Free Press.

Bersin, J. (2014). Spending on corporate training soars: Employee capabilities now a priority. *Forbes*. Retrieved from www.forbes.com/sites/joshbersin/2014/02/04/the-recovery-arrives-corporate-training-spend-skyrockets/#7fce90fdc5a7

Boatman, J., & Wellins, R. (2011). *Time for a leadership revolution: Global leadership forecast 2011* [pdf]. Retrieved from www.ddiworld.com/ddi/media/trend-research/globalleadershipforecast2011_globalreport_ddi.pdf

Brown, P., & Brown, V. (2012). *Neuropsychology for coaches: Understanding the basics.* Milton Keynes: Open University Press.

Chartrand, T.L., & Bargh, J.A. (1999). The chameleon effect: The perception–behavior link and social interaction. *Journal of Personality and Social Psychology, 76*(6), 893–910.

Chiu, C., Hong, Y., & Dweck, C.S. (1997). Lay dispositionism and implicit theories of personality. *Journal of Personality and Social Psychology, 73*(1), 19–30.

Day, D.V. (2000). Leadership development: A review in context. *The Leadership Quarterly, 11*(4), 581–613.

Day, D.V., & Harrison, M.M. (2007). A multilevel, identity-based approach to leadership development. *Human Resource Management Review, 17*(4), 360–373.

Day, D.V., Fleenor, J.W., Atwater, L.E., Sturm, R.E., & McKee, R.A. (2014). Advances in leader and leadership development: A review of 25 years of research and theory. *The Leadership Quarterly, 25*(1), 63–82.

Den Hartog, D.N., House, R.J., Hanges, P.J., Ruiz-Quintanilla, S.A., Dorfman, P.W., Abdalla, I.A., . . . & Akande, B.E. (1999). Culture specific and cross-culturally generalizable implicit leadership theories: Are attributes of charismatic/transformational leadership universally endorsed? *The Leadership Quarterly, 10*(2), 219–256.

Dijksterhuis, A., & Van Knippenberg, A. (1998). The relation between perception and behavior, or how to win a game of trivial pursuit. *Journal of Personality and Social Psychology, 74*(4), 865–877.

Dulebohn, J.H., Bommer, W.H., Liden, R.C., Brouer, R.L., & Ferris, G.R. (2012). A meta-analysis of antecedents and consequences of leader-member exchange: Integrating the past with an eye toward the future. *Journal of Management, 38*(6), 1715–1759.

Dweck, C.S. (1986). Motivational processes affecting learning. *American Psychologist, 41*(10), 1040–1048.

Dweck, C.S. (1999). *Self-theories: Their role in motivation, personality, and development.* Philadelphia, PA: Psychology Press.

Dweck, C.S. (2012). Implicit theories. In P.A.M. Van Lange, A.W. Kruglanski, & E.T. Higgins (Eds.), *Handbook of theories of social psychology* (pp. 43–61). Thousand Oaks, CA: Sage.

Eden, D. (1984). Self-fulfilling prophecy as a management tool: Harnessing Pygmalion. *Academy of Management Review, 9*(1), 64–73.

Eden, D. (1990). *Pygmalion in management: Productivity as a self-fulfilling prophecy.* Lexington, MA: DC Heath.

Eden, D., & Ravid, G. (1982). Pygmalion versus self-expectancy: Effects of instructor-and self-expectancy on trainee performance. *Organizational Behavior and Human Performance, 30*(3), 351–364.

Eden, D., & Zuk, Y. (1995). Seasickness as a self-fulfilling prophecy: Raising self-efficacy to boost performance at sea. *Journal of Applied Psychology, 80*(5), 628–635.

Eden, D., Geller, D., Gewirtz, A., Gordon-Terner, R., Inbar, I., Liberman, M., . . . & Shalit, M. (2000). Implanting Pygmalion leadership style through workshop training: Seven field experiments. *The Leadership Quarterly, 11*(2), 171–210.

Engle, E.M., & Lord, R.G. (1997). Implicit theories, self-schemas, and leader–member exchange. *Academy of Management Journal, 40*(4), 988–1010.

Epitropaki, O., & Martin, R. (2004). Implicit leadership theories in applied settings: Factor structure, generalizability and stability over time. *Journal of Applied Psychology*, 89(2), 293–310.

Epitropaki, O., Kark, R., Mainemelis, C., & Lord, R.G. (2017). Leadership and followership identity processes: A multilevel review. *The Leadership Quarterly*, 28(1), 104–129.

Epitropaki, O., Sy, T., Martin, R., Tram-Quon, S., & Topakas, A. (2013). Implicit leadership and followership theories "in the wild": Taking stock of information-processing approaches to leadership and followership in organizational settings. *The Leadership Quarterly*, 24(6), 858–881.

Feldman, J.M. (1981). Beyond attribution theory: Cognitive processes in performance appraisal. *Journal of Applied Psychology*, 66(2), 127–148.

Festekjian, A., Tram, S., Murray, C.B., Sy, T., & Huynh, H.P. (2014). I see me the way you see me: The influence of race on interpersonal and intrapersonal leadership perceptions. *Journal of Leadership and Organizational Studies*, 21(1), 102–119.

Festinger, L. (1957). *A theory of cognitive dissonance*. Stanford, CA: Stanford University Press.

Goodwin, V.L., Wofford, J.C., & Boyd, N.G. (2000). A laboratory experiment testing the antecedents of leader cognitions. *Journal of Organizational Behavior*, 21(7), 769–788.

Graen, G.B., & Uhl-Bien, M. (1995). Relationship-based approach to leadership: Development of leader–member exchange (LMX) theory of leadership over 25 years – Applying a multi-level multi-domain perspective. *The Leadership Quarterly*, 6(2), 219–247.

Higgins, M.C., & Kram, K.E. (2001). Reconceptualizing mentoring at work: A developmental network perspective. *Academy of Management Review*, 26(2), 264–288.

House, R.J., & Aditya, R.N. (1997). The social scientific study of leadership: *Quo vadis? Journal of Management*, 23(3), 409–473.

House, R.J., Javidan, M., Hanges, P., & Dorfman, P. (2002). Understanding cultures and implicit leadership theories across the globe: An introduction to project GLOBE. *Journal of World Business*, 37(1), 3–10.

Ibarra, H. (1999). Provisional selves: Experimenting with image and identity in professional adaptation. *Administrative Science Quarterly*, 44(4), 764–791.

Ibarra, H. (2004). *Working identity: Unconventional strategies for reinventing your career*. Boston, MA: Harvard Business School Press.

Keller, T. (1999). Images of the familiar: Individual differences and implicit leadership theories. *The Leadership Quarterly*, 10(4), 589–607.

Keller, T. (2003). Parental images as a guide to leadership sensemaking: An attachment perspective on implicit leadership theories. *The Leadership Quarterly*, 14(2), 141–160.

Kirkpatrick, D. (1959). Techniques for evaluating training programs. *Journal of the American Society for Training and Development*, 13(11–12), 3–9.

Kram, K.E., & Isabella, L.A. (1985). Mentoring alternatives: The role of peer relationships in career development. *Academy of Management Journal*, 28(1), 110–132.

Lacerenza, C.N., Reyes, D.L., Marlow, S.L., Joseph, D.L., & Salas, E. (2017). Leadership training design, delivery, and implementation: A meta-analysis. *Journal of Applied Psychology*, 102(12), 1686–1718.

Lewandowsky, S., Oberauer, K., & Gignac, G.E. (2013). NASA faked the moon landing –therefore, (climate) science is a hoax: An anatomy of the motivated rejection of science. *Psychological Science*, 24(5), 622–633.

Lord, R.G., & Hall, R.J. (2005). Identity, deep structure and the development of leadership skill. *The Leadership Quarterly, 16*(4), 591–615.

Lord, R.G., & Maher, K.J. (1991). *Leadership and information processing: Linking perceptions and performance.* Boston, MA: Unwin Hyman.

Lord, R.G., Foti, R.J., & De Vader, C.L. (1984). A test of leadership categorization theory: Internal structure, information processing, and leadership perceptions. *Organizational Behavior and Human Performance, 34*(3), 343–378.

Markus, H., & Nurius, P. (1986). Possible selves. *American Psychologist, 41*(9), 954–969.

Markus, H., & Wurf, E. (1987). The dynamic self-concept: A social psychological perspective. *Annual Review of Psychology, 38*(1), 299–337.

McGregor, D. (1960). *The human side of enterprise.* New York: McGraw-Hill.

McNatt, D.B., & Judge, T.A. (2004). Boundary conditions of the Galatea effect: A field experiment and constructive replication. *Academy of Management Journal, 47*(4), 550–565.

Miscenko, D., Guenter, H., & Day, D.V. (2017). Am I a leader? Examining leader identity development over time. *The Leadership Quarterly, 28*(5), 605–620.

Oyserman, D., & Markus, H. (1998). Self as social representation. In U. Flick (Ed.), *The psychology of the social* (pp. 107–125). New York: Cambridge University Press.

Payne, B.K., Brown-Iannuzzi, J.L., & Loersch, C. (2016). Replicable effects of primes on human behavior. *Journal of Experimental Psychology: General, 145*(10), 1269–1279.

Rizzolatti, G., Fogassi, L., & Gallese, V. (2001). Neurophysiological mechanisms underlying the understanding and imitation of action. *Nature Reviews Neuroscience, 2*(9), 661–670.

Roberts, W.A. (2002). Are animals stuck in time? *Psychological Bulletin, 128*(3), 473–489.

Rosenthal, R. (1993). Interpersonal expectations: Some antecedents and some consequences. In P.D. Blanck (Ed.), *Interpersonal expectations: Theory, research, and applications – Studies in emotion and social interaction* (pp. 3–24). New York: Cambridge University Press.

Rosenthal, R., & Jacobson, L. (1968). *Pygmalion in the classroom.* New York: Holt, Rinehart, & Winston.

Salas, E., & Cannon-Bowers, J.A. (2001). The science of training: A decade of progress. *Annual Review of Psychology, 52*(1), 471–499.

Salas, E., Tannenbaum, S.I., Kraiger, K., & Smith-Jentsch, K.A. (2012). The science of training and development in organizations: What matters in practice. *Psychological Science in the Public Interest, 13*(2), 74–101.

Schwartz, J., Bersin, J., & Pelster, B. (2014, March 7). Human capital trends 2014 survey: Top 10 findings. Retrieved from www2.deloitte.com/insights/us/en/focus/human-capital-trends/2014/human-capital-trends-2014-survey-top-10-findings.html

Schyns, B., & Meindl, J.R. (2005). *Implicit leadership theories: Essays and explorations.* Greenwich, CT: Information Age.

Sy, T. (2010). What do you think of followers? Examining the content, structure, and consequences of implicit followership theories. *Organizational Behavior and Human Decision Processes, 113*(2), 73–84.

Sy, T., & Eden, D. (2014, May). *The art of followership: Applying organizational aesthetics to trigger implicit followership theories and corresponding action tendencies.* Poster session presented at the meeting of the Society of Industrial Organizational Psychology, Honolulu, HI.

Sy, T., Reiter-Palmon, R., Shaughnessy, S., Leung, A., Horton, C., Royston, R., & Scheller, E. (2018). *I am the follower and the leader: Advancing a model of follower–leader identity integration* [Unpublished manuscript].

Sy, T., Shore, L.M., Strauss, J., Shore, T.H., Tram, S., Whiteley, P., & Ikeda-Muromachi, K. (2010). Leadership perceptions as a function of race–occupation fit: The case of Asian Americans. *Journal of Applied Psychology, 95*(5), 902–919.

Thaler, R.H., & Sunstein, C.R. (2008). *Nudge: Improving decisions about health, wealth, and happiness.* New Haven, CT: Yale University Press.

Wakefield, N., Abbatiello, A., Agarwal, D., Pastakia, K., & van Berkel, A. (2016). Leadership awakened: Generations, teams, science. In *Global Human Capital Trends 2016: The New Organization – Different by Design* (pp. 27–36) [pdf]. Retrieved from www2.deloitte.com/content/dam/Deloitte/global/Documents/HumanCapital/gx-dup-global-human-capital-trends-2016.pdf

Weaver, S.J., Rosen, M.A., Salas, E., Baum, K.D., & King, H.B. (2010). Integrating the science of team training: guidelines for continuing education. *Journal of Continuing Education in the Health Professions, 30*(4), 208–220.

Weick, K.E. (1995). *Sensemaking in organizations.* Thousand Oaks, CA: Sage.

Wentworth, D. (2016, November 30). Top spending trends for training, 2016–2017. *Training.* Retrieved from: https://trainingmag.com/top-spending-trends-training-2016-2017/

Whiteley, P., Sy, T., & Johnson, S.K. (2012). Leaders' conceptions of followers: Implications for naturally occurring Pygmalion effects. *The Leadership Quarterly, 23*(5), 822–834.

Yammarino, F. (2013). Leadership: Past, present, and future. *Journal of Leadership and Organizational Studies, 20*(2), 149–155.

14

CRITICAL LEADERSHIP STUDIES

Exploring the Dialectics of Leadership

David L. Collinson

In his seminal text *Leadership*, James McGregor Burns (1978, p. 19) argued that transformational and transactional leadership comprised "two fundamentally different forms" of leadership. Approximately 30 years later, Burns (2007) acknowledged that his original concepts were "over-dichotomized" and that he could not now explain why he had neglected "the mixture" between them. *Leadership* is one of the most celebrated and cited books in the history of leadership studies. The concepts of transformational and transactional leadership have dominated the field, and it is these themes that those outside the discipline frequently associate with leadership research. As one of the founding fathers and most influential writers in leadership studies, Jim Burns' disclosure is particularly significant: It demonstrates that even the most influential ideas in leadership studies can be prone to over-dichotomization.

This chapter argues that studies of leadership are quite successful in identifying conceptual distinctions and differentiations, but are often much less effective in exploring interconnections and tensions. In place of dichotomization, the chapter proposes the value of more dialectical forms of analysis that explicitly attend to interrelationships, ambiguities, and contradictions in leadership theories and practices. This emphasis on interconnections in turn highlights the need to explore a number of neglected and interrelated leadership dialectics. The chapter considers recent work in critical leadership studies (CLS) that embraces "the dialectical turn" by examining the importance of power, conformity, and resistance in leadership dynamics.

Covering a diverse set of theories and perspectives, critical approaches share a concern to highlight the interrelated significance of situated power relations, multiple identity constructions, and their various interrelations and tensions. From a CLS standpoint, it is through these interweaving processes that leadership dynamics are typically enacted, frequently rationalized, sometimes resisted, and occasionally transformed. Critical perspectives acknowledge that, for good or ill, leaders exercise considerable power and influence in organizations. They demonstrate that leaders' power takes many forms, sometimes mutually reinforcing and sometimes contradictory. Power can be constructive and empowering and/or destructive and oppressive. Exploring organizational power dynamics in all their asymmetrical, shifting, intersecting, and contradictory forms, CLS seeks to open up new and innovative thinking about leadership dynamics.

From this critical lens, it is possible to view the leadership field as comprising at least three main paradigms: heroic, post-heroic, and critical studies. Heroic approaches focus primarily on (effective) leaders' qualities and practices (for example, trait, style, contingency, path–goal, charisma, emotional intelligence, social identity, and authentic theories). This leader-centred literature represents the overwhelming majority of studies on leadership. It tends to focus primarily on individuals, paying less attention to the socially and discursively constructed contexts, relations, and meanings of leadership dynamics, or to their structural and cultural conditions and consequences. By privileging leaders, heroic perspectives leave unquestioned assumptions that it is "leaders" who are in charge and make decisions, whilst "followers" are those who merely carry out orders from "above." They tend to assume that the interests of leaders and followers automatically coalesce.

Post-heroic perspectives replace this leader-centric emphasis with a focus on relational and collective dynamics (for example, distributed, shared, collaborative, discursive, and complexity leadership). Shifting the analytical lens from the individual to the collective, post-heroic perspectives highlight the importance of followers, cultures, and contexts. In so doing, they build on the rather individualistic and leader-centric lens of conventional approaches. But what unites heroic and post-heroic paradigms is a recurrent tendency to ignore or downplay issues of power and control; hence the need for critical approaches. Highlighting the typically asymmetrical and contested nature of leader–follower relations, CLS respond to the failure of heroic and post-heroic leadership studies to address important questions of power, privilege, asymmetries, and inequalities. Before elaborating on critical, dialectical approaches to the study of leadership, the first section of this chapter begins by discussing the nature and extent of dichotomization in leadership studies.

Dichotomizing Leadership

As one of the few writers to highlight the overlaps between transformational and transactional leadership, Hollander (2009) argues that transformational leadership remains an exchange relationship. He asserts that Burns' distinction is predicated on a narrow concern with tangible rewards. When intangibles are also considered, Hollander (2009) suggests, it becomes evident that these concepts are more interconnected than originally assumed. Hollander (2009) contends that transformational leaders provide followers with personal attention, support, fairness, and intellectual stimulation, and that followers reciprocate with loyalty, esteem, and trust, allowing leaders greater latitude, or "idiosyncracy credit." Observing that most effective leaders incorporate both transformational and transactional elements, Hollander (2009) also questions the recurrent tendency to elevate transformational leadership as the "good mode" of leadership, whilst transactional leadership is often portrayed as inferior. His arguments illustrate how dichotomization tends to overemphasize conceptual difference and to create unwarranted asymmetries within distinctions. It privileges one side of an apparent polarity above the other, exaggerating its (perceived) positive aspects, whilst overstating (perceived) negative features of the downplayed polarity.

The conceptual separation of transformational and transactional leadership is only one example of this dichotomizing impulse in mainstream leadership studies. Other binaries include: leadership/management, leadership/followership, born/made leaders, task/people, theory X/theory Y, one best way/contingent, organic/mechanistic, autocratic/participative, rational/emotional, and saviours/scapegoats. Dichotomies primarily emerge as "either/or," mutually exclusive alternatives, but they can also surface as "2 × 2" quadrants, or as multilevel analyses (for example, society, organization, group, and individual). Identifying different levels can be a useful heuristic device, but, in their concern with differentiation, multilevel studies sometimes fail to consider how different analytical levels are simultaneously implicated and interwoven in particular practices. The literature is replete with numerous distinctions often treated as "either/or" dichotomies. As Harter (2006, p. 90) observes, in the study of leadership "dualisms pop up everywhere." This "bi-polar shopping list approach" (Grint, 1997, p. 3) is particularly prevalent in mainstream heroic studies, in which leaders' personas and practices tend to be privileged, and psychological perspectives predominate.

In leadership studies, dichotomization also appears quite intractable, with one binary often reinforcing others. For example, studies of transformational leadership sometimes rely on and reproduce leader/manager and leader/follower dichotomies. Here, the transformational pole is typically connected with leadership, while the transactional polarity is often associated with management. Accordingly, leading and managing are viewed as mutually exclusive (Rost, 1993), with leaders and managers being defined as different types of person (Zaleznik, 1975). Transformational leaders are often privileged as visionary change agents, whereas transactional managers are downgraded as more narrowly concerned with rules, routinization, and risk-aversion. The reverse dichotomy is also evident. Lease (2006, p. 15) criticized the "good leader/bad manager dichotomy" for "glamorizing" leadership and "denigrating" management. Inverting the binary, Lease (2006) argues that leadership is better seen as one aspect of the broader construct of management. A critical, dialectical approach holds that power in organizations is typically exercised through leadership and management: Not one or the other, but both. Leadership and management are interwoven forms of organizational power.

In relation to the leader/follower dichotomy, transformational studies have been criticized for privileging leaders and neglecting the active role of followers (Linstead, Fulop, & Lilley, 2009). This dichotomy is particularly intractable, as Burns (1978, p. 3) noted: "[L]eader–follower bifurcation is one of the most serious failures in the study of leadership." Some 30 years later, Burns (2008, p. xii) acknowledged that, in the ensuing period, making the linkage between leadership and followership has "proved exceptionally difficult." The tendency to dichotomize leaders and followers remains a particular challenge for researchers, not least because dichotomization seems to reflect and reinforce leadership romanticism.

Meindl, Ehrlich, and Dukerich (1985) criticized the literature for an excessive belief in the (exaggerated) potency of leaders and for privileging leaders over followers. Arguing that romanticized perspectives frequently exaggerate what leaders are able to achieve, they asserted that leaders' contribution to a collective enterprise is inevitably more constrained and closely tied to external factors outside a leaders' control, such as those affecting whole industries. Meindl and colleagues' (1985) arguments paved the way for the emergence of post-heroic leadership – an approach that emphasizes that leadership is better understood as socially constructed, and as more collective and relational.

Post-heroic perspectives also sometimes engage in dichotomization, typically by inverting the leader/follower binary. In a later paper, Meindl (1995, p. 329) proposed a "follower-centric" approach to leadership studies. He recommended that researchers should ignore leaders and concentrate instead on followers' views of leaders and of themselves as followers. Meindl's (1995) approach valuably highlights the importance of followership, but his recommendation tends to reverse the prevailing dichotomy, replacing the privileging of leaders with the analytical prioritization of followers.

Similarly, Chaleff (2009, 2015) recommends that "courageous" followers need to voice constructive criticism and engage in "intelligent disobedience," particularly when they believe that leaders are not acting in the best interests of the organization. While these are important recommendations about followership, they tend to underestimate the costs and overestimate the possibilities of explicit dissent in organizations. Studies of whistle-blowing reveal that followers who express their concerns in precisely the way advocated by Chaleff need to recognize that their actions might be career-damaging and may even result in them being fired (Miceli & Near, 2002). For many employees, the prospect of being disciplined for expressing dissent and of having to find another job can be daunting. Focusing on collective processes generally, some post-heroic perspectives seem to underestimate the hierarchical nature of organizations and to replace the privileging of leaders with a romanticism of followers.

In a similar way, post-heroic interest in "leadership as practice" (LAP) explicitly rejects any concern with the traits and behaviours of individual leaders (Raelin, 2016), preferring instead to view leadership "as an agency emanating from an emerging collection of practices" (Raelin, Kempster, Youngs, Carroll, & Jackson, 2018, p. 372). Whereas mainstream perspectives can be criticized for being narrowly focused on individual leaders, post-heroic theories such as LAP often focus on collective practices to the neglect of any examination of individual leaders. Rejecting these polarized positions, critical perspectives argue that it is not a question of one or the other; rather, *both* (collective) practices *and* (individual) traits/behaviours are conceptually important, as are the ways in which they interrelate in particular practices. The dichotomizing impulse of LAP is also evident in its neglect of organizational and social structures, and of the interrelationships between practices and power relations (Collinson, 2018).

Problematizing dichotomization does not mean rejecting the value of distinctions per se. Indeed, distinctions can help to create meaning, clarity, and transparency, and thus avoid confusion and manipulation. As sociologist Simmel (1994, p. 5) observed, human beings typically "separate the connected" and "connect the separate," adding that "things must first be separated from one another in order to be together." Human beings routinely distinguish and contrast to make sense, learn, and organize. Language typically relies on subject–object separations (for example, "leader" and "follower"). Differentiation is also fundamental to organization: The principle of separating processes into their constituent parts informs the division of labour. However, when distinctions are viewed as dichotomies, they can reduce complex leadership relationships to "either/or" polarities that downplay or neglect interrelations, tensions, asymmetries, and contradictions. Drawing on Simmel's terminology, it can be argued that leadership researchers sometimes can disproportionately "separate the connected" to the neglect of "connecting the separate." Recent leadership research displays a growing interest in "connecting the separate" through a focus on dialectical perspectives.

From Dichotomies to Dialectics

Dialectical approaches highlight the analytical importance of deep-seated tensions and contradictions in relations based on opposing, but interdependent, forces that produce conflict and change: "a dynamic knot of contradictions, a ceaseless interplay between contrary or opposing tendencies" (Baxter & Montgomery, 1996, p. 3). Dialectical thinking was, historically, a significant feature of both classical philosophy (for example, Plato, Socrates, Aristotle) and early social science (for example, Hegel, Marx, Engels, Sartre, Weber, Simon). Yet, with the rise of management science in the twentieth century, many earlier insights about ambiguities, tensions, and contradictions were lost as new perspectives focused increasingly on creating analytical order and tidiness (Storey & Salaman, 2009). In recent years, there has been a re-emergence of interest in dialectical studies of society (Giddens, 1984; Latour, 1993), of organization (Putnam, Fairhurst, & Banghart, 2016; Mumby, 2011), and of communication (for example, Tracy, 2004, Barge, Lee, Maddux, Nabring, & Townsend, 2008).

Dialectical analyses have started to inform research on leadership effectiveness. In the United States, Collins (2001) found that the "level 5" leaders of "good to great" companies consistently displayed a paradoxical and flexible blend of seemingly irreconcilable qualities: They were modest, but wilful; humble, yet fearless; both resolute and stoic. Cameron, Quinn, Degraff, and Thakor (2014) argue that effective leaders tend to be "simultaneously paradoxical," integrating factors usually seen as competing and even incompatible. In the UK, Storey and Salaman (2009) recommend that leaders learn how to creatively use the tensions between seemingly conflicting priorities. Advocating organizational systems that "thrive on paradox," Storey and Salaman (2009, p. 22) hold that the management of dilemma and paradox is "the essence of leadership."

Yet Storey and Salaman (2009) also acknowledge that in practice leaders frequently look for "tidy solutions" and respond to dilemmas by adhering to ingrained, polarized ways of thinking. Similarly, Kaplan and Kaiser (2006) discovered that many American leaders tended to be "lop-sided." Most leaders in their large-scale study were deemed to be either too task-focused (and not sufficiently people-oriented), or too big-picture-oriented (with little concern for implementation). Most importantly, these leaders also preferred to be lop-sided, typically favouring their current skills and downgrading the alternatives. Hence escaping the limits of dichotomization appears to constitute a major challenge for practising leaders.

A number of leadership researchers have sought to reframe the persistent leader/follower dichotomy in dialectical terms. Fairhurst (2001) observed that leadership research typically concentrates either on leaders, in ways that overlook the collective, or on the collective, thereby neglecting the leader's basis for action. She advocates dialectical forms of inquiry that go beyond these seemingly oppositional binaries to explore their "dynamic tension" and "interplay." Gronn (2011) argues that, historically, the leadership literature is characterized by a recurrent pendulum effect that swings between individual perspectives followed by renewed interest in more distributed, collective leadership. He argues that leadership is fundamentally "a hybrid configuration," invariably comprising both leaders and followers, both individual and collective dimensions, in varying mixtures. This focus on dialectics in leadership studies has, in turn, informed the emergence of more critical leadership studies that explicitly examine power in leadership dynamics.

The Dialectics of Power

Critical leadership studies (CLS) draw on dialectical perspectives to examine asymmetrical power relations in leadership dynamics. They emphasize that leaders exercise considerable power, that this can be paradoxical and contradictory, that followers' practices are frequently proactive, knowledgeable, and oppositional, and that gender and other key aspects of diversity and identity crucially shape control/resistance dialectics. In addition to viewing leadership dynamics as coproduced within asymmetric relationships, critical perspectives draw on the dialectics of power to reconsider leader–follower relations.

Foucault's (1977, 1979) ideas have been particularly influential in CLS. Arguing that power is intimately connected to knowledge and subjectivity, he addressed the ways in which "power/knowledge" regimes are inscribed on subjectivities. Foucault explored the "disciplinary power" of surveillance that produces detailed information about individuals, rendering them visible, calculable, and self-disciplining selves. He suggested that, by shaping identity formation, power can be enabling and productive, as well as subordinating. One implication of Foucault's ideas is that leaders can exercise power by measuring and evaluating followers' performance – especially when the latter internalize and reproduce this discipline through self-surveillance. Foucault also highlighted the dialectical relationship between power and resistance. He argued that power creates the conditions for its own resistance and that dissent typically draws on the very power it opposes. Even in the most totalitarian of power regimes, inconsistencies and contradictions arise that provide opportunities for resistance, especially in the form of localized acts of defiance. As Foucault (1979, p. 95) argued, "where there is power, there is resistance."

Giddens' (1979, 1984, 1993) structuration theory has also been influential in CLS particularly because of its emphasis on the dialectics of power relations. This perspective demonstrates how structure and action are embedded in, and reproduce, one another as their medium and outcome. Central to Giddens' approach is the notion of "the dialectic of control," which holds that, no matter how asymmetrical, power relations are always two-way, contingent, and to some degree interdependent. Emphasizing an intrinsic relation between agency and power within all social relations, Giddens asserts that human beings are knowledgeable social agents who, acting within historically specific (sometimes unacknowledged) conditions and (sometimes unintended) consequences, always retain a capacity to "make a difference." With regard to leadership, an important implication is that leader–follower relations can be understood as fundamentally characterized by both interdependencies and power asymmetries. Since asymmetrical power relations are always two-way, leaders will remain dependent to some extent on the led, while the latter retain a degree of autonomy and discretion.

Critical leadership studies argue that mainstream leadership research tends to be excessively positive in orientation and, as a result, is often reluctant to address issues of power and privilege (Collinson, 2012). Heroic studies are frequently informed by the assumption that leaders are invariably a source of good, that leaders' efforts unfailingly produce positive outcomes, and that causal links can be made directly between leaders' positive contribution and organizational performance. Concentrating on identifying the "essential" characteristics of "successful" leaders, many studies tend to view leadership primarily in terms of its inherently positive "influence," while questions of power disappear from view.

Leader-centred research often dichotomizes "power" and "influence": a binary that fails to appreciate that the latter is often one aspect of the former, or that power and control are important conditions and consequences of leadership dynamics. In his classic text, Burns (1978) differentiated "leaders" (who successfully engage and satisfy followers' motives) from "power holders" (who use followers for their own purposes and utilize "brute" power to achieve their ends). Arguing that "power wielders" should not be considered to be leaders at all, Burns (1978, p. 3) held that Hitler was not a leader, but a tyrant – "an absolute wielder of brutal power" who crushed all opposition: "A leader and a tyrant are polar opposites." Differentiating between "leaders" and "tyrants" in this way tends to sanitize the concept of leadership: Brutal dictators and autocrats are no longer considered to be leaders at all.

In subsequent years, this tendency to "purify" leadership studies of questions related to power has increasingly characterized leadership research. Focusing more narrowly on leaders' "influence" and capacity to inspire, many studies continue to take for granted that power and control are unproblematic forms of organizational authority, and that the interests of leaders and followers inevitably coalesce. A recent example of this tendency is "authentic leadership" theory, which typically depicts authentic leaders as dynamic, self-aware visionaries who make transparent, highly ethical decisions. Authentic leaders' positivity is viewed as infectious, creating "positive psychological capital," "positive moral perspective," and "positive climate" throughout the organization. Accordingly, issues of asymmetrical power and control disappear from view.

More critical perspectives rethink leadership as a set of dialectical relationships in which the exercise of power is central. Informed by various perspectives (from labour process theory to radical psychology and post-structuralism), they show how power is not so much a "dependent variable" as it is a deeply embedded and inescapable feature of leadership structures, cultures, relations, and practices. Critical studies challenge hegemonic views that take for granted that (white, middle-aged men) are the people in charge who create visions and make decisions, while followers are an undifferentiated collective who carry out orders from "above." They recognize that leaders' power and control can take multiple economic, political, discursive, and embodied forms, acknowledging, for example, that power is both structural and practice-based: Power can be conferred by hierarchical position, as well as enacted more informally through knowledge, relationships, networks, and agency. Critical studies emphasize that power can be both enabling and disciplinary: It can be positive, productive, and empowering, as well as toxic, corrupt, and destructive (see also Schyns, Neves, Wisse, & Knoll, Chapter 10, in this volume).

Critical leadership studies emphasize that power (and identity) can be enacted in overt, subtle, disguised, and sometimes invisible ways within leadership dynamics (Collinson, 2011). They recognize that, for good and/or ill, leaders exert significant power and influence over contemporary organizational processes, especially through key decision making (Tourish, 2013). For example, leaders typically play a key role in defining strategies and visions, shaping structures and cultures, monitoring work and performance, providing rewards, applying sanctions, and in hiring and firing. Leaders can also exercise power by "managing meaning" and defining situations in ways that suit their purposes (Smircich & Morgan, 1982). Critical leadership studies address the dangers of concentrating organizational control in the hands of a few: As Finkelstein (2003, p. 43) noted, "being [chief executive officer] of a sizeable corporation is probably the closest thing in today's world to being king of your own country." They also reveal how the exercise of power can be disguised – for example, through ideologies that seek to redefine sectional as universal interests, through discourses that construct excessively positive definitions of reality, and by leaders "distancing" themselves from particular local practices. Critical studies also examine the effects of power on leaders themselves. While power confers status and privilege, it may also facilitate hubris and arrogance (Sadler-Smith, Akstinaite, Robinson, & Wray, 2017). This, in turn, can inform a failure to consult – even a disregard for others' views – and a desire to hold onto power even when support for the leader has faded away.

Critical feminist studies argue that gender continues to be a key dynamic through which leadership power is enacted. Bowring (2004) emphasizes that the binary opposition between leaders and followers is often reinforced by a gender dualism in which men are viewed as the universal, neutral subject and women, as "the other." Feminist research shows how romanticized notions of the heroic, "tough," and "strong" leader are often saturated with masculinity, that women continue to be largely excluded from senior positions, and that they can experience considerable hostility in male-dominated managerial cultures (Sinclair, 2007). Critical studies of men examine the dominance of "hegemonic masculinity" in shaping leadership decisions, values, styles, language, cultures, identities, and practices (Hearn & Collinson, 2018).

The paid workplace (as well as the domestic sphere) is an important site for the reproduction of men's power and status. Studies suggest that masculine values can shape formal (for example, recruitment) and more informal (for example, joking relationships) organizational practices. Masculine cultures at work can also be reproduced through men's sexuality and the sexual harassment of women. There is emerging evidence that competition and conflict between men in senior positions within and between competing organizations can have damaging organizational and personal effects (for example, Martin, 2013). These contradictory dynamics of excessive competition between (male) leaders indicate the need for more research on men and masculinities in leadership positions.

Similar arguments can be made for other intersecting sources of power and identity, such as race, ethnicity, religion, disability, and sexual orientation: important themes for more critical work on leadership. Critical studies of management and organization illustrate how certain gendered, ethnic, and class-based voices are routinely privileged in the workplace, whilst others are marginalized (Ashcraft & Mumby, 2004). Feminist perspectives also suggest that dichotomization may itself constitute a gendered process: an exercise of gendered power, reflecting a masculine concern with enacting control by creating distinctions and hierarchies.

Relatedly, critical studies also highlight the embodied nature of leadership power (Liu, 2017). They demonstrate, for example, that, in education, the police, and orchestras, women and men leaders can utilize their bodies as positive modes of power, influence, and communication (Sinclair, 2005, 2013; Ropo & Sauer, 2008), and how corporeality, emotions, and aesthetics may shape leaders' practices (Hansen & Bathurst, 2011; Melina, Burgess, Falkman, & Marturano, 2013). In this way, critical writers reframe the Cartesian mind/body dualism in dialectical terms. For Descartes, logic and the scientific method required the separation of "the rational mind" from the "emotional body." Leadership research has traditionally focused on leaders' minds to the neglect of their bodies, treating leadership as an inherently cerebral, rational, and disembodied process. In terms of the ways in which leaders in practice can utilize emotions in communication, the election of U.S. President Trump focused attention on "why irrational politics appeals" (Fitzduff, 2017).

Similarly, critical studies of men and masculinities indicate that men can be quite detached from their own bodies (that is, disembodied), especially in relation to illness (Connell, 2005). Often reluctant to confront possible physical fragilities, men may try – frequently unsuccessfully – to distance themselves from their own bodies (Hearn & Collinson, 2018). This sense of mind/body separation, or disembodiment (as leaders and as men), may be compounded by new digital and virtual technologies (Hearn, 2012). The use of information and communication technologies (ICT) can intensify (men) leaders' distance, potentially compounding their tendency to view employees and customers as numbers on a spreadsheet.

Giddens' dialectic of control reminds us that whilst power is important for understanding social dynamics, it should not be overstated or seen as all-determining. A focus on leadership dialectics warns against treating leaders as if they were all-powerful. One example of the limitations on leaders' power is the frailty of the human body itself. Research has revealed the extent to which American presidents (Post & Robbins, 1993) and British prime ministers (Owen, 2009) have been detrimentally impacted by mental and/or physical illness whilst in office, as well as the lengths to which those around the leader may go to conceal such illness from the public. Another important potential constraint on leaders' power may be followers themselves and the degree to which leaders remain (inter)dependent on subordinates, as the next section elaborates.

Conformity, Compliance, and Resistance

Heroic studies tend to portray followers as "an empty vessel waiting to be led, or even transformed, by the leader" (Goffee & Jones, 2001, p. 148). They tend to view followers only in relation to their susceptibility to certain leader behaviours or styles. In recent years, however, there has been growing interest in followership research (for example, Shamir, Pillai, Bligh, & Uhl-Bien, 2007; Riggio, Chaleff, & Lipman-Blumen, 2008; Kellerman, 2008). Post-heroic perspectives have argued that "exemplary" and "star" followers are a precondition for high-performing organizations – particularly in the contemporary context of flatter hierarchies and greater team-working (for example, Kelley, 2004).

Critical approaches view the study of followership as a significant element in a dialectical approach to leadership. But they argue that the analysis of followership needs to be located within asymmetric power relations. In the heroic paradigm, followership is often assumed to be freely chosen. Critical perspectives argue that such overly voluntaristic arguments fail to locate followers in their structural, cultural, and economic context – the asymmetrical conditions and consequences of action. Precisely because of the ways in which power and control are typically enacted in contemporary organizations, many employees may have to follow or accept a strategic direction decided by leaders, even when they disagree with the selected path.

Critical perspectives also recognize that followership can have many different meanings, including, for example, political supporters, disciples, fans (for example, of sports teams and musicians), customers, fanatics, and even Twitter "followers." Within this broad range of possibilities, an employee can be seen as a specific kind of follower who sells their labour to an employer. In that sense, employment can be treated as a particular kind of commodified followership: one that is more contingent and constrained, sometimes insecure and potentially disposable, and much less "freely chosen." This, in turn, also means recognizing a much broader spectrum of possible follower agencies, ranging from deference, unquestioning loyalty, commitment, conformity, and compliance, to indifference, cynicism, disguised dissent, and overt resistance.

The disciplinary nature of power is revealed by studies that explore follower conformity, compliance, and consent. Although conformity tends to be viewed positively in heroic leadership studies, and frequently treated as an expression of commitment and loyalty, more critical writers highlight its potentially detrimental consequences. As a stark reminder of its potential dangers, they point to the Nazi extermination of 6 million Jews and the explanation of those involved that they were "just obeying orders." Milgram's (1963) experiments highlighted people's willingness to obey authority. Fromm (1977) pointed to "the fear of freedom," whereby individuals try to shelter in the perceived security of being told what to do, viewing this as a less-threatening alternative to the responsibility of making decisions for themselves. Bratton, Grint, and Nelson (2004) highlight the negative organizational effects of "destructive consent" and the potentially positive consequences of "constructive dissent."

Various researchers observe that followers often attribute exceptional qualities to charismatic leaders through processes such as transference (Maccoby, 2007), fantasy (Gabriel, 1997), and idealization (Shamir, 1999). Lipman-Blumen (2005) contends that followers frequently seem to be fascinated by toxic leaders despite – possibly even because of – the latter's dysfunctional characteristics (insatiable ambition, enormous ego, arrogance, etc). From a leadership perspective, we need to know a great deal more about how, why, and with what consequences men and women followers conform, comply, or remain committed to their leaders and organizations.

Whilst emphasizing the importance of power dynamics, there is also a growing recognition in CLS that leadership relations are typically not so asymmetrical and top-down that they are invariably one-way and all-determining. Three related points follow. First, by recognizing followers as skilled and knowledgeable agents, we can begin to see that they have at their disposal a repertoire of possible agencies. Critical leadership studies highlight the significance of followers' potential for resistance, whether this dissent is explicit (for example, strikes) and/or more disguised (for example, output restriction). This view contrasts with much of the literature, which tends to treat resistance as abnormal or irrational. Second, CLS emphasize that leadership dynamics can have unintended and contradictory consequences that leaders do not always understand or anticipate, and/or of which they are unaware. Third, practices of control and resistance may be mutually reinforcing and simultaneously linked, often in contradictory ways. From this perspective, power is seen as both disciplinary and enabling, while practices of control and resistance are viewed as mutually reinforcing and simultaneously linked, often in contradictory ways.

Although issues of dissent have only recently been addressed in leadership studies (for example, Banks, 2008), there is a considerable literature in organization studies indicating that employees often draw on strategic agencies and cultural resources to express disaffection in organizations (Mumby, Thomas, Marti, & Seidl, 2017). Critical researchers have revealed that oppositional practices can take numerous forms (Courpasson & Vallas, 2016). These include strikes, working to rule, working the system, output restriction, whistle-blowing, and sabotage (Gagnon & Collinson, 2017). In exceptional cases, subordinates may even (seek to) depose leaders.

Feminist studies demonstrate that resistance can take gendered forms. Research reveals, for example, how male-dominated shop-floor counter-cultures are frequently characterized by highly masculine breadwinner identities, aggressive and profane forms of humour, ridicule and sarcasm, and the elevation of "practical," manual work as confirmation of working-class manhood. Cockburn (1983) illustrates how male-dominated shop-floor counter-cultures and exclusionary trade union practices in the printing industry advantaged men, while subordinating women. Research in female-dominated factories and offices suggests that women workers often engage in (feminine) counter-cultures characterized by similarly aggressive joking and sexualized practices.

Some critical writers argue that employee resistance is more likely to emerge when followers believe that leaders are exercising control in unfair, dictatorial, coercive, and/or nepotistic ways. Equally, followers are more likely to resist when they feel that their views have not been considered, when they perceive leaders to be "out of touch," and when they detect discrepancies between leaders' policies and practices. Where followers perceive such inconsistencies, they can become increasingly cynical about leaders. Fleming's (2005) research in an Australian call centre found that, in the face of a corporate culture that treated workers like children, cynicism enabled employees to construct oppositional identities.

My own research in organizations over the past 40 years has consistently found that followers are potentially more oppositional than is often recognized not only in the leadership literature, but also by leaders themselves. Research in a British truck manufacturer found that a corporate culture campaign introduced by the new American senior management team to establish trust with the workforce had precisely the opposite effect, fuelling a shop-floor counter-culture (Collinson, 1992). Manual workers dismissed senior management's definition of the company as a team. Informed by perceptions of leaders' apparent disregard for their views and workers' own sense of job insecurity, employees resisted by "distancing" themselves, restricting output and effort, and by treating work purely as a means of economic compensation. The company's leaders remained unaware of how their strategies produced contrary effects on the shop floor. This study showed how leaders' control can have unintended effects, and how power/resistance dialectics can become embedded and mutually reinforcing.

Where followers are particularly concerned to avoid sanctions, they may resist in more disguised ways. While employees might be highly critical of leaders' practices, they may censor their views and camouflage their actions through a kind of resistance that "covers its own tracks" (Scott, 1985, p. 278). Anticipating the possibility of disciplinary sanctions, they might shape their actions accordingly. Subtle and routine subversions, such as absenteeism, "foot dragging," and "disengagement," can be difficult to detect. Employees may even undermine leaders' change initiatives simply by doing nothing. Such inertia can result in leaders making all sorts of mistakes (Grint, 2005). Disguised dissent is particularly likely where surveillance has become increasingly pervasive. Under the gaze of authority, individuals are increasingly aware of themselves as visible objects, and, as a consequence, they can become increasingly skilled choreographers of self and information, learning to disguise their response to "the gaze." By concealing and massaging knowledge and information, they respond to surveillance by engaging in impression management (Goffman, 1959).

Research on North Sea oil installations found that, despite extensive leadership commitment to safety, many offshore workers were either not reporting accidents and "near misses," or else they sought to downplay the seriousness of particular incidents (Collinson, 1999). While company leaders talked proudly about the organization's "learning culture," offshore workers complained about a "blame culture" on the platforms. Believing that disclosure of accident-related information would have a detrimental impact on their annual appraisals, pay, and employment security, offshore workers felt compelled to conceal or downplay information about accidents, injuries, and near misses. Precisely because such practices constituted a firing offence, workers also disguised their underreporting.

Hence, while heroic approaches tend to assume that it is primarily leaders who use impression management, followers may also disguise dissent. Critical perspectives suggest that such dramaturgical practices can take primarily conformist (for example, telling leaders what they want to hear) or more oppositional (for example, knowledge and output restriction) forms. They may also embody elements of both conformity and resistance. Accordingly, workplace power asymmetries can generate subtle forms of disguised dissent. Rather than being polarized dichotomies, dissent and consent may be inextricably linked within the same practices.

Kondo (1990, p. 224) criticizes the tendency to artificially separate conformity or resistance into "crisply distinct categories." She contends that there is no such thing as an entirely "authentic" or "pristine space of resistance," or of a "true resister." Her arguments have important implications for CLS. Observing that people "consent, cope, and resist at different levels of consciousness at a single point in time," Kondo (1990, p. 224) questions the meaning of the term "resistance," and warns about the dangers of romanticizing followers' oppositional practices – that is, of imputing a subversive or emancipatory motive or outcome to resistance.

Indeed, a number of other studies also suggest that resistance and dissent can have unintended and contradictory outcomes. Willis (1977) describes how working-class "lads" creatively constructed a counter-culture that celebrated masculinity and the so-called freedom and independence of manual work. Yet this counter-culture facilitated the lads' smooth transition into precisely the kind of shop-floor work that then subordinated them, possibly for the rest of their working lives. Similarly, Ashcraft (2005) shows how resistance can symbolically invert dominant values and meanings, but in ways that sometimes cut across emancipatory agendas, reinforcing the status quo. She reveals how airline captains engaged in subversive practices, but, in this case, their intentions were to undermine a change programme, and to preserve their power and identity. Viewing the corporate enactment of a "crew empowerment system" as a threat to their masculine authority and identity, pilots resisted their loss of control, whilst giving the appearance of supporting the change programme.

In sum, critical studies of followership point to the importance of conformity and resistance in leadership processes. They also address the paradoxical processes and outcomes that can ensue from resistance: Apparently oppositional practices can actually reinforce the conditions of control that stimulated dissent in the first place. This discussion of power/resistance dialectics does not seek to imply that followers will invariably engage in resistance (in a mechanical way), or that dissent is necessarily effective; control may produce compliance and even conformity, while resistance can also have unintended and contradictory consequences. These arguments in turn raise important questions about the meaning of resistance – about who resists, how, why, and when they do so, what strategies inform their practices, and what outcomes ensue.

Conclusion

This chapter has explored the emergent field of critical leadership studies (CLS), which emphasizes the conceptual importance of power asymmetries and dialectical perspectives. Critical approaches recognize that leaders exercise considerable control, enjoy considerable privilege, and that their power and status can have contradictory and ambiguous outcomes, which leaders either do not always understand or of which they are unaware. From a critical perspective, leader–follower relations always contain the potential for conflict and dissent. Leaders cannot simply assume followers' obedience or loyalty. Although control can stimulate resistance, it may also discipline, shape, and restrict the very opposition it provokes. Critical leadership studies therefore view control and resistance as mutually reinforcing, ambiguous, and potentially contradictory processes.

Given the asymmetrical nature of workplace power, it is hardly surprising that followers may conform (or at least give the outward appearance of compliance), but, from a leadership point of view, we need to know more about the conditions and consequences of such practices. For example, leaders can surround themselves with sycophants, thereby stifling dialogue, new ideas, and innovation (Bratton et al., 2004). Hence, from a practitioner perspective, it is important that leaders develop a critical way of thinking that can question excessively positive upward communication. Critical perspectives also emphasize that, far from being passive "followers" whose identities are shaped by charismatic leaders, employees can express opposition in multiple ways. They may utilize knowledge and information in ways that simultaneously enact, but also conceal, their resistance. Disguised dissent incorporates self-protective practices that sometimes blur the boundaries between resistance and consent.

The implications for leadership studies of these emergent critical perspectives are potentially far-reaching – particularly when we consider the multiple and intersecting nature of power/identity dialectics. Critical feminist studies demonstrate that differences and inequalities can take multiple forms (for example, gender, ethnicity, class, age, disability, faith, sexual orientation, national origin, etc.). When questioning one dichotomy, researchers can still reproduce others. For example, in addressing leader/follower dialectics, it is possible to ignore how these dynamics are also shaped by gender, ethnicity, and race, with the consequence that other inequalities are reinforced. Equally, focusing exclusively on the need for more women to occupy leadership positions can neglect race, ethnicity, and/or class. Whereas white, middle-class women are beginning to occupy leadership and management positions, women of colour typically predominate in lower-paid jobs (Holvino, 2010). Finding ways of theorizing the intersecting and cross-cutting nature of these multiple dialectics remains a pressing challenge for CLS. These arguments also highlight the need to develop new forms of more inclusive and integrated leadership practices that value multiplicity, diversity, and difference.

While the notions of "leader" and "follower" are deeply embedded identities, especially in Western societies, there is a growing recognition that such traditional identities no longer adequately characterize leadership power relations, which are increasingly seen as blurred, fluid, and contradictory. For example, distributed leadership encourages followers to act as "informal leaders." In many contemporary organizations, leaders are subject to intensified pressures of accountability that render them "calculable followers." In such contexts, individuals are expected to act as both leaders and followers, either simultaneously or at different times and under different circumstances. Accordingly, critical research could examine further the implications of these multiple, shifting, and often paradoxical identities of "leaders" and "followers" in particular contexts.

In sum, this chapter has suggested that critical approaches have the potential to develop new insights into the asymmetrical and dialectical nature of leadership dynamics. Critical perspectives also raise a number of underexplored issues about what it means to be a "leader" and a "follower" in contemporary organizations and societies. In the current context, in which many high-profile cases of destructive, corrupt, and/or ineffective leadership have recently emerged in various organizations, sectors, and societies, it would seem particularly appropriate that CLS should contribute to debates about the future direction of leadership research and practice.

References

Ashcraft, K.L. (2005). Resistance through consent? *Management Communication Quarterly*, 19(1), 67–90.
Ashcraft, K.L., & Mumby, D.K. (2004). *Reworking gender: A feminist communicology of organization*. London: Sage.
Banks, S. (2008). *Dissent and the failure of leadership*. Cheltenham: Edward Elgar.
Barge, K.M., Lee, B.M., Maddux, K., Nabring, R., & Townsend, B. (2008). Managing dualities in planned change initiatives. *Journal of Applied Communication Research*, 36(4), 364–390.

Baxter, L.A., & Montgomery, B.M. (1996). *Relating: Dialogues and dialectics*. New York: Guilford Press.
Bowring, M.A. (2004). Resistance is not futile: Liberating Captain Janeway from the masculine–feminine dualism of leadership. *Gender, Work and Organization*, 11(4), 381–405.
Bratton, J., Grint, K., & Nelson, D. (2004). *Organizational leadership*. Mason, OH: South Western/Thomson.
Cameron, K.S., Quinn, R.E., Degraff, J., & Thakor, A.V. (2014). *Competing values framework* (2nd ed.). Cheltenham: Edward Elgar.
Chaleff, I. (2009). *The courageous follower* (3rd ed.). San Francisco, CA: Berrett-Koehler.
Chaleff, I. (2015). *Intelligent disobedience*. San Francisco, CA: Berrett-Koehler.
Cockburn, C. (1983). *Brothers*. London: Pluto.
Collins, J. (2001). *Good to great*. London: Random House.
Collinson, D.L. (1992). *Managing the shopfloor: Subjectivity, masculinity and workplace culture*. Berlin: Walter de Gruyter.
Collinson, D.L. (1999). Surviving the rigs: Safety and surveillance on North Sea oil installations. *Organization Studies*, 20(4), 579–600.
Collinson, D.L. (2011). Critical leadership studies. In A. Bryman, D.L. Collinson, K. Grint, B. Jackson, & M. Uhl Bien (Eds.), *The Sage handbook of leadership* (pp. 179–192). London: Sage.
Collinson, D.L. (2012). Prozac leadership and the limits of positive thinking. *Leadership*, 8(2), 87–107.
Collinson, M. (2018). So what is new about leadership-as-practice? *Leadership*, 14(3), 384–390.
Connell, R. (2005). *Masculinities*. Cambridge: Polity Press.
Courpasson, D., & Vallas, S. (Eds.). (2016). *The Sage handbook of resistance*. London: Sage.
Fairhurst, G. (2001). Dualisms in leadership research. In F.M. Jablin & L.L. Putnam (Eds.), *The new handbook of organizational communication* (pp. 379–439). Thousand Oaks, CA: Sage.
Finkelstein, S. (2003). Seven habits of spectacularly unsuccessful people. *Business Strategy Review*, 14(4), 39–50.
Fitzduff, M. (2017). *Why irrational politics appeals*. Santa Barbara, CA: Praeger.
Fleming, P. (2005). Metaphors of resistance. *Management Communication Quarterly*, 19(1), 45–66.
Foucault, M. (1977). *Discipline and punish*. London: Allen & Unwin.
Foucault, M. (1979). *The history of sexuality*. London: Allen & Unwin.
Fromm, E. (1977). *The fear of freedom*. London: Routledge Kegan Paul.
Gabriel, Y. (1997). Meeting God: When organizational members come face to face with the supreme leader. *Human Relations*, 50(4), 315–342.
Gagnon, S., & Collinson, D. (2017). Resistance through difference: The co-constitution of dissent and inclusion. *Organization Studies*, 38(9), 1253–1276.
Giddens, A. (1979). *Central problems in social theory*. London: Macmillan.
Giddens, A. (1984). *The constitution of society*. Cambridge: Polity Press.
Giddens, A. (1993). *New rules of sociological method* (2nd ed.). Cambridge: Polity Press.
Goffee, R., & Jones, G. (2001). Followership: It's personal too. *Harvard Business Review*, 79(11), 148.
Goffman, E. (1959). *The presentation of self in everyday life*. Harmondsworth: Penguin.
Grint, K. (Ed.). (1997). *Leadership: Classical, contemporary, and critical approaches*. Oxford: Oxford University Press.

Grint, K. (2005). *Leadership: Limits and possibilities*. New York: Palgrave Macmillan.
Gronn, P. (2011). Hybrid configurations of leadership. In A. Bryman, D.L. Collinson, K. Grint, B. Jackson, & M. Uhl-Bien (Eds.), *The Sage handbook of leadership* (pp. 437–454). London: Sage.
Hansen, H., & Bathurst, R. (2011). Aesthetics and leadership. In A. Bryman, D.L. Collinson, K. Grint, B. Jackson, & M. Uhl-Bien (Eds.), *The Sage handbook of leadership* (pp. 255–266). London: Sage.
Harter, N. (2006). *Clearings in the forest: On the study of leadership*. West Lafayette, IN: Purdue University Press.
Hearn, J. (2012). Male bodies, masculine bodies, men's bodies. In B.S. Turner (Ed.), *Routledge handbook of body studies* (pp. 307–320). London: Routledge.
Hearn, J., & Collinson, D.L. (2018). Men, masculinities and gendered organizations. In R. Aldag & S. NKomo (Eds.), *Oxford research encyclopedia of business and management* (pp. 1–35). Oxford: Oxford University Press.
Hollander, E. (2009). *Inclusive leadership*. London: Routledge.
Holvino, E. (2010). Intersections: The simultaneity of race, gender and class in organization studies. *Gender, Work and Organization, 17*(3), 248–277.
Kaplan, R., & Kaiser, R. (2006). *The versatile leader*. San Francisco, CA: John Wiley & Sons.
Kellerman, B. (2008). *Followership*. Cambridge, MA: Harvard Business School Press.
Kelley, R.E. (2004). Followership. In G.R. Goethals, G. Sorenson, & J.M. Burns (Eds.), *Berkshire encyclopedia of world history* (pp. 504–513). London: Sage.
Kondo, D.K. (1990). *Crafting selves: Power, gender and discourses of identity in a Japanese workplace*. Chicago, IL: University of Chicago Press.
Latour, B. (1993). *We have never been modern*. Cambridge, MA: Harvard University Press.
Lease, D.R. (2006, April). *Management reviled: Is leadership just good management repackaged?* Paper presented at the Academy of Business Education Conference, <AQ Place?>.
Linstead, S., Fulop, L., & Lilley, S. (Eds.). (2009). *Management and organization*. Basingstoke: Palgrave Macmillan.
Lipman-Blumen, J. (2005). *The allure of toxic leadership*. Oxford: Oxford University Press.
Liu, H. (2017). The masculinisation of ethical leadership dis/embodiment. *Journal of Business Ethics, 144*(2), 263–278.
Maccoby, M. (2007). *The leaders we need*. Boston, MA: Harvard Business School Press.
Martin, I. (2013). *Making it happen: Fred Goodwin, RBS and the men who blew up the British economy*. London: Simon & Schuster.
McGregor Burns, J. (1978). *Leadership*. New York: Harper Row.
McGregor Burns, J. (2007). Foreword. In R. Couto (Ed.), *Reflections on leadership* (pp. v–viii). Lanham, MD: University Press of America.
McGregor Burns, J. (2008). Foreword. In R.E. Riggio, I. Chaleff, & J. Lipman-Blumen (Eds.), *The art of followership* (pp. xi–xii). San Francisco, CA: Jossey-Bass.
Meindl, J. (1995). The romance of leadership as a follower-centric theory: A social constructionist approach. *The Leadership Quarterly, 6*(3), 329–341.
Meindl, J., Ehrlich, S., & Dukerich, J. (1985). The romance of leadership. *Administrative Science Quarterly, 30*(1), 78–102.
Melina, L., Burgess, G.J., Falkman, L.L., & Marturano, A. (2013). *The embodiment of leadership*. San Francisco, CA: Jossey-Bass.
Miceli, M.P., & Near, J.P. (2002). What makes whistle-blowers effective? Three field studies. *Human Relations, 55*(4), 455–479.

Milgram, S. (1963). Behavioral study of obedience. *Journal of Abnormal and Social Psychology, 69*(2), 137–143.

Mumby, D. (Ed.). (2011). *Reframing difference in organizational communication studies.* London: Sage.

Mumby, D., Thomas, R., Marti, I., & Seidl, D. (2017). Resistance redux. *Organization Studies, 38*(9), 1157–1183.

Owen, D. (2009). *In sickness and in power.* London: Methuen.

Post, J., & Robbins, R. (1993). *When illness strikes the leader.* New Haven, CT: Yale University Press.

Putnam, L., Fairhurst, G., & Banghart, S. (2016). Contradictions, dialectics, and paradoxes in organizations: A constitutive approach. *Academy of Management Annals, 10*(1), 65–171.

Raelin, J. (Ed.). (2016). *Leadership-as-practice: Theory and application.* London: Routledge.

Raelin, J., Kempster, S., Youngs, H., Carroll, B., & Jackson, B. (2018). Practicing leadership-as-practice in content and manner. *Leadership, 14*(3), 371–383.

Riggio, R.E., Chaleff, I., & Lipman-Blumen, J. (Eds.). (2008). *The art of followership.* San Francisco, CA: Jossey-Bass.

Ropo, A., & Sauer, E. (2008). Corporeal leaders. In D. Barry & H. Hansen (Eds.), *New approaches in management and organization* (pp. 469–478). London: Sage.

Rost, J. (1993). *Leadership for the twenty-first century.* Westport, CT: Praeger.

Sadler-Smith, E., Akstinaite, V., Robinson, G., & Wray, T. (2017). Hubristic leadership: A review. *Leadership, 13*(5), 525–548.

Scott, J. (1985). *Weapons of the weak: Everyday forms of peasant resistance.* New Haven, CT: Yale University Press.

Shamir, B. (1999). Taming charisma for better understanding and greater usefulness: A response to Beyer. *The Leadership Quarterly, 10*(4), 555–562.

Shamir, B., Pillai, R., Bligh, M., & Uhl-Bien, M. (2007). *Follower-centered perspectives on leadership.* Greenwich, CT: Information Age.

Simmel, G. (1994). Bridge and door. *Theory, Culture and Society, 11*(1), 5–10.

Sinclair, A. (2005). Body possibilities in leadership. *Leadership, 1*(4), 388–406.

Sinclair, A. (2007). *Leadership for the disillusioned.* London: Allen & Unwin.

Sinclair, A. (2013). A material dean. *Leadership, 9*(3), 436–443.

Smircich, L., & Morgan, G. (1982). Leadership: The management of meaning. *Journal of Applied Behavioural Science, 18*(3), 257–273.

Storey, J., & Salaman, G. (2009). *Managerial dilemmas.* Chichester: John Wiley & Sons.

Tourish, D. (2013). *The dark side of transformational leadership: A critical perspective.* London: Routledge.

Tracy, S.J. (2004). Dialectic, contradiction, or double bind? Analyzing and theorizing employee reactions to organizational tension. *Journal of Communication Research, 32*(2), 119–146.

Willis, P. (1977). *Learning to labour.* Aldershot: Saxon House.

Zaleznik, A. (1975). Managers and leaders: Are they different? *Harvard Business Review, 55*(3), 67–78.

15

LEADERSHIP FOR WHAT?

Eric Guthey, Steve Kempster, and Robyn Remke

Would it really matter in the broader scheme of things if leadership studies didn't exist? In its current state, we are not so certain that it would. When you pause to think about it, leadership research and development have not really made any sort of substantial contribution to society, nor have they provided much in the way of meaningful support for collective efforts to address major societal and global challenges. With a few laudable exceptions, leadership studies have had next to nothing to say about such complex problems as food waste, famine, or obesity, discrimination and sexual harassment in the workplace, the global refugee crisis, the rise of racist and anti-immigrant sentiments, the resurgence of nationalist and populist movements or political demagoguery, or the very real threats posed by human-made climate change. This is a major failing, we argue here, because leadership research and leadership development practice have the potential to address such pressing social and environmental challenges, to help to repair fractured communities, and to contribute to the betterment of society on a global scale. Furthermore, we argue, engagement in multistakeholder efforts to address these sorts of complex challenges could, in turn, help to rejuvenate leadership research and development in more conventional contexts, generating new connections, ideas, and practices, and spinning off vital new approaches to leadership that could also benefit commercial organizations and the persons who work for them.

Nearly two decades ago, Starkey and Madan (2001) sparked a debate that has continued to engage scholars of management and organization up to the present day: They argued that the predominance of an overly academic and theoretical mode of knowledge production ("Mode 1") had given rise to a relevance gap between business school research and the managerial organizations that such research should serve. They suggested that management research should adopt a more practice-based, problem-driven mode of knowledge production ("Mode 2"), which would more directly address the challenges confronting managerial organizations. Joining the debate, Huff and Huff (2001) responded that even a combination of Modes 1 and 2 was not sufficient to fix the problems facing business schools, because both modes of knowledge production were primarily directed at the wrong problems. They proposed a new mode of knowledge production ("Mode 3"), which would address problems of concern to humanity at large and, in so doing, would revitalize business schools as well.

This debate – especially Huff and Huff's (2001) notion of Mode 3 knowledge production – remain particularly important with respect to leadership research, because scholars have responded to a perceived relevance gap within this area in ways that threaten to render their work increasingly irrelevant and obsolete. The problem, we argue here, is that much of leadership studies has also been pursuing the wrong kind of relevance: primarily, relevance to bureaucratic organizations and to the managers who run them, rather than relevance to the complex societal problems that matter. We propose that the solution to this problem will require that leadership scholars engage and collaborate with a wider variety of public and private stakeholders to redirect the power of leadership research and leadership development to address complex social, and even global, challenges – rather than merely to generate new theory or to attempt to fix organizational performance gaps.

In this chapter, we return to the debate that Starkey and Madan (2001) started, aiming to map out a new approach to the production of leadership knowledge and, ultimately, to the production and reproduction of leadership itself. We explain how this new approach combines and extends elements of action research, service learning, collaboratory design science, research on the links between leadership and purpose, and complexity leadership theory. We illustrate the connections between these various ideas and practices by means of an extended description of the design of a proposed collaboratory engagement with public-sector managers in the Gaunteng City Region, an area that spans Johannesburg, Soweto, and Pretoria, and which constitutes the most heavily populated province in South Africa. We build on this proposal, and on other examples of collaboratory engagements in public and cross-sector contexts, to discuss how we might leverage leadership research and development as a collective endeavour, rather than an individual journey of self-discovery, so that it can address pressing social challenges both within and across commercial organizations, and produce new leadership knowledge in the process. The interconnected and admittedly ambitious goals behind asking the question "Leadership for what?" are therefore threefold: to contribute to efforts toward meaningful social change, and thereby to transform the way in which we study and practise leadership, and to benefit public and private organizations along the way.

Modes of Knowledge Production and Debates about Relevance

In their article "Bridging the relevance gap: Aligning stakeholders in the future of management research", Starkey and Madan (2001) delivered a bracing critique of the overly academic and theoretical way in which most business schools, in their view, conduct research. To make this point, they drew heavily on Gibbons and colleagues' (1994) discussion of new modes of knowledge production as forces for change, and they drew in particular on the sharp distinction that those authors drew between what they called Mode 1 and Mode 2 knowledge production. Mode 1 knowledge production "is what we traditionally conceive of as the scientific approach to knowledge creation and is what universities have historically concerned with" (Starkey & Madan, 2001, p. S5). Starkey and Madan argued that an obsession with academic disciplinary boundaries, and with the primacy of theory over practice, was threatening to render management studies irrelevant, unsustainable, and increasingly obsolete. As a result, they observed, there was "a growing concern among management academics that Mode 1 knowledge is losing touch with higher education's stakeholders" (Starkey & Madan, 2001, p. S5).

Starkey and Madan proposed to bridge this relevance gap by embracing what Gibbons and colleagues had termed Mode 2 knowledge production: a transdisciplinary, context-specific approach to "knowledge as it works in practice in the context of application" (Starkey & Madan, 2001, p. S5). Mode 2 knowledge production is a problem- and opportunity-driven approach, rather than a theory-driven approach like Mode 1 (MacLean, MacIntosh, & Grant, 2002). It values utility and efficacy over scientific validity (Van de Ven, 2007). And, to the extent that Mode 2 knowledge production develops theories, they are not abstract, but rather descriptive of how things are done and normative concerning what should be done (Burgoyne & Turnbull James, 2006, p. 312).

Starkey and Madan did not go quite so far as to maintain that management scholars should simply abandon Mode 1 pursuits in favour of Mode 2. At several points during their argument, they appeared to endorse Tranfield and Starkey's (1998) call for business school research that could straddle the "double hurdle of academic rigour and managerial relevance, embedded in both the social science canons of best practice and the worlds of policy and practice" (quoted in Starkey & Madan, 2001, p. S8). At the end of the day, however, Starkey and Madan were arguing that business schools remained far too stodgy and academic, and that they needed, for the most part, to jettison Mode 1 in favour of Mode 2 so as to climb down from the ivory tower and get about the business of producing knowledge that was relevant for helping practising managers to do their jobs. "Arguably, the Mode 1 approach to research and knowledge production is no longer sustainable," they stated clearly: "Universities are the last bastions of [Mode 1] in a world where greater accountability and the speed of change in relevant knowledge encourage [a Mode 2] approach" (Starkey & Madan, 2001, p. S5).

Starkey and Madan's article has been hotly debated ever since. A number of scholars have followed their lead and tried earnestly to bridge the gap they highlighted. For example, Aram and Salipante (2003) sought to reinterpret Modes 1 and 2 within a broader epistemological frame and to bridge the relevance gap by focusing on the common interest that both sides of the divide share with regard to problems drawn from practice. They argued that a common focus on problems, and on the questions that such problems generate, could help to set in motion a continuous, iterative cycle of switching between contextualized knowing and general/abstract knowing that would amount to what they called "bridging scholarship." "Since problems are the stimuli for learning, bridging scholarship identifies the problematic experience of individuals who are puzzling out the challenges that environmental change presents to them," they maintained (Aram & Salipante, 2003, p. 201).

Other scholars have remained considerably more sceptical about Starkey and Madan's call to render business school research more relevant to managers, to the point of characterizing the implications of such efforts problematic, if not also ideologically suspect (Knights, 2008). Working from this critical perspective, Butler, Delaney, and Spoelstra (2015) interviewed leadership scholars about their experiences of engaging with practitioners to question the whole notion of relevance. They found that these sorts of experiences often forced scholars to choose between managerial relevance, on the one hand, and their professional/academic ideals, on the other. "Put bluntly, the idea that scholars must produce work that has a direct and practical application within organizations already serves to shape the nature and purpose of academic research around corporate imperatives at the outset," they argued (Butler et al., 2015, p. 741). For this reason, they proposed that rejecting the call for relevance should be considered a viable and legitimate option. "Our hope is to challenge the idea that 'relevance' is an unconditional good in itself," they concluded: " . . . [W]e also aim to provide legitimacy for scholars who wish to refrain from practitioner engagement altogether" (Butler et al., 2015, p. 742).

In defending scholars who would resist the pressure for relevance, Butler and colleagues were rejecting a decidedly narrow definition of the terms "relevance," "problems," and "practice," and advocating for a more pluralistic understanding of what these terms might mean. But their own argument very narrowly conceived of practitioners exclusively as corporate managers and did not include other types of manager, practitioner, or activist engaged in addressing major societal challenges inside government organizations, non-government organizations (NGOs), or social movements. For this reason, they also glossed over the countercurrent of pluralist approaches to the notion of relevance that had already characterized the debate that Starkey and Madan started from its very beginning.

Writing in the same 2001 journal issue as Starkey and Madan, Huff and Huff (2001) delivered their own bracing critique of business school research – albeit one based on a very different conception of what constitutes relevance. In contradistinction to Starkey and Madan, they argued that even a combination of Mode 1 and Mode 2 knowledge production would not render management research relevant to problems and constituencies that really matter. Finalizing their response just after the terrorist attacks of September 11, 2001, and building like Starkey and Madan on James March's earlier call to "deepen an intellectual understanding of the relation between activities in business and the major issues of human existence" (Schmotter, 1998, quoted in Starkey & Madan, 2001, p. S24), they proposed instead a third mode of knowledge production that would leverage the strengths of Modes 1 and 2 to tackle social challenges of concern to humanity at large. "The purpose of Mode 3 knowledge production," they proposed, would be "to assure survival and to promote the common good, at various levels of social aggregation" (Huff & Huff, 2001, p. S51).

Huff and Huff were expanding the definition of the terms "relevance," "practice," and "problems" to address complex societal challenges above and beyond the operational problems faced by managers in commercial organizations. They were also significantly expanding the ranks of the stakeholders with a vested interest in management education to include not only corporate managers and policymakers, but also NGOs, charitable causes, the committed people working in these contexts, and many others involved in social movements for significant and constructive change. According to Huff and Huff, these many different stakeholders would have to find new ways of interacting and collaborating with each other to tackle the challenges in question. "Inputs from diverse stakeholders will be required, contributors from NGOs, the media and electronic sources of information seem particularly important," they pointed out: "The process will not be easy, because the differences in values and interpretation are remarkably broad. As we frame it, more participatory practices than followed in many organizations also will be required" (Huff & Huff, 2001, p. S53).

Huff and Huff's argument in favour of Mode 3 knowledge production raised important questions about the broader purpose of business schools in relation to both business and society at large. Over the past several years, leadership scholars have struck up a parallel conversation about the nature and function of leadership, and its connection to purpose. This connects back to our original point: If leadership research and development can't, or won't, address societal and global challenges, then what is it really for, and why do we need it? A brief review of the state of this conversation about leadership and purpose will help to tie Huff and Huff's notion of Mode 3 knowledge production back to our main point about the need for a new way of going about conducting leadership research and development.

Leadership for What? From Unity of Purpose to Multiple Purposes

In their article "Leadership as purpose: Exploring the role of purpose in leadership practice," Kempster, Jackson, and Conroy (2011) distinguish sharply between notions of vision, mission, shared goals, objectives and plans, on the one hand, and the notion of purpose, on the other. The former have come to refer primarily to corporate imperatives and strategies, they argue, while they use the latter notion to refer to major social challenges and societal goals. "When conceptualized as a process of sensemaking," they argue, "leadership can provide an opportunity for notions of societal purpose to come to the fore in countervailing balance with corporate purposes" (Kempster et al., 2011, p. 323). With this in mind, they argue for the realignment of the concept of leadership around the notion of purpose.

Kempster and colleagues point out that many popular and standard academic texts do not mention any notion of purpose in the process of defining leadership – that is, they don't really stop to ask what leadership is ultimately for (Daft, 2015; Gill, 2006; Kouzes & Posner, 2017; Yukl, 2005). One standard text that does touch on such issues, they allow, is Drath (1998, p. 406), who maintains that leadership should be understood not only as a person, but also as a sense of purpose and as a force that gives people a common direction. Drath anchors this argument about purpose and meaning in the literature on transformational leadership, which emphasizes the role of idealized influence and the interpersonal skills of the leader in motivating followers. But he also predicts that future discussions of leadership would place an increasing emphasis upon systemic relationships and mutual meaning-making (Drath & Palus, 1993).

Kempster and colleagues (2011) explore the philosophical underpinnings of this point about the need for a broader sense of purpose and common direction by drawing on the ideas of Aristotle by way of Scottish philosopher Alistair MacIntyre – specifically, his gloss on Aristotle's concept of *telos*. *Telos* has been defined as "a vision anticipating the moral unity of life, given in the form of a narrative history that has meaning within a particular community's traditions" (McCann & Brownsberger, 1990, p. 221). As Kempster and colleagues (2011, p. 322) elaborate: "The *telos* is a meta-goal . . . MacIntyre suggests that a meaningless life is one that lacks movement towards a *telos*." Kempster and colleagues argue further that processes of socialization within commercial organizations lead to the minimization of room for *telos*, or for any kind of broad societal purpose in leadership discourse, and they follow MacIntyre's lead in suggesting that such minimization results inevitably from managers' fiduciary duty to maximize value to only one stakeholder, rather than to a multiplicity of stakeholders.

Parry and Jackson (2016) have elaborated on Kempster and colleagues' (2011) point that leadership should function to champion societal purpose as a countervailing force to corporate purpose. They begin with a full-throated critique of the culture of shareholder value and the complicity of business school education in promoting such an ideal. Ultimately, Parry and Jackson (2016) argue, we should be teaching that the purpose of leadership is to integrate corporate and societal purpose in a manner that gives priority to the latter. "Perhaps a responsible leadership message coming from business schools will integrate the goals of societal purpose and corporate purpose," they conclude: "Perhaps accountability will be matched with responsibility" (Parry & Jackson, 2016, p. 161).

Writing in the same volume, Guthey (2016, pp. 212–213) has praised the intent of this point about leadership and purpose, but has critiqued the assumptions undergirding the whole conversation about this topic. At issue, he argues, is the use of the term "purpose" to refer to an overarching societal meta-goal or unitary *telos*. Working from a relational perspective, he points out that "a radically relational perspective on responsible leadership would emphasize not just one purpose, but many purposes." He goes on to argue that:

> . . . the bulwark of a healthy society is a multiplicity of different purposes, competing visions of responsibility, different political perspectives, diverse ethnic, racial, cultural, regional, and gendered identities and interests, along with a vital and functioning political system that allows for debate, negotiation, and compromise among these different groups and interests.

From this pluralist perspective, he observes, "the notion of corporate or societal purpose is not quite adequate to address the multiple purposes attached to either business, or society, or the combination of the two." And he concludes that "a radically relational approach to responsible leadership would begin from a recognition of the social, political, and often contentious give-and-take between different purposes and interests at play in a pluralistic democratic society."

Recent advances in relational and complexity leadership theory provide support for this argument and for the idea that even the members of a single organization often strive for a multiplicity of different purposes to productive effect. From the perspective of complexity leadership theory, for example, the impulse to seek out a single or overarching societal or corporate purpose that can unite a variety of different stakeholders appears very similar to what Uhl-Bien and Arena (2017) describe as an "order" response to complexity. As Uhl-Bien and Arena (2017, p. 10) explain:

> [S]napping back to previously successful, ordered solutions provides a sense of control that satisfies not only the needs of managers who have been trained in traditional leadership models, but also organizational members who look to leaders to take care of them and make things "right" again.

As they explain further, "the problem with this is that order is the enemy of adaptability, and ordered responses can stifle out the interactive dynamics needed by organizations to respond effectively to complexity."

In a similar vein, Ospina and Foldy (2010) have characterized leadership in social change organizations as a form of "bridging" that facilitates coordination across organizations without erasing substantial differences in interests, values, and missions among such organizations under the umbrella of some assumed common purpose. In their discussion of intergroup leadership, Pittinsky and Simon (2007) have detailed how such appeals to unity of purpose can be highly counter-productive to collaboration in interorganizational contexts.

The "Collaboratory" as Multi-stakeholder Leadership Development

The preceding discussion gives rise to an important question: How can we transform leadership research and development so that it can mobilize multiple, diverse stakeholders and perspectives to confront major social challenges, in the manner of Mode 3 knowledge production, drawing on their collective strengths, while not smoothing over the real differences between them – even differences of purpose – precisely because those differences provide diversity of perspective and new, unexpected ideas and connections? This is where we invoke the "collaboratory" process (Wulf, 1993). The word "collaboratory" describes a joint process of collaboration and laboratory research fused together as an ongoing dynamic of experimenting through application to develop innovations in practice (Muff, 2014, p. 12). Wulf (1993) first conceived of the practice as a space without walls in which scientists could come together around themes and projects to undertake research collaboratively. Still working within the physical sciences, Bly (1998) extended the concept to describe a partnership between researchers and the community served by the research – that is, it is envisaged as a continual flow between Mode 1 and Mode 2 knowledge contributions. Cogburn (2003, p. 86) emphasized that collaboratories consist not only of technical research practices, but also of social processes, including "collaboration techniques; formal and informal communication; and agreement on norms, principles, values, and rules." Collaboratories are not one-offs; if they were, then this would be no more than a fancy-sounding title for a workshop. Collaboratories offer a longitudinal action research approach that tests emerging ideas in a multitude of settings and repeatedly interrogates what has been discovered in subsequent collaboratory gatherings (Kempster, Guthey, & Uhl-Bien, 2017).

Perhaps the most prominent example of a collaboratory is that established at Cern, the largest particle physics laboratory in the world. In this context, Mabey and Nicholds (2015) have explored the social processes of knowledge production associated with the research being undertaken through the ATLAS collaboration within the CERN Large Hadron Collider. Their examination of this particular collaboratory suggested a horizontal approach to knowledge management. The empirical evidence pointed to a relational, rather than a positional, form of leadership (Marion & Uhl-Bien, 2001; Uhl-Bien, Marion, & McKelvey, 2007). Mabey and Nicholds (2015, p. 44) offered the term "knowledge leadership" to describe the most salient relational process in this context, which provides a compelling way of understanding the leadership dynamic anticipated in a collaboratory "as being co-determined by a range of actors and as a shared activity appropriate for tasks that are highly interdependent, complex and requiring high levels of creativity."

The experimental and ongoing nature of a collaboratory reflects many of the core principles that inform the reconceptualization of management as a design science. Design science is a transdisciplinary problem-led approach that can help to "create systems of management and economy that are a better fit for purpose than we have currently" (Hodgkinson & Starkey, 2011, p. 609). Drawing from such fields as medicine, architecture, engineering, or psychotherapy (Van Aken, 2004, p. 224), design science can address the relevance gap by connecting knowledge production from Modes 1, 2, and 3. As Hodgkinson and Starkey (2011) suggest, design science focuses on "what works" from a pragmatic perspective, rather than simply what is true from a positivist one. It also enables interaction between those generating knowledge and those seeking to apply the knowledge (Kelemen & Bansal, 2002). Romme's (2003, p. 562) description helps to explain why design science is uniquely positioned for addressing complex social and global challenges:

> The idea of design involves inquiry into systems that do not yet exist. Will it work rather than is it valid or true? Rooted in pragmatism as underpinning epistemology, design science seeks to produce knowledge that is both actionable and open to on-going validation. Importantly it has a latent aspirational orientation to action where approaches to design involves human beings using knowledge to create what should be.

Design science reflects many principles of action learning — which often inform best practices in leadership development (Burgoyne & Turnbull James, 2001). The major difference is the manner in which design science blends an anticipatory vision of what might, or should, be with a set of principles and prescriptions for guiding the research journey. Because design science seeks to develop an evidence base to help to refine the principles for guidance in subsequent settings, it enables academics to participate within the process to retrieve Mode 1 outputs. Yet design science similarly allows academics and practitioners from a range of backgrounds to collaborate in an interdisciplinary manner to produce Mode 2 knowledge that is connected with Mode 3. At the same time, those engaging in design science within the context of a collaboratory travel together through a process of leadership development. Thus the process simultaneously produces Mode 3 outputs relevant for stakeholder communities and policymakers, and Mode 2 outputs for participating managers and their organizations. Figure 15.1 illustrates how we see these various modes of knowledge production interacting with each other in a virtuous circle to address important societal challenges in the collaboratory context.

Branching out from their use in the natural sciences, collaboratories have entered the lexicon of management education. In this context, they exhibit prominent dimensions of responsible leadership (Kempster & Carroll, 2016; Miska & Mendenhall, 2018) – namely, multiple levels of responsibility, spanning the individual, the team, the organization, suppliers, customers, communities, and broadly society and the environment (Doh & Quigley, 2014; Voegtlin, Patzer, & Scherer, 2012), addressed through alignment of personal, organizational, and societal purposes (Kempster et al., 2011); balancing shareholder value with stakeholder value (Maak & Pless, 2006; Waldman & Galvin, 2008); ethical assumptions of doing no harm and a duty of care to such stakeholders by addressing Elkington's (2004) triple bottom line, which embraces a broader humanitarian perspective and a sense of worldly appreciation (see also Maak & Pless, 2009; Stahl & Sully de Luque, 2014; Turnbull, 2012); and an approach that suggests a shared orientation (Pearce, Wassenaar, & Manz, 2014), and is relational and collaborative (Pless, Maak, & Waldman, 2012).

For these reasons, we suggest that collaboratories can function as a crucible for engaged leadership research, as well as a model for a new kind of multi-stakeholder leadership development. On the level of content, the collaboratory process provides a deeply informing educational process for managers with respect to many issues beyond the normal vista of everyday management concerns.

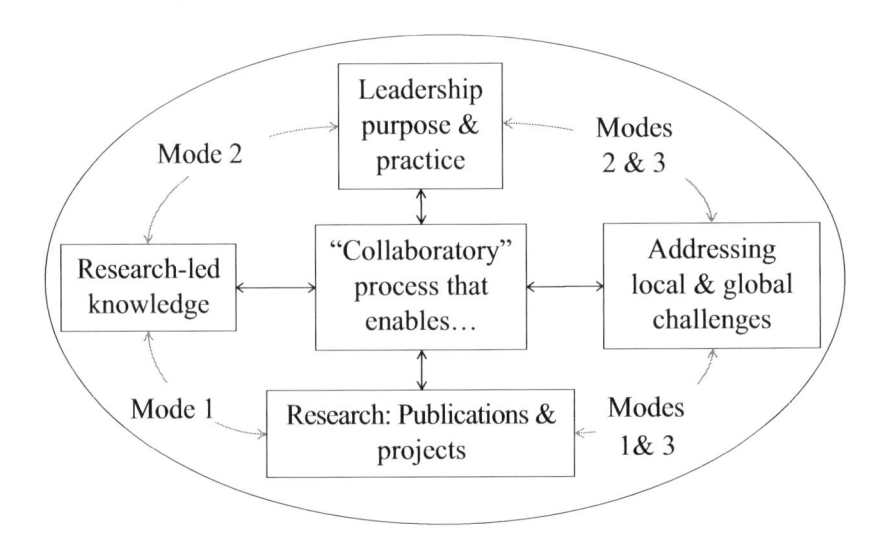

FIGURE 15.1 Collaboratory leadership development.

The collaboratory immerses participants into the thick of complex challenges and sparks an emerging sense of ownership of the problem(s), together with a growing commitment to address these – reflecting Gosling and Mintzberg's (2003) argument for developing the global and worldly mindset. On the level of process, the collaboratory provides an effective mechanism for the transfer of learning back to the organization (Belling, James, & Ladkin, 2004; Burgoyne & Turnbull James, 2001).

Our description of the collaboratory process bears several points of resemblance to the social change model of leadership development designed for use in student leadership development contexts (Dugan, 2011; Komives & Wagner, 2017), but the differences are instructive and serve to highlight three key characteristics of collaboratories as we have described them. First of all, implementations of the social change model "almost uniformly take the developmental perspective and focus on individual outcome achievement" (Dugan, Turman, & Torrez, 2015, p. 7), whereas the collaboratory rejects an individualistic, inner-directed, or leader-centric view in favour a leadership-centred focus on collaboration and interaction. Second, the social change model foregrounds the importance of the "Seven Cs" – essentially a list of core values that are critical for leadership efforts to drive social change – whereas the collaboratory process places a premium on the emergence via interaction and practice not only of values, but also of purposes, practices, and solutions. Third, the social change model of leadership development overemphasizes common purpose as a core leadership value in the context of social change, whereas the collaboratory stresses the importance of multiple purposes and the necessity of negotiating among them in the process of addressing major societal challenges.

Collaboratory Design: The Guateng City Region Academy

In this section, we exemplify these many aspects of the collaboratory as a form of multi-stakeholder leadership research and development through problem solving by describing the design of one such set of collaboratory practices in the context of a partnership between the Gauteng City Region Academy (GCRA) in South Africa and the Lancaster University Leadership Collaboratory (LLC). Management at the GCRA wanted to develop a new programme for leading strategic change in their local organization and region. The programme will be offered to the 14 departments (consisting of the three clusters Economic, Governance, and Social), initially commencing in spring 2018. The goal of the programme is to expose senior managers to thought-provoking content in leading strategic change, as well as to afford them the time to create a leadership value change network.

First, some crucial background: The Gauteng province of South Africa is located in the north-eastern part of South Africa. While it is the smallest province in terms of land mass, it is the most populous province, with approximately 13.2 million people calling Gauteng home, which is about 24 per cent of the total South African population (Stats SA, n.d.). A mixture of both urban and rural, the cities of Johannesburg, Soweto, and Pretoria are centrally located within the province and are the main financial districts in the region. The province contributes approximately a third of total South African gross domestic product (GDP) (Gauteng Provincial Government, n.d.). Most of Gauteng's inhabitants are young: Only 4 per cent are over the age of 65.

A closer look at the statistics make clear that the Gauteng City Region is a study in contrasts. While it serves as one of the key economic engines of the South African economy, it also shares in the country's crippling unemployment. Roughly 25 per cent of the South African population, and 50 per cent of young people (the GCRA's core constituency), are without jobs. Consequently, the region is also characterized by massive disparity in economic well-being: a contemporary reality deeply connected to South Africa's long history of racial disparity and Apartheid. Income inequality in South Africa is among the highest in the world, and the Gauteng region shares in this unfortunate statistic as well, with a full 10 per cent of the regions inhabitants living below the poverty line. While the recent growth of a black middle class in South Africa appears as a bright spot in this landscape, it has the unfortunate side-effect of increasing income inequality among South Africa's roughly 80 per cent black population itself. South Africa also currently contains between 5 million and 8 million undocumented immigrants – upwards of 5 per cent of the population – and these numbers are higher in major urban centres such as Johannesburg. The large number of migrants contributes to major problems in employment, housing, and other services. Meanwhile, education in South Africa has experienced major problems over the past several years with respect to quality in secondary education and with respect to access in higher education (GCRO, 2013). One of the most newsworthy consequences of these latter interconnected problems over the last two years was the rolling lockdowns of South African universities, including those in the Gauteng City Region, as a result of the "Fees Must Fall"/"Afrikaans Must Fall" protest movements spearheaded by disaffected university students across the country (Hauser, 2016).

These complex and interconnected problems exert considerable, often very challenging, impacts on youth development, jobs, and education, and therefore they directly confront the GCRA, which is a branch of the Gauteng Department of Education and a part of the regional government. According to its own website, the mandate of the GCRA is:

> . . . skills development for both the public sector and the youth of Gauteng Province, which is central to building skills for the economy and to ensure an efficient, effective and developmental oriented public service. The role of the Academy is therefore, to contribute to socio-economic transformation.
>
> *(GCRA, n.d.)*

The GCRA's strategic goals include: "To develop interventions which respond to the skills development needs of the Gauteng public servants; and to enable young people to make the transition from school to work, through relevant work training opportunities" (GCRA, n.d.).

The GCRA works with and for its own governmental employees, members of the public and private sectors, its youth, and those seeking support. As the GCRA's strategic goals and mission make clear, the focus and objective of the Academy is not merely leadership development, but leadership for social change. From the very outset, leadership is purposefully and explicitly defined as a mechanism and tool for larger social and cultural change. Driven by the vision of the GCRA, therefore, the force motivating the Gauteng/Lancaster Collaboratory stems from a need to better equip GCRA managers to facilitate better practices and processes at work, as well as to enable them to work as individual citizens to bring about social change. More specifically, the GCRA seeks to be better at responding to practical and emergent realities such as resource constraints, organizational conflict, and conflicting stakeholder interests.

The GCRA's partner in this initiative, the Lancaster Leadership Collaboratory, comprises academics from the Lancaster University Management School who teach and research issues related to leadership, organizational communication, and organizational behaviour. Members of the LLC have experience working with the Collaboratory in other projects that span youth empowerment, healthcare management, human rights recognition, human migration and social integration, and organizational cultural/structural change. Past Collaboratory experiences have included working with groups from Europe, North America, Asia, Australia, and Africa. A number of these collaboratories were joint efforts among a network of leadership scholars from several different countries, alongside practitioners in leadership development and social change work. These included: a workshop on the dynamics of cross-sector partnerships between the Danish Red Cross and a number of private-sector organizations working to support refugees in the process of integration, hosted in Copenhagen, Denmark, in May 2016; a NATO-funded workshop, together with the Center for Creative Leadership and the Geneva Center on Security Policy, on the dynamics of leadership in fragile and post-conflict environments, hosted in Geneva, Switzerland, in September 2016; a workshop on inclusive and grassroots leadership in the context of refugee resettlement, hosted jointly by the Annual Conference of the International Leadership Association and the Candler School of Theology at Emory University in Atlanta, Georgia, in November 2016; and a two-day collaboratory with South African university students, parents, faculty, representatives of university administration, and student protesters and activists, conducted in collaboration with the Albert Luthuli Centre for Responsible Leadership at the University of Pretoria in March 2017, on the challenges facing university stakeholders in connection with the "Fees Must Fall" and "Afrikaans Must Fall" protests that had led to incidents of violence

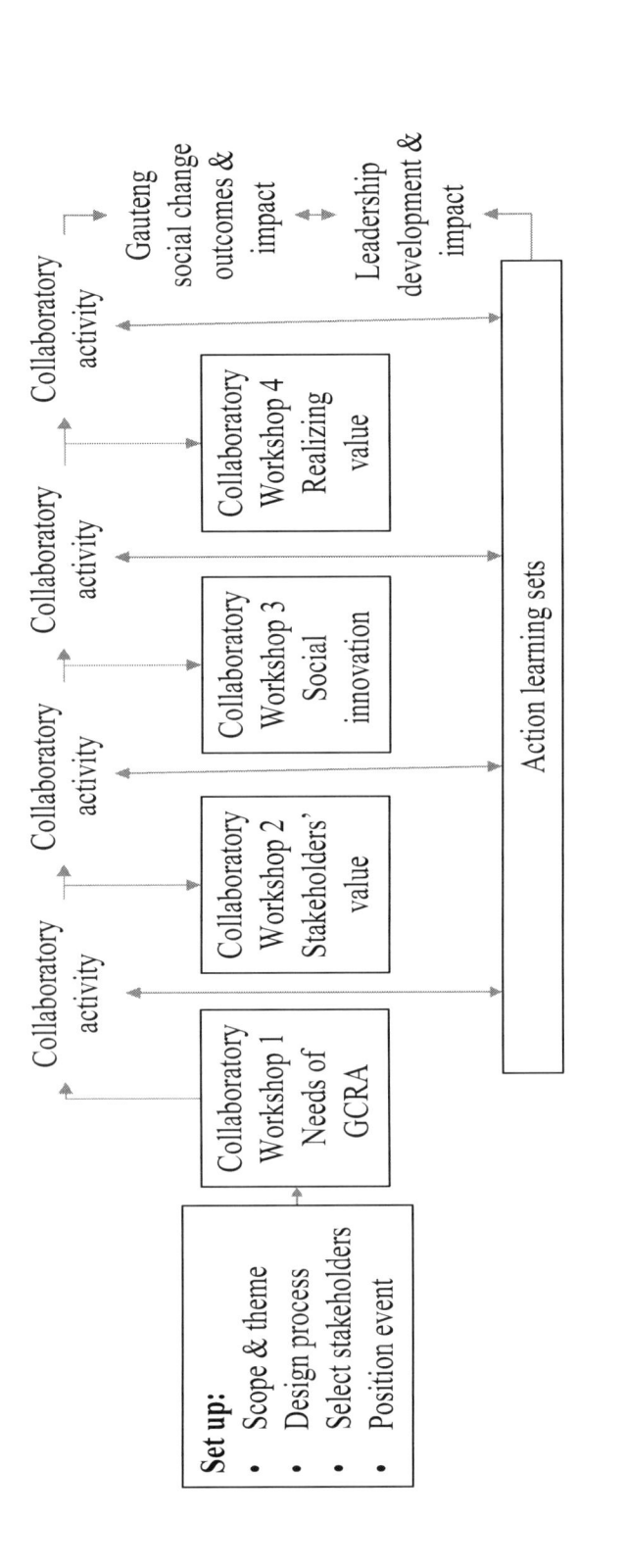

FIGURE 15.2 GCRA/Lancaster Collaboratory Design.

and the lockdown of Pretoria and many other South African universities in 2016 and 2017.

As explained earlier, a collaboratory is a blend of *collaboration* of stakeholders and *laboratory* – it is a collective experiment with the aim of addressing a specific problem or challenge. This is a process that unfolds over a predetermined length of time. The GCRA determined that it had 18 months for the Gauteng/Lancaster Collaboratory. Figure 15.2 illustrates the flow of the collaboratory process.

Central to this process is the act of naming, examining, and confirming the issues, challenges, or problems facing the GRCA. The specifics of these challenges and contributing factors are understood best by the local participants: the employees and stakeholders. Therefore, the first thing the Collaboratory will do is seek to build stronger relationships and to develop trust between the members of the GCRA and other relevant stakeholders. To help to accomplish this, the Gauteng/Lancaster Collaboratory will use collaboratory workshops, actions, and action learning sets to help to facilitate rapport and trust among GCRA members and stakeholders. The Collaboratory workshops (four in total) provide space and opportunity to begin (and continue) the process of blending the vision and aspirations of the participants with the practical realities that constrain or complicate change. Expert input to help to facilitate this process is provided by the members of the LCC.

Unlike most leadership development programmes and change management schemes, a key feature of the collaboratory is that it provides the mechanisms by which ideas are created, tested, and refined. The collaboratory is intended to create a safe space in which to fail, so to speak. This safe space consists of the collaboratory activities, in which participating stakeholders work together to test emerging ideas, which are subsequently examined in the following workshops. In other words, after the initial workshop, the ideas generated in the workshop discussion will be tried and tested to determine their efficacy, appropriateness, and usefulness. Further, possible unanticipated consequences and/or outcomes will be noted.

In this latter regard, action learning sets serve a crucial support function for the members of the collaboratory. Through the use of a facilitator, the action learning sets catalyse conversations among groups of participating stakeholders (approximately 6–9 people) about what is working or not working, and about alternative plans, unforeseen consequences, hidden assumptions, and new challenges or problems. In this manner, they provide a forum for collective leadership development in which participants together explore aspirations, identities, and skills associated with their roles within the collaboratory and, more importantly, within their organization. The focus of this mode of development is not directed inward toward individual leader traits and skills, emotional intelligence, or competency profiles; the focus remains on the collective effort – or, more specifically, on the thorny task of negotiating and forging collective effort via collaboration across difference, marshalling the strengths of multiple purposes and perspectives to the task of addressing the complex challenges at hand. The collaboratory approach we have designed for the GCRA/Lancaster Collaboratory does not take productive collaboration for granted nor does it simply assume that common effort provides a ready starting point for leadership development, but instead it approaches productive collaboration as a fragile achievement – one that can emerge from the sense of urgency that stakeholders bring to the task of addressing common complex challenges.

Conclusion

Where will new leadership ideas come from? A leadership development consultant asked one of us this question a few years back. He was not asking rhetorically: He really wanted to know, because, in his opinion, the leadership development and consulting industries had not produced any truly new ideas in quite some time. From the perspective we have developed in this chapter, we would answer his question as follows: New leadership ideas will not come from pure academic research or theorizing – that is, from Mode 1 knowledge production –because, as Starkey and Madan (2001) were not completely wrong to point out, academic theorizing can often become too distanced and detached from pragmatic concerns and pressures. Neither will new leadership ideas come from simply engaging directly in practical managerial challenges themselves – from Mode 2 knowledge production – because practical organizational activities come with their own set of blinders, roadblocks, and biases in the form of daily performance pressures, bottom-line short-termism, management fashions and buzzwords, organizational politics, and sometimes even corruption and greed. As we have argued here, new leadership ideas will emerge as a by-product of various forms of engaged and interdisciplinary Mode 3 knowledge production. This will require that leadership scholars connect and collaborate with a wider variety of public and private stakeholders to redirect the power of leadership research and development to address complex social, and even global, challenges – rather than merely to generate new theory or to attempt to fix organizational performance gaps.

To reiterate an important point, it would be a mistake to think of this Mode 3 approach to leadership knowledge production as simply providing a new common ground or meta-purpose that unites or aligns a variety of different stakeholders and agendas around a shared vision. Drawing again on complexity leadership theory, and on Ospina and Foldy's (2010) insights about bridging difference, we would argue that this kind of very traditional leadership vocabulary is not adequate to address wicked societal problems or complex global challenges. These sorts of imposing challenges require that multiple, and even conflicting, interests and purposes connect, coordinate, and work together without erasing the very real differences that constitute the sources of their respective strengths.

By this same token, we would argue, confronting complex societal and global challenges via Mode 3 engagement requires the valuable contributions of both Mode 1 and 2 knowledge production, each with its own agenda, but each with something important to offer. In other words, the three modes are distinct, yet interconnected and mutually reinforcing. Mode 1 research is a close bedfellow of Mode 3, because pure research clearly seeks to enhance society by understanding and explaining phenomena and ideas to advance the human condition. At the same time, Mode 3 knowledge production recognizes the need for research breakthroughs to address complex challenges in a socially useful manner (Willmott, 2012), and it offers the side benefit of opening up new topic areas, contexts, and connections for Mode 1 research. Mode 2 brings practical experience, know-how, operational discipline, and sometimes considerable financial and organizational resources to the table. And by engaging in Mode 3 efforts to address major social and global challenges, managerial organizations and the people who work in them will encounter new ideas about leadership and new organizational practices of relevance to their Mode 2 challenges.

We cannot predict the exact outcome of the GCRA/Lancaster Leadership Collaboratory in advance – not only because it has not yet taken place at time of writing, but also, and more importantly, because the collaboratory process hinges on the emergence out of the rough-and-tumble of multi-stakeholder collaboration and experimentation of new connections, new ideas, and new solutions that participants have not yet even anticipated. Neither can we predict the exact outcome of leveraging this and future collaboratories to nudge leadership research and development toward an interdisciplinary and multi-stakeholder approach to Mode 1, 2, and 3 engagement with major societal and global challenges that matter. It is our hope that such an effort would help to fix what's wrong with leadership, and would lead to the emergence of new connections, new ideas about leadership, and new solutions to some of the pressing and complex challenges facing humankind. Perhaps, as a long-term result of such an effort, leadership research and development could even fulfil their potential as very powerful mechanisms for social and global change.

References

Aram, J.D., & Salipante, P.F. (2003). Bridging scholarship in management: Epistemological reflections. *British Journal of Management*, 14(3), 189–205.
Belling, R., James, K., & Ladkin, D. (2004). Back to the workplace: How organisations can improve their support for management learning and development. *Journal of Management Development*, 23(3), 234–255.
Bly, S. (1998). Special section on collaboratories. *Interactions*, 5(3), 31.
Burgoyne, J., & Turnbull James, K. (2001). *Leadership development: Best practice guide for organisations*. London: Council for Excellence in Management and Leadership.

Burgoyne, J., & Turnbull James, K. (2006). Towards best or better practice in corporate leadership development: Operational issues in mode 2 and design science research. *British Journal of Management*, *17*(4), 303–316.

Butler, N., Delaney, H., & Spoelstra, S. (2015). Problematizing "relevance" in the business school: The case of leadership studies. *British Journal of Management*, *26*(4), 731–744.

Cogburn, D.L. (2003). HCI in the so-called developing world: What's in it for everyone. *Interactions*, *10*(2), 80–87.

Daft, R.L. (2015). *The leadership experience* (6th ed.). Stamford, CT: Cengage Learning.

Doh, J.P., & Quigley, N.R. (2014). Responsible leadership and stakeholder management: Influence pathways and organizational outcomes. *Academy of Management Perspectives*, *28*(3), 255–274.

Drath, W.H. (1998). Approaching the future of leadership development. In C. McCauley, R. Moxley, & E. Van Velsor (Eds.), *Handbook of leadership development* (pp. 403–432). San Francisco, CA: Jossey-Bass.

Drath, W.H., & Palus, C.J. (1993). Leadership as meaning-making in communities of practice. *Issues & Observations*, *13*(4), 12.

Dugan, J.P. (2011). Pervasive myths in leadership development: Unpacking constraints on leadership learning. *Journal of Leadership Studies*, *5*(2), 79–84.

Dugan, J.P., Turman, N.T., & Torrez, M.A. (2015). Beyond individual leader development: Cultivating collective capacities. *New Directions for Student Leadership*, *148*, 5–15.

Elkington, J. (2004). Enter the triple bottom line. In A. Henriques & J. Richardson (Eds.), *The triple bottom line: Does it all add up?* (pp. 1–16). London: Routledge.

Gauteng City Region Academy (GCRA). (n.d.). Retrieved from www.gauteng.gov.za/services/youth/Pages/GCRA.aspx

Gauteng City-Region Observatory (GCRO). (2013). *The state of the Gauteng City-Region review 2013* [pdf]. Retrieved from http://2013.legacy.gcro.unomena.net/

Gauteng Provincial Government. (n.d.). Retrieved from www.gauteng.gov.za

Gibbons, M., Limoges, C., Nowotny, H., Schwartzman, S., Scott, P., & Trow, M. (Eds.). (1994). *The new production of knowledge: The dynamics of science and research in contemporary societies*. London ; Thousand Oaks, CA: Sage.

Gill, R. (2006). *Theory and practice of leadership*. Thousand Oaks, CA: Sage.

Gosling, J., & Mintzberg, H. (2003). The five minds of a manager. *Harvard Business Review*, *81*(11), 54–63.

Guthey, E. (2016). Romanticism, antimodernism, and a pluralist perspective on responsible leadership. In S. Kempster & B. Carroll (Eds.), *Responsible leadership: Realism and romanticism* (pp. 203–214). London: Routledge.

Hauser, C. (2016, September 22). "Fees must fall": Anatomy of the student protests in South Africa. *New York Times*. Retrieved from www.nytimes.com/2016/09/23/world/africa/fees-must-fall-anatomy-of-the-student-protests-in-south-africa.html

Hodgkinson, G.P., & Starkey, K. (2011). Not simply returning to the same answer over and over again: Reframing relevance. *British Journal of Management*, *22*(3), 355–369.

Huff, A.S., & Huff, J.O. (2001). Re-focusing the business school agenda. *British Journal of Management*, *12*, S49–S54.

Kelemen, M., & Bansal, P. (2002). The conventions of management research and their relevance to management practice. *British Journal of Management*, *13*(2), 97–108.

Kempster, S., & Carroll, B. (Eds.). (2016). *Responsible leadership: Realism and romanticism*. New York: Routledge.

Kempster, S., Guthey, E., & Uhl-Bien, M. (2017). Collaboratory as leadership development. In S. Kempster, A. Turner, & G. Edwards (Eds.), *Field guide to leadership development* (pp. 251–271). Cheltenham: Edward Elgar.

Kempster, S., Jackson, B., & Conroy, M. (2011). Leadership as purpose: Exploring the role of purpose in leadership practice. *Leadership, 7*(3), 317–334.

Knights, D. (2008). Myopic rhetorics: Reflecting epistemologically and ethically on the demand for relevance in organizational and management research. *Academy of Management Learning & Education, 7*(4), 537–552.

Komives, S.R., & Wagner, W. (2017). *Leadership for a better world: Understanding the social change model of leadership development* (2nd ed.). San Francisco, CA: Jossey-Bass.

Kouzes, J.M., & Posner, B.Z. (2017). *The leadership challenge: How to make extraordinary things happen in organizations* (6th ed.). Hoboken, NJ: John Wiley & Sons.

Maak, T., & Pless, N.M. (2006). Responsible leadership in a stakeholder society: A relational perspective. *Journal of Business Ethics, 66*(1), 99–115.

Maak, T., & Pless, N.M. (2009). Business leaders as citizens of the world: Advancing humanism on a global scale. *Journal of Business Ethics, 88*(3), 537–550.

Mabey, C., & Nicholds, A. (2015). Discourses of knowledge across global networks: What can be learnt about knowledge leadership from the ATLAS collaboration? *International Business Review, 24*(1), 43–54.

MacLean, D., MacIntosh, R., & Grant, S. (2002). Mode 2 management research. *British Journal of Management, 13*(3), 189–207.

Marion, R., & Uhl-Bien, M. (2001). Leadership in complex organizations. *The Leadership Quarterly, 12*(4), 389–418.

McCann, D.P., & Brownsberger, M.L. (1990). Management as a social practice: Rethinking business ethics after MacIntyre. *Annual of the Society of Christian Ethics, 10*, 223–245.

Miska, C., & Mendenhall, M.E. (2018). Responsible leadership: A mapping of extant research and future directions. *Journal of Business Ethics, 148*(1), 117–134.

Muff, K. (Ed.). (2014). *The collaboratory: A co-creative stakeholder engagement process for solving complex problems*. Sheffield: Greenleaf.

Ospina, S., & Foldy, E. (2010). Building bridges from the margins: The work of leadership in social change organizations. *The Leadership Quarterly, 21*(2), 292–307.

Parry, K., & Jackson, B. (2016). Promoting responsibility, purpose and romanticism in business schools. In S. Kempster & B. Carroll (Eds.), *Responsible leadership: Realism and romanticism* (pp. 149–162). London: Routledge.

Pearce, C.L., Wassenaar, C.L., & Manz, C.C. (2014). Is shared leadership the key to responsible leadership? *Academy of Management Perspectives, 28*(3), 275–288.

Pittinsky, T.L., & Simon, S. (2007). Intergroup leadership. *The Leadership Quarterly, 18*(6), 586–605.

Pless, N.M., Maak, T., & Waldman, D.A. (2012). Different approaches toward doing the right thing: Mapping the responsibility orientations of leaders. *Academy of Management Perspectives, 26*(4), 51–65.

Romme, A.G.L. (2003). Making a difference: Organization as design. *Organization Science, 14*(5), 558–573.

Schmotter, J.W. (1998). An interview with Professor James March. *Selections, 14*(3), 56–62.

Stahl, G.K., & Sully de Luque, M. (2014). Antecedents of responsible leader behavior: A research synthesis, conceptual framework, and agenda for future research. *Academy of Management Perspectives, 28*(3), 235–254.

Starkey, K., & Madan, P. (2001). Bridging the relevance gap: Aligning stakeholders in the future of management research. *British Journal of Management, 12*, S3–S26.

Statistics South Africa (Stats SA). (n.d.). Retrieved from www.statssa.gov.za/

Tranfield, D., & Starkey, K. (1998). The nature, social organization and promotion of management research: Towards policy. *British Journal of Management, 9*(4), 341–353.

Turnbull, S. (Ed.). (2012). *Worldly leadership: Alternative wisdoms for a complex world.* Basingstoke: Palgrave Macmillan.

Uhl-Bien, M., & Arena, M. (2017). Complexity leadership. *Organizational Dynamics, 46*(1), 9–20.

Uhl-Bien, M., Marion, R., & McKelvey, B. (2007). Complexity leadership theory: Shifting leadership from the industrial age to the knowledge era. *The Leadership Quarterly, 18*(4), 298–318.

Van Aken, J.E. (2004). Management research based on the paradigm of the design sciences: The quest for field-tested and grounded technological rules – Paradigm of the design sciences. *Journal of Management Studies, 41*(2), 219–246.

Van de Ven, A.H. (2007). *Engaged scholarship: A guide for organizational and social research.* Oxford: Oxford University Press.

Voegtlin, C., Patzer, M., & Scherer, A.G. (2012). Responsible leadership in global business: A new approach to leadership and its multi-level outcomes. *Journal of Business Ethics, 105*(1), 1–16.

Waldman, D.A., & Galvin, B.M. (2008). Alternative perspectives of responsible leadership. *Organizational Dynamics, 37*(4), 327–341.

Willmott, H. (2012). Reframing relevance as "social usefulness": A comment on Hodgkinson and Starkey's "not simply returning to the same answer over and over again." *British Journal of Management, 23*(4), 598–604.

Wulf, W. (1993). The collaboratory opportunity. *Science, 261*(5123), 854–855.

Yukl, G. (2005). *Leadership in organizations* (6th ed.). Prentice Hall.

INDEX

Locators for figures are in *italics* and those for **tables** in bold.

360-degree feedback **65**, 69–72, **71**

abilities *see* knowledge, skills, and abilities (KSAs)
abusive supervision 194–199; *see also* destructive leadership
academic context *see* future research; leadership research; leadership research methods; purpose of leadership
action learning 287–288, 293
Adobe Systems 80
adolescence: leader identity 176; leadership development 212–217
adulthood, leader identity 176–179
affective motivation 96
affirmative action 130
agent-based modeling 29–30, 50, 166; *see also* role modeling
agentic attributes 125–126
analysis *see* levels of analysis
annual performance review *see* appraisals
appraisals: arguments for eliminating 77, **78–79**; assessment methods 63, **65**; vs. continued oversight/feedback 80–81; performance management 74–76
Arena, M. 285–286
assessment 58, 82; leadership development 72–74; methods 63–72; performance management 74–81; reluctant leaders 98–99; what to assess 59–63
assessment centers **64**, 66, 69

balanced scorecard 76–77
Bales, Robert 10, 19
behaviors: destructive leadership 194–195; gender differences 122–123, 127; leadership research methods 14–15, 19; leadership style 142–143; training in leadership 245–246, 248–249, 252–253
bias: extinction of bias myth 124–126; gender in leadership assessment 81; training in leadership 242; youth leadership development 218; *see also* cultural bias; male-centric bias; self-selection bias
biological factors, claiming leadership 92–93
blame culture 273
bodies, power relations 269
brain functions, time 161
Browne, C. G. 10, 17
buddy leaders **178**, 183–184
buffer leaders **178**, 182–183
bullying, destructive leadership 189
Burns, James MacGregor 115, 260, 263, 267

careers: assessment methods 58; leadership development 72–74; motivation to lead 95–96; *see also* recruitment
case analysis 28
change management 293

character *see* personal characteristics
character first assessment 67
childhood: informal and formal leadership 209; leader identity 176, 181; leadership development 212–217
citations 113–114
claiming leadership 90–93; *see also* self-selection bias
Coca-Cola 80
cognition: assessment methods **64**, 68; Eastern and Western culture 138–142; temporal context 162–164
the collaboratory leadership development 286–294, *288*, *292*
collective focus: Eastern culture 140–142; leadership development 234–235
collectives, levels of analysis 45, 47, 48, 52, 54–55
communal traits 124–126
communication *see* interactions; leader-follow relationships
companies *see* organizations
competency modeling, assessment 61–62
complexity: leader identities 173; leadership development 227–228; purpose of leadership 285–286; temporal context 152–156, **154**
compliance, critical leadership studies 270–274
computational modeling 29–30, 50–51
conformity, critical leadership studies 270–274
content analysis 28
context for learning (CFL) 30
context of leadership: assessment 59–60; destructive 198–201; leadership development 210–212, 234–235; research methods 18, 22–23, 115–116
continuous rating assessment (CRA) approach 26–27
critical leadership studies 4–5, 260–261, 274–275; conformity, compliance, and resistance 270–274; dialectical approaches 264–269; dichotomizing leadership 261–264; power relations 265–274
cross-sectional surveys 16, 184
cultural bias 3, 138–139; cognitive differences between East and West 138–142; future research avenues 145–147; individual focus 140, 142–143, 147; paternalistic leadership 143–145

cultural context: destructive leadership 198–199; humanities 111–118; leadership development 73–74; sciences 108–109

'dark side' of leadership 189, 190, 196, 202, 267
decision making, levels of analysis 51–52
Deloitte 80
demonstration-based training 246–248
depth of time 163–165, **164**
design science 287–288
destructive leadership 4, 189–192, 201–203; concepts and results 192–194; contextual factors 198–201; definition 192–193; intentions 196–198; perception vs. behavior 194–195; tyranny 267
development *see* leadership development
developmental process 4
dialectical approaches 264–269
dichotomizing leadership 261–264
digital natives 211–212
discrimination: female leaders 129–130; gender 124–125; youth leadership development 216–217, 221
divorce, leader identity 181
dominant leaders, personal characteristics 62–63
Dragoni, L. 163–164
dyadic methods 23–25
dyads: levels of analysis 44, 45–46, 53; temporal context 155
dynamic computational modeling 50–51
dynamic systems, temporal context 152–156, **154**

Eastern culture *see under* cultural bias
effectiveness: dialectical approaches 265; leadership research 5
efficacy 97
Einarsen, S. 192–193, 197
emergence: claiming leadership 90; leadership research methods 14–15
emotional intelligence 238
emotions, temporal context 162–163
entrepreneurship, growth mindset 219–220
ethics, and leadership 107–119
ethnic context, youth leadership development 216–217, 221
ethnographical research 28
executive assessment 66–67

executives: appraisals 74; assessment 60, 66–68, 80; claiming leadership 91; gender 121–122, 129; global leadership 61; narcissism 91; temporal context 152, 163
exemplary leadership 4, 5, 189
experience: adolescence 176–179; childhood 176, 181; leader identities 173, 175–184; leadership development 217–221; youth leadership development 217–221
experience sampling measurement (ESM) 25–27
explaining, social sciences 112–113

feedback: vs. appraisals 80–81; assessment methods 63, 68–72, **71**; destructive leadership 196; performance management 74–76
feminism: conformity, compliance, and resistance 271–272; power relations 268–269; *see also* gender
Fenestra 68
firms *see* organizations
Fischer, T. 18
flat hierarchies 131
Foldy, E. 286, 294
followers *see* implicit followership theories; leader-follow relationships
Foucault, Michael 266
future research: cultural bias 145–147; destructive leadership 201–202; leader identities 184–185; leadership development 237–239; leadership research methods 30–31; male-centric bias 126–131; time 167
futures, temporal context 162–163

Galatea effect 253–254
Gardner, W. L. 10
gender: behavioral differences 122–123; claiming leadership 91; leadership assessment 81; male-centric bias 121–131; power relations 268–269; reluctant leaders 95; youth leadership development 216–217, 220–221
gender-neutral theories of leadership 126–128
Generation Z 211–212
generational differences 211–212
genetic factors, claiming leadership 92–93
Gibbons, M. 281
Giddens, A. 266, 269–270

global leadership: assessment 61; levels 18
GLOBE Project 138–139
goals: assessment 76–77, 81; single and multiple purposes 284–285; *see also* purpose of leadership
grounded theory 28
groups: levels of analysis 44–45, 52, 54; temporal context 155; *see also* collectives
growth mindset 218–220
Guateng City Region Academy 289–294, *292*
Gustafson, S. B. 22

hermeneutics 113
heroic perspectives 261, 270, 273
heterogeneity, levels of analysis 47
high potentials (HiPo) 98–99
historiometric studies 29
holistic focus, Eastern culture 140–142, 147
Hollander, E. 261–262
home life, leader identity 180–181
homogeneity, levels of analysis 47
homology thesis 49
Huff, A. S. 280, 283
Huff, J. O. 280, 283
humanities: ascent of the sciences 107–109; ethics 107–118; leadership research 2, 107, 118–119; methods 109–111; three cultures 111–118

identity *see* leader identities
idiosyncrasy credit 146, 147
implicit followership theories (IFTs) 26, 244–245, 252–255
implicit leadership theories (ILTs) 26, 96, 244–245, 252–255
individual characteristics *see* personal characteristics
individual focus: cultural bias 140, 142–143, 147; leadership development 234–235; levels 17–18; levels of analysis 44, 51–52; person-oriented methods 20–23
information-based training 246–248
intentions, destructive leadership 196–198
interactions: computational modeling 29–30; dyadic methods 24; leadership research methods 14–15, 18; observational methods 19–20; person-oriented methods 20–23
interdisciplinarity, sciences 109, 117–118

interpersonal relationships *see* interactions; leader-follow relationships; relationships
intersectionality 269
interviews: assessment methods **64**, 67; content analysis 28; leader identity 177, **178**

Jackson, B. 284–285
Johnson, S. K. 219

Kagan, Jerome 111–118
Kempster, S. 284
Kimberly-Clark 80
knowledge, skills, and abilities (KSAs): reluctant leaders 97–98; what to assess 59–63; *see also* talent shortage
knowledge leadership 287
knowledge production modes 279–280, 281–283, 286–289, 294–295

Lancaster University Leadership Collaboratory (LLC) 289–294
leader efficacy 97
leader identities 4, 173–175, 185; development 175–179; future research 184–185; mindset 243–244, 249–250; refinement 179–184; reluctant leaders 93–95; skills 97–98; taxonomy of 177–179, **178**; youth leadership development 212–217, 220–221
leader traits, assessment 59–60; *see also* personal characteristics
leader-follower relationships: conformity, compliance, and resistance 270–274; cultural context 146, 147; destructive leadership 200–201; dialectical approaches 265; leader identities 174; male-centric bias 127–128; research methods 19–20; self-concept 145; social exchange 144, 146–147
leader-member exchange (LMX) theory 146–147
leadership: definition 9; process-orientated definition 11, **12–13**
leadership as practice (LAP) 264
leadership as process 2
leadership assessment *see* assessment
leadership development 209–210, 221; assessment 72–74; childhood and adolescence 212–217; the collaboratory 286–294, *288*; context 210–212, 234–235; future research 237–239;

mindset 242–246, 248–251; practice in 232–237; programs and models 217–221, 233–234; reluctant leaders 96–97, 98–99; research 229–232; as theory 227–229; 'what's wrong with?' 226–227; *see also* training in leadership
leadership industry 5
leadership inference drawing 53–54
leadership logos 249–252, *251*, 254–255
leadership mindset 242–246, 248–251
leadership research: book audience 5; humanities 2, 107, 118–119; levels of analysis 41–44; 'what's wrong with leadership?' 1–5; *see also* future research; purpose of leadership
leadership research methods 9–11; computational models 29–30; future directions 30–31; leadership development 229–232; process-oriented 9–10, 11–18; qualitative approaches 27–29; quantitative approaches 27; recommendations 19–27; sciences and humanities 109–111
leadership style: cultural context 142–145; destructive leadership 192–193; gender 122–124; identity taxonomy 177–179, **178**; personal characteristics 62–63; Pygmalion 252–255; youth leadership development 217–221
leadership theory building, levels of analysis 53, 54
leadership theory testing, levels of analysis 53, 54
leadership training *see* training in leadership
Lear 80
learning culture 273
levels: dyadic methods 23–25; leadership research methods 17–18
levels of analysis 41; collectives 45, 47, 48, 52, 54–55; definitions 44–45; dyads 44, 45–46, 53; dynamics and analytics 49–51; fixes and guidelines 51–55; management 45, *46*; multiple levels in combination 48–49; networks 47–48; temporal context 156; 'what's wrong with leadership?' 41–44
Leverhulme Foundation 1
life experience *see* experiences
lifespan approach *213*, 213, 227–228, 229–230, 234; *see also* experiences
literature *see* leadership research
Liu, D. 197–198

longitudinal research: cultural bias 144; leadership development 229–230, 231–232; time 16; *see also* shortitudinal studies
Lord, Robert 1, 30
Lowe, K. B. 10

Madan, P. 279–283
Magnusson, D. 22
male-centric bias 3, 121–122; claiming leadership 91; future research 126–131; myths about 122–126
management structure 45, **46**; *see also* executives; performance management
Martinko, M. J. 194–195
masculinity 269; *see also* male-centric bias
mathematical modeling 29–30, 50–51
measuring leadership *see* assessment; performance measures
mentor leaders **178**, 183
methods *see* leadership research methods
Millennials 211–212
modeling *see* agent-based modeling; competency modeling; computational modeling; role modeling
motivation to lead (MTL): leadership development 228; male-centric bias 124; self-selection bias 95–96
multilevel theory 17–18; dyadic methods 23–25; grounded theory 28; leadership development 232; levels of analysis 43–44, 48–49, 51–55; temporal context 163–165, **164**; *see also* levels of analysis
multisource feedback **65**, 69–72, **71**
multi-stakeholder leadership development 286–289
Murphy, S. E. 17, 219
Myers-Briggs Type Indicator (MBTI) 238

narcissism 90–91
negatives *see* destructive leadership
networks, levels of analysis 47–48
neurology, time 161
nonlinear effects, temporal context 156–159
nontraditional leaders: claiming leadership 90–93; gender-neutral theories of leadership 126–128; leadership development 220–221; leadership reluctance 93–99
nontraditional leadership structures 131

observational methods 19–20
online assessments **64**, 68
organizations: conformity, compliance, and resistance 273; destructive leadership 199–200; leadership development 234–235; purpose of leadership 285–286; temporal context 155, 156–159; training in leadership 241–242
Ospina, S. 286, 294

parent-child relationships, self-concept 144–145
parenthood, leader identity 180–181, 184
Parry, K. 284–285
paternalistic leadership, cultural bias 143–145, 147
people-oriented behavior 142–143, 265
perception: destructive leadership 194–195; training in leadership 245–246
performance management systems 74–81
performance measures 2–3; leadership development 73–74; what to assess 59–63; *see also* appraisals; assessment
personal characteristics: assessment 62–63; claiming leadership 90–91; destructive leadership 189, 193, 196–197; gender differences 122–123, 124–126; leader traits 59–60; leadership development 230–231; youth leadership development 212–217
person-oriented methods 20–23
persons *see* individual focus; personal characteristics
philosophy: ethics 107, 117; leadership research 2, 107; purpose of leadership 284; and the sciences in history 107–109
pluralistic understanding 282–283, 285
positivism 109–110
post-heroic perspectives 261, 263–264
poverty, claiming leadership 92
power relations 265–274
practice-based training 246–248
practitioners, as book audience 5
pragmatic prospecting 160–162
the present, temporal context 156–159
prestige leaders 62–63
process-orientation 9–10
process-oriented methods: key elements 11–18; recommendations 19–27; typical studies 10–11
professional life *see* workplace

promotion: leadership development 72–74; motivation to lead 95–96
prospection theories 160–162
purpose of leadership 279–280, 294–295; the collaboratory 286–294, *288*; Guateng City Region Academy 289–294; knowledge production modes 279–280, 281–283, 286–289, 294–295; multiple or single purpose 284–286; multi-stakeholder leadership development 286–289
Pygmalion leadership 252–255

qualitative approaches, research methods 27–29
quantitative approaches, research methods 27
quantum theory 156–159
questionnaires 10–11

racial context, youth leadership development 216–217, 221
ratings *see* appraisals; performance measures
rationality 269
recruitment: and destructive leadership traits 189; growth mindset 218–220; talent shortage 210, 218–221, 226; *see also* leadership development
relational focus: Eastern culture 140–142, 147; purpose of leadership 285–286
relationships, levels of analysis 48–49, 52; *see also* leader-follower relationships
reluctant leaders 93–99; *see also* self-selection bias
representativeness heuristic 130
research *see* future research; leadership research; leadership research methods; purpose of leadership
resistance 270–274
reviews *see* appraisals
role congruity theory 91, 125
role modeling 182, 216–217, 231
Rousseau, D. 17

scholars, as book audience 5
sciences: ascent of 107–109; design science 287–288; social 2, 3, 107–118
scientist-practitioner gap 242
self-concept: cultural context 141, 144–145; mindset 243–244; reluctant leaders 93–95; temporal context 159–160

self-efficacy 214–216, 219–220, 228
self-managed teams 131
self-regulation: motivation to lead 95–96; youth leadership development 215–216
self-report questionnaires 10–11
self-selection bias 3, 89, 99; claiming leadership 90–93; reluctant leaders 93–99
senior leadership *see* executives
sensemaking, purpose of leadership 284
shortitudinal studies 25–26
simulation investigation for empirical network analysis (SIENA) 25
skills *see* knowledge, skills, and abilities (KSAs); talent shortage
Snow, C.P. 108–109, 111
social capital 28, 235
social context, leadership research methods 14–15
social exchange 144, 146–147
social network analysis (SNA) 24–25
social sciences: ethics 107–118; leadership research 2, 3
society-oriented behavior 142–143, 265
socio-economic status (SES), claiming leadership 92
South Africa, Guateng City Region Academy 289–294, *292*
spouses, leader identity 181
stakeholders, the collaboratory 286–289, 293
Starkey, K. 279–283
stereotype threat 91, 92
stereotypes, male/female leaders 121, 128–129
Stogdill, Ralph 9
structuration theory 266
students, as book audience 5
subjectivity, research methods 114–115
surveys: cross-sectional 16, 184; multisource feedback **65**, 69–72, **71**; time 16
systems approach: destructive leadership 198–200; temporal context 152–156, **154**

talent shortage 210, 218–221, 226; *see also* knowledge, skills, and abilities (KSAs)
task-oriented behavior 142–143, 265
teaching leadership *see* leadership development; training in leadership
teams *see* collectives; groups

technology, leadership development 211–212
telos 284–285
temporal construal theory 160–161
temporal exponential random graph model (TERGM) 25
Tepper, B. J. 191, 197, 198
tests **64**, 68, 69; *see also* assessment
'three cultures', humanities 111–118
time 3–4; depth of 163–165, **164**; dynamic systems 152–156, **154**; futures 162–163; implications for research and practice 165–167; leader identity 179–180, 182–184, *183*; leadership development 229–230, 231–232; leadership research methods 15–16, 22–23; levels of analysis 49–50; as medium 150–152, 166–167; the present and nonlinear effects 156–159; shortitudinal studies 25–26; travel through and exploration of 159–162; uncertainty and emotions 162–163; youth leadership development 212–217; *see also* longitudinal research
top leadership *see* executives
training in leadership 4, 241–242, 255; assessment 73; behaviors and mindset alignment 248–249; destructive leadership 202; leadership development 236–237; leadership mindset 242–246, 249–251; methods overview 246–247; Pygmalion leadership 252–255; *see also* leadership development
transactional leadership: critical leadership studies 260, 261–263; personal characteristics 62
transformational leadership: critical leadership studies 260, 261–263; personal characteristics 62; research methods 26
tyranny 267; *see also* destructive leadership

Uhl-Bien, M. 285–286
uncertainty: reluctant leaders 94; temporal context 162–163
understanding, social sciences 112–113
US Army research 1, 176–177, 181, 182

verbal discourse analysis 20
vertical dyadic linkage (VDL) 146
vision, temporal context 157

Western culture *see under* cultural bias
within-person methods 25–27
women: behavioral differences 122–123; claiming leadership 91; leadership assessment 81; male-centric bias 121–131; power relations 268–269; reluctant leaders 95; youth leadership development 216–217, 220–221
workplace: leader identity 176–179, 182–184; power relations 268

youth leadership development 212–221

Zimbardo, Philip 150